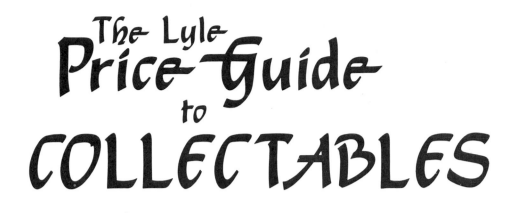

The Lyle
Price Guide
to
COLLECTABLES

The publishers wish to express their sincere thanks to the following for their kind help and assistance in the production of this volume:

CHARLES BORTHWICK (Sub Editor)
ANNETTE CURTIS (Sub Editor)
EELIN McIVOR (Sub Editor)
TRACEY BLACK
GILLIAN EASTON
LESLEY MARTIN
NICKY FAIRBURN
JONN DUNLOP
KERRY McCONNEL
ANTONIA MURPHY
FRANK BURRELL
ROBERT NISBET
EILEEN BURRELL
RICHARD SCOTT

Text by Liz Taylor, Eelin McIvor, Annette Curtis, Tony Curtis, Paul Sheppard.

While every care has been taken in the compiling of information contained in this volume the publishers cannot accept any liability for loss, financial or otherwise, incurred by reliance placed on the information herein.

ISBN 0-86248-116-3

Printed and bound by
Butler & Tanner Ltd., Frome, Somerset.

Introduction

Collecting is a world governed by uncommon rules, which allow everyone to participate in the fascinating game at any chosen level from attractive yet inexpensive home furnishings to big money investments.

It is a passion that can become a way of life. The lure of the chase, the search for the elusive treasure, the fascination of knowing almost, but not quite, everything about some out-of-the-ordinary subject is what makes the collector's adrenalin surge. They thrive most of all on the teasing certainty that fortunes can be made and that just around the corner they could find the one thing that will make their collection complete and unique.

When bitten by 'the bug' men and women of all ages and walks of life have become collectors and their specialities range from banknotes to Bairnsfatherware, from motor bikes to mustard pots. Everything and anything can be collected, from 18th century prints to today's throwaway beer cans.

If nobody collected golfing books then the first edition of 'The Golf' written in 1743 wouldn't be worth £17,000, and for the same reason an old Guinness bottle wouldn't be worth £150 and Marilyn Monroe's autograph wouldn't be worth £750.

Whilst scarcity value can take even the most commonplace artefacts of a past age into a high price range, it is still possible to build a fascinating collection for a minimal outlay and, of course, with many items being newly collectable, valuable pieces can still be found for a few pounds. Rarity however, does not always herald instant wealth, for one of the most important rules of the game is supply and demand. The bigger the collecting field—the bigger the market therefore, the greater the chance of a rare item being fully appreciated—and that means money. With a little of the right knowledge there is always the real possibility of turning a modest investment into a considerable nest egg.

Obviously condition is of great importance when establishing value. The prices quoted here are based on collectables which are in fair and average condition. There is still a rich source of material available and an example which has survived in good condition will prove to be a better investment than one damaged or showing signs of wear and tear.

This book is specifically designed to aid both the busy specialist and the enthusiastic beginner by creating an awareness of the vast scope of this fascinating field and by providing a guide to the sometimes surprising current market value of thousands of items.

The sky really is the limit for successful collectors, so—join the treasure hunt.

TONY CURTIS

Acknowledgements

Abridge Auction Rooms, Market Place, Abridge, Essex RM4 1UA
Helen Anderson, Page Galleries, 29 High Street, Kington
Aviation Antiques, 369 Croydon Road, Caterham, Surrey
R. Bannister, Cowleigh Bank, Malvern, Worcestershire (G.W.R. Jigsaws)
Bearnes, Rainbow, Avenue Road, Torquay, Devon TQ2 5TG
Bermondsey Antique Market, Tower Bridge Road, London
J. J. Binns, Alpha Antiques, High Street, Kington, Hereford
Border Bygones, The Vallets, Forge Crossing, Lyonshall, Kington HR5 3JQ
British Antique Exporters, School Close, Queen Elizabeth Avenue, Burgess Hill, West Sussex
Brown & Merry, 41 High Street, Tring, Herts HP23 5AB
Shirley Butler, Oddiquities, 61 Waldram Park Road, Forest Hill, London (Fire Irons)
Capes Dunn & Co., The Auction Galleries, 38 Charles Street, Manchester M1 7DB
Chancellors Hollingsworth, 31 High Street, Ascot, Berkshire SL5 7HG
Christie's, 8 King Street, St James's, London SW1Y 6QT
Christie's South Kensington Ltd., 85 Old Brompton Road, London SW7 3LD
Robert C. Coley, Droitwich, Worcestershire (Fishing Tackle)
Courts Miscellany, (George Court), 48 Bridge Street, Leominster
Dacre, Son & Hartley, 1-5 The Grove, Ilkley, West Yorkshire LS29 8HS
Dreweatt Neate, Donnington Priory, Donnington, Newbury, Berks RG13 2JE
Du Mouchelles Art Galleries Co., 409 E. Jefferson Avenue, Detroit, Michigan 48226 USA
Gwen Edwards, Lyonshall, Herefordshire
G. Eggleton, 4 Sarum Green, Oatlands Chase, Weybridge, Surrey (Trophies)
The Enchanted Aviary, 63 Hall Street, Long Melford, Sudbury, Suffolk (Taxidermy)
Jock Farquharson, Brandyden of Farmerton, Fern, Forfar DD8 3QU (Toy Vehicles)
Judith Gardener, The Childrens Bookshop, Hay on Wye (Just William Books)
Gorringes, Auction Galleries, 15 North Street, Lewes, East Sussex
Michael Gosling, Philmont, 78 Skip Lane, Walsall, West Midlands (Baden Powell Items)
Goss & Crested China Ltd., 62 Murray Road, Horndean, Hants PO8 9JL (Bairnsfatherware)
W. R. J. Greenslade & Co., 13 Hammet Street, Taunton, Somerset TA1 1RN
Gerald N. Gurney, Guildhall Orchard, Gt Bromley, Colchester, Essex CO7 7TU (Racketana)
Hat Pin Society of Great Britain, 26 Fulwell Road, Bozeat, Wellingborough, Northants NN9 7LY
Giles Haywood, The Auction House, St John's Road, Stourbridge DY8 1EW
Heathcote Ball & Co., 47 New Walk, Leicester
Hobbs & Chambers, 'At the Sign of the Bell', Market Place, Cirencester, Gloucestershire
Paul Jones, Hereford Alternative Arts Centre, Dilwyn, Hereford (Stained Glass, Taps)
Spike Jones, Scammells Rest, Shobdon, Hereford (Fairground Memorabilia)
G. A. Key, Aylsham Salerooms, Palmers Lane, Aylsham, Norfolk NR11 6EH
Kingsland Auction Services, Kingsland, Leominster
Lalonde Fine Art, 71 Oakfield Road, Clifton, Bristol, Avon BS8 2BE
Lawrence Fine Art, South Street, Crewkerne, Somerset TA18 8AB
David Lay, The Penzance Auction House, Alverton, Penzance, Cornwall TR18 4RE
Min Lewis, The Vine, St Davids Street, Presteigne, Powys (Pianola Rolls)
Tim Lewis, Woonton, Herefordshire
Locke & England, Walton House, 11 The Parade, Leamington Spa
Lots Road Chelsea Auction Galleries, 71 Lots Road, Chelsea, London SW10 0RN
R. K. Lucas & Son, 9 Vietoria Place, Haverfordwest SA61 2JX
Lynn Private Collection, Tyne & Wear (Royalty Books)
Miller & Co., Lemon Quay Auction Rooms, Truro, Cornwall TR1 2LW
Onslow's Auctioneers, Metrostore, Townmead Road, London SW6 2RZ
Osmond Tricks, Regent Street, Auction Rooms, Clifton, Bristol, Avon BS8 4HG
Hoggs Parker, Romney House, Ashford Market, Ashford, Kent TN23 1PG
Phillips, Blenstock House, 7 Blenheim Street, New Bond Street, London W1Y 0AS
Prudential Fine Art Auctioneers, 5 Woodcote Close, Kingston upon Thames, Surrey KT2 5LZ
Reeds Rains Prudential, Trinity House, 114 Northenden Road, Manchester M33 3HD
Record Collector, 45 St Marys Road, Ealing, London W55RQ
Brenda Riley, Kaleidescope, London House, Presteigne, Powys (Umbrellas)
Russell, Baldwin & Bright, The Fine Art Saleroom, Rylands Road, Leominster HR6 8JG
The Peter Savage Antique Bottle Museum, Cambrook House, Nr Warwick CV35 9HP
Lacy Scott (Fine Art Dept) 10 Risbygate Street, Bury St Edmunds, Suffolk IP33 3AA
Robt. W. Skinner Inc., Bolton Gallery, Route 117, Bolton, Massachusetts, USA
David Stanley Auctions, Stordan Grange, Osgathrope, Leicester LE12 9SR
Street Jewellery, 16 Eastcliffe Avenue, Newcastle on Tyne NE3 4SN (Finger Plates)
Louis Taylor & Sons, Percy Street, Hanley, Stoke on Trent, Staffordshire ST1 1NF
M. Veissid & Co., Hobsley House, Frodesley, Shrewsbury SY5 7ND
Trevor Vennett-Smith, 11 Nottingham Road, Gotham, Nottingham NG11 0HE (Signed Photographs)
Wallis & Wallis, West Street Auction Galleries, West Street, Lewes, East Sussex BN7 2NJ
Neil Wayne, Old Chapel, Bridge Street, Belper, Derbyshire (Razors)
John Wilson, 50 Acre End Street, Eynsham, Oxford OX8 1PD (Signed Photographs)
Peter Wilson Fine Art Auctioneers, Victoria Gallery, Market Street, Nantwich, Cheshire
Woolley & Wallis, The Castle Auction Mart, Salisbury, Wiltshire SP1 3SU
Worsfolds Auction Galleries, 40 Station Road West, Canterbury, Kent
Yesterday's News , 43 Dundonald Road, Colwyn Bay, Clwyd LL29 7RD

Contents

Aeronautical 9
Albums 11
American Indianware 12
Anchovy Pot Lids 15
Armour 17
Art Pottery 20
Art Nouveau Postcards 23
Autographs 25
Automatons 27
Avon Bottles 30
Baden Powell Items 31
Bairnsfatherware 33
Banknotes 36
Barometers 40
Beadwork Bags 43
Belleek 44
Bells 46
Berlin Woolwork 47
Bicycles 49
Biggles Books 51
Books 52
Boxes 56
Bronze 59
Butter Stamps 62
Car Mascots 63
Card Cases 66
Carved Stone 67
Carved Wood 69
Chairs 72
Chelsea 75
Chiparus Figures 77
Cigarette Cases 79
Claret Jugs 82
Clocks Bracket 83
    Carriage 84
    Lantern 85
    Longcase 86
    Mantel 88
    Skeleton 90
    Wall 91
Cloisonne 92
Coal Boxes 94
Commemorative China 95
Conversation Pieces 98
Corkscrews 102
Cricketana 105
Crystal Sets 107
Daum 108
Decanter Labels 110

Decanters 112
Decoys 114
Delft 116
De Morgan 118
Dolls 119
Dolls Houses 123
Doorstops 125
Drinking Sets 126
Enamel 128
Etuis 130
Eye Baths 131
Fairground Memorabilia 133
Fairings 135
Fans 138
Finger Plates 141
Fire Irons 142
Firemarks 144
Fishing Reels 147
Flambe 150
Fuchi Kashira 151
Galle 152
Ginger Beer Bottles 154
Goldscheider 156
Golfing Books 158
Goss Cottages 160
Grueby 163
Guiness Bottles 164
G.W.R. Jigsaws 166
Hair Clips 167
Handbags 168
Hans Coper 169
Hardstone 170
Hat Pins 172
Helmets 175
Horn 178
Icons 179
Inhalers 181
Inros 183
Ivory 185
Jade 188
Jewellery 190
Just William Books 194
Keys 195
Kingsware 196
Lacquer 198
Lalique 200
Leach 202
Liberty 203
Louis Wain Postcards 204

CONTENTS

Loving Cups 205
Maps 207
Martinware 210
Masonic Items 212
Match Strikers 214
Medals 218
Medical Items 222
Meissen 224
Micro Mosaics 226
Military Badges 227
Mineral Water Bottles 230
Minton 232
Mirrors 234
Model Engines 236
Model Ships 239
Models 242
Moorcroft Pottery 245
Motorbikes 246
Musical Boxes 248
Musical Instruments 250
Mustard Pots 253
Napoleonic Memorabilia 254
Nautical Items 258
Netsuke 261
Ointment Pots 264
Paperweights 267
Parian 271
Patch Boxes 273
Phonographs 274
Pianola Rolls 276
Picture Frames 277
Pistols 279
Playing Cards 282
Polyphones 284
Pomanders 285
Portrait Miniatures 286
Pot Lids 289
Powder Flasks 291
Prams 292
Preiss Figures 295
Prints 297
Racketana 300
Rattles 304
Razors 305
Rifles 307
Rookwood 310
Royal Dux 311
Royalty Books 313
Ruskin Pottery 316
Samplers 317
Sardine Dishes 320
Scrimshaw 321
Seals 322
Series Ware 324
Sevres 326
Shaker 328
Shaving Cream Pot Lids 330
Shaving Mugs 332
Shells 334
Ships Figureheads 335
Silhouettes 336
Signed Photographs 339
Snuff Bottles 342
Snuff Boxes 345
Sporting Stoneware 348
Stained Glass Windows 350
Stands 352
Stevengraphs 355
Stickley 357
Stoneware 359
Swords 361
Syphons 363
Tapestries 365
Taps 367
Tassie Medallions 368
Taxidermy 369
Terracotta 372
Textiles 374
Thimbles 377
Tickets 379
Tiles 381
Tobacco Jars 383
Tobacco Silks 385
Toleware 387
Toy Cars 388
Trade Cards 391
Transport 393
Trays 397
Treen 399
Trophies 402
Truncheons 403
Tsubas 404
Tunbridgeware 407
Umbrellas 409
Uniforms 410
Veterinary Items 413
Vinaigrettes 414
Violins 417
Walking Sticks 420
Watch Stands 423
Watches 424
Wax Models 428
Weathervanes 429
Wedgwood 432
Wemyss 434
Wine Glasses 435
Wood, Ralph 438
Worcester 439

AERONAUTICAL

The honour of being first in the air belongs to America — the first aeroplane was invented by Samuel Pierpoint Langley in 1896 and the first powered flight was made in 1903 by the Wright brothers. Since those early days enthusiasts have vied to possess relics of flight and books, photographs, log books, airmail letters, posters and even bits of old planes are all collected. The field is enormous, ranging from autographs or photographs of flying aces like Amy Johnston and Jim Mollison, Douglas Bader, Sheila Scott or space age astronauts to ashtrays and cigarette lighters made in the shape of aeroplanes or zeppelins. Most old aeroplanes are in historical collections or museums but there are a few enthusiasts, especially in America, rich and daring enough to buy them and even to fly them. More cautious collectors confine themselves to collecting plane parts like wooden propellors, or mundane items like airline baggage tickets.

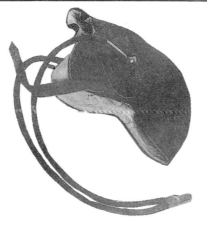

Geoffrey Watson — Women's Royal Air Force, published by Employment Exchange, 30 x 20in. (Onslow's) $498 £330

A brown leather lined flying helmet by Lewis of Oxford Street, with vocal intercom. (Onslow's) $306 £180

Schneider Trophy, 1931, Official Souvenir Programme, together with two others. (Christie's) $155 £110

A Royal Flying Corps propeller boss clock with French movement, 41cm. high (Onslow's) $204 £120

Poster by A. Brenet, Imperial Airways Through Africa, 102 x 64cm. (Onslow's) $646 £380

One of four silver place-setting holders depicting a Wright flyer, 1½in. high, in presentation case. (Christie's) $589 £350

A blue enamel oval snuff box, the cover painted with a hot air balloon over the countryside, 2¼in. long. (Christie's) $646 £420

A chromium plated and enamelled Brooklands Aero-Club badge inscribed 21, 3¾in. high. (Christie's) $520 £420

Blackpool Aviation Meeting, 1910, a silver cup with three reeded handles on acanthus legs, 8½in. diam. (Christie's) $1,551 £1,100

The Aerial Derby, published by The Dangerfield Printing Co., London, '15, on linen, 29¾ x 20in. (Onslow's) $270 £180

A sheepskin-lined U.S. Army flying jacket, type B-3, size 48. (Christie's) $231 £150

W. G. Barrett — The Schneider Trophy, published by Pools Advertising Service Ltd., 30 x 20in. (Onslow's) $75 £50

Safety axe from a Wellington bomber, with Air Ministry ordinance marks, 1940. $25 £15

Geoffrey Watson — Special Shell Aviation Petrol, No. 356, published by Vincent Brooks Day & Son, 30 x 45in. (Onslow's) $166 £110

A silk Stevengraph depicting a balloon and entitled 'Many happy returns of the day, made by T. Stevens of Coventry on 28th Feb. 1874', 10in. long. (Christie's) $92 £65

ALBUMS

The age of photography opened all sorts of possibilities for record-keeping, but early daguerreotypes were expensive, and it was not until the later 19th century that the art became generally affordable. It was then that the photograph album came into its own as a prized Victorian family possession. Often of richly tooled leather, gold-embossed with heavy clasps, their bindings rivalled those of the family Bible. Fascinating collectables, they are usually worth more if the pictures are identified or identifiable.

Late 19th century Japanese photographic album with a finely painted frontispiece. $175 £100

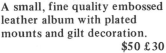

A small, fine quality embossed leather album with plated mounts and gilt decoration. $50 £30

Late Victorian photographic album with finely printed mounts. $105 £60

Late 19th century black lacquered album decorated with mother of pearl and ivory. $105 £60

Early 20th century black leather album with finely cut silver plated mounts. $130 £75

Late 19th century embossed brown leather album with floral decoration and gilt brass clasp, complete with photographs. $125 £70

Edwardian tooled red leather album with gilded brass clasp, containing family photographs. $140 £80

AMERICAN INDIANWARE

The American Indian has for long been a figure of romance and many collectors are interested in amassing anything connected with them. These range from "Cigar Store Indians", wooden figures carved in the likeness of Red Indians wearing feather headdresses that used to stand outside cigar stores in America, to pieces of their costume, head-dresses or bead necklaces. Buffalo hide was used by Indian tribes for making their clothes to their tents and they painted the hide in colourful patterns. Collectors also vie to possess Indian totem poles, carved and painted in characteristic ways. Tribespeople used bone, ivory, quills, corn husks, willow twigs and beads in making their artefacts and the beadwork is particularly interesting because it was first introduced among southern tribes in the 16th century by the white man as a kind of currency and spread north and east during the 18th and 19th centuries. Certain types of beads provide clues about the extent of contact between Indian tribes and white settlers.

Plains pony beaded and fringed hide dress, 19th century, formed of two skins, 51in. long. (Robt. W. Skinner Inc.) $7,200 £4,044

Classic Navajo chief's blanket, woven in single strand home-spun and ravelled yarn, 82 x 62in. (Robt. W. Skinner Inc.) $30,000 £20,978

Plains beaded hide boot moccasins, Southern Cheyenne/Arapaho, 1880's, 15in. high. (Robt. W. Skinner Inc.) $1,800 £1,011

Navajo pictorial weaving, woven on a burgundy ground in white, green, brown, black and pink, 43 x 57in. (Robt. W. Skinner Inc.) $900 £505

Eskimo/Northwest Coast polychrome wood mask, 19th century, cedar, 8½in. long. (Robt. W. Skinner Inc.) $2,200 £1,235

A Verneh horse blanket, the blue field with rows of stylised animals, 5ft.5in. x 4ft.7in. (Christie's) $1,163 £825

Southern Plains painted buffalo fur robe, 92in. long, 67in. wide. (Robt. W. Skinner Inc.) $500 £347

An Indian-style covered woven basket, 1916, 8¼in. high, 10½in. diam. (Robt. W. Skinner Inc.)$450 £267

Nez Perce twined cornhusk bag, 13½ x 18in. (Robt. W. Skinner Inc.) $475 £266

Tlingit twined spruce root rattle top basket, 5¼in. diam. (Robt. W. Skinner Inc.) $500 £280

Hopi polychrome wood Kachina doll, possibly the clown figure, 'Piptuka', early 20th century, 8½in. high. (Robt. W. Skinner Inc.) $900 £505

Northwest coast polychrome wood face mask, carved and incised cedar, 9½in. high. (Robt. W. Skinner Inc.) $2,500 £1,748

Great Lakes loom beaded cloth bandolier bag, late 19th century, 36in. long. (Robt. W. Skinner Inc.) $850 £477

Southwestern polychrome pottery jar, Zia, 14in. diam. (Robt. W. Skinner Inc.) $2,100 £1,179

Plains beaded and fringed hide cradleboard, Ute Reservation Period, 39in. high. (Robt. W. Skinner Inc.) $650 £365

A Hopi polychrome pottery canteen, painted over a creamy yellow slip in dark brown linear and 'Koshare' figural decoration, 3¼in. high. (Robt. W. Skinner Inc.) $200 £136

Southwestern pottery dough bowl, Cochiti, the interior painted over a cream slip in black foliate motifs, 14in. diam. (Robt. W. Skinner Inc.) $1,200 £816

Pacific Northwest Coast Attu circular basket with cover, 4in. high. (Christie's) $1,980 £1,131

Woodlands husk face mask, composed of bands of braided cornhusks, 11½in. high. (Robt. W. Skinner Inc.) $1,000 £699

Navajo fringed Germantown rug, woven on a bright red ground in navy-blue, dark red, pink, white and green, 76 x 83in. (Robt. W. Skinner Inc.) $7,750 £4,353

A Southwestern polychrome storage jar, San Ildefonso, of tall rounded form, 12½in. high. (Robt. W. Skinner Inc.) $700 £476

A Southwestern polychrome basketry tray, Yavapai, woven in red and dark brown designs on a golden field, 14½in. diam. (Robt. W. Skinner Inc.) $950 £646

Late 19th century Hopi polychrome wood Kachina doll, possibly 'Qoia', a Navajo singer, 16½in. high. (Robt. W. Skinner Inc.) $4,000 £2,247

Northwest coast mask, Bella/Bella Coola, of polychrome cedar wood, 12.5/8in. high. (Robt. W. Skinner Inc.) $49,000 £33,333

ANCHOVY POT LIDS

Anchovy paste with its salty taste is not everyone's idea of a tasty tea time snack but the Victorians loved it and consumed it on toast in vast quantities. To attract customers, paste manufacturers put their products in eye-catching tins or jars with brightly patterned lids. Those that have survived provide a rich field of interest for collectors. The most sought after are made of Prattware and decorated with transfer printed designs. Patriotic themes were especially popular and Royal coats of arms or pictures of Queen Victoria were very common — inferring that the paste was as popular with the Royals as with their subjects. The best known makers of anchovy paste were Burgess, Osborn and Thorne who made a brand called Thorne's Inimitable Anchovy Paste which came in a pot with a flag decorated lid.

Small lid by E. Lazenby & Son 6 Edwards Street, Portman Square, London. $25 £15

Gorgona anchovy paste lid by R.T.N., printed in black on a white background. $45 £25

Small lid by E. Lazenby & Son of London, bearing the word 'Manufactory'. $30 £18

Anchovy paste lid by Morel Bro' Cobbett & Son Ltd., 18 Pall Mall, London. $25 £15

Rare lid by J. N. Osborn with the design in pastel shades of blue and red on a white background. $435 £250

Anchovy paste lid by G. F. Sutton & Co., 100 High Holborn, London. $18 £10

Hannell's Real Gorgona anchovy paste lid, 35 Davies Street, Berkeley Square, London. $25 £15

Real Gorgona anchovy paste lid by Manfield's, 20 Poland St., Oxford Street, London. $35 £20

Large size Burgess's genuine anchovy paste lid, '107 Strand, corner of the Savoy steps'. $20 £12

Edward VII lid by Burgess's, Hythe Rd., Willesden, London. $14 £8

Anchovy paste lid referred to as 'London Lid', with no maker's name. $55 £30

Anchovy paste lid by Burgess's 'The Original Fish Sauce Warehouse'. $10 £6

Early 1860's lid by Cross & Blackwell, 21 Soho Square and Ilking St., Soho. $55 £30

E. Lazenby & Son lid, Edward Street, Portman Square, London. $45 £25

Small lid by G. F. Sutton, Sons & Co., Osborne Works, Brandon Road, King's Cross. $14 £8

Crosse & Blackwell lid, 21 Soho Square, London, established 1706. $14 £8

Real Gorgona anchovy paste lid by Harry Peck's, Snow Hill, London. $20 £12

A pictorial lid by Crosse & Blackwell, in sepia on a white background. $60 £35

Anchovy paste lid by G. F. Sutton & Co., Osborne Works, King's Cross, W.C. $18 £10

'London' lid printed in black on a white background. $35 £20

George V anchovy paste lid by Burgess's, Hythe Road, Willesden, N.W. $20 £12

ARMOUR

During the days of chivalry a few knights went out to fight in full suits of armour but the fashion did not last as long as people imagine because the weight and unwieldiness of the suits made the men inside vulnerable to attack from lighter and more nimble opponents. The suit of armour is perhaps more highly regarded by collectors today than it was by serious fighting men of the past. Genuine old suits, often made in Germany for ceremonial use only, are very expensive but care has to be taken because they have been copied for many years and it takes an expert to tell a 15th century suit from one made in the 19th century. Individual pieces of armour are less bulky, less problematic and much easier to find. Gauntlets, arm and shoulder covers, helmets, face guards and breastplates are all collected but they too are sometimes not as old or as genuine as they seem. Unwary 19th century collectors were even duped by clever forgers working around Waterloo immediately after the battle.

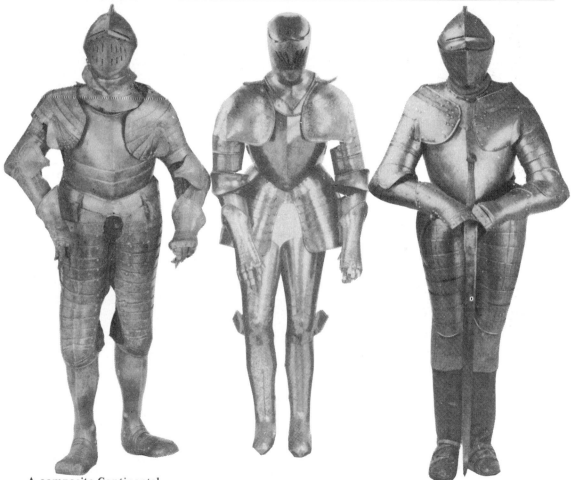

A composite Continental armour mainly in early 17th century style, mounted on a fabric-covered wooden dummy, with realistically-carved, painted and bearded head set with glass eyes. (Christie's) $6,674 £3,800

A composite Continental armour in mid 16th century style, with roped borders and etched decoration, on a wooden stand. (Christie's) $3,560 £2,000

A composite Cuirassiers three-quarter armour, circa 1600, fingers lacking from gauntlets, pitted and cleaned overall. (Phillips) $4,536 £2,800

A 15th century Turkish breastplate, Krug, struck with the St. Irene arsenal mark. (Wallis & Wallis) $207 £190

A 17th century Indian chiselled steel arm defence bazu band, 13in. (Wallis & Wallis) $91 £64

A 17th/18th century mail coat with short sleeves. (Christie's) $267 £190

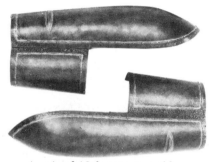

A breastplate probably adapted in the early 19th century. (Wallis & Wallis) $302 £200

A pair of 18th century gold damascened Indian arm defences Bazu-Band, 12¾in., of solid shaped form. (Wallis & Wallis) $266 £230

A 17th century Continental breastplate with twin studs for fastening and shoulder straps. (Wallis & Wallis) $214 £150

A Georgian copy of a fully articulated and fluted 16th century Maximilian full suit of armour. (Wallis & Wallis) $7,150 £5,000

Early 17th century pikeman's breastplate together with associated simulated five lame tassets. (Christie's) $846 £600

A suit of armour dated Tenmon gonen (1536). (Christie's) $3,706 £2,592

A pair of 17th century Indian arm guards bazu band made for a princeling, 10in. (Wallis & Wallis) $286 £200

An early 19th century Indo-Persian gold damascened steel shield dhal, 13¼in.. (Wallis & Wallis) $224 £145

A left hand gauntlet circa 1580, deep roped knuckle-piece, four lames, and cuff. (Wallis & Wallis) $270 £155

A breastplate struck with maker's mark and a musket ball proof test, circa 1600. (Wallis & Wallis) $567 £430

A pair of 17th century iron stirrups decorated in silver and gilt with massed cherry-blossom and meyuimon, signed Kitamura. (Christie's)
$1,698 £1,188

Prussian Regt. of Garde du Corps officer's parade cuirass. (Christie's)
$6,525 £4,500

A kebiki-laced kuchiba-iro-odoshi tosei-gusoku. (Christie's) $4,406 £3,240

A composite armour comprising: lacquered iron four-plate momonari kabuto with four lame shikiro and modern kuwagata, all contained in a wood box, some restoration. (Phillips) $2,464 £1,400

A decorative composite armour mainly in 16th century style, on a wooden display-stand with square base. (Christie's)
$1,602 £900

ART POTTERY

Art pottery is the work of an individual potter which shows that person's artistry, style and originality. It is not mass produced. From earliest times artist/potters have made one-off items of beauty and in the 19th century there was a great demand for individually created pieces. The Martin brothers were art potters par excellence. One of the first big pottery concerns to encourage and provide facilities for art potters was Doulton's for, from the 1860's onwards, Henry Doulton invited students from the nearby Lambeth College of Art to work in his Studio which was financed by the more prosaic side of his business. He never attempted to impose an "house style" on his protégés who were encouraged to give their art full expression. Among many who worked at Doulton's were George Tinworth, the Barlows, William Rix, who discovered ways of producing marbling effects in pottery glazes, and Charles J. Noke who invented the famous Flambe and Chang glazes.

A faience vase decorated with entwined leaves and fruit, 8½in. high, circa 1877. $150 £85

A large Royal Doulton Burslem Holbein Ware jardiniere decorated with four cavaliers playing cards, 13¼in. high, signed W. Nunn. $785 £450

Royal Doulton vase painted by Ethel Beard, 13in. high. $210 £120

A Doulton Lambeth coffee pot painted with a purple iris, circa 1879. $385 £220

A pair of Doulton Lambeth faience oil lamp bases decorated by Esther Lewis, 10¼in. high. $785 £450

Royal Doulton Chang vase by Noke and Moore, 7½in. high, circa 1935. $960 £550

Doulton Lambeth faience vase with the artist's monogram for Mary Butterton, circa 1880.
$315 £180

A Royal Doulton Sung vase by Charles Noke and Fred Moore, 7in. high, circa 1930. $260 £150

A Royal Doulton Sung vase by Noke, 6¾in. high, circa 1928.
$700 £400

Royal Doulton faience vase by John H. McLennan, decorated with panels representing Earth and Water, 13½in. high.
$315 £180

Doulton Art Pottery jardiniere with a blue ground and applied flowers, 8¾in. high. $105 £60

A Doulton Burslem baluster vase painted with an Edwardian lady, by H. G. Theaker, 10¼in. high. $575 £330

A Doulton Lambeth faience vase painted with stylised flowers, by Emily Gillman, 9¼in. high. $150 £85

A Doulton Burslem Morrisian ware teapot decorated with a band of dancing maidens, 7¾in. high, circa 1899. $140 £80

An oviform pate-sur-pate vase decorated with birds by Florence Barlow, 15in. high.
$610 £350

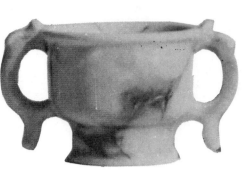

Royal Doulton Sung vase by
Charles Noke and Fred Moore,
10¼in. high, circa 1930.
$455 £260

Royal Doulton Chinese jade
two-handled bowl in white and
green, 3½in. high. $560 £320

A Doulton Lambeth Silicon
ware oviform vase, by Edith
D. Lupton and Ada Dennis,
20.5cm. high, dated 1885.
$330 £190

Doulton Lambeth faience vase
decorated with daffodils and
narcissi, 10½in. high. $140 £80

A large Royal Doulton Sung
vase by Arthur Eaton, decorated with dragons amongst
clouds, 13in. high, circa 1930.
$1,400   £800

A Royal Doulton jug decorated
with a maiden wearing a flowing
dress, 10½in. high. $260 £150

A Royal Doulton earthenware
globular vase, 21.8cm. high.
$95 £55

A Royal Doulton Titanian ware
teapot, 6½in. high, circa 1920.
$55 £30

Royal Doulton Chang vase by
C. J. Noke and Harry Nixon,
7½in. high, circa 1930.
$2,100 £1,200

ART NOUVEAU POSTCARDS

Of all types, Art Nouveau postcards are the most prestigious and can fetch hundreds and even thousands of pounds. Many were originally designs for posters by such artists as Alphonse Mucha or Jules Cheret (worth £50-£300 each). Look out for the Collection des Cent, a series of 100 cards published in 1901, or Editions Cino (1898) a series of 35 cards including work by Toulouse Lautrec, which can be worth £50-£500 each.

Art Nouveau postcard embossed and overlaid with silver, by Raphael Tuck. $12 £7

'Autumn', an Art Nouveau study by A. K. Macdonald. $25 £15

'Mikado', an Oriental study by Raphael Kirschner, Series 600. $35 £20

Velkonocni Pozdrav, an Art Nouveau Easter postcard printed in Czechoslovakia. $10 £6

'In the Eventide', a study by A. K. Macdonald. $25 £15

'Der Verrufene Weiher', by M. Webenwein, Viennese artist. $10 £6

An embroidered Continental study by Hans Volkert. $14 £8

ART NOUVEAU POSTCARDS

Art Nouveau study of a girl
with a goblet, printed in black.
$9 £5

Art Nouveau study of a girl
with a cigarette, by S.
Hilderscheimer. $18 £10

An Art Nouveau Easter card
printed in Czechoslovakia by
Velkonocni Pozdrau. $10 £6

'Cartolina Postale', a set of four cards by Raphael Kirchner. $210 £120

'Femme a L'Eventail' by
Brunelleschi, printed in France.
$105 £60

'My hope and heart is with thee',
a series postcard by Raphael
Tuck, No. 3571. $30 £18

'Peacock Feathers' by Raphael
Kirschner, series 660. $35 £20

AUTOGRAPHS

Autographs of the famous and infamous have always held a certain fascination, but it is since the rise of the film and pop star that they have become popular as never before and they can sometimes fetch surprising sums at auction.

A simple autograph on its own is obviously prone to forgery, particularly on photographs, and many pop stars did in fact employ people to sign photographs for them! Needless to say, these are worth much less than the real thing, and any expensive autograph really must be authenticated before purchase. Personal letters from celebrities are much preferable. In terms of value, the autographs of most modern personalities are only worth a few pounds, with prices rising the further back they date eg Laurel and Hardy or Harry Houdini. The ones which fetch a premium are those of people who were known rarely to sign autographs, and, of course, Royalty.

Sir William Richmond, the artist, 1863. (Border Bygones) $35 £20

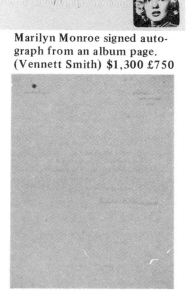

Marilyn Monroe signed autograph from an album page. (Vennett Smith) $1,300 £750

Hiram Powers, the American sculptor, 1866. (Border Bygones) $85 £50

Charles Darwin autographed letter about the orangutan. (Phillips) $4,420 £2,600

Signed letter from Winston Churchill on Chartwell notepaper, dated 5 January 1958. $500 £300

English £1 note, signed by Winston Churchill, F. D. Roosevelt and Stanley Matthews. (Onslow's) $830 £500

Samuel Prout, the artist. (Border Bygones) $60 £35

AUTOGRAPHS

Jack Doyle, the boxer.
(Border Bygones) $25 £15

Walt Disney signed album page.
(Vennett Smith) $350 £200

Charles Dickens envelope
stuck down on card, addressed
and signed to his son at Eton.
(Phillips) $110 £65

The original contract signed
by Jacob Epstein for 'A
Monument in Memory of the
Late Oscar Wilde', commissioned
by Robert Ross, 1909. (Phillips)
$7,820   £4,600

Enrico Caruso, together with
caricature, 1910. (Border
Bygones) $175 £100

Sir Charles Eastlake, the
artist, 1862. (Border Bygones)
$45 £25

Lady Halle, the violinist,
1888. (Border Bygones)$35 £20

Autographed letter from David
Livingstone, 1865. (Vennett
Smith) $525 £300

C. Babbage, mathematician,
inventor of the calculating
machine. (Border Bygones)
$50 £30

AUTOMATONS

The Victorian age was the hey-day of the automaton for not only were hundreds of ingenious mechanical toys produced but there was a huge demand for automatons for adults as well — automatic writers, piano players, shoe cleaners, music makers and pier-end machines figured among the hundreds of them.

The earliest automatons were devised in the 18th century by a Swiss family called Jacquet-Droz and they were the wonder of the sophisticated world at that time. Some early automatons were made in the form of animal orchestras with monkeys in powdered wigs and silken jackets playing instruments with musical accompaniments, or elegant singing birds in gilded cages, opening their beaks and turning their heads as they poured out their songs. The first automatons were, like watches, powered by ingeniously coiled springs but other inventors propelled their machines with compressed air, water, sand, mercury or steam. It was the spring however that proved to be the most popular and most efficient.

Early automatons by such famous names as Vaucanson, Robertson or Rechsteiner, particularly the writing and drawing machines, are worth thousands of pounds today. Talking dolls developed by Von Kempelen are in the same price bracket.

In the 19th century German manufacturers saw the possibility of mass producing automatic toys for children and their tin plate industry began to boom around the 1870's. These toys were not so sophisticated as the earlier automatons for they were pressed out by machines and their works were rudimentary but they were cheap and popular and were exported widely, especially to England.

Mid 19th century Swiss musical automaton of singing birds, on oval base, 60cm. high. (Christie's)
$1,980 £1,381

Mid 19th century automaton of a singing bird in a cage, the movement signed Bontems, Paris, 21½in. high. (Christie's)
$1,760 £1,075

A French musical clock diorama, signed Hy Marc, 37¾ x 26¾in. (Lawrence Fine Arts)
$2,774 £1,550

Late 19th century 'Boy Feeding Pig' automaton, the bisque head marked Jumeau SGDG 4, 18¾in. high. (Robt. W. Skinner Inc.) $2,600 £1,805

A musical automaton of a bisque headed doll beside a dressing table, marked Simon & Halbig S & H 6, the doll 15in. high. (Christie's)
$3 000 £2,000

27

AUTOMATONS

Late 19th century Continental singing bird automaton in repousse sterling silver gilt casket, 4¼in. wide. (Reeds Rains) $769 £520

A 19th century clockwork lady knitting automaton, Germany, 21in. high. (Robt. W. Skinner Inc.)
$1,800 £1,250

A varicoloured gold musical fob seal with commemorative portraits of Napoleon I and Josephine and an erotic automaton, Swiss, early 19th century, 42mm. high. (Christie's) $17,600 £10,757

A singing bird automaton with clock, Swiss, probably by Jacquet Droz, circa 1785, 20in. high. (Christie's)
$44,000 £30,703

A clockwork fur covered rabbit automaton, emerging from a green cotton covered cabbage, 7½in. high, French, circa 1900. (Christie's)
$544 £330

A mid 19th century German portable barrel organ automaton, 52cm. wide. (Phillips)
$9,000 £6,000

A composition headed automaton modelled as a standing Chinese man, 30in. high, French 1880. (Christie's)
$9,000 £6,000

A French automaton dancing couple by Theroude, on velvet lined circular base, 12in. high. (Lawrence Fine Art)
$1,700 £950

A Leopold Lambert musical automaton doll, 'The Flower Seller', the Jumeau bisque head impressed 4, 19½in. high. (Lawrence Fine Art)
$6,265 £3,500

AVON BOTTLES

Most women will remember at least some of the pretty and imaginative containers in which the Avon company have marketed their products since their launch on the UK market in the early 60s, and it seems somehow obvious that these should now be a subject for collection. To attract top prices, bottles should be in pristine condition, accompanied by original boxes where these existed. Full bottles, however, do not attract a premium, so the contents of your Christmas gift can be used with impunity!

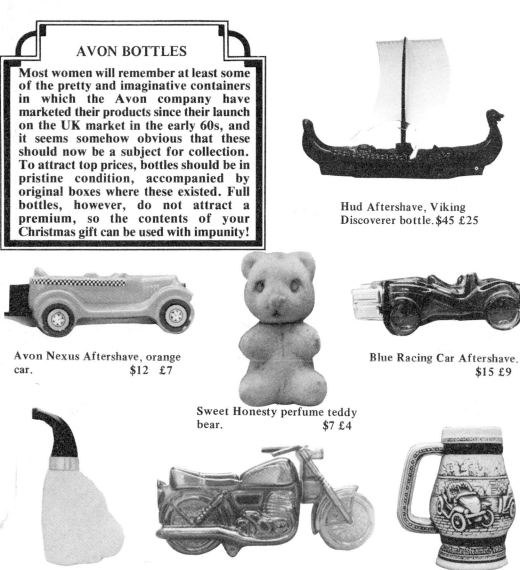

Hud Aftershave, Viking Discoverer bottle. $45 £25

Avon Nexus Aftershave, orange car. $12 £7

Sweet Honesty perfume teddy bear. $7 £4

Blue Racing Car Aftershave. $15 £9

Tai Winds Aftershave, blood-hound pipe bottle. $14 £8

Aftershave motor bike bottle. $25 £15

Stanley Steamer mug, hand-painted in Brazil for Avon, 1982. $35 £20

Wild Country aftershave in blue train bottle. $20 £12

Tai Winds Aftershave, Dutch pipe bottle. $25 £15

Moonwind eau de cologne, black cat bottle. $9 £5

AVON BOTTLES

Avon Moonwind Pierot bottle.
$10 £6

Moonwind eau de cologne,
gold telephone bottle. $9 £5

Occur eau de cologne,
gramophone bottle. $7 £4

Tai Winds Aftershave, veteran
car bottle. $18 £10

Wild Country Aftershave,
siege cannon bottle. $12 £7

Tai Winds Aftershave, pointer
dog bottle. $10 £6

Andy Cap Blue Blazer body
powder, 1969. $175 £100

Exclusive Bath Oil in green
marbled jug. $7 £4

Nexus Aftershave, footballer
bottle. $35 £20

Xmas decoration bubble bath
oil. $15 £9

Elegance, blue bell bottle.
$10 £6

Moonwind bath oil, orange
teapot. $14 £8

BADEN POWELL ITEMS

Although Robert Stephenson Smyth Baden-Powell is remembered today as the founder of the Scouting movement, he was a hero before that. The people of Victorian Britain lauded him as the defender of Mafeking during the Boer War because he held the town against the besieging Boers for many months in 1900 and when it was relieved, the general populace rejoiced wildly up and down the country. Baden-Powell became a popular hero and pieces of commemorative pottery, statuettes, biscuit tins, cigarette cards, badges and Vesta cases were decorated with his image. It was not until 1908 that he started the Boy Scout movement and its worldwide success has provided Baden-Powell collectors with a second string of possibilities. Not only can they look for relics and mementoes of the military hero but they also seek out early Scouting items which range from copies of his book "Scouting for Boys", to early badges, photographs, pieces of uniform and other mementoes of the great jamborees of the movement.

Staffordshire cup depicting Major General R. S. S. Baden Powell. $45 £25

Colourful biscuit tin with 'View of Mafeking and Baden Powell', in brown and blue. $35 £20

Small Staffordshire fluted cream jug with portrait of Baden Powell. $35 £20

Wooden butter dish with Staffordshire centre depicting Baden Powell in sepia, 7in. diam. $45 £25

Brass bust of Baden Powell on a marble plinth, 3in. high. $70 £40

Nicely shaped Staffordshire jug with a portrait of Baden Powell. $35 £20

Two-handled loving cup with the portrait of Lieut-Col. R. S. S. Baden Powell. $35 £20

Unusual clay pipe in good condition, the bowl formed in the image of Baden Powell. $45 £25

German made teapot of pale orange ground with sepia image of Baden Powell and gilt decoration. $55 £30

BADEN POWELL ITEMS

Silver vesta case embossed with the image of Baden Powell. $45 £25

An unusual teapot featuring Baden Powell in Boer War uniform together with scouts in a camping scene. $60 £35

A small tin pin tray, 'Souvenir of South Africa 1899—1900', featuring Baden Powell, 3in. diam. $25 £15

A plaster bust of Baden Powell, 10in. high. $60 £35

Royal Worcester plate featuring Col. R. S. S. Baden Powell, decorated with garlands of flowers. $70 £40

Staffordshire figure of Baden Powell with cannon, 22in. high. $260 £150

Wedgwood style blue and white coffee pot by Dudson, England, 6in. high. $45 £25

Stamped brass hanging wall plaque of Baden Powell, 5½in. high. $35 £20

Tall Staffordshire milk jug with gilt decoration and portrait of Baden Powell. $35 £20

BAIRNSFATHERWARE

If ever a war needed a leavening of humour to help men survive its horrors, it was the Great War of 1914-18. Not surprisingly humour was rather short at the time however and when the cartoons of Bruce Bairnsfather made their first appearance in a military newspaper, featuring the character of "Ol' Bill" the long suffering Tommy, they were greeted with enthusiasm. Perhaps the best known of Bairnsfather's cartoons shows two Tommies sharing a shell hole and one saying to the other who is obviously grumbling . . . "Well, if you knows a better 'ole, go to it".

Ol' Bill became a cult figure, a sort of pro-war propaganda to divert attention from the reality of the carnage. He was reproduced in hundreds of different ways — not only in Bairnsfather's own "Fragments from France" cartoons but also in pottery figures including one made by Carlton Ware showing Ol' Bill with the arms of the City of London stamped over his greatcoat. There were Ol' Bill mugs, car mascots, ashtrays and badges. His image was printed onto handkerchiefs, scarves, posters, postcards and magazines. There were films and plays about him and Bairnsfather's cartoons were made into jig saw puzzles and prints. More than 50 different ones were available.

There is now an illustrated catalogue of Bairnsfatherware called "In Search of the Better 'Ole" published by Milestone Publications, 62 Murray Road, Horndean, Hampshire, PO8 9JL.

Beswick 'Old Bill' coloured mug, tooth brush moustache. $105 £60

Grimwade shaving mug, 'Where did that one go to?' with Margate Coat of Arms. $105 £60

Grimwade vase, 'Where did that one go to?' 33cm. high. $114 £65

Old Bill 'Humpty Dumpty' shape cloth doll with no arms, 18cm. high. $140 £80

St Dunstans Collecting Box with 'Three Happy Men of St Dunstans' and 'Old Bills' Appeal', tin, 14cm. high. $105 £60

BAIRNSFATHERWARE

Grimwade vase depicting 'Old Bill', 'At present we are staying at a farm'.
$85 £50

Grimwade pottery plate with decorative edging 'Where did that one go to?' $85 £50

Grimwade vase 'Well if you knows of a better 'ole, go to it'. $85 £50

'Old Bill' pottery head in white. $85 £50

Bystander 'Fragments' Playing Cards, by Chas. Goodall & Son Ltd. $50 £30

Carlton ware standing figure of 'Old Bill', with coloured face and balaclava, 'Yours to a cinder Old Bill'. $190 £110

Grimwade vase 'Well Alfred, 'ow are the cakes'. $105 £60

Shaped pottery plate with decorative border in relief 'What time do they feed the sea lions Alf?' $80 £45

'Old Bill' brass car mascot.
$263 £150

BAIRNSFATHERWARE

Old Bill cloth doll on wire frame. Used as Red Cross fund raiser, 13cm. high. $105 £60

Carlton ware standing figure of 'Old Bill', 'British Empire Exhibition'. $150 £85

'Old Bill' brass circular ashtray, 14cm. diam., with inscribed signature. $79 £45

'Fragments' magazine, Christmas 1919 edition. $26 £15

Carlton ware 'Shrapnel Villa', 'Tommies Dugout Somewhere in France!' $70 £40

Glass slide 'Where did that one go to?' $12 £7

Small shouldered Grimwade vase, 'Where did that one go?' $85 £50

Grimwade circular fruit bowl, 'Coiffure in the trenches', 25cm. diam. $88 £50

'Old Bill' coloured pottery head. $105 £60

BANKNOTES

The oldest surviving paper money dates from the Chinese Ming dynasty of the 14th century when 12 inch long bank notes were printed on mulberry paper bark. Though the notes were worth a small fortune in their time, today they can be bought for around £400 each. More valuable are Scottish notes issued by banks which crashed spectacularly. The first to go was **Douglas Heron's** bank in Ayr which had a three year life span in the 1770's but more sought after by collectors are notes issued by the City of Glasgow Bank which closed in 1878. One of its £5 notes is today worth around £1,000.

Collectors of bank notes seek out notes issued by transitory regimes – French Revolution notes, American Confederate notes, notes made as currency in concentration camps and notes issued by dictators like Idi Amin or governments like the Sandinista regime in Nicaragua. Even more desirable are notes with mistakes or one of the very rare million pound notes issued by the Bank of England in 1948 but quickly withdrawn. Condition is an important factor in the pricing of old bank notes so they should be handled as little as possible.

Portugal: 1910 100 milreis. (Phillips)
$284 £160

J. G. Nairne Bank of England Note £5
21 September 1916 issued at Hull. (Phillips)
$783 £440

Great Britain: Cruikshank Anti-Hanging note. (Phillips) $302 £170

Ireland: Ulster Bank: £100 1941. (Phillips)
$284 £160

United States of America: 1890 $20 National
Currency for 1st National Bank of San
Francisco. (Phillips) $284 £160

J. B. Page Bank of England Note £10
1971-75 error with most of reverse image
appearing on front of note. $640 £360

New Zealand: 1916 Band of New Zealand
£1 uniface colour trial in green, yellow and
multicolour. (Phillips) $445 £250

Henry Hase Bank of England Note £2
13 April 1811, tears in body of note and
damaged upper right. (Phillips) $356 £200

Ireland: Central Bank: £100 1949. (Phillips)
                                     $231 £130

St Kitts: 1938 Royal Bank of Canada $5.
(Phillips) $462 £260

Ireland: Provincial Bank: £1 July 1924,
10mm tear bottom of centre crease. (Phillips)
                                     $106   £60

K. O. Peppiatt Bank of England Note £20
16 December 1939. (Phillips) $605 £340

Trinidad: 1940 $100. (Phillips)$462 £260

C. P. Mahon Bank of England Note 10/-
1928 A01 prefix. (Phillips) $302 £170

Australia: 1870 Bukkulla Vineyards £1.
(Phillips) $320 £180

1914 Banque Industrielle de Chine $1.
(Phillips) $133 £75

Isle of Man: Manx Bank £1 1919. (Phillips)
$605 £340

Russia: 1811 25 roubles Assignat. (Phillips)
$462 £260

1871-72 Bank of South Australia unissued
set of £1, £5, £10, £20 and £50. (Phillips)
$4,628 £2,600

China: 1918 Yokohama Specie Bank $1
issued at Tientsin. (Phillips) $302 £170

J. Bradbury Treasury Note £1 August 1914, (Phillips) $516 £290

British Guiana: 1929 Government £1. (Phillips) $249 £140

Devon and Cornwall Banking Company: £5 proof on card for Exeter. (Phillips) $462 £260

J. Bradbury Treasury Note 10/- 1918-19. (Phillips) $356 £200

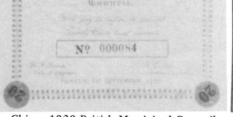

China: 1939 British Municipal Council (Tientsin) note "Will Pay to Bearer on Demand, Twenty Cents Local Currency". (Phillips) $160 £90

New Zealand: £10 uniface colour trial in dark blue, mauve and multicolour. (Phillips) $515 £290

United States of America: 1872 $1 National Currency for The Pomeroy National Bank (Ohio). (Phillips) $587 £330

Belgian Congo: 1921 5 francs uniface colour trials, front in blue and green for Stanleyvill and back in brown for Kinshasa. (Phillips) $267 £150

BAROMETERS

The principle of the barometer was invented in 1643 by a Florentine mathematician called Evangelista Torricelli and in 1660 British born Robert Boyle adapted the technique to the production of a weather glass. The earliest barometers were produced by famous horologists like Tompion, Quare, John Patrick, Henry Jones and Charles Orme and examples of their craftsmanship that survive today are exorbitantly expensive. However the possibility of being able to forecast the weather appealed to people in every walk of life and soon cheaper barometers were produced in large numbers. By the end of the 18th century, the banjo shaped barometer made its appearance and the Victorians bought them as essential pieces of decoration for their halls. The finest examples were made in mahogany or satinwood frames with boxwood stringing round the edges and silvered dials. Some incorporated thermometers, hygrometers, spirit levels or clocks and the more dials there were, the more expensive the barometer was and still is.

A grande sonnerie calendar carriage clock cum barometer, the barometer inscribed R. W. Inglis 1897, 6½in. high.
$4,375 £2,500

Brass ship's barometer, circa 1860. (British Antique Exporters) $130 £75

A walnut cased combined time-piece, barograph, aneroid barometer and thermometer, signed Chadburn & Son, 26¾ x 14in. (Lawrence Fine Arts)
$800 £460

A brass and nickel plated yacht barometer modelled as a turret with simulated cannons, 4½in. high. $125 £70

A George I walnut signal barometer, the brass plate inscribed Made by John Patrick in the Old Bailey London, 36¼ x 29½in. (Christie's)
$12,250 £7,000

A late 19th century oxodised brass surveying aneroid barometer, by Pidduck & Sons, Hanley, 6in. diam. $260 £150

BAROMETERS

A large Victorian oak wheel barometer, inscribed Fletcher and Sons, London, 46½in. high. (Christie's)
$569   £308

A late 17th century walnut stick barometer, the engraved brass plates for Summer and Winter, 48in. high. (Christie's)
$2,499 £1,700

A Sheraton period wheel barometer, by J. B. Roncheti. (Woolley & Wallis)
$5,904 £4,100

A late 17th century walnut stick barometer, unsigned, 39½in. high. (Christie's)
$3,234 £2,200

A large 19th century rosewood wheel clock barometer, signed J. Amadio, 128cm. high, circa 1835. (Phillips)
$3,620 £2,000

A late 19th century oak American Forecast or Royal Polytechnic bulb Cistern barometer, 107cm. high. (Phillips)
$536 £360

A mid Victorian papier-mache barometer, 38in. high. (Christie's)
$471 £330

An early 19th century mahogany Sheraton shell wheel barometer, 8in. diam. silver dial signed Lione, Somalvico & Co., 100cm. high. (Phillips) $457 £320

BAROMETERS

A George III mahogany barometer, the dial signed Malacrida, London, 37½in. high. (Christie's)
$3,052 £1,650

A mahogany wheel barometer, inscribed Dring and Fage, London, 38½in. high. (Christie's) $447 £242

George II mahogany stick barometer with silvered face, signed F. Watkins, London, 40½in. high: $39,204 (Christie's) £24,200

A late 19th century mahogany wheel barometer, dial signed Leoni Taroni & Co., London, 36¼in. high. (Christie's) $865 £528

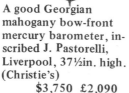

An oak wheel barometer, inscribed Gulliford, Dunster, 42in. high. (Christie's)
$407 £220

A good Georgian mahogany bow-front mercury barometer, inscribed J. Pastorelli, Liverpool, 37½in. high. (Christie's)
$3,750 £2,090

A Victorian mahogany wheel barometer with architectural pediment, inscribed A. Corti, Fecit, 38in. high. (Christie's)
$794 £418

A late 18th century mahogany stick barometer, signed Cary, London, 96cm. high. (Phillips) $1,086 £600

BEADWORK BAGS

Beadwork bags became popular in the 19th century, and the beads could be made from various materials, such as glass, steel, jade, leather, etc. Some were made of 'crochet' beadwork (worked outward in circles from the centre) or were knitted in rows. 20th century beadwork was often embroidered on a patterned canvas, while loom beadwork was used for more commerical bags. Look out for rare large bags with good landscapes or animal subjects worked on silk or satin.

Beadwork evening bag circa 1910, with chain link strap. $18 £10

19th century beadwork bag with tortoiseshell fittings and chain. $60 £35

19th century beadwork 'Dolly' bag with steel beads and tassel, satin lined. $105 £60

1920's black jet beaded evening bag with chain strap. $30 £18

1940's beadwork bag decorated with sequins, foreign made, with mirror inside. $20 £12

Early 1920's beadwork bag of black beads and sequins with satin lining. $40 £24

Late 19th century beadwork bag with gilded fittings and gold beads. $95 £55

(Brenda Riley)

BELLEEK

Belleek pottery has a characteristic, iridescent pearl-like glaze and has been produced at Fermanagh, Northern Ireland, since 1863. It first attracted popular attention when it was shown at the Dublin Exhibition of 1865. Some of the most attractive Belleek pieces were made in marine forms and date from between 1865 and 1880. They were modelled by the pottery's Art Director, R. W. Armstrong. As well as making glazed objects Belleek also produced parian china figures and statuettes while, in a later period, the firm made very attractive basketware dishes and thin moulded tea ware. High prices are paid today by collectors for the rarer and more ornate items produced by the company, particularly for basketware pieces trimmed with realistic looking roses. There is a Belleek Collectors' Society which publishes a magazine and operates from the pottery which is still based at Fermanagh and can be visited by appointment.

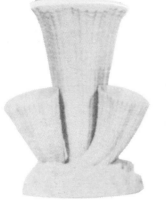

A Belleek cornucopia vase on shell moulded base, 9¼in. high. (Christie's) $382 £242

A Belleek porcelain trefoil basket, osier pattern, 5in. diam. (Hobbs & Chambers) $238 £150

One of a pair of Belleek flasks, circa 1863-91, 6in. high. $862 £770

Late 19th century Belleek figure of a young lady dressed in a classical style pink robe, 14¼in. high. (Outhwaite & Litherland) $1,131 £780

A Belleek earthenware spirit flask for rum, 1863-91, printed dog and harp mark, 11¾in. high. $739 £660

One of a pair of Belleek ewers of waisted form, black printed marks, second period, 20cm. high. (Christie's) $484 £432

A Belleek 'dolphin' candle-stick, modelled as a putto seated on a dolphin, 19.5cm. high, no. D343. (Phillips) $1,078 £700

A pair of Belleek candlestick figures of a boy and girl basket bearer, 22cm. high. (Phillips) $5,328 £3,600

A Belleek figure of a cooper standing before two barrels forming vases, 21cm. high. (Christie's) $3,080 £2,000

A Belleek model of a light-house, impressed Belleek and black printed marks, registration mark for 1873, 23cm. high. (Christie's) $1,078 £700

A Belleek rectangular plaque painted by Horatio H. Calder, black printed Belleek mark, First Period, 17 x 11.3cm. (Christie's) $3,850 £2,500

A Belleek First Period figure of 'The Crouching Venus', 18¼in. high. (Christie's) $1,160 £800

A Belleek 'tulip' vase, standing in a circular basket base encrus-ted with leaves, 31cm. high, no. D93. (Phillips) $3,388 £2,200

A pair of Belleek figures of 'Meditation' and 'Affection', 35cm. high, nos. D1134 and D20. (Phillips) $2,772 £1,800

One of a pair of Belleek nautilus vases, naturally modelled and heightened in pink, 21cm. high. (Christie's) $1,540 £1,000

BELLS

In the days before electric alarms, bells were essential items of life. They were in churches, on doors, in servants' halls and drawing room tables or hung round animals' necks. Basically there are two kinds of bell — the open church bell shape with a clapper swinging inside and the closed variety with a loose clapper moving freely inside the globe of the bell.

Bells were and still are used for a myriad different purposes from alerting people to fires to calling children to school or people to worship. Shepherds kept track of their flock with bells and tradesmen alerted customers to their approach by ringing a handbell. Collectors are fond of little bells that were used for summoning servants. They were made in a variety of materials ranging from china and glass to brass or silver. Favourites are in Cranberry, Bristol, Nailsea or Tiffany glass or the delicately carved Oriental bells that travellers brought home from India or Burma.

A table bell by Godert Van Ysseldijk, 14.5cm. high, maker's mark, The Hague, 1767, 306gr. $742 £495

An archaic bronze bell, nao, mid-1st Millenium B.C., 40cm. high, fitted box, wood stand and bell striker. (Christie's) $3,146 £2,200

A 19th century clear and cranberry glass bell, 13in. high, complete with clapper. (Robt. W. Skinner Inc.) $245 £140

20th century Welsh brass souvenir bell with lion handle, 7in. high. $9 £5

A small bronze ship's bell, almost certainly of European origin, circa 1750, 10.5cm. high. (Christie's) $3,004 £1,951

A French table bell, 10.2cm. high, maker's mark J.D., Paris, 1761, 138gr. $5,009 £3,604

BERLIN WOOLWORK

Embroidery was a pastime of the leisured lady from the Middle Ages on but in the 19th century, the rise of a new middle class meant that more women had time on their hands but no training for specialist sewing. The invention of a "painting by numbers" embroidery kit was a stroke of genius on the part of a manufacturer in Berlin who, from around 1804, started selling embroidery patterns printed on squared paper that were easy to copy onto canvas. Berlinwork was used to cover chairs and footstools or firescreens and occasionally a piece of work was framed in rosewood or maple and hung on the wall.

The designs were sometimes based on famous paintings or patterns of exotic flowers and birds. A popular subject was a sailing ship and these were often worked by sailors on long voyages. It was an easy art for all that had to done was to copy the pattern onto a canvas and fill it in with tent or cross stitch in wool. Sometimes the sewer included beads and cut pile patches to give texture and variety to the composition. By the 1830's the designs were sold printed direct onto canvas and more than 14,000 patterns were available in Britain alone. Later examples tended to be gaudy in colour because purple aniline dye was used extensively and after 1870 it became less fashionable because skilled needlewomen looked down on the practitioners of Berlinwork.

A Berlin woolwork cushion, the central medallion worked with raised plush roses, circa 1860, 18in. square. (Christie's)
$2,035 £1,404

A circular Berlin woolwork picture of an Indian Nabob, in black glass mount framed and glazed, circa 1840, 16in. high. (Christie's) $249 £172

Mid 19th century Berlin woolwork picture of a Turk, 29 x 25½in. (Christie's)
$548 £378

A large Berlin woolwork
bag with leather clasp and
brass handle, circa 1860.
(Christie's) $171 £118

A Victorian walnut framed
sewing chair on cabriole
legs. (G. A. Key) $619 £350

A rectangular needlework
cushion with summer flowers
on a brown ground, 18in. wide.
(Christie's) $311 £176

A mid Victorian black, gilt
and mother-of-pearl japanned
firescreen, 52in. high.
(Christie's) $2,674 £1,870

A 'Turkeywork' picture,
circa 1850, 21 x 19½in.
$326 £286

An early Victorian rose-
wood firescreen with glazed
panel, 40in. wide, 63in. high.
(Christie's) $826 £540

A raised work picture on an
ornamental pheasant against
a Berlin woolwork ground,
mid-19th century, 22 x 17½in.
(Christie's) $78 £54

A mid Victorian walnut
open armchair, the cartouche-
shaped padded back with gros
and petit point needlework
panel. (Christie's) $1,276 £880

A Victorian shield-shaped
petit point picture worked
in coloured wools with a
parrot perched on a branch,
21 x 17in. (Christie's)
$391 £270

BICYCLES

The first bicycle recorded in history is depicted in a stained glass window in a Stoke Poges church. It shows a figure seated on a wheeled instrument using his feet to propel himself along the ground. A better bicycle was exhibited before the court of Louis XVI and Marie Antionette in 1779 and in 1816 came the invention of the hobby horse, a simple device of two wheels and a cross bar on which the feet were again used for propulsion. The first real bicycle however was invented in Scotland in 1840 by Kirkpatrick MacMillan of Dumfries. Riding his machine, the inventor was fined for 'furious driving'. The first crank driven bicycle was the velocipede or 'bone shaker' of the 1860's and after that a wave of interest in bicycling swept both Britain and America. Even the lowest paid workers were able to achieve independence and mobility at a low cost. Today early bicycles, especially those made in the mid 19th century by the Coventry Sewing Machine Co or the Swift Cycle Co Ltd fetch high prices and examples from the early years of the 20th century are also rising in value.

A 1930's baker's iron framed delivery tricycle with original wooden boxed front and rear wheel brake, 85in. long. (Andrew Hartley) $743 £425

Dursley-Pedersen pedal cycle, circa 1905, with three-speed gearing. $1,435 £820

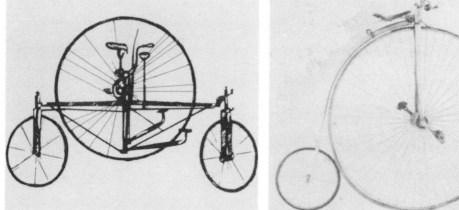

A James Starley Coventry lever tricycle built by Haynes & Jeffy's, 1877.
                                        $3,500 £2,000

Nickel plated steel high wheel bicycle, the 'Expert Columbia' model, by The Pope Manufacturing Co., wheel diam. 52in. (Robt. W. Skinner Inc.) $1,800 £1,440

A wood velocipede with canvas covered wheels, straight backbone and turned handlebars, 26in. diam., probably French, circa 1880. (Christie's) $1,821   £990

A fine, wooden framed Pedestrian Hobby Horse bicycle. (Phillips) $3,500 £2,000

Swift pedal tricycle with steering by twin hand grips, circa 1880. $3,250 £1,850

English BSA safety bicycle, circa 1885. $3,850 £2,200

A late 19th century child's bicycle with 16in. detachable driving wheel. (Christie's) $665 £380

A Royal Mail pennyfarthing bicycle painted in black with red coachline, with original leather seat. (Anderson & Garland) $1,662 £1,250

BIGGLES BOOKS

The story goes that when a journalist asked a famous fighter pilot in 1944 to what he owed his success, he replied simply 'Biggles.' The character was created by Capt. W. E. Johns, an ex-RFC pilot, after the Great War, and new titles continued to appear right up to his death almost half a century later.

It's true-blue Boys' Own Paper stuff, of England, Empire and Honour, which, perhaps because of the undying attraction of a 'rattling good yarn' has continued to fire the imagination of succeeding generations.

Recent attempts to remarket the image in more contemporary terms, in the form of a rather tongue-in-cheek film and a spoof biography have failed to make any real impression on the Faithful. Most titles are now out of print and hardly to be found even on library shelves because, as one librarian explained, they had long since been 'liberated' by not-so-honest addicts and collectors.

'Biggles Hits the Trail', pub. Brockhampton Press, 1960's reprint. $6 £3.50

'Biggles of 266', collection of short stories reprinted by Dean & Son 1960's. $9 £5

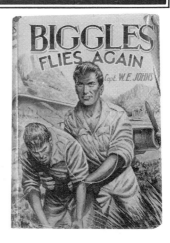

'Biggles Flies Again', pub. Dean & Son, 1960's reprint. $8 £4.50

'Biggles in The Cruise of the Condor', pub. Dean & Son, 1960's reprint. $5 £3

'Biggles Pioneer Air Fighter', collection of short stories pub. Thames Publishing Co. Originally published in 1932 under title 'The Camels Are Coming'. $12 £7

'Biggles in the South Seas', pub. Brockhampton Press 1962, originally published 1940, 6th impression 1952. $8 £4.50

BOOKS

For centuries books have been a favourite item for collection and more love has been lavished on them than on any other kind of collectable. They are treasured for their content as well as for their appearance. Book collecting is one of the more specialised areas of the market, one much practised by millionaires, and books are regarded as a safe resort for money against inflation. It is now rare for a box of mixed books with a first edition tucked away among them to be picked up in a local auction house for a few pence because each sale is attended by knowledgeable dealers.

Since books deal with every aspect of the world and life, a serious collector must specialise. Among the most highly sought after areas is topography because of the magnificent plates that illustrate many books — however they are expensive. Similarly "blue chip" are books on wild life, flowers and horticulture. Single plates of Redoute's roses or lilies fetch enormous prices. Victorian travel books and sporting books are also highly desirable.

Children's books, especially if illustrated by artists like Shepherd, Tenniel, Jessie M. King, Kay Neilsen or Kate Greenaway are very sought after as are Victorian children's books with attractive embossed covers. There is a strong market too in modern first editions with the ebb and flow of fashion and favour flowing from one author to another. Anniversaries of a certain author tend to put up their price. Even paperback books are collected — first edition Penguins, especially "Ariel", the first of them all, fetch hundreds of pounds. Modern first editions must have their dust covers and be in good condition to fetch premium prices.

Combe (William): The English Dance of Death, 2 vol.s, hand-col. front, and vig. title, 72 hand-col. plates by Rowlandson, 1 cover detached. (Phillips) $1,337 £700

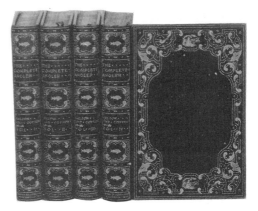

Walton (I.) and Cotton (C.): The Complete Angler, ed Sir H. Nicolas, extended to 4 vols with specially printed titles. (Phillips) $3,490 £1,950

Combe (W.): The Tour(s) of Doctor Syntax. (Phillips) $930 £520

Sydenham Edwards: The new Flora Britannica, 61 hand-coloured plates, quarto, 1812. (Phillips) $1,680 £1,050

Lunardi (Vincent): An Account of the First Aerial Voyage in England, 2nd Edn., small 4to, 1784. (Phillips) $264 £180

The Bible bound with Book of Common Prayer, engraved title dated 1672, printed title 1679. (Phillips) $3,200 £2,000

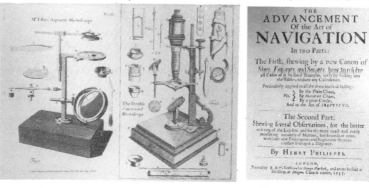

Omar Khayyam, Rubaiyat, trans. E. Fitzgerald, 16 colour plates, by W. Pogany, g.e. by Riviere, circa 1930. (Phillips) $987 £700

George Adams, Essays On The Microscope, with atlas of plates, First Edition, London 1787, 2 vols., 4to and oblong 4to (the atlas). (Christie's) $1,100 £759

Philippes (Henry: The Advancement of the Art of Navigation, First Edn., 3 parts in 1 vol., illus. in text, 4to, 1657. (Phillips) $1,764 £1,200

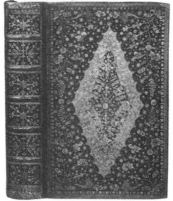

Koch and Kellermeistern von Allen Speison Getrenken, title printed in red and black woodcuts, Frankfurt, 1554. (Phillips) $4,160 £2,600

Irish Binding: Book of Common Prayer, contemporary red morocco, lined case, Cambridge, John Baskerville, 1760. (Phillips) $1,434 £880

Doves Press, Alfred Lord Tennyson, Seven Poems and two Translations, Limited Edition, by Cobden-Sanderson, signed and dated 1903. (Phillips) $1,128 £800

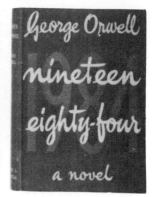

John Watson Stewart, The Gentleman's and Citizen's Almanack, g.e., Dublin, T. and J. W. Stewart, 1755. (Phillips) $1,015 £720

Halford (F. M.): Dry Fly Entomology, 2 vols., No. 22 of 75 copies signed by the author, 1897. (Phillips) $1,249 £850

Orwell (G.): Nineteen Eight-Four, First Edn., 1949. (Phillips) $750 £500

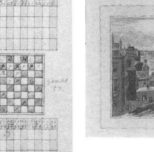

Gianutio (Horatio): Libro nel Quale si tratta della Maniera di Giuocara Scacchi, modern vellum, Turin, A. de Bianchi, 1597. (Phillips) $3,200 £2,000

Greco Gioachino, 1600-c.1634, Manuscript entitled 'The Royall Game of Chess', comprising 95 games executed in pen, ink and green wash. (Phillips) $1,408 £880

W. Daniell and R. Ayton: A Voyage Round Great Britain, 8 volumes in 4, 2 vols. of plates, folio, 1814-26. (Phillips) $19,200 £12,000

T. S. Eliot: The Waste Land, Ltd. Edn., No. 92 of 300, Officina Bodoni, 1961. (Phillips) $992 £620

James Scott of Edinburgh Binding, The Holy Bible containing the Old and New Testaments, London, J. Baskett, 1741 bound with Psalms of David, Edinburgh, A. Kincaid, 1772. (Phillips) $1,762 £1,250

James Scott of Edinburgh Binding, The Holy Bible bound with Psalms of David, dark blue morocco gilt, g.e., Edinburgh, A. Kincaid, 1772. (Phillips) $1,410 £1,000

Vale Press, R. Browning,
Dramatic Romances and
Lyrics, Limited Edition of
210, 1899. (Phillips)
$958 £680

Bridges (R): Sketches Illustrative of the Manners and
Costumes of France, Switzer-
land and Italy, 49 col. plates,
4to, 1821. (Phillips)
$447 £300

Fowles (J.): The Collector,
First Edn., 1963. (Phillips)
$135 £90

E. Dodwell: Views in Greece,
30 hand-coloured views, folio,
1821. (Phillips) $6,400 £4,000

A 17th century miniature
Book of Psalms with embroi-
dered cover, England, 2 x 3¼in.
(Robt. W. Skinner Inc.)
$2,000 £1,398

Capt. Robert Melville Grindlay:
Scenery Costume and Architecture on the Western Side of
India, folio, R. Ackermann,
1826. (Phillips) $2,880 £1,800

'The Story of a Passion", by
Irving Bacheller, published
by Roycrofters, 1901, hand-
illuminated by Abby Blackmar,
suede cover. (Robt. W. Skinner
Inc.) $150 £81

C. Dickens: Great Expectations,
3 vols., 1st Edn., 32pp. of
advertisements, original cloth
gilt, 1861. (Phillips)
$19,200 £12,000

Eragny Press, R. Browning,
Some Poems, Limited Edition
of 215 col. woodcut front, by
L. Pissarro, 1904. (Phillips)
$846 £600

BOXES

A box as a place of safe keeping was an essential item in homes from earliest times. Even Egyptian tombs and sparsely furnished castles contained boxes in which clothes and precious items could be securely locked. They range from tiny ones for keeping items of jewellery to large dower chests that young girls filled with items for their dowry. The Victorians loved boxes and bought them in vast quantities for a myriad of purposes ranging from travelling medicine chests to snuff, pill or tobacco boxes. They can be found in almost any material — Tunbridge ware, wood, ivory, silver, gold, china, cardboard, papier maché . . . . Specialist collectors often concentrate on the boxes used by specific professions like the ones full of fearsome looking instruments carried by surgeons or boxes with cupping bowls used by bloodletters. There are also barber's boxes, picnic boxes, writing boxes and needlework boxes — all have their devotees.

Late 16th century Momo-yama period Christian host box or pyx, 9cm. diam. (Christie's)
$38,720 £24,200

One of a pair of Federal mahogany and mahogany veneer inlaid knife boxes, America or England, circa 1790, 14½in. high. (Robt. W. Skinner Inc.) $950 £664

A 17th century Flemish ebony and ivory table cabinet, on later bun feet, 21in. wide. (Christie's) $1,995 £1,512

A wooden, painted gesso and gilded casket, by W. Cayley-Robinson, 35cm. wide. (Phillips) $1,224 £850

A Spanish 17th century rosewood and ivory inlaid table cabinet, 40cm. wide. (Phillips) $2,624 £1,600

A 19th century French gold mounted tortoiseshell jewel casket, 5in. high. (Christie's)
$8,250 £5,811

A 19th century leather covered document box, the dome top with brass bail handle, 11½in. wide. (Christie's) $242 £146

Bird's-eye maple Academy painted polychrome box, circa 1820, 12¼in. long. (Robt. W. Skinner Inc.) $3,600 £2,142

A 19th century leather covered document box, with brass bail handle and brass stud trim, 5¾in. high, 14in. wide. (Christie's) $275 £166

Early 19th century wallpaper hat box, 'A Peep at the Moon', America, 12½in. high, 17in. wide. (Robt. W. Skinner Inc.) $200 £129

A George III satinwood travelling necessaire box, the hinged lid enclosing a well-fitted interior, with leather label inscribed 'Manufactured by Bayley & Blew, 5 Cockspur Street, London', 15½in. wide. (Christie's) $2,645 £1,430

A 19th century cylindrical cosmetic box with an inner tray and three small containers, 9.3cm. diam., 8.8cm. high. (Christie's) $15,895 £9,350

Late 18th century document box (bunko), decorated in gold and silver hiramakie, takamakie and hirame on a nashiji ground, 40 x 30 x 15cm. (Christie's) $9,350 £5,500

A French straw-work workbox worked in a three-coloured diapered pattern, pink, gold and green, 7½ x 5½ x 4in., circa 1750. (Christie's) $1,443 £825

A 19th century English Colonial camphorwood and ebony chest, 32½in. wide. (Parsons, Welch & Cowell) $1,771 £1,150

A mid Victorian black and gilt japanned papier-mache cigar box with hinged lid, 7¾in. wide. (Christie's) $125 £88

Late 16th century Momo-yama period small domed travelling casket, 21 x 12 x 10.5cm. (Christie's) $748 £440

A 19th century pine Scandin-avian bride's box, 11½in. high, 21½in. wide. (Christie's) $495 £323

A 19th century rounded rectangular suzuribako, 23 x 19.8cm. (Christie's) $3,366 £1,980

An Anglo-French silver and silver mounted dressing table set contained in a brass inlaid rosewood case, by C. Rawlings, 1821, and P. Blazuiere, Paris, 1819-38. (Christie's) $25,740 £14,300

Late 16th/early 17th century gourd-shaped roironuri suzuribako, 25.5cm. long. (Christie's) $11,220 £6,600

Mid 19th century Victorian rosewood and mother-of-pearl inlaid sewing box with fitted interior. (G. A. Key) $462 £280

One of a pair of George III mahogany vase-shaped cutlery boxes, 26in. high. (Christie's) $3,888 £2,700

A travelling dressing set with silver mounts, dated 1901, Birmingham, in an alligator skin case. (Lots Road Chelsea Auction Galleries) $680 £420

BRONZE

The malleability of bronze makes it an ideal medium for sculptors and in the 19th century there was a great upsurge in the manufacture of decorative items made from the material. Animals were favourite subjects and sculptors like P. J. Mene, Isidore Bonheur, Jules Moigniez and Christophe Fratin followed the lead of Antoine-Louis Bayre in creating lifelike bronze figures of animals. Bayre created a sensation at the Paris Salon of 1831 when he exhibited a vibrant bronze of a tiger devouring a gavial which inspired a school of sculptors known as "les animaliers" whose aim was realism. Bonheur, for example, was highly regarded among connoisseurs for the realistic way he created galloping horses. During the 19th century there was a great upsurge of interest in Japanese bronzes, especially figures and vases with metal work and enamel decoration. The best ones date from the Meiji period of 1868-1912. Bronze was also used along with ivory by figure sculptors like Chiparus and Preiss.

Early 20th century bronze bust of Woman, signed Wigglesworth, stamped Gorham Co. Founders, 13¾in. high. (Robt. W. Skinner Inc.) $800 £555

Huntress, a silvered bronze figure cast from a model by G. None, Paris, 34cm. high. (Christie's) $1,887 £1,320

A 19th century bronze bust of a bearded 16th century scholar, his cloak cast with allegorical figures, 28cm. high. (Phillips) $1,304 £800

A French bronze figure of a Neapolitan mandolin player, bearing the inscription Duret, 55cm. high. (Phillips) $1,222 £750

A 19th century French bronze group of a python attacking an Arab horseman, cast from a model by Antoine Louis Barye, circa 1835-40, 22 x 29cm. (Christie's) $23,595 £14,300

Egyptian Dancer, a gilt bronze and ivory figure cast and carved from a model by C. J. Roberte Colinet, 42.5cm. high. (Christie's) $28,512 £19,800

BRONZE

A late 19th century French
bronze statuette of Diana,
signed Denecheau, 60cm.
high overall. (Christie's)
$6,380 £4,400

A 16th/17th century late
Ming bronze group cast as
Budai, 32.5cm. wide.
(Christie's) $2,831 £1,980

A Viennese cold painted
bronze of a seated Indian
brave, bearing the inscription
C. Kauba and stamped
Geschutzt 5806, 17cm. high.
(Phillips) $1,271 £780

Late 19th century bronze
lobed koro on karashishi
mask and scroll tripod feet,
61cm. high. (Christie's)
$1,405 £990

Pair of 19th century French bronze,
copper and silver plated busts of 'La
Juive d'Alger' and the 'Cheik Arabe de
Caire', by Charles-Henri-Joseph Cordier,
86cm. high. (Christie's)
$161,656 £96,800

A 19th century French
bronze head of a child, 'Bebe
Endormi', cast from a model
by Aime-Jules Dalou, 19cm.
high. (Christie's)
$3,993 £2,420

A late 19th/early 20th century
bronze memorial relief, attributed to Sir Alfred Gilbert,
25cm. high. (Christie's)
$551 £330

Morning Walk, a parcel gilt
bronze and ivory group cast
and carved after a model by
A. Becquerel, 26.8cm. high.
(Christie's) $1,900 £1,320

A 19th century French
bronze statue of Cupid, after
Denis-Antoine Chaudet,
60cm. high. (Christie's)
$3,122 £1,870

Europa and the Bull, a bronze figure cast from a model by H. Muller, 25.4cm. high. (Christie's) $1,022 £715

An Art Deco bronze group of a male and female nude, 65cm. high. (Christie's) $3,304 £2,160

A 19th century bronze group of a mounted African Hunter, incised P. J. Mene, 46cm. high. (Phillips) $3,423 £2,100

A 19th century French bronze group of Hebe and the Eagle of Jupiter, inspired by Rude, the base inscribed E. Drouot, 78cm. high. (Phillips) $4,564 £2,800

A pair of French 19th century bronze busts of a Nubian man and woman, also known as 'Venus Africaine', both signed Cordier, 83cm. and 79cm. high. (Christie's) $166,980 £101,200

Bear Hug, a bronze figure cast after a model by F. Rieder, 30.8cm. high. (Christie's) $2,044 £1,430

An early 19th century French romantic bronze portrait plaque of Albert Bertin, cast from a model by A. Etex, 43 x 32cm. (Christie's) $1,514 £990

A 19th century bronze of Actaeon kneeling on a wounded stag, incised Holme. Cardwell Fect. Roma 1857, 83cm. high. (Christie's) $14,520 £8,800

Bronze bust of 'Dalila', by E. Villanis, circa 1890, seal of Societe des Bronzes de Paris. (Worsfolds) $1,440 £900

BUTTER STAMPS

In the days when butter came direct from the dairy and not off a supermarket shelf, it was the custom to mark it with curls or patterns, often signifying the dairy from which it came. The implement used for doing this was a butter stamp. It was small and carved from wood, often sycamore or less usually boxwood and it always incorporated a motif — a swan and bullrushes if the farm was beside a river or a sheep if it was on a hillside. Other motifs included birds, dates, wheatsheafs, thistles or hearts. American butter stamps often had the motif of tulips and sometimes they stamped out little messages like "Eat Good Butter". Stamps are usually quite cheap and those commemorating special events are of particular interest to collectors.

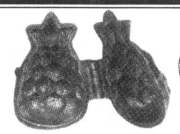

Sycamore wood butter marker, circa 1830, 5in. diam. $90 £50

19th century pewter pineapple butter mould, 3¾in. long. (Christie's) $100 £60

19th century American wooden oval butter stamp with carved eagle, 5½in. long. $435 £250

A carved wood butter stamp with wheatsheaf design, 4½in. diam. $60 £35

A 19th century American carved wood butter stamp, depicting a standing pig on grass, and a cylindrical cover, top 5¾in. diam. (Christie's) $264 £148

A 19th century American carved wood butter stamp, 4¼in. diam. (Christie's) $242 £136

19th century American wooden butter stamp carved with a running fox, 2½in. diam. $210 £120

19th century American butter stamp carved with a lamb, 3in. diam. $315 £180

19th century American wooden butter stamp showing a bird on a branch, 3in. diam. $260 £150

CAR MASCOTS

Around 1905 the first mascots appeared perched on the sleek bonnets of cars. The earliest examples were made of cast metal but later they appeared in carved wood or glass. The most famous car mascot is perhaps the Rolls Royce Spirit of Ecstasy which the company adopted as their trademark and the American Lincoln company followed by adopting a greyhound as their symbol. Mascots can be found — but at a price — in a large variety of shapes; skiers, nude goddesses, eagles, horses, swallows and flying spirits, rabbits, policemen, leaping deer or herons and they were designed by some of the most accomplished artists of the time. The most famous mascots of all however are those made in glass by Rene Lalique who produced 46 different designs in clear, coloured or frosted crystal between the late 1920's and the late '30's. Any one of them is worth several thousand pounds today.

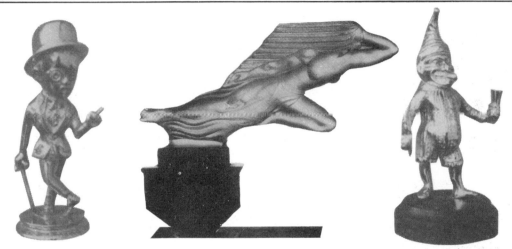

'Sir Kreemy Knut', chrome plated mascot of Sir Kreemy was the trade mark and Company mascot of Sharp's Toffee Co. $260 £150

'Spirit of the Wind', a red-ashay car mascot on chromium plated metal mount, 11.5cm. high. (Christie's) $1,353 £825

'Punch', British made, chrome plated mascot, early 1930's, no markings or indication of the manufacturer. $175 £100

'Coq Nain', a coloured car mascot, the topaz and satin finished glass moulded as a cockerel, 20.2cm. high. (Christie's) $4,510 £2,750

'Dragonfly', chrome plate with mother of pearl wings by Desmo, 1930's. $910 £525

'Stag's Head', an accessory mascot, produced in the 1920's by A. E. L., nickel plated brass. $210 £120

CAR MASCOTS

'Touch Wud', a good luck mascot with a leather head, glass eyes and a brass body, circa 1908. $290 £165

'Girl on a Goose', British made mascot signed L.L. for Louis Lejaune. $785 £450

A brass car mascot of Minerva, inscribed 'Minerva P. de Soete', 6in. high. (Christie's) $403 £260

'Sanglier', a Lalique car mascot in clear and satin finished glass, moulded as a boar, 6.5cm. high. (Christie's) $1,022 £715

'Lady Skater', chrome plated Desmo mascot from the 1930's was for skating enthusiasts. $260 £150

'Tete de Coq', a Lalique car mascot, in clear and satin finished glass, 18cm. high. (Christie's) $2,044 £1,430

A chromium plated car mascot figure of 'Puss in Boots', 6in. high. (Christie's) $465 £300

A rosewood and ivory toucan radiator cap, inscribed Howett, London, 5in. high. (Christie's) $248 £160

'Pharaoh', a Red-Ashay, car mascot in clear and satin finished glass, 11.5cm. high. (Christie's) $1,321 £864

CAR MASCOTS

A brass stylised car mascot bust of Minerva, inscribed P. de Soete, 5½in. high. (Christie's) $589 £380

'The Dummy Teat', nickel plated mascot manufactured by J. Grose & Co., 1926, for the Austin 7 fondly known as the Baby Austin.$525 £300

'Tete de Belier', a Lalique car mascot, moulded as a ram's head, 9.5cm. high. (Christie's)$27,060 £16,500

A Lalique clear and frosted glass car mascot of 'Victoire — Spirit of the Wind', 10in. long. (Prudential Fine Art)
            $9,454 £5,800

An early 20th century cold painted metal car mascot of a dragonfly golfer seated on a composition golf ball, 6in. high. (Woolley & Wallis)
            $693 £420

'Grand Libellule', a Lalique car mascot in clear and satin finished glass, 21cm. high. (Christie's) $5,783 £3,780

A Lalique car mascot, Longchamps, in clear and satin-finished glass, 13cm. high. (Christie's)
        $12,672 £8,800

'Vitesse', a Lalique car mascot moulded as a naked female, 18.5cm. high. (Christie's)
        $9,020 £5,500

'Archer', a Lalique car mascot in clear and satin finished glass, 12cm. high. (Christie's)
        $2,044 £1,430

CARD CASES

During the 19th century and right up to the Second World War there was a strict protocol to be observed in the leaving of calling cards on friends, neighbours and social acquaintances. Everyone who aspired to a position in society had cards printed and knew how and when they should be distributed. Sometimes it was necessary to leave two or even three at a time and if a corner was turned down they knew what that meant as well. Cards had to be immaculately clean so it was necessary to keep them in special cases which were always slim and rectangular in shape. Card cases were made of gold, tortoiseshell, ivory, silver, Tunbridge ware, mother of pearl, papier maché or leather. Some of the prettiest were made of interlocked squares of mother of pearl with silver fittings and were marked with the owner's initials or monogram. Card cases were frequently given as gifts.

A Victorian shaped rectangular silver card case, by Edward Smith, Birmingham 1852, 10.1 cm. (Lawrence Fine Art) $330 £264

A papier mache card case, inlaid with mother-of-pearl and gilt with a Chinese river scene. (Lawrence Fine Art) $13 £11

A tortoiseshell card case, inlaid in engraved mother-of-pearl . (Lawrence Fine Art) $82 £66

A Chinese ivory card case, deeply carved with numerous figures and buildings in landscapes. (Lawrence Fine Art) $88 £71

A fine Swiss gold and enamel card case, one side painted with a gallant taking leave of his loved one, circa 1830, 3¾in. long. (Christie's) $5,667 £3,080

A mother-of-pearl card case, inlaid in a trellis pattern with an engraved bird and flowers, with paua shell. (Lawrence Fine Art) $32 £25

CARVED STONE

Carved stone is one of the earliest forms of artistic expression and one which, because of its very nature, can survive indefinitely, as the prehistoric stones of Easter Island, and elsewhere bear witness. Age, indeed does not seem to play a great part in determining value, since an ancient Sumerian tablet, for example, can be picked up for £100 or so, while modern examples, by such practitioners as Henry Moore and Barbara Hepworth, sell for huge sums.

A pair of carved stone putti the plump figures standing, one holding a bird, the other a basket of fruit, 38in. high. (Christie's) $3,300 £2,200

A carved stone figure of Hercules, partly draped with lion's skin, holding golden apples of the Hesperides, 40in. high. (Robt. W. Skinner Inc.) $800 £559

A Sumerian brick fragment impressed with four lines of cuneiform —'Ur Namma, King of Ur, who built the temple of Namma', 27 x 29cm. overall. (Phillips)
$290 £190

Late 17th century English stone figure of 'Prometheus Bound', in the manner of Cibber, 175cm. high. (Phillips) $15,750 £10,500

Late 17th century Buddhist stone stela of typical form, dated Genroku 5 (1692), with a later inscription and date Meiji 34 (1901), 77.5cm. high. (Christie's)
$1,389 £972

Contemporary Eskimo carving of a wrestling man and bear in mottled greenish-grey stone, 18in. high. (Robt. W. Skinner Inc.) $700 £476

A greenish-grey and black stone figure of a seated roaring lion, Tang Dynasty, 13cm. high. (Christie's)
$1,746 £1,188

CARVED STONE

One of a pair of carved granite Foo dogs and stands; China, 19th century, 28½in. high. (Robt. W. Skinner Inc.) $4,200 £2,818

A dark stone figure of Guanyin, seated in dhyanasana, Tang Dynasty, 39.5cm. high, mounted on black marble stand. (Christie's) $14,157 £9,900

A naturalistically coloured stone carving of a chimpanzee, 53.5cm. high. (Phillips) $460 £320

A sandstone head of rounded form, on a long cylindrical neck, 27cm. high, perhaps Romano-Celtic. (Phillips) $229 £150

A stone horse's head, Han Dynasty, 12.9cm. high. (Christie's) $13,500 £9,000

One of a pair of 5th century A.D. large stone figures of chimera, heavily carved from a matt grey material of limestone type, approx. 55.5cm. high. (Christie's) $157,300 £110,000

A Northern Qi stele with two figures of Buddha seated side by side, dated Tianbao 6th year, tenth month, tenth day, corresponding to AD555, 29cm. high. (Christie's) $15,000 £10,000

A carved limestone sculpture of Mother and Child, by W. Edmondson, circa 1934/39, 15in. high. (Christie's) $9,900 £6,827

A Buddhist stone stele, dated to the 2nd year of Zheng Guan of the N. Wei Dynasty, 36cm. high. (Christie's) $943 £660

CARVED WOOD

Wood carving is one of the most ancient and universal arts, found in a multitude of objects from altars to nutcrackers. Many early toys were of wood—a Charles II carved wooden doll sold recently for over £70,000. Carved furniture demands a book on its own, while another interesting speciality field consists of tribal arts—weapons, figures and utensils.

Wood carving is perhaps at its finest when applied to religious subjects, as the many glorious carvings in Christian and other places of worship bear ample witness.

A stained wood smoker's compendium in the form of a motor car, 6½ x 11½in. (Christie's) $322 £260

A Shinto wood sculpture of a seated deity wearing Heian/Kamakura style robes and hat, Edo period, 58.8cm. high. (Christie's) $2,400 £1,600

A pair of Chinese painted carved wooden figures, late 18th/early 19th century, the gentleman 46¼in. high, the lady 21¼in. high. (Christie's) $17,820 £11,000

A carved walnut figure of St. Lucy, traces of original polychrome, the reverse hollowed, 44.5cm. high, probably S. German. (Phillips) $720 £500

A 19th century carved walnut panel with a coat-of-arms and motto Le Main Tiendrai, 46in. wide. (Christie's) $2,478 £1,620

A stylised figure of a carved wooden horse, America, 23in. high, 23in. long. (Robt. W. Skinner Inc.) $1,200 £674

A late 16th century polychromed and carved limewood relief panel of a bearded saint, possibly St. Christopher, 37cm. high. (Phillips) $652 £400

CARVED WOOD

A carved oak panel depicting the martyrdom of St. Lawrence, 1764, 96cm. high. (Phillips) $2,100 £1,400

A gilt bronze and carved wood figure of a Spanish flamenco dancer cast and carved from a model by Hagenauer, 23.9cm. high. (Christie's) $939 £648

A 19th century Japanese carved hardwood okimono of humorous deity, 5½in. high. (Hobbs & Chambers) $264 £160

A 16th century Flemish oak relief carved group of a moustachioed soldier and his female companion, 42cm. high. (Phillips) $5,542 £3,400

One of a pair of giltwood jardinieres with overhanging reeded lips, 11in. wide. (Christie's) $1,837 £1,100

A painted wooden hollow standing horse, American, circa 1850/90, 49in. long, possibly used as a harness-maker's sign. (Christie's) $3,520 £2,427

A 19th century boxwood wrist-rest, unsigned, 5.5cm. long. (Christie's) $880 £550

A Charles X period carved walnut cradle on foliate scroll dolphin supports. (Phillips) $7,000 £4,000

An Egyptian Anthropoid wood mask, 18cm. high, Ptolemaic Period. (Phillips) $254 £140

CARVED WOOD

A 19th century wooden model of a seated camel, 50in. wide, 27½in. high. (Christie's)
$20,358 £14,040

A Netherlandish oak panel carved in relief with the Adoration of the Magi, 17th/18th century, 71 x 81cm. (Phillips) $2,934 £1,800

A 19th century lacquered wood mask of Ayagiri, 4.6cm. high. (Christie's)
$1,487 £880

A 16th/17th century carved and polychromed limewood group of the Madonna and Child, 52cm. high. (Phillips)
$1,630 £1,000

A North Italian late 18th/early 19th century walnut panel. (Parsons, Welch & Cowell) $1,087 £720

Late 18th century carved hard pine spoon rack with chip carved decoration, New Jersey, 21in. high. (Robt. W. Skinner Inc.) $1,800 £1,071

A Continental carved wooden tankard with hinged cover, 8in. high. (Prudential Fine Art) $2,184 £1,300

A Momoyama period Christian folding lectern (shokendai), decorated in aogai and hira-makie, circa 1600, 50.5cm. high. (Christie's)
$38,880 £27,000

A 19th century American carved wooden rooster, 12½in. high. (Robt. W. Skinner Inc.)
$1,500 £1,041

CHAIRS

Since man gave up squatting on the floor, the chair has become one of the most essential items of household furniture and it can range from the strictly utilitarian to the positively luxurious. As far as style goes, the buyer has a huge range from which to pick — what about a Tudor chair with a high wooden back and deep carving? Or if a softer seat is required, a nice deeply padded Victorian ladies' chair with short cabriole legs might do very well. The Georgian arm chair with its lug eared sides and lion's paw feet fits in with most people's idea of a comfortable seat while others may prefer a round armed 1930's fireside chair reminiscent of nights spent listening to the wireless.

Sets of dining table chairs have soared in price over the past few years and those specially sought after are Georgian chairs with sabre legs or in Chinoiserie designs. Victorian dining room chairs tend to be heavier and more stolid than the Georgian but they too fetch high sums. Sets of twelve including two carvers are at a premium. Kitchen chairs are selling well, especially those with ladder or spar backs; bedroom chairs are lighter and more frivolous but are also popular and bentwood chairs, chairs with basket work seats or bergere backs and sides do well. There is a growing vogue for chairs dating from the 1940's and 1950's, especially those made of chromium and leather. On the Continent, buyers are especially keen on chairs dating from the 1930's and the bizarre chairs made by the designer Bugatti.

Two of a set of twelve Regency simulated rosewood and parcel gilt dining chairs comprising six armchairs and six side chairs. (Christie's)   Twelve $28,512 £17,600

Two of a set of six Federal painted fancy chairs, N.Y., 1800-15, 33¾in. high. (Christie's)   Six $3,850 £2,327

A Federal carved mahogany side chair and armchair, possibly by John Carlile Jr., Rhode Island. (Christie's) $3,080 £2,138

An Italian Directoire white painted and parcel gilt elbow chair. (Phillips) $2,592 £1,800

One of a pair of walnut bergeres upholstered in green velvet, on moulded cabriole legs and scrolled toes. (Christie's) $1,633 £990

An early Victorian oak open armchair attributed to A. W. N. Pugin, the back and seat upholstered in contemporary foliate cut velvet. (Christie's) $8,910 £5,500

A Regency mahogany armchair with cane-filled back and seat with red leather squab cushion. (Christie's) $1,262 £770

One of a pair of Finimar laminated birchwood open armchairs designed by Alvar Alto. (Christie's) $2,044 £1,430

One of a pair of Regency blue-painted and parcel gilt armchairs with padded arm rests and seats, both stamped T. Gray. (Christie's) $19,057 £11,550

A mid Victorian open armchair of Gothic style with drop-in seat. (Christie's) $1,473 £1,045

A George III mahogany 'cockpen' open armchair with pierced trelliswork back and arms. (Christie's) $1,982 £1,296

A Regency mahogany library armchair, the cane filled back and seat with red leather squab cushions. (Christie's) $3,406 £2,090

CHAIRS

A blue PVC inflatable armchair. (Christie's)
$578 £378

One of a pair of upholstered easy armchairs by Howard & Sons. (Christie's)
$3,306 £1,980

A wicker patio chair designed by Terence Conran. (Christie's) $134 £88

A George III mahogany Windsor armchair with comb-back and yoke-shaped arms. (Christie's)
$10,692 £6,600

A late Regency mahogany hall porter's chair with arched hooded back and seat covered in brown leather, 61½in. high. (Christie's)
$4,303 £2,640

A Chippendale mahogany corner chair, Newport, Rhode Island, 1750-70, 32½in. high. (Christie's)
$27,500 £16,626

An inlaid rosewood curule-type armchair, attributed to Pottier and Stymus, circa 1870, 34in. high, 31in. wide. (Robt. W. Skinner Inc.)
$1,100 £763

Early 20th century wicker arm rocker, 31in. wide. (Robt. W. Skinner Inc.)
$200 £119

One of a pair of early Victorian rosewood armchairs, each with a spoon-shaped back and serpentine seat, on cabriole legs. (Christie's) $4,712 £3,080

CHELSEA

The most famous British porcelain factory is Chelsea which is thought to have started around 1745 when a series of small, well moulded cream or milk jugs called "goat and bee jugs" were made. The earliest pieces bore an incised triangle mark and were usually made of white porcelain. Chelsea porcelain was always marked with an anchor in various colours and shapes but it was much faked and marks should not be taken at their face value. Later examples of Chelsea became more richly decorated and followed Meissen or Oriental patterns. The Chelsea factory produced a large range of different forms — tea, dessert and dinner services as well as ornaments, figures and groups. It always catered for a higher class of client and no earthenware was produced. After 1784 it is usually referred to as Chelsea-Derby because it was taken over by a Derby manufacturer called William Duesbury.

A Chelsea 'Hans Sloane' botanical plate, red anchor and 43 mark, circa 1755, 23.5cm. diam. (Christie's) $6,463 £4,860

A Chelsea group of two goats, painted in the workshop of Wm. Duesbury , raised red anchor mark, circa 1751, 16.5cm. wide. (Christie's) $14,256 £9,900

A Chelsea-Derby Jardiniere of 'U' shape, Chelsea style with fabulous birds on rockwork and in the branches of leafy trees, 17cm. high. (Phillips) $1,485 £900

A Chelsea flared and fluted coffee cup with scroll handle, circa 1750, 7.5cm. high. (Christie's) $2,692 £1,870

A pair of Chelsea masqueraders, gold anchor marks at back, circa 1765, 30cm. high. (Christie's) $2,059 £1,430

A Chelsea apple tureen and cover naturally modelled and coloured in green and russet, the base with red 3 mark, circa 1755, 10.5cm. high. (Christie's) $6,134 £4,320

A Chelsea fluted oviform teapot and cover painted in the Kakiemon palette, circa 1752, 12.6cm. high. (Christie's) $5,214 £3,672

A Chelsea group of two children, naked except for a white and gold drapery, seated on a rocky mound, 17.5cm. high. (Lawrence Fine Art) $1,539 £950

A Chelsea fluted teabowl painted in a vivid Kakiemon palette with birds perched and in flight, 1750-52, 5cm. high. (Christie's) $1,900 £1,320

A Chelsea double scent bottle modelled as a parrot and a rooster, circa 1755, 7cm. high. (Christie's) $2,692 £1,870

Pair of Chelsea Derby candlestick figures of a gallant and his companion, 6½in. and 6in. high, no nozzles. (Graves Son & Pilcher) $830 £550

A Chelsea acanthus leaf moulded white chocolate pot on four feet, 1745-49, 24cm. high overall. (Christie's) $1,346 £935

A Chelsea octagonal dish, painted in the Kakiemon palette with pheasants, circa 1750, 20.5cm. wide. (Christie's) $1,925 £1,100

A Chelsea group of two children, naked except for a pink drapery, with large fish, 24cm. high. (Lawrence Fine Art) $1,458 £900

A Chelsea silver shaped plate painted in the Kakiemon palette with The Red Tiger Pattern, 1750-52, 23cm. diam. (Christie's) $6,336 £4,400

CHIPARUS FIGURES

Of all the practitioners of bronze and ivory Art Deco models, the Rumanian born Dmitri Chiparus is perhaps the most familiar to the public at large, if only because such modern personalities as Paul McCartney and Elton John are known collectors. Chiparus' figures range from nudes and women in everyday clothes, through pierrots to theatrical and exotic dancers (many of which show the Egyptian influence engendered by the discovery of Tutenkhamun's tomb), often in amazing, gravity-defying postures.

A gilt bronze and ivory group of three young girls, signed Chiparus, 6in. high. $2,600 £1,500

An Art Deco period figure in bronze and ivory of a lady holding a muff, signed D. H. Chiparus, 12½in. high. (R. H. Ellis & Sons) $2,743 £2,160

A bronze and ivory figure cast and carved after a model by D. H. Chiparus, 16in. high. (Christie's) $6,930 £4,500

'Actress', a bronze figure cast from a model by D. H. Chiparus, of a maiden standing on tip-toe, 29.5cm. high. (Christie's) $2,431 £1,430

'Young Girl', a bronze figure cast from a model by Demetre Chiparus, of a maiden standing on tip-toe with one foot held before her, signed in the onyx Chiparus, 29.5cm. high. (Christie's) $2,244 £1,320

'Les Amis de Toujours', a bronze and ivory figure by Demetre Chiparus, of a standing lady, flanked by two borzois, on a rectangular amber coloured onyx base, 63cm. high. (Christie's) $22,440 £13,200

'Dancer', a bronze and ivory figure cast and carved from a model by D. H. Chiparus, of a young woman dancing with one foot pointing outwards and arms outstretched, signed in the marble D. Chiparus, 41.5cm. high. (Christie's) $8,415 £4,950

CHIPARUS FIGURES

A painted bronze and ivory figure, 'Hush', 42cm. high, inscribed D. H. Chiparus. (Phillips) $3,888 £2,700

Lioness, a bronze figure cast after a model by Demetre Chiparus, 57.8cm. long. (Christie's) $1,494 £1,045

A painted bronze and ivory figure, 'Oriental Dancer', 40.20cm. high, inscribed on the marble Chiparus. (Phillips) $6,624 £4,600

'Priestess', a gilt bronze and ivory figure cast and carved from a model by D. Chiparus, 43cm. high. (Christie's) $4,384 £3,024

'The Fan Dancer', a bronze and ivory figure by Chiparus, on marble and onyx base, 15in. high. (Christie's) $6,615 £4,500

An ivory figure of a girl, 'Invocation', carved from a model by D. Chiparus, 24.5cm. high. (Phillips) $1,584 £1,100

'Apres la lecture', a bronze and ivory figure cast and carved from a model by D. Chiparus, 36.5cm. high. (Christie's) $10,824 £6,600

'Sheltering from the Rain', a bronze and ivory group cast and carved from a model by D. Chiparus, 26cm. high. (Christie's) $2,534 £1,760

'Nubian Dancer', a bronze and ivory dancing girl, cast and carved after a model by D. H. Chiparus, 15½in. high. (Christie's) $18,120 £12,000

CIGARETTE CASES

Early cigarette cases were meant to be carried by men so they usually have a more solid and weighty appearance than those made later for the use of women when the cigarette smoking habit became accepted in both sexes and all classes of society. These cases can be made of a variety of materials from gold and silver downwards through tortoiseshell, papier maché or mother of pearl to base metal. Some of the most attractive cases are those made for women in the 1920's which were decorated with brightly coloured enamels in bold Modernist designs. A few of the more expensive cases were designed as evening bags and incorporated cigarette lighters and lipsticks. The best cigarette cases are often works of art, displaying the skill of the silversmith and the engraver. Interesting collections can still be built up for modest outlays.

A jewelled two-colour gold cigarette case, the reeded body set with diamonds, St. Petersburg, 1908-17, 9.8cm. $3,395 £2,342

A Continental cigarette case, cover enamelled with a nude lying on the edge of the shore, with English import marks for 1906. (Phillips)
$528 £350

An oblong gold coloured cigarette case with cabochon bluestone pushpiece, with Swedish control marks, 3¼in. long. (Christie's)
$1,166 £810

A Portuguese enamel cigarette case, the cover depicting a bare-breasted Classical girl, circa 1900. (Phillips) $573 £380

A Victorian cheroot case, by Yapp & Woodward, Birmingham, 1854, 12.7cm. high, 4.75oz. (Phillips) $271 £180

Late 19th century Austrian enamel cigarette case, the cover enamelled with an Ancient Egyptian scene, circa 1895. (Phillips)
$906 £600

An Austrian cigarette case applied with two-colour gold and gem set monograms and facsimile signatures, circa 1895. (Phillips) $774 £520

A Victorian cigarette case, the cover enamelled with a nude girl lying beside a stream, Birmingham, 1887. (Phillips) $588 £400

An Austrian white metal and enamel eight-sided cigarette case, the enamel by F. Zwichl, depicting a Samson car in black, red and cream. (Christie's) $783 £540

A Continental plated cigarette case enamelled with a collie dog on a sky background, circa 1910. (Phillips) $223 £150

An Edwardian gilt lined cigarette case, polychrome-enamelled with a picture of a lady, R.C., Birmingham, 1905. (Christie's) $284 £200

A German cigarette case enamelled on cover with a spaniel carrying a dead duck in its mouth, circa 1900. (Phillips) $367 £250

An Austrian enamel cigarette case, signed 'Schleiertanz', circa 1895. (Phillips) $735 £500

A white metal and enamel cigarette case, the enamel by F. Zwichl, circa 1920. (Christie's) $2,818 £1,944

A late Victorian gilt lined cigarette case, enamelled with a scene from R. Kipling's poem 'Absent minded beggar', C.S. & F.S., Birmingham, 1899. (Christie's) $372 £250

A late Victorian cigarette case enamelled on cover with a coaching scene, by J. Wilmot, Birmingham, 1896. (Phillips) $509 £280

A good 19th century Russian niello cigarette case, cover depicting a despatch carrier being driven by a peasant in a horse-drawn carriage, Gustav Klingert, Moscow, 1888, 8.5cm. long. (Phillips) $618 £340

A Russian cigarette case with separate hinged vesta compartment, probably by Dmitri Nikolaiev, Moscow, circa 1890. (Phillips) $402 £230

An enamelled silver cigarette case, probably German, circa 1910, thumbpiece missing, 3½in. high. $502 £440

An Omar Ramsden 9ct. beaten gold cigarette case with cut steel relief decoration, gold mark for 1922, 11.3 x 8.8cm. (Christie's) $950 £660

An enamelled cigarette case, German, circa 1905, 9cm. high. $401 £352

A 1930's cigarette case, silver and two-colour gold coloured metal, with stripes of black lacquer, 11.75cm. wide. $451 £350

An Omar Ramsden silver cigarette case, with gilt interior, 1923, 9.5cm. $170 £132

An Art Deco sterling silver cigarette case with black and silver ground in a crackle pattern with red enamel zigeraut decoration on one side. (Robt. W. Skinner Inc.) $200 £161

CLARET JUGS

Claret jugs, as their name suggests, were designed to hold wine at table. Usually pear-shaped, and with a handle, English jugs from the early 19th century were often of silver with corked necks, while later glass examples favoured silver mountings with hinged lids.

Claret jugs were designed by such leading practitioners as Christopher Dresser, while George Fox in the mid 19th century produced animal and other shapes as novelties.

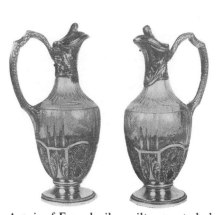

A pair of French silver gilt mounted clear glass claret jugs, by Risler & Carre, Paris, circa 1870, 11¾in. high. (Christie's) $4,924 £3,240

A Victorian claret jug, by Marshall & Sons, Edinburgh, 1865, 35cm. high, 30oz. (Christie's) $1,110 £740

A late Victorian mounted glass claret jug in the form of a cockatoo, by Alex. Crichton, 1882, 27cm. high. (Phillips)
$3,450 £2,300

A Victorian silver mounted glass claret jug, by Elkington & Co., Birmingham, 1878, 10½in. high. (Reeds Rains) $1,512 £1,050

A Hukin & Heath EPNS mounted large cut glass claret jug, 12in. high. (Hetheringtons Nationwide) $304 £190

A George IV claret jug, maker's mark probably that of Joseph Angell, 1829, 29cm. high, 31oz. (Lawrence Fine Art)
$2,392   £1,650

An ovoid glass claret jug with a star design, the plain mount with bracket handle, 7¾in. high. (Christie's) $144 £88

BRACKET CLOCKS

Bracket clocks have handles on top to enable them to be carried from room to room and a glazed door at the back through which the working of the mechanism can be seen. The backplate is usually finely engraved. The most desirable bracket clocks are those made by English clockmakers and all of them run for at least eight days without rewinding and nearly all early examples have a fusee movement which is a top-shaped brass compartment housing the mainspring. Unwinding of the spring is controlled by a length of gut or wire according to the same principle as a miniature bicycle chain which is coiled around the outside of the 'top'. English bracket clocks have no gear teeth on their drums but Continental bracket clocks can be recognised by gear teeth set on the drum that contains the mainspring.

A Regency Gothic mahogany bracket clock, the painted dial signed Manners & Sons, Stamford, 21½in. high. (Christie's) $1,542 £935

A Georgian green lacquered bracket clock, signed Stepn. Rimbault, London, 1ft.8in. high.   (Phillips)
$2,805   £1,700

A Queen Anne kingwood striking bracket clock, the dial signed Cha. Gretton, 14in. high. (Christie's)
$29,040 £17,600

A William III quarter repeating ebony bracket clock, signed Claudius Du Chesne, Londini Fecit, 16½in. high. (Christie's)
$19,694 £10,475

A Victorian walnut bracket clock, the case in Gothic style, 2ft.2in. high. (Phillips)
$660 £400

An 18th century C. European red lacquered quarter chiming bracket clock, the backplate signed Iohan Maurer in Prag, 57cm. high. (Phillips)
$8,736   £5,200

CARRIAGE CLOCKS

As the name suggests these clocks were used by travellers and they had handles which enabled them to be hung up in carriages. They were bought only by the very rich until the 19th century when travelling became more universal and French clockmakers began to produce those attractive small clocks in large numbers. They are usually very sturdy with finely cast brass cases and thickly bevelled glass windows resting in grooves in the frame. In later examples the glass at the top was small and let into a metal plate, allowing a sight of the mechanism inside. In early 19th century clocks the carrying handles were round, tapering towards the ends and, because there was often a repeat button on the front, the handles only folded backwards.

A brass calendar carriage timepiece, enamel dial with chapter disc above gilt mask, 4¾in. high. (Christie's) $363 £220

A 19th century French gilt brass carriage clock, the lever movement striking on a gong with push repeat, 19cm. high. (Phillips) $924 £550

A 19th century French gilt brass and porcelain mounted grande sonnerie carriage clock, with trademark P.M., 18cm. high. (Phillips) $7,728 £4,600

A quarter-repeating and cloisonne enamel carriage clock, 3in. high. (Christie's)
$5,808 £3,300

A 19th century English timepiece, the backplate signed French Royal Exchange, London, 17.5cm. high. (Phillips) $7,540 £5,200

An ornate gilt repeating carriage clock, signed Bolviller a Paris, 6¼in. high. (Christie's)
$1,322 £715

LANTERN CLOCKS

Lantern clocks are the first truly domestic timepieces ever made and they either stood on a bracket or had an iron ring at the back to enable them to be hung on a nail driven into the wall. Then the clock was levelled and steadied by spikes at the base. The weights of the earliest lantern clocks had a weight on a rope hanging from them. Old lantern clocks never ran for more than thirty hours and they had only one hand because minute hands were not introduced until around 1690. For at least a century after that however rural clockmakers still turned out one handed clocks because they were far less complicated to build.

A lantern clock with engraved dial plate, 15in. high. (Christie's) $1,496 £935

A N. European striking lantern clock, dated 1672, 8in. high. (Christie's)
$2,992 £1,870

A Germanic iron chamber clock, the posted frame 30-hour movement with fabricated wheels, 22in. high. (Christie's)
$4,118 £2,860

A Georgian brass miniature lantern clock made for the Turkish market, signed Robt. Ward, London, 5½in. high. (Phillips)
$2,145 £1,300

A Japanese brass lantern clock, the posted frame 30-hour iron movement with double foliot verge escapement, 11½in. high. (Christie's) $2,120 £1,404

A late Stuart brass quarter chiming carillon lantern clock, dial signed Edw. Hemins of Bister, 15in. high. (Christie's) $6,160 £3,850

LONGCASE CLOCKS

There are two kinds of longcase clocks — firstly, the type commonly called the grandfather clock and, secondly, its smaller counterpart, the grandmother clock. In early longcase clocks, the face was small, only about eight to nine inches across, made of brass and engraved with flowers or scrolls. It was not until around 1680 that wider faces were introduced and they went on growing larger until the 18th century when they were at least twelve inches across or even larger. Brass faces were universal until around 1790 when they were superceded by faces made of painted wood or iron. About that time there was a great demand for longcase clocks and manufacturers were anxious to meet the demand from people with less deep pockets as well as the rich.

Top of the longcase clocks in present day popularity are those dating from the period of George III especially the ones with mahogany cases. Oak cases have until recently proved more difficult to sell unless they had brass faces. The difference in price because of the case is most marked in the case of grandmother clocks where an example with a figured walnut veneered case can fetch at least five times as much as another with a plain oak case. Very high prices are paid for longcase clocks with good quality marquetry cases or in Chinoiserie cases.

Federal birch inlaid tall case clock, New England, circa 1780, 90in. high. (Robt. W. Skinner Inc.)
$3,200 £2,133

Art Nouveau mahogany tall case clock, late 19th century, by Gerr Suss, Hamburg, 96½in. high. (Robt. W. Skinner. Inc.) $1,750 £930

An early 18th century walnut and panel marquetry longcase clock, the 11in. square brass dial signed Thos. Stubbs, London, 2.10m. high.(Phillips)
$19,320 £11,500

A Georgian mahogany quarter chiming longcase clock, the 12in. dial signed Wm. Haughton, London, 2.46m. high. (Phillips)
$6,720 £4,000

Federal cherry inlaid tall case clock, back of dial inscribed 'Wm. Prescott', circa 1790, 91¾in. high. (Robt. W. Skinner Inc.) $12,000 £8,391

A gilt metal mounted marquetry long case clock of Louis XV style, 90in. high. (Christie's) $3,421 £2,592

Late 19th century mahogany 8 day rack striking longcase clock, by Seddon & Moss. (Peter Wilson) $5,984 £3,400

Scottish 19th century mahogany longcase clock by D. Robinson, Airdrie, 7ft. tall. (Chancellors Hollingsworths) $1,472 £920

A Gustav Stickley oak tall case clock, circa 1902-04, 71in. high. (Robt. W. Skinner Inc.) $7,750 £5,381

A mahogany longcase sidereal regulator with break circuit work, signed Wm. Bond & Sons, Boston, circa 1858, 64½in. high. (Christie's) $28,600 £17,480

An Arts & Crafts oak tallcase clock, by the Colonial Mfg. Co., Zeeland, Michigan, circa 1914, 84in. high. (Robt. W. Skinner Inc.) $2,000 £1,081

An American carved walnut longcase regulator, signed Howard & Davis, Makers — Boston, circa 1851, 8ft.0½in. high. (Christie's) $24,200 £16,886

MANTEL CLOCKS

Victorian householders all wanted a fine clock on their drawing room mantlepieces and the 18th and 19th centuries were the heyday of clock makers. The more fancy and ornate the clocks, the better pleased were the customers. French clockmakers in particular had a flair for creating the most ornate clocks while those in England tended to concentrate on the clock itself rather than its trappings. By the end of the 17th century clocks began to appear with much scrollwork on their cases and French clockmakers like Lepine, Janvier, Amand, Lepaute and Thuret were masters of this art. Their clocks always had a verge escapement which is marked by a horizontally turning crown wheel with sharp teeth just above the pendulum; painted faces or porcelain numbers and cunningly sited winding holes. The pendulums of these French clocks were usually pear shaped and suspended on brass rods.

Copies of French clocks were very popular in the 19th century and customers were particularly fond of the more florid examples, especially the ones made of ormolu and elaborately decorated. Ormolu is a hard metal, usually brass, which is rough cast and then chiselled and engraved by hand. It is given its shine by the application of a thin coat of gold and mercury. Because ormolu was expensive however, clock makers also produced copies of fancy clocks made of spelter which looked very similar at first glance but which are worth only about a quarter of a genuine ormolu clock. To find out whether a clock is ormolu or spelter, scratch the underside. If the gold colour comes away to reveal grey metal underneath, it's spelter. Spelter also gives a dull note when tapped sharply with a coin. Genuine ormolu has a sharp sound.

A French Empire ormolu mantel clock, the movement mounted on a chariot, 44cm. high. (Phillips) $1,728 £1,200

Early 18th century German gilt brass octagonal table clock, the top plate signed L. Petitot, Berlin, 4¼in. diam. (Christie's)
$4,445 £3,024

A Charles X ormolu and malachite mantel clock, the dial flanked by the brothers Horatii taking their oath, after J-L David, 21½in. wide. (Christie's) $6,980 £4,180

MANTEL CLOCKS

A Victorian strut clock with enamel dial signed Baudin Freres, Geneve, 8in. high. (Christie's) $792 £550

A Sevres pattern gilt bronze mantel clock, the movement by Gasnier a Paris, circa 1875, 41cm. wide. (Christie's) $1,361 £825

Empire mahogany carved mantel clock, by Eli Terry & Son, Conn., circa 1825, 31in. high. (Robt. W. Skinner Inc.) $1,000 £666

A brass Eureka mantel timepiece, the enamel dial inscribed S. Fisher Ltd., 1ft.1in. high, under a damaged glass shade. (Phillips) $660 £400

A Japanese gilt brass striking spring clock, the case engraved with stylised flowers and with turned angle columns, 6in. high. (Christie's) $1,956 £1,296

A French 19th century bronze ormolu and red marble mantel clock, the enamel dial signed Guibal A Paris, 57cm. high. (Phillips) $2,175 £1,500

A 19th century French brass mantel clock, the enamel dial signed for Payne, Tunbridge Wells, 1ft.8in. high. (Phillips) $2,062 £1,250

A Charles X ormolu mantel clock with glazed circular dial, 19in. high. (Christie's) $1,483 £1,045

A Charles X ormolu and porcelain clock, the movement signed Le Roy, Paris 1102, 16in. high. (Christie's) $1,370 £770

SKELETON CLOCKS

Skeleton clocks are usually to be found beneath glass domes and sitting on wooden bases because they are so designed that their workings can be examined without difficulty and as a result they are prone to dust damage. At one time skeleton clocks were made by apprentice clockmakers who had to create a clock that the examiners could see working without the barrier of a case. However those glass covered clocks soon became popular with the public and they can now be found in a large variety of types and sizes. English skeleton clocks were made of fret-cut brass with silvered brass chapter rings while the French variety was usually much smaller with enameled chapter rings and solid fronts and backs. In later examples the front and back plates were often engraved.

A Victorian brass skeleton chiming clock of York Minster type, 27½in. high overall. (Christie's) $4,827 £3,240

A Eureka electric striking clock, signed Eureka Clock Co. Ltd., London, 11in. high overall. (Christie's) $2,516 £1,760

A small skeleton timepiece, on mahogany base with glass dome, 11in. high. (Christie's) $1,144 £715

A quarter chiming skeleton clock, the pierced plates of open and angular design, 21in. high. (Christie's) $3,261 £2,160

An early Victorian brass striking skeleton clock, signed Harrison Darlington, 12¼in. high, excluding dome. (Christie's) $2,164 £1,320

A brass three-train 'Westminster Abbey' skeleton clock, striking on gong and nest of eight bells having mercury pendulum, 24in. high. (Andrew Grant) $6,048 £4,200

WALL CLOCKS

In 1797 William Pitt devised a neat way of raising revenue and imposed a tax on clocks which was a clever way of soaking the rich because they were usually the only people who were able to afford timepieces. As a result of this tax, it became the custom for a community to have one clock displayed in a central point where everyone could go to find out the time. They were often hung in inns and were given the name of Act of Parliament clocks. Most of them were large and fairly unsophisticated in style. The advantage of having a clock displayed in an eye catching situation became popular and better off households started buying smaller wall clocks, about eighteen inches in width and encased in veneered rosewood cases with brass scroll inlays. The Victorians bought clocks called Vienna regulators which had mahogany cases and elaborate pendulums. The ones driven by weights were usually of better quality than those powered by a spring.

An 18th century striking Act of Parliament clock, signed Ino. Wilson, Peterborough, 56½in. high. (Christie's) $1,881 £990

Early 19th century inlaid mahogany clock with brass bezel and convex 10in. dial. (Reeds Rains) $701 £420

A cherry wall regulator time-piece, by Seth Thomas Clock Co., Conn., circa 1880, 36in. long. (Robt. W. Skinner Inc.) $650 £419

A George III eight-day wall clock, the dial inscribed Gray and Reynolds, Wimborne, 16in. high. (Woolley & Wallis) $1,872 £1,300

Early 19th century Federal mahogany giltwood and eglomise banjo clock, 33½in. long. (Christie's) $1,760 £1,064

A George III giltwood cartel clock with associated silvered dial signed Wm. Linderby, London, 34in. high. (Christie's) $4,989 £3,080

91

CLOISONNE

In cloisonne enamelling, every detail of the design is defined with narrow bands of metal, gold, silver or copper, in such a way as to cover the whole surface to be decorated. These are then filled with the appropriate enamel colours, ground to a fine powder, moistened and fired. After firing, the wires remain visible and become an integral part of the design. The method differs from Champleve enamelling in which depressions are cut into a metal base and filled with enamel paste before firing.

It is thought that the Chinese adopted cloisonne techniques from the West, particularly from Byzantium, but it became very popular again in Europe during the 19th century when Alexis Falize, a French silversmith, began importing and selling articles of Chinese cloisonne as well as adopting the technique for his own products.

A cloisonne enamel candle holder formed as a standing elephant, late Qing Dynasty, overall 33cm. wide.
(Christie's) $3,775 £2,640

Two 18th century cloisonne enamel and gilt bronze Ruyi sceptres, 31cm. long.
(Christie's) $3,000 £2,000

A cloisonne enamel circular box and flat cover, Qianlong, 32.7cm. diam., wood stand.
(Christie's) $3,460 £2,420

Late 19th century cloisonne cabinet decorated in various coloured enamels, 14.5 x 9 x 12cm. (Christie's)
$1,110 £750

A Namikawa compressed globular tripod censer and domed cover, circa 1900, 10.3cm. diam. (Christie's)
$3,124 £2,200

A cloisonne enamel and gilt bronze tripod censer and domed cover, Qianlong/ Jiaqing, 39cm. high.
(Christie's) $2,516 £1,760

CLOISONNE

A 16th century Ming cloisonne enamel globular tripod censer, 12.8cm. diam. (Christie's) $2,831 £1,980

One of a pair of cloisonne enamel vases and covers, 6in. high. (Lawrence Fine Art) $446 £308

A 16th century cloisonne enamel shallow tripod dish on three short feet, 16.5cm. diam. (Christie's) $1,125 £750

Late 19th century cloisonne enamel oviform vase with flaring neck, 61.5cm. high. (Christie's) $4,440 £3,000

A pair of 19th century cloisonne enamel and gilt bronze cockerels, 17½in. high. (Bermondsey) $2,100 £1,500

Late 19th century large cloisonne enamel hexagonal vase with flaring neck and spreading foot, 66.4cm. high. (Christie's) $4,440 £3,000

Late 19th century cloisonne lacquer on porcelain covered jar, Japan, 18in. high. (Robt. W. Skinner Inc.) $875 £638

A cloisonne enamel barrel shaped bowl on three small gilt metal lingzhi feet, 10cm. diam. (Christie's) $820 £540

An early 19th century cloisonne enamel vase with ring handles, 15¼in. high. (Bermondsey) $1,250 £850

COAL BOXES

The coal box was a product of the age when designers turned their attention to the fireplace as the focal point of the room, rather than just a functional feature. 'Purdoniums', named after their inventor, Purdon, became part of the standard accoutrements of the fireside, and were often richly decorated and ornamented. Some can fetch several hundred pounds at auction today, which is surprising, bearing in mind their humble function.

Victorian mahogany coal box, 1860. (British Antique Exporters) $130 £75

A Regency black and gilt japanned coal box with rounded rectangular domed lid, and another, 19in. wide. (Christie's) $6,350 £4,320

A late Victorian brass coal box with domed lid and pierced finial, 17in. wide. (Christie's) $551 £330

A late Victorian black and gilt japanned papier-mache purdonium, on later rosewood bracket feet, 18¾in. wide. (Christie's) $1,573 £1,100

A mid Victorian black, gilt and mother-of-pearl japanned papier-mache purdonium, 20in. wide, and another. (Christie's) $1,573 £1,100

Late 19th century Art Nouveau style brass coal box. (British Antique Exporters) $130 £75

An early Victorian walnut coal bin of sarcophagus form with coffered top and hinged front with metal liner, 21in. wide. (Christie's) $1,533 £1,080

COMMEMORATIVE CHINA

The arrival of Queen Victoria on the throne opened the floodgates for the manufacture of commemorative china. Her predecessors as rulers were more often lampooned than venerated, but Victoria changed the popular attitude towards royalty. China commemorating events in the reigns of William and Mary, George III, George IV and William IV are rare but pieces with pictures of Victoria and Albert were made in their thousands and enjoyed pride of place on the walls and mantlepieces of rich and poor up and down the land. Plates, tobacco jars, mugs, vases, pipes, teapots, doorstops and spill jars marked every event in the royal life. The china cost little to buy and proved so popular that the range spread to include political happenings, military displays, exhibitions and even famous crimes and criminals. One of the most rare items are mugs celebrating Victoria's coronation — before the commemorative china boom really took off — which can be worth around £500 today if in good condition. Her Jubilee mugs were produced in such vast numbers that their value is much less.

A Staffordshire blue and white cylindrical mug printed with equestrian figures of The Duke of Wellington and Lord Hill, 4¾in. high. (Christie's) $260 £200

An oviform vase made to commemorate the Coronation of Edward VII and Queen Alexandra in 1902, 27.5cm. high. $225 £150

An 18th century blue and white pottery jug with loop handle, 7.75in. high. (Prudential Fine Art)
                    $214 £130

A 19th century Liverpool transfer-printed pitcher of baluster form with pulled spout and applied C-scroll handle. (Christie's)
        $1,100 £665

An Obadiah Sherratt group of Polito's menagerie, circa 1830, 29.5cm. high. (Christie's)
        $21,546 £16,200

A Liverpool creamware inscribed and dated armorial oviform jug with loop handle, 1792, 14.5cm. high. (Christie's) $766 £540

A black glazed terracotta teapot and cover, printed in yellow and decorated in enamels and gilt, 16cm. high. (Phillips) $80 £50

A Doulton stoneware three handled mug commemorating the hoisting of the flag at Pretoria, 6½in. high. $127 £85

A Staffordshire jug depicting Wellington at Salamanca, 5½in. high. (Christie's) $117 £90

A creamware tall cylindrical mug, circa 1785, 12.5cm. high. (Christie's) $726 £440

Pair of mid 19th century copper lustre jugs with blue band decoration and painted figures of Queen Victoria and Prince Albert, 5½in. high. (Reeds Rains) $372 £240

A vase with a grey Doulton & Slater lace ground with an applied white bust of the Prince of Wales, circa 1885, 6¼in. high. $195 £130

A Staffordshire brown and white part glazed Parian jug with portraits of Wellington and Blucher, inscribed Jane Roberte, 7½in. high. (Christie's) $247 £190

Queen Caroline: a small lustre pottery cream jug, printed in black with portrait and national flora, 8cm. high. (Phillips) $480 £300

A Liverpool creamware jug, 21cm. high. (Phillips) $1,252 £750

A tankard designed by John Broad commemorating the 1897 Jubilee, circa 1897, 6½in. high. $135 £90

A Staffordshire saltglaze tartan ground Royalist teapot and cover with loop handle, circa 1750, 14cm. high. (Christie's) $15,336 £10,800

A jug with a portrait of H.M. Stanley below the inscription 'Emin Pasha Relief Expedition 1887-1889', 7½in. high. $120 £80

A Liverpool creamware oviform jug, inscribed in black script W.B., 6¾in. high, circa 1800. (Christie's) $209 £110

A Royal Doulton two-handled loving cup commemorating King George V silver jubilee, 10in. high, No. 584 of a limited edition of 1,000. (Christie's) $338 £260

A Worcester small cylindrical mug transfer-printed in black by R. Hancock with The King of Prussia, date 1757, 9cm. high. (Christie's) $1,185 £770

A jug commemorating the hoisting of the flag at Pretoria, circa 1900, 8¼in. high. $165 £110

A Doulton stoneware double handled tankard commemorating War in the Sudan, 1883, 6in. high. $127 £85

A coronation jug commemorating the accession of Edward VII and Queen Alexandra, circa 1902, 7½in. high. $142 £95

CONVERSATION PIECES

The essential criteria for these is that they must be either bizarre or not immediately recognisable. The category covers everything from a bath chair to a painted refrigerator, and a number of antiques, such as a mid-Victorian chicken drumstick holder could easily fit the bill. They may or may not be valuable – it's really beside the point. Basically, they're fun things to collect.

Thirteen Star American flag, circa 1810, 28 x 45in. (Robt. W. Skinner Inc.) $450 £357

A Spanish Colonial dress saddle with white leather seat and pommel, also a pair of 'Botas' leggings, 30in. long. (Robt. W. Skinner Inc.) $925 £642

A decorative cartridge display board, arranged geometrically in stylised floral motif, 43in. square. $4,323 £3,300

A pair of fireside companions painted with a boy and a girl in 18th century costume, 42in. and 45in. high. (Christie's) $4,347 £2,860

One of two sheets of Chinese wallpaper painted in fresh colours, 18th century, 92 x 38in. (Christie's) $1,749 £1,296

A Dutch oak birdcage of architectural design, the seven compartments with black-painted metal bars and refuse-trays, basically 18th century, 44½in. wide. (Christie's) $10,120 £5,500

Mid 19th century North Italian parcel gilt and painted sedan chair, 30½in. wide, 69in. high. (Christie's) $14,696 £8,800

CONVERSATION PIECES

A wooden artist's palette, belonging to Pierre Matisse, circa 1907, a label on reverse bears the inscription *'Matisse Palette of 1907 – (Blue Still Life)*,' 9½ x 14in. (Christie's) $13,200 £7,542

A Victorian three-wheeled bath chair, with metal rimmed wooden wheels, painted olive green with maroon and yellow lining, 78in. overall. (Lawrence Fine Arts) $597 £330

A papier mache lacquer match case holder, the top painted with a peasant woman seated and eating, by the Lukutin Factory, 19th century. (Christie's) $446 £264

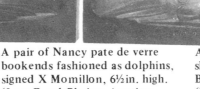

Two fragments of early George III printed wallpaper, after C. N. Cochin the Younger, 44½ x 22½in. and 47½ x 22¾in. (Christie's) $482 £324

A pair of Nancy pate de verre bookends fashioned as dolphins, signed X Momillon, 6½in. high. (Lots Road Chelsea Auction Galleries) $4,550 £2,500

An Art Deco glass cocktail shaker with silver mounts, Birmingham, 1936, 8in. high. (Dreweatt Neate) $748 £400

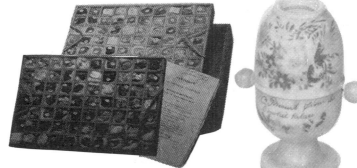

A refrigerator decorated by Piero Fornasetti, on black painted tubular steel framed base, 70cm. wide. (Christie's) $861 £594

Early 19th century cabinet of geological specimens, by M. le Prof. Jurine et M. Brard. (Christie's) $1,320 £910

An alabaster peep egg with three scenes of the Crystal Palace, 4½in. high. (Christie's) $175 £104

President Chester A. Arthur's Parade flag, red wool field of several sections, American, circa 1883, 69 x 45in. (Robt. W. Skinner Inc.)
$1,400 £1,111

'Hires' syrup dispenser, Phila., patented 1920, 14¼in. high. (Robt. W. Skinner Inc.)
$340 £263

Edwardian novelty desk clip and pen brush in the form of a muzzled bear, Birmingham, 1908. (Prudential Fine Art)
$462 £280

'The Tap Dancer', a life-size metal figure of a young negro, 185cm. high. (Christie's) $3,608 £2,200

A pair of 19th century glass specie jars enamelled in white on the inside and enamelled colours with the Royal Arms, 18.1/8in. high. (Christie's) $844 £528

An Egyptian mummified hawk, 22cm. long, Late Dynastic Period. (Phillips) $473 £260

A group of yacht 'Gore' sail design books, by the Ratseys and Lapthorn sailmaking firm, New York, 1902-60. (Christie's) $8,250 £6,021

A Victorian child's sledge, painted red on shaped metal runners. (Lots Road Chelsea Auction Galleries)
$486 £300

A circular, gilt lined love token box, probably French, 2½in. diam. (Christie's) $492 £308

Late 19th century Oriental carved coral figural group, 8in. long. (Robt. W. Skinner Inc.) $296 £200

An American 19th century papercut picture, depicting two eagles with flags, 5¾ x 7½in. (Christie's) $1,100 £620

Cast zinc St. Bernard dog figure, probably Mass., circa 1880, 45in. wide. (Robt. W. Skinner Inc.) $2,600 £1,818

One of twenty sheets of Chinese wallpaper painted in fresh colours.(Christie's) $78,408 £59,400

Two plate glass Royal Warrant Holder's display signs, bearing the coat of arms of H.M. Queen Alexandra, 18½ x 18in. (Christie's) $393 £275

An Eley 'Sporting and Military' cartridge board, including brass rifle and pistol cartridge cases and tins of primers etc., in its oak frame. (Christie's) $205 £140

A lead winged cherub with dolphin fountain, 26in. high. (Lots Road Chelsea Auction Galleries) $992 £620

A WMF plated corkholder, each cork surmounted by a sculptural figure, 15.5cm. high. (Christie's) $896 £550

A 19th century pouch 8 x 7.5cm, with a boxwood seated baku netsuke, signed Gyokumin, 4.6cm. long. (Christie's) $5,205 £3,080

CORKSCREWS

The corkscrew is a fine example of a simple gadget which has undergone much elaboration. A screw device with a simple steel spiral fixed to a wooden handle for pulling corks out of bottles was in common use in the 17th century — before that wine was sold in flagons or kegs and there was no need for corkscrews. By 1850 however, the Victorian love for elaboration and invention meant that the corkscrew was embellished and prettified with handles made of inlaid or engraved silver, brass, ivory or horn often carved in the shape of animals or birds. Sometimes various gadgets, including a brush for dusting the necks of bottles, was added to the basic corkscrew and collectors prize the more fantastic and complicated examples most highly. Miniature corkscrews in silver were made for the use of ladies drawing tiny corks out of necks of perfume bottles and other tiny ones were to be found included in the gadgets hanging from a Victorian housekeeper's chatelaine or ornamental bunch of keys, pencils and scissors that swung from the waist. Some corkscrews inscribed with messages were given as gifts from house guests to their hosts.

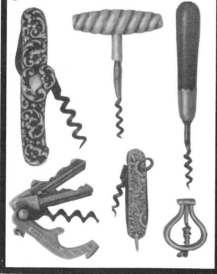

A Dutch silver corkscrew, struck with date letter for 1895, 4in. high. (Christie's) $880 £515

A silver corkscrew by John Reilly. $3,500 £2,000

Late 18th century silver corkscrew by Cocks & Bettridge of Birmingham, 3in. high. (Christie's) $255 £145

A Dutch silver and mother-of- pearl corkscrew, apparently unmarked, circa 1775, 3in. high. (Christie's) $770 £451

Early 19th century variant of Thomason's double action corkscrew with elliptical brass turning handle and helical worm. (Christie's) $1,540 £902

A cast iron bar corkscrew, black painted with gold decoration, origin unknown. (Christie's) $1,100 £644

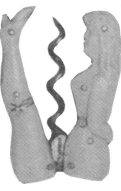

Early 19th century Thomason-type double action corkscrew with open frame, turned bone handle and helical worm. (Christie's) $528 £309

A German 'folding lady' corkscrew, circa 1900, height closed 2.5/8in. (Christie's) $605 £354

Early 19th century Thomason-type double action corkscrew, with turned bone handle and helical worm. (Christie's) $825 £483

A Dutch silver and mother-of-pearl corkscrew, struck with indistinct maker's mark, circa 1780, 3.1/8in. high. (Christie's) $880 £515

A Dutch silver corkscrew, by Johannes Van Geelen, Gouda, 1799, the handle cast in the form of a lion passant on a scroll base, 3¾in. high. (Christie's) $1,320 £773

A Dutch silver corkscrew, by L. Olfers, Groningen, the handle cast as a galloping horse on a scroll base, 3¾in. high. (Christie's) $935 £548

A George II silver combination corkscrew and nutmeg grater, apparently unmarked, circa 1750, 3½in. long. (Christie's) $1,540 £902

Late 19th century silver 'lady's legs' folding corkscrew, probably American, marked Sterling, height closed 2in. high. (Christie's) $418 £245

A 19th century Dutch silver corkscrew, the curled platform handle with the cast figure of a cow, 3½in. high. (Christie's) $605 £354

CORKSCREWS

A Dutch silver corkscrew by J. J. Koen of Amsterdam, 3¼in. high. (Christie's) $305 £175

A rotary eclipse bar corkscrew, in brass, with steel helical worm and wood side handle. (Christie's) $770 £451

A Dutch silver and mother-of-pearl corkscrew, circa 1800, maker's mark apparently **DP** with vase of flowers between, 3¼in. high. (Christie's) $1,100 £644

A 19th century Dutch silver corkscrew, the platform handle with the cast figures of a man in 18th century dress and two rearing horses, 4in. high. (Christie's) $880 £515

Late 19th century American silver mounted and mother-of-pearl corkscrew, stamped Sterling, 4¼in. wide. (Christie's) $528 £309

A Dutch silver corkscrew, struck with date letter for 1908, 4in. high. (Christie's) $935 £548

Early 19th century King's screw double action corkscrew, with turned bone handle and helical worm, nickel side handle. (Christie's) $462 £270

'Amor', a German figural folding corkscrew, formed as a Bakelite soldier and his lady, circa 1900, height closed 2¾in. (Christie's) $572 £335

Hull's 'Royal Club' side lever corkscrew, with helical worm. (Christie's) $880 £515

CRICKETANA

With devotion to the national game amounting almost to a religion in some quarters, it is small wonder that a ready market exists for 'cricketana.' The Grand Old Man of the game, W. G. Grace, always attracts a premium, while older cricketing books are also in demand. Many potteries too have found it worthwhile to produce mugs, plates etc, either as special commemorative issues or simply because they are confident that a cricketing theme will always find a market.

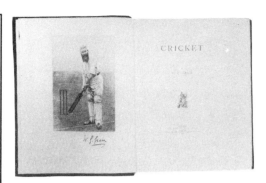

W. G. Grace. Cricket, pub. 1891, crown quarto edn. de luxe. (Phillips) $436 £260

Henry Scott Tuke, by W. G. Grace, 1905, sketch in charcoal, 20 x 26cm. (Phillips) $3,696 £2,200

The Cricket Match Played at Toronto, Canada, 1872, lithograph designed by R. Smith, 90 x 50cm. (Phillips) $1,596 £950

A Staffordshire pottery mug, decorated with cricket figures in white relief and silver lustre, 10cm. high. (Phillips) $184 £110

A Minton pottery tankard for M.C.C. 1787-1937, 13cm. high. (Phillips) $218 £130

J. Nyren: The Young Cricketer's Tutor, pub. 1833. (Phillips) $285 £170

A Robinson & Leadbetter parian bust of W. G. Grace, 17cm. high. (Phillips) $1,260 £750

V.A.A.A.C.C.C. Team 1892: An Australian navy-blue velvet and gold braid cap for 1892. (Phillips) $336 £200

An inscription from an Edwardian two-handled silver tray for Teignbridge Cricket Club, 70cm. long. (Phillips) $1,512 £900

A Minton pottery ashtray for M.C.C. 1787-1937, 13.5cm. (Phillips) $100 £60

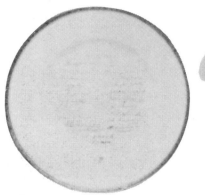

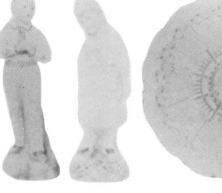

A Royal Worcester porcelain plate, the centre printed in gilt with signatures of the Australian Touring Side, 1964, 27cm. diam. (Phillips) $168 £100

A pair of Continental porcelain figures of Young England and His Sister, approx. 32cm. high. (Phillips) $756 £450

A Coalport porcelain plate commemorating W. G. Grace's century of centuries, 23cm. diam. (Phillips) $218 £130

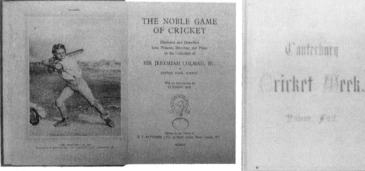

J. Wisden: Cricketers' Almanack 1864-1985, bound in blue calf and gilt with Scarborough Cricket Club badge on front cover. (Phillips) $16,800 £10,000

Sir Jeremiah Colman: The Noble Game of Cricket, pub. 1941, ltd. edn. of 150. (Phillips) $772 £460

The Canterbury Cricket Week. Volume First, pub. 1865. (Phillips) $436 £260

CRYSTAL SETS

With the commencement of commercial radio broadcasting in the early 20's, the crystal set arrived on the scene. The earliest commercially made ones were primitive, consisting usually of a hardwood base with headphones. More elaborate cabinet design, whether of bakelite or hardwood, followed, as did 'home-made' versions. Early crystal sets were taken to the Post Office, and the licence stamp actually stuck on the set! Many home-made sets therefore remained unregistered.

The Curry Super Low Loss crystal set coil. $5 £3

Brownie Wireless Co. of Great Britain, No. 2 Model, crystal set, patent no. 9117/25, in a bakelite case. $175 £100

Brownie Wireless Co., No. 3 Model crystal set with built in coil in a bakelite case. $175 £100

Ivalek crystal set, in the shape of a radio, early 1950's.
$45 £25

Home-made kit form crystal set on a bakelite baseplate.
$35 £20

T.M.C. crystal set No. 351, wave length 300—500 metres and 1580 to 1680 in a red mahogany case with brass fittings. $235 £135

British Thompson Houston Co. Ltd., Rugby, England, Radiola 'Bijou' crystal receiver Form B, G.P.O. Reg. No. 861, mahogany boxed. $260 £150

DAUM

In 1875 Jean Daum started a glassworks at Nancy in France and it was continued by his two sons Jean-Louis and Jean-Antonin who made Art Nouveau glass in the style of Emile Galle. The glassworks has continued in the hands of the Daum family ever since and their products have been distinguished by exquisite quality and style. Much of their output was coloured glass with etched floral decorations and also cased glass but they also created new shapes including the long necked Berluze vase. Since 1966, th firm has made a great deal of Pate de Verre glass with designs by artists like Salvador Dali. All wares produced by the factory since its inception carry the Daum signature which has changed in form many times over the years.

A Daum overlaid and acid-etched table lamp with wrought-iron mount, 60cm. high. (Christie's)
$11,088   £7,700

A Daum limited edition pate-de-verre and fibre glass surrealist sculpture by Salvador Dali, depicting a soft clock slumped on a coat hanger. (Christie's) $2,975 £2,052

A Daum Art Deco acid etched vase, the smoky-blue glass deeply etched with oval and circular panels, 33.5cm. high. (Christie's)
$2,345 £1,430

One of two Daum Cameo glass rosebowls, crimped ruffled rim decorated with cameo-cut sprays of violets, signed 'Daum/Nancy', diam. 7in. (Robt. W. Skinner Inc.)
$800 £446

A Daum cameo landscape vase, the tapering cylindrical body with swollen collar, 27cm. high. (Christie's)
$783 £540

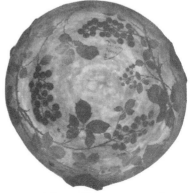

A large Daum cameo glass hanging lampshade of shallow domed form, 46cm. diam., signed. (Phillips)
$3,024 £2,100

A Daum enamelled and acid etched vase of rounded cube form, 11.5cm. high. (Christie's) $2,345 £1,430

Daum Cameo and enamelled glass perfume bottle with conforming stopper, signature 'Daum/Nancy', height 4½in. (Robt. W. Skinner Inc.) $1,400 £782

A small Daum rectangular section cameo glass jug, circa 1900, 11cm. long. (Christie's) $380 £302

A Daum Nancy acid etched glass table lamp, France, circa 1900, 14in. high. (Robt. W. Skinner Inc.) $2,000 £1,388

A Daum Art Deco acid etched vase, bell-shaped, 28cm. high. (Christie's) $992 £605

A Daum cameo table lamp with wrought-iron, three-branch neck mount, 44.1cm. high. (Christie's) $8,712 £6,050

A Daum acid textured two-handled vase, engraved signature Daum Nancy with the Cross of Lorraine, France, 25.5cm. high. (Christie's) $1,443 £880

A Daum cameo and engraved martele baluster vase, engraved Daum Nancy with Cross of Lorraine, 25.4cm. high. (Christie's) $2,674 £1,870

A Daum bowl, the white, green and red mottled glass acid-etched with primroses and foliage, 13.9cm. high. (Christie's) $865 £605

DECANTER LABELS

In the days when many decanters were made of opaque or coloured glass it was the custom to hang a label round the necks telling what was inside. Some of the labels were very beautifully made in silver, enamel, porcelain or Sheffield plate and could be finely chased or decorated. They were used in wealthy homes from around 1730 onwards and until the mid 19th century most of them were individually made by craftsmen. Later however they were mass produced. After 1860, they dropped out of general use because the Grocers' Licences Act of that year made it possible for wine to be sold in single bottles with paper labels indicating the contents.

Old labels can be valuable, especially the ones made of Battersea enamel and dating from between 1753-56. They were quite large with a wavy outline and could be worth several hundreds of pounds today. Other valuable labels are those which were originally printed with the name Madeira but later overprinted with titles like brandy or whisky. There are many die-stamped reproduction labels on the market but they can usually be distinguished from the genuine ones which are heavier.

An early 19th century wine label of cast openwork fruiting vine design, possibly Irish, circa 1820. (Phillips) $422 £280

A Victorian stamped-out hunting horn wine label, incised 'Port', by G. Unite, Birmingham, 1857. (Phillips) $474 £300

A Victorian cast wine label, title scroll incised 'Red Constantia', by Rawlings & Sumner, 1843. (Phillips) $573 £380

A George IV Irish wine label, incised 'St. Peray', by L. Nolan, Dublin, 1825. (Phillips) $474 £300

DECANTER LABELS

A George III cast openwork wine label with a reclining satyr beside a barrel, by Phipps & Robinson, probably 1817. (Phillips)
$210 £120

One of a pair of George IV Irish oval wine labels, by James Scott, Dublin, circa 1825. (Phillips) $560 £320

A Victorian Provincial escutcheon wine label, possibly by Thomas Wheatley of Newcastle, circa 1850. (Phillips)
$113 £65

A pair of George III wine labels of shell and fruiting vine design, by Richard Turner, 1819. (Phillips) $402 £230

A Victorian silver bottle ticket for Sherry, in the form of a bat, English or Indian Colonial, circa 1880, 4¼in. wide. (Christie's) $880 £515

A George IV armorial wine label of openwork ribbed disc form, by Riley & Storer, 1829. (Phillips) $630 £360

A set of four Victorian wine labels, each engraved with a crest, by Rawlings & Sumner, London, 1859 and 1860. (Christie's) $281 £176

One of three George III silver gilt wine labels for Port, Claret and Champagne, by Benjamin Smith, 1808, 3in. high, 7oz.5dwt. (Christie's) $3,676 £2,484

A George III wine label modelled as a putto, by Peter, Anne and William Bateman, 1799. (Phillips) $1,435 £820

A George II Provincial wine label, formed as two putti, by Isaac Cookson, Newcastle, circa 1750. (Phillips) $367 £210

A George III Provincial rectangular thread-edge wine label, by Hampston & Prince, York, 1784/5. (Phillips)
$122 £70

A Victorian wine label of fruiting vine and leafy scroll design, circa 1840. (Phillips)
$210 £120

DECANTERS

Elegant glass bottles for holding wines and spirits are very favourite with collectors and there is a large variety to be found ranging from fragile, etched ones with long necks to the more chunky shapes of thicker glass which were favoured by Victorian householders. A good collection has to include as many different shapes and styles as possible and it is unlikely that the possibilities will ever be exhausted. Best known are ships' decanters with heavy bases which could be slipped into decanter boxes to prevent them being toppled over in a gale. Similar styles were popular during the days of coach travel when a glass of brandy would help wile away the tedium of a journey. Decanters became less popular after the invention of the tantalus which was a locking frame round two or three glass decanters. It was intended to keep them locked away from thieving servants or tippling members of the household and it was named after Tantalus, son of Zeus, whose punishment for a misdeed was to suffer terrible thirst and be forever reaching for a bunch of grapes that dangled above his head.

A green baluster decanter with lozenge stopper, 9½in. high, and a blue decanter, 9in. high. (Christie's)
$236 £160

A Netherlands blue-tinted decanter, the metal mounted cork stopper secured by a chain, 25cm. high. (Phillips)
$2,772 £1,800

A 'Lynn' decanter of club shape with horizontally ribbed sides and kick-in base, circa 1775, 23.5cm. high. (Christie's) $945 £528

A dated enamelled carafe, the opaque white panel inscribed Thos. Worrall 1757, 22cm. high. (Christie's)
$8,393 £6,264

A Hukin & Heath 'Crow's foot' decanter, designed by Dr. C. Dresser, electroplate and glass, with registration lozenge for 1879, 24cm. high. (Christie's)
$11,275 £7,776

A Guild of Handicraft hammered silver and green glass decanter, the design attributed to C. R. Ashbee, with London hallmarks for 1903, 22.5cm. high. (Christie's)
$1,892 £1,296

DECANTERS

A Bohemian engraved and cut decanter, circa 1730, 27.5cm. high. (Christie's) $475 £330

A cylindrical file-cut decanter and stopper, cut with three rings to the neck, 10in. high. (Christie's) $88 £60

Victorian glass decanter, 1870. (British Antique Exporters) $70 £52

A Venini 'Vetro pesante inciso' carafe, dark brown cased in clear glass, circa 1957, 25.5cm. high. (Christie's) $1,232 £770

An Archimede Seguso 'Compisizione Piume' carafe, circa 1960, 29cm. high. (Christie's) $7,920 £4,950

A George III glass decanter, Indian club-shaped with wide neck, circa 1790, overall height 29cm. (Christie's) $935 £548

An English Jeroboam decanter, the reverse engraved March 8th 1791, 38cm. high. (Phillips) $1,925 £1,250

A Venini 'Vetro pesante inciso' decanter and stopper designed by Paolo Venini, circa 1957, 18.5cm. high. (Christie's) $1,232 £770

An Orrefors decanter and stopper, by Nils Landberg. (Christie's) $2,516 £1,760

DECOYS

Some bird decoys are uncannily realistic looking, as they ought to be to deceive other birds. Hunters from earliest times have fashioned decoys to reassure their prey that, because other birds are acting calmly, they have nothing to fear. In order to reinforce this feeling of security, duck decoys were often accompanied by decoys of gulls and crows which were placed along river banks to give an appearance of normality. Decoys are usually made of wood and painted with flat paint to give a lifelike effect. They are generally slightly larger than lifesize because the larger they are the more quickly they can be spotted. Decoys dating from the 18th and 19th century are the most valuable and they have a primitive appeal which makes them perfect room decorations.

Early 20th century Summer Yellow Legs carving, G. Shaw, Chatham, Mass., 5 in. high, 9 in. long. (Robt. W. Skinner Inc.) $1,100 £617

Black-bellied plover by A. Elmer Crowell, East Harwich, Mass., full sized, original paint, filler chipped from part of each leg, oval stamp on carved clam shell base. $17,500 £10,000

A miniature Canada goose, by A. Elmer Crowell, Mass., original paint. (Robt. W. Skinner Inc.) $1,000 £595

A life size carved and painted black duck, Birchler, circa 1925, full length 18 in., 19 in. high. (Robt. W. Skinner Inc.) $2,700 £1,824

Canada goose by Oliver Lawson, Chrisfield, Maryland, signed on bottom and dated 1965, unusual preening position with intricate carving of wings and primaries. $4,375 £2,500

Sandpiper, tinny, factory made, in excellent original paint and original stick. $435 £250

114

DECOYS

A painted cedar hen canvas-back decoy, made by L. T. Ward Bros, 1936, 15in. long. (Christie's) $3,850 £2,655

A painted wooden Maine Flying Scoter decoy, by 'Gus' Aaron Wilson, circa 1880/1920, together with two black-painted wooden duck decoys. (Christie's) $4,620 £3,136

A Canada Goose decoy, by George Boyd, early 20th century, 29in. long. (Christie's) $1,760 £1,213

Two late 19th century painted wooden decoys, one 10in. long, the other 11½in. long. (Christie's) $330 £220

A pair of painted wooden American Merganser decoys, a hen and drake, by L. T. Holmes, circa 1855/65. (Christie's) $93,500 £64,482

Two late 19th century painted wooden decoys, 9½in. long. (Christie's) $300 £200

A painted wooden hollow constructed Canada Goose decoy, by Chas. H. Hart, Mass., circa 1890/1915, 20½in. long. (Christie's) $4,400 £3,034

A painted wooden Primitive Brant decoy, three-piece laminated construction, 18in. long. (Christie's) $242 £166

A painted wooden oversized Golden Eye decoy, by 'Gus' Aaron Wilson, circa 1880/1920, 20in. long.(Christie's) $1,760 £1,213

DELFT

When Chinese porcelain arrived in the West, Europe was literally dazzled. Nothing of such beauty and brilliance had ever been manufactured there, and the indigenous pottery industries now had to compete with the flood of imports. Majolica had been made in small workshops throughout Holland by potters who were experienced yet open to new techniques. A result of this was delft, a decorated, tin-glazed earthenware, known elsewhere as faience. It first appeared in the early 17th century and the next 120 years were to see the steady development of both technique and quality. Majolica had been mainly multicoloured, but delft was nearly all blue and white, imitating Chinese porcelain. Decoration too at first followed Chinese traditions, but later pieces saw innovative themes, such as the peacock jar, with a motif of two peacocks facing a central basket.

The finest period lasted until about 1730, when the seduction of enamel colours and the prettiness of porcelain began to sap the vitality of the medium.

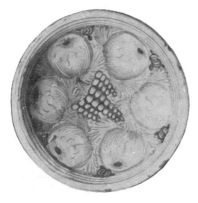

A mid 17th century English delft charger, probably Southwark, 37cm. diam. (Christie's) $920 £648

A Dublin delft blue and white baluster vase, circa 1750, 32cm. high. (Christie's) $1,456 £1,026

A Bristol delft blue and white barber's bowl, circa 1740, 25.5cm. diam. (Christie's) $1,292 £972

A massive London delft dated polychrome armorial drug jar of swelling form, circa 1656, 36cm. high. (Christie's)
          $25,855 £19,440

Early 18th century Dutch Delft blue and white seated Magot, 18cm. high. (Christie's) $1,188 £825

A London delft dated blue and white wet drug jar for S. Cichorei.Sympi with date 1659, 20cm. high. (Christie's)
          $1,226 £864

An English delft polychrome posset pot, either London or Bristol, circa 1695, 24.5cm. wide. (Christie's)
$2,359 £1,430

One of a pair of 18th century Dutch Delft polychrome cows with yellow horns, 21cm. long. (Christie's) $2,453 £1,728

A Bristol delft blue and white footed bowl, circa 1730, 26.5cm. diam. (Christie's) $2,178 £1,320

A London delft blue and white Royalist portrait plate, circa 1690, 22cm. diam. (Christie's)
$2,541 £1,540

A Delft mantel garniture, comprising two covered jars and a vase, vase 13in. high. (Christie's) $770 £434

A Lambeth delft blue and white octagonal pill slab, circa 1780, 26cm. high. (Christie's) $3,085 £1,870

A Bristol delft plate painted in a bright palette with a peacock, circa 1740, 21cm. diam. (Christie's)
$1,540 £880

A London delft vase painted in blue 24cm. high. (Phillips)
$835 £500

A late 17th century Lambeth blue and white delftware dish, 14in. wide. (Dacre, Son & Hartley) $656 £400

DE MORGAN

One of the most remarkable tile makers and potters of the Arts and Crafts movement in England was William de Morgan (1839-1917). He was a friend of William Morris and collaborated with him to produce tile designs including flowers, fish, ships and mythical birds and beasts. He also worked with Joe Juster, Halsey Ricardo and Frederick and Charles Passenger. De Morgan had a pottery and showroom at Cheyne Row, Chelsea and later, at Merton Abbey, he and Morris made tiles, dishes and vases with predominantly purple, blue and green colours which imitated 15th and 16th century Iznik tiles. He established a factory in Fulham which produced pottery, tiles, panels and murals. After 1892 De Morgan spent a great deal of time in Italy where he was influenced by the work of Florentine artists. His marks include DM, a tulip and leaves, a Tudor rose or an A forming the steeple of a ruined abbey.

A De Morgan charger, decorated by Chas. Passenger, 1890's, 41.5cm. diam.
$9,223 £7,150

A De Morgan vase, decorated by Joe Juster, 1880's, 31.2cm. high.$2,128 £1,650

A small William de Morgan lustre bowl, 5½in. diam. (Christie's) $297 £220

A De Morgan lustre vase, decorated by Fred Passenger, 1890's, 32.6cm. high.
$1,135 £882

A William de Morgan wall plate designed by Chas. Passenger, 47cm. diam. (Christie's) $1,879 £1,296

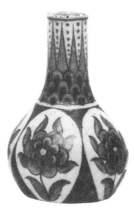

A De Morgan vase decorated in shades of mauve, green, blue and turquoise with panels of flowers, 1890's, 15.6cm. high.
$397 £308

DOLLS

Since earliest times children have played with dolls and some of their roughly made toys turn up on archaeological sites to give mute testimony to distant childhoods. However, the sophisticated dolls which fetch high prices at auction were often never intended to face the rough and tumble of a nursery for they were made to be played with by adult women. The neatly jointed wooden dolls of the 17th and 18th centuries are examples of this. They were treasured by their owners and dressed up in the latest fashions. Many of them had their own trunks full of beautiful costumes.

In the 19th century doll making became big business and bisque headed dolls with rolling eyes and hair that could be combed made their appearance. Queen Victoria was a great collector and spent many hours dressing up her dolls. They were far too precious to be played with by children. It was not until a less rigorous attitude to the young prevailed that doll making became a mass industry and the French and German doll makers dominated the market. In the 20th century there was a great vogue for making dolls in the form of popular heroines like Shirley Temple or Snow White and dolls based on the little princesses Elizabeth and Margaret Rose had a huge vogue.

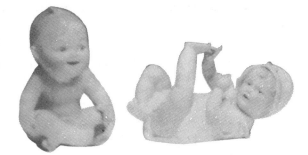

A bisque figure of a chubby baby, impressed No. 9902, 4½in. high, and a bisque figure of a baby playing with his toes, 5½in. long, impressed Gebruder Heubach. (Christie's)
$635 £385

A set of composition dolls representing the Dionne quintruplets with doctor and nurse, 7½in. high, the adults 13in. high, by Madame Alexander. (Christie's) $639 £418

Set of six late 19th century all bisque dolls, German, mounted in candy box, inscribed on cover 'found in the nursery of a ruined old chateau — Verdun, France — 1917', 4in. high. (Robt. W. Skinner Inc.) $650 £393

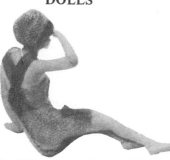

Early 20th century German bisque bathing belle, resting on one hand, the other raised shielding her eyes, 3½in. high. (Lawrence Fine Art) $587 £330

A composition mask faced googlie eyed doll, with smiling watermelon mouth, wearing spotted dress, 10½in. high. (Christie's) $610 £330

A composition headed Motschmann type baby doll with dark inset eyes, painted curls and floating hands and feet, 8in. high, circa 1850. (Christie's) $689 £418

A 'Chad Valley' boxed set of Snow White and the Seven Dwarfs in Original clothes, Snow White with painted pressed felt face, jointed velvet body, the blue velvet bodice with pale blue and pink slashed sleeves and short cape, 17in. high, the Dwarfs 9½in. high. (Christie's) $5,291 £2,860

A composition mask faced googlie eyed doll, with smiling watermelon mouth, wearing pinafore and bonnet, 9in. high. (Christie's) $345 £187

A French bisque headed doll with cork pate, the leather shoes impressed with a number 11, a bee and a Paris Depose, 25in. high. (Ambrose) $2,430 £1,350

A Hebe bisque headed doll, marks indistinct, with open mouth and upper teeth, sleeping blue eyes and long fair plaited hair, 24in. high. (Lawrence Fine Art) $332 £187

A painted head doll with blue
eyes, the felt body in original,
clothes, 16in. high, marked
Lenci, circa 1930. (Christie's)
$202   £121

A bisque headed child doll,
marked SFBJ Paris 14, 32in.
high, original box marked
Bebe Francais. (Christie's)
$1,128 £800

A bisque headed character
child doll, marked 231
DRMR 248 FANY A2/0M,
14in. high. (Christie's)
$3,993 £2,420

An 18th century group of Italian creche figures, six average height 9in., four average
height 11½in., and two at 14½in. (Robt. W. Skinner Inc.) $3,700 £2,242

A papier mache mask faced doll
with turquoise blue eyes, the
cloth and wood body in original
Central European costume, 15½
in. high, circa 1860. (Christie's)
$330 £198

Two all bisque doll's house dolls
with fixed blue eyes, blonde wigs
and moulded socks and shoes in
original national costume, 4in.
high. (Christie's) $183 £110

A bisque headed child doll
with fixed brown eyes and
blonde wig, 10in. high,
marked 1079 DEP S&H.
(Christie's) $312 £187

DOLLS

A cloth character doll, the head in five sections, 16in. high, by Kathe Kruse, and The Katy Kruse dolly book, published 1927. (Christie's) $1,745 £1,045

Simon & Halbig/Kammer & Reinhardt bisque-headed doll, 1914-27, 26in. high. (Hobbs & Chambers) $789 £470

A bisque headed clockwork Bebe Premier Pas with kid upper legs and blonde wig, 17½in. high, by Jules Nicholas Steiner, circa 1890. (Christie's) $1,837 £1,100

A terracotta headed creche figure modelled as a Turk with moustache and pigtail, painted wooden hands and feet, 19in. high. (Christie's) $610 £330

A pair of advertising dolls modelled as the 'Bisto Kids', designed by Will Owen, 11in. high, circa 1948. (Christie's) $386 £209

A composition character headed doll modelled as Lord Kitchener, in original clothes with Sam Browne hat and puttees, 19in. high. (Christie's) $305 £164

A German bisque head doll, marked 283/297, Max Handwerck, 24¾in. high. (Geering & Colyer) $468 £260

A bisque headed doll's house doll modelled as a man with cloth body and bisque hands, 6in. high. (Christie's) $235 £143

A German bisque head doll, marked Heubach-Koppelsdorf, 250-4, 25¾in. high. (Geering & Colyer) $468 £260

DOLLS HOUSES

Like early dolls, the first dolls' houses were made to be played with by adults and even today they have an undeniable appeal to mothers just as train sets appeal to fathers. Some early dolls' houses were exquisitely furnished with brocade on the walls and silver on the tables, recreating in miniature the life of the great house of the time with servants in the kitchen, babies in the nursery and carriages at the front door. The earliest dolls' houses are thought to have come from Germany around 1660 but the most sophisticated were those made in France in the 19th century. Some later ones even had lights that worked and lifts that went up and down. Prices for pieces of miniature furniture to furnish a dolls' house can be high and Victorian houses were furnished down to the last aspidistra with plaster pies and legs of mutton on the kitchen table. There is an excellent display of dolls' houses at the Bethnal Green Museum in London and another in Wallington Hall, Northumberland.

A printed paper on wood doll's house, by Lines Bros., 43in. wide. (Christie's)
$1,542 £935

Late 19th century yellow Victorian doll's house and furniture, 26¾in. wide. (Robt. W. Skinner Inc.)
$300 £230

Early 20th century American wooden gabled roof doll's house with glass windows, 24¾in. high. (Robt. W. Skinner Inc.)
$435 £250

A painted wooden doll's box type town house of three bays and three storeys, 25in. high. (Christie's)
$544 £330

An early 20th century two-storeyed doll's house, facade 20 x 18in., depth 12in. (James Norwich Auctions) $448 £280

Victorian wooden doll's house, cottage style, with working door with brass knob at front, circa 1890. (Theriault's) $1,450 £1,082

A custom crafted Colonial style doll's house, circa 1980, with ten rooms of furniture, rugs, textiles and accessories, 28in. high, 5¾in. long. (Robt. W. Skinner Inc.) $1,500 £1,200

19th century wooden Mansard roof doll's house with painted brick front, 23¾in. high. (Robert W. Skinner Inc.) $400 £225

An early 20th century doll's house, paper covered to simulate brickwork, 88cm. high. (Osmond Tricks) $542 £290

A Jacobean style wood and composition doll's house of four bays and two storeys, 27in. wide. (Christie's) $635 £385

DOORSTOPS

Why were the Victorians so keen on propping their doors open? Perhaps it was the cult of fresh air but whatever the reason, a vast quality and variety of doorstops survives from that period. Because of the job it had to do, a doorstop must be heavy and the usual material was cast iron, lead or brass in the shape of baskets of fruit, Mr Punches, stout old gentlemen or shire horses. Some doorstops were cast in the likeness of famous people like Queen Victoria or the Duke of Wellington. Even Jumbo, the elephant star of London Zoo, was made into a doorstop after he was sold and exported to America with Barnum and Bailey's circus. He died trying to charge a steam train there. Drawing room doorstops tended to be slightly lighter than those for doors in less elegant parts of the house and were often made of Nailsea glass with air bubbles trapped inside.

Late 19th century cast iron cat doorstop. $60 £35

19th century cast iron lion rampant doorstop. $70 £40

Victorian painted iron stick-stand and doorstop of a boy holding a serpent. (Lots Road)
$400 £250

Late 19th century cast iron Mr Punch doorstop. $130 £75

Pair of Georgian brass door stops, the moulded bases with weighted iron insets, 13¾in. high. (Woolley & Wallis) $736 £460

19th century eagle and serpent cast iron doorstop. $260 £150

125

DRINKING SETS

While some punch sets, for example, date from the 19th century and beyond, the drinking set really became fashionable in the Art Nouveau/Art Deco periods, with such leading designers as Lalique, Daum and Galle. While they were originally intended as largely functional items, in the hands of these craftsmen they could also be highly decorative and can now fetch surprising sums. Like all sets, they are prone to breakage or loss of some of their parts, so complete surviving sets always attract a premium.

A Victorian liqueur set with crimped heart-shaped tray, by Heath & Middleston, Birmingham, 1891, the liqueur bottle 8¼in. high, 12.75oz. free. (Christie's) $480 £300

An Art Deco decanter and glasses, the decanter 22.5cm. high and six liqueur glasses 5cm. high (one glass chipped). (Phillips) $264 £150

An Art Deco glass decanter set, the decanter 20.5cm. high and six octagonal glasses, 6.5cm. high. (Phillips) $774 £440

A Japanese cocktail set decorated in high relief with iris, circa 1900. (Phillips) $1,640 £1,000

A Schott & Gen 'Jena er Glas' clear glass tea-set, designed by Wm. Wagenfeld, teapot, cover and filter, 11cm. high. (Phillips) $316 £220

A WMF electroplated liqueur set and tray, the decanters 9in. high, the tray 16in. wide, all with stamped marks. (Christie's) $705 £480

Bohemian gold decorated cobalt blue glass punch set, late 19th century, 9½in. high. (Robt. W. Skinner Inc.) $900 £548

A Patriz Huber liqueur set, white metal and glass, stamped with 935 German silver mark and PH, circa 1900, decanter 18.4cm. high. (Christie's) $4,099 £2,808

A Gabriel Argy-Rousseau pate-de-verre eight-piece liqueur service, the tray 40.1cm. wide. (Christie's) $3,132 £2,160

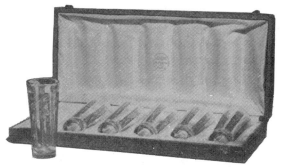

A Lalique oviform clear and frosted glass decanter and stopper, 7in. high, and eight glasses en suite. (Christie's) $288 £200

A set of six Lalique aperitif glasses moulded in clear glass with amethyst tinted panels of Grecian maidens, circa 1930, 9.8cm. high. (Christie's) $1,644 £1,134

ENAMEL

The star of the British enamels are those made at Battersea's York House for a period of only three years from 1753 to 1756. Not unnaturally, when any of these turn up today they fetch very high prices indeed. Genuine old Battersea has a copper base and looks as if it had been coated with an opaque material similar to glass. However the name Battersea is often misleadingly applied to other enamels which were really made in Wednesbury, South Staffordshire, Bilston or even Czechoslovakia. Old pieces are very pretty and are sometimes decorated with paintings of landscapes or seaside scenes and some of them carry loving messages because they were often given as presents or made as mementoes of certain resorts.

A 19th century Limoges polychrome enamel plaque, in the 16th century style, after Pierre Reymong, 7.1/8 x 5.1/8in. (Christie's) $990 £565

A South German double-ended enamel snuff box of waisted form, circa 1740, 2.5/8in. high. (Christie's) $3,920 £2,420

A German rectangular enamel snuff box painted in colours with battle scenes from the Seven Years' War, circa 1760, 3in. wide. (Christie's) $5,445 £3,300

A 19th century French enamel plaque of Eve, signed L. Penet, in ebonised frame, 39 x 27cm. (Christie's) $2,388 £1,430

Two Staffordshire white enamel tapersticks with gilt metal mounts, circa 1765, one 6.3/8in. and one 6½in. high. (Christie's) $1.866 £1,296

An Austrian enamelled cigarette case, the cover depicting a Caucasian warrior. (Phillips) $1,050 £600

A white metal and enamel box with parcel gilt interior, circa 1900, 10.3cm. diam. (Christie's) $861 £594

A George III enamel bottle ticket, Birmingham or South Staffordshire, circa 1770, 3in. long. (Christie's) $264 £154

A South Staffordshire George III enamel bonbonniere, circa 1770, 3in. long. (Christie's) $4,180 £2,388

One of a pair of late 19th century Viennese silver mounted enamel cornucopiae, by Hermann Bohm, 8½in. long. (Christie's) $3,036 £1,944

Two Staffordshire oval enamel portrait plaques, circa 1765, probably Birmingham, each 3¼in. (Christie's) $2,799 £1,944

An enamel wine funnel, South Staffordshire, circa 1770, 4¼in. long. (Christie's) $1,980 £1,160

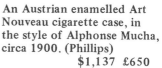

An 18th century Limoges style enamel on copper plate, 7.7/8in. diam. (Robt. W. Skinner Inc.) $600 £437

A Viennese enamel sweetmeat dish with gilt metal mounts, circa 1900, 6.3/8in. high. (Christie's) $1,174 £810

An Austrian enamelled Art Nouveau cigarette case, in the style of Alphonse Mucha, circa 1900. (Phillips) $1,137 £650

ETUIS

An etui sounds like a useful word for crossword puzzle addicts but in fact it was a ladies' companion, a small ornamental case designed to be worn from a chatelaine around the waist or carried in a purse. Etuis contained miniature manicure sets, sewing implements, a snuff spoon, a pencil, a button hook and sometimes a pocketknife – the elegant ladies' Swiss knife kit in fact. They were worn for over 200 years but went out of fashion at the end of the 19th century. Some etuis were very pretty and could be made of gold or hardstone but more commonly of silver, porcelain, ivory or painted enamel.

A German silver gilt mounted white enamel etui, circa 1765, some of the contents with later Dutch control marks, 4in. high.(Christie's) $737 £702

Mid 18th century etui, oval tapered body, fully fitted. $1,000 £600

A George II gold mounted etui, circa 1750, 3¾in. high. (Christie's) $3,139 £2,052

A Staffordshire enamel etui of upright form, with original gilt metal mounts, circa 1770, 4.1/8in. high. (Christie's) $1,399 £972

George II etui, circa 1745, in green shagreen case. $1,300 £750

A gold etui case, the body chased with flowers and bearing the Royal cypher. (Wellington Salerooms) $8,064 £4,800

EYE BATHS

At first sight eye baths look very utilitarian items but they have changed little in basic shape since they were first introduced more than 300 years ago and therefore their design must be more or less perfect for their purpose. The most common eyebaths, which are still on sale today, are made of blue glass but collectors are able to hunt them out in such a wide variety of materials as pottery, lignum vitae, celluloid, bakelite, plastic, ivory, pewter, aluminium and rubber – they were even made in silver and a Georgian silver one can sell for around £700. Some chemists produced their own eyebaths for special eye-lotions and a few had realistic looking eyes painted on them. The price varies according to the rarity of the piece and the material with which it is made.

Stemmed moulded amber glass eye bath. $25 £15

Aluminium squat eye bath by Kress & Owen, with original box. $20 £12

An early green freeblown eye bath with embellished stem.
                    $35 £20

Clear glass stemmed eye bath with wrythened bowl. $14 £8

Clear waisted glass eye bath.
                    $9 £5

Milkglass stemmed eye bath.
                    $18 £10

EYE BATHS

Squat pink glass eye bath by Maws of London. $7 £4

Squat bakelite eye bath with foot. $18 £10

Squat blue stoneware eye bath. $5 £3

Rubber eye bath advertised as suitable for motorists. $20 £12

Squat white stoneware eye bath, Culuval Roberts. $20 £12

Squat white stoneware eye bath with 'Woodheads' in green print. $25 £15

Yellow stemmed stoneware eye bath. $25 £15

Blue and white Meissen porcelain eye bath with gold rim. $95 £55

Blue glass eye bath with reservoir and foot. $50 £30

White stoneware stemmed eye bath. $20 £12

Maw's Eye Douche with rubber ball. $35 £20

Blue glass short stemmed free-blown eye bath. $35 £20

FAIRGROUND MEMORABILIA

Childhood memories of visits to the fair bring back exciting sensations of loud music and bright colour and there is an enthusiastic circle of collectors who seek out everything connected with the fair from gypsy caravans or wooden fronted coconut stalls to merry-go-rounds with their galloping horses. Fair ground art work was always very stylised with brash, vivid colours and simple designs. The most popular item with collectors are the wonderful merry-go-round animals – horses, ostriches, dragons and galloping zebras which carried screaming children round and round on their backs. They are very popular with interior decorators today and prices vary depending on the condition and the quality of the carving of the animals which have a primitive appeal. The best ones can soar into six figures especially in America.

The brightly coloured and often highly ornate signs for stalls, merry-go-rounds and so on were usually painted by someone belonging to the fairground itself. The stylised decoration was sometimes even extended to their own caravans, and became quite an art form. Even small offcuts of these can make interesting collectables.

Small carousel stander, mounted as a rocking horse, circa 1900, 27in. high, 29in. long. (Robt. W. Skinner Inc.) $1,500 £892

A Burton type showman's horse-drawn living van, circa 1920, of standard ribbed and planked construction. (Bearne's) $5,632 £3,200

A carved and painted wooden zebra carousel figure, attributed to H. Speilman, circa 1880, 33in. high. (Robt. W. Skinner Inc.)
$3,400 £2,361

A carved and painted carousel horse, attributed to I. D. Loof, circa 1885, 60½in. high. $14,000 £8,000

Voigt 52 keyless fairground organ, built in 1880 as a barrel operated organ converted to the book system in 1912. $24,500 £14,000

Horsedrawn showman's van, built by Brayshaws, circa 1910. (Spike Jones) $2,600 £1,500

'Golden Marenghi', 46 key fairground organ, circa 1905, 7 x 7ft. (Onslow's) $28,764 £18,800

Late 1940's showman's wagon, internally fitted in walnut and mahogany, 24ft. long. (Spike Jones) $21,000 £12,000

Wooden carousel rooster, mounted on spiral brass and wrought iron post, possibly Europe, circa 1900, 48in. high. (Robt. W. Skinner Inc.) $1,800 £1,395

FAIRINGS

In the mid 19th century the prizes on fairground stalls were often little china figures with humorous or risque legends written along the base. These were 'fairings' and today they are among the most sought after collectables.

They were very unsophisticated in creation and were small, rarely more than four inches high and standing on rectangular bases between two and three inches square. They showed children, politicians, soldiers and sailors and people wooing each other or getting married. In all there are more than 400 different types of fairings.

The Last Match. $100 £60   Attack. $150 £90

They were given as fairground prizes because they cost very little to buy from the manufacturers who were based in Germany and turned them out for only a few coppers each. The principal makers were Springer and Oppenheimer of Elbogen and Conte and Boehme of Possneck who mass produced fairings in huge numbers and exported them to England. Many of the subjects they represented were taken from sheets of popular music. "Champagne Charlie is My Name" represents a music hall song sung by George Leybourne called 'Champagne Charlie' which was all the rage in the 1860's. Others include "Pluck" and "The Decided Smash" also taken from a song sheet called "Full Cry Gallop". Some fairings were also scenes from the Franco-Prussian War which was raging at the time.

You Dirty Boy. $100 £60   Champagne Charlie Is My
                           Name. $260 £150

A Lucky Dog. $100 £60   Before Darwin. $55 £30

When A Man's Married His Troubles Begin $55 £30

The Shoemaker In Love $875 £500

Let Us Be Friends $150 £90

I Am Going A-Milking Sir, She Said $150 £90

Caught In The Act $350 £200

English Neutrality 1870/71 Attending The Sick And Wounded $875 £500

The Broken Hoop $260 £150

Returning At One O'Clock In The Morning $100 £60

Children's Meeting $100 £60

FAIRINGS

Welsh Costume $55 £30

Home From The Club He Fears
The Storm $260 £150

Hark Tom Somebody's Coming
$150 £90

Now They'll Blame Me For This
$150 £90

Twelve Months After Marriage
$100 £60

Our Best Wishes $350 £200

(Happy Father) What Two? Yes
Sir. Two Little Beauties!!
$100 £60

The Long And Short Of It
$260 £150

God Save The Queen $150 £90

FANS

The folding fan is said to have been invented in Japan around 670 A.D. and introduced first into China and then Europe about the time of Vasco da Gama. Fan sticks were made of ivory, mother of pearl or various woods and covered with paper, parchment, skin, lace or "chicken skin", specially prepared kid skin. They were usually decorated with painting.

The vogue for the folding fan in Europe dates from the 16th century and Elizabeth I is known to have had a good collection. In popularity it supplanted the feather fan which had been used before then. Special conventions were developed for the use of fans and gestures in handling them grew into code signals of an amorous nature.

The Fanmakers' Company was formed in England in 1709 and for a while the importation of foreign fans was prohibited. It was not till the end of the 18th century that the most extravagant and luxurious fans were carried by ladies of fashion and by the 19th century, the fan had become an indispensible fashion accessory.

Fan sticks are often very decorative and made of exotic materials gilded and painted to suit the designs on the leaf. They went through various fashions, growing smaller and then becoming bigger and more flamboyant again. During the Art Nouveau period the shape of the leaves and sticks reflected the artistic style of the time. In the 1920's women carried fans when they went to dances but with the growth in popularity of smoking, this fashion died away. Fan collecting is very popular because it is still possible to find attractive examples at fairly low prices.

An ivory brise fan painted with a lady fishing, 9in., circa 1730. (Christie's) $5,736 £3,850

A fan, the leaf painted with the return of a hero, the verso with chinoiserie, 10in., French, circa 1760, in glazed case. (Christie's)
$3,278 £2,200

A fan, the leaf painted with a court scene, 10in., circa 1770. (Christie's) $655 £440

A fan, the ivory sticks carved, pierced and gilt with the Altar of Love, 10½in., Italian, circa 1780. (Christie's) $1,346 £935

A French fan with gilded ivory sticks and ivory silk leaf painted with lovers at an altar, circa 1770, 28cm. long. (Phillips) $405 £250

A gilded horn brise fan with pique work, painted with figures on a quay overlooking a bay, circa 1810, 16cm long. (Phillips) $324 £200

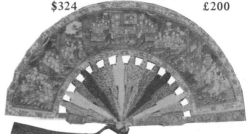

A fan with carved, pierced, silvered and gilt mother-of-pearl sticks and the chicken-skin leaf painted and gilded, circa 1760, 30cm. long, probably German. (Phillips) $777 £480

A Chinese fan with carved and pierced shaped sticks of tortoiseshell, mother-of-pearl, stained and unstained ivory and metal filigree with enamel decoration, circa 1840, 28cm. long, in box. (Phillips) $777 £480

A Chinese cabriolet fan with black, pink, silver and gilt lacquer sticks, circa 1830, 28.5cm. long, in original box with label printed in Spanish. (Phillips) $1,053 £650

A fan with carved, pierced, silvered and gilt mother-of-pearl sticks and an 18th century pastiche, signed Donzel, circa 1870, in a shaped, glazed case. (Phillips) $2,268 £1,400

A 19th century painted fan, the guards inlaid with green enamel, porcelain plaques, semi-precious stones and pearls, probably French, 11¼in. long. (Christie's) $880 £502

A French fan, the carved, pierced and painted ivory sticks decorated with red and green florets, circa 1760, 26cm. long, and a shaped case. (Phillips) $1,053 £650

FANS

A Flemish fan with ivory sticks, the guards inlaid with mother-of-pearl and decorated with silver pique, 26.5cm, long. (Phillips)
$479 £340

An ivory brise fan painted and lacquered with a classical scene, 8½in., circa 1730. (Christie's)
$3,933 £2,640

A late 18th century Italian fan with pierced ivory sticks, 28cm. long. (Phillips)
$535 £380

La Contre Revolution, a printed fan edged with green silk fringe, 11in., French, circa 1790. (Christie's) $901 £605

A French painted pierced ivory brise fan with tortoiseshell guards decorated with silver pique, early 18th century, 21cm. long. (Phillips)
$479 £340

A fan, the dark leaf painted with a Biblical scene of figures drinking from a mountain torrent, 10¼in., Italian, circa 1770, in silk covered box. (Christie's) $1,147 £770

A late 18th century fan with carved, pierced and silvered ivory sticks, 24.5cm. long, and a box. (Phillips) $155 £110

An early 19th century fan with carved shaped ivory sticks, the vellum leaf painted with Flora attended by maidens and suitors, 28cm. long. (Phillips) $513 £340

FINGER PLATES

Finger plates were put on doors to prevent hands marking the paintwork and they were made of brass, steel, cut glass or fine porcelain and some were very ornate indeed, made to match the rest of the door fittings or the architectural design of the house. Because it was only in upper class houses that finger plates were used in the 18th and early 19th centuries, most of the ones that survive from that time are of fine quality and very expensive today. Victorian finger plates, especially those used in bedrooms, were often made of porcelain and painted with attractive bunches of flowers. In the 1920's they began being used in middle class homes and especially during the Art Deco period some attractive ones were made from bakelite, tin or perspex. Some finger plates were used as advertising notices and fixed to the doors of shops. These are highly prized by collectors and sometimes they can be found in old properties covered with layers of paint. It is worthwhile cleaning them with care. A few shop finger plates incorporated a match striker.

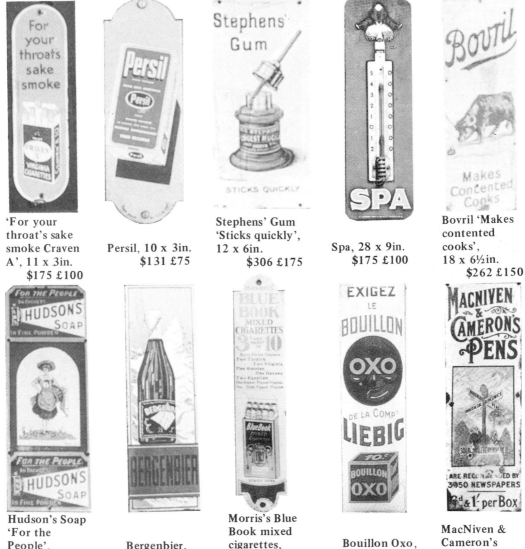

'For your throat's sake smoke Craven A', 11 x 3in. $175 £100

Persil, 10 x 3in. $131 £75

Stephens' Gum 'Sticks quickly', 12 x 6in. $306 £175

Spa, 28 x 9in. $175 £100

Bovril 'Makes contented cooks', 18 x 6½in. $262 £150

Hudson's Soap 'For the People', 9½ x 3½in. $350 £200

Bergenbier, 18 x 7in. $175 £100

Morris's Blue Book mixed cigarettes, 10 x 2¼in. $219 £125

Bouillon Oxo, 21 x 6in. $131 £75

MacNiven & Cameron's Pens, 24 x 8in. $262 £150

FIRE IRONS

Before central heating, a blazing hearth was the focal point of a home and the gleaming fire irons used for tending the fire were very much the housewife's pride and joy. They were made of brass, steel, wrought iron, cast iron or copper and fashioned in a wide range of designs. It was necessary to have a shovel, a poker, tongs and a brush and some sets also incorporated a set of bellows for blowing life into reluctant blazes. Then there were also fire dogs for resting the implements on and a fender which gave protection against burning logs or coal tumbling into the room. The Club fender which made its appearance around 1860 is an excellent idea because not only does it form a safety barrier for the fire but it also had little upholstered seats at each corner or all along its front where favoured people could perch near the warmth. In recent years there has been a great rise in popularity of old fashioned, long handled Victorian fire irons, especially the ones made of brass.

There is also a following for "companion sets" of fire-irons hung round a central stem which were made for suburban homes from the 1920's and '30's onwards.

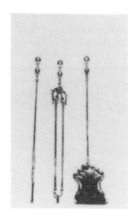

A heavy set of Victorian brass fire irons, 32in. long. $175 £100

An Edwardian brass companion set, 21in. high. $90 £50

Victorian brass barley twist fire irons, 30in. long. $210 £120

A fine set of Georgian steel fire irons, 32in. long. $350 £200

Four-piece Edwardian brass companion set, 30in. high. $175 £100

An early set of steel and brass fire irons, 32in. long, circa 1810. £110 $260 £150

FIRE IRONS

A fine pair of brass and enamelled andirons, 26in. high. (Christie's)
$3,344 £2,200

Late Victorian brass companion set, 1880. (British Antique Exporters)
$29 £22

A pair of Federal brass andirons and matching fire tools, New York, 1800-25, andirons 20in. high. (Christie's) $1,980 £1,117

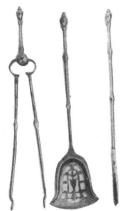

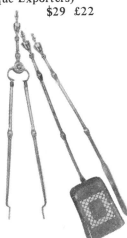

A set of three George III brass fire-irons, 31¼in. long. (Christie's) $775 £550

A set of three George III polished steel fire-irons comprising a poker, a pair of tongs and a pierced shovel with brass vase-pommels, the shovel 30¼in. long. (Christie's)
$3,908 £2,090

A set of three polished steel fire-irons with baluster pommels, 36in. long. (Christie's)
$1,144 £715

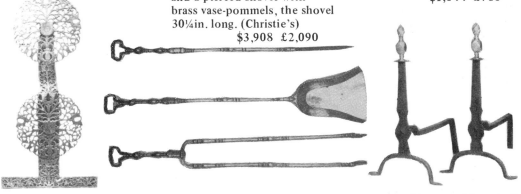

One of a pair of cast iron foliate andirons, attributed to E. Gimson, circa 1905, 22¼in. high. (Robt. W. Skinner Inc.) $5,500 £3,846

A set of three George III brass fire-irons with shaped ring handles and baluster shafts, 24in. long. (Christie's) $1,960 £1,210

A pair of brass and iron knife-blade andirons, American, circa 1800, 22¼in. high. (Christie's) $880 £539

FIREMARKS

Before 1830 there was no municipal fire brigade and when a fire broke out in a private residence, the occupants had to put it out themselves or else look for help from one of the fore crews employed by insurance companies which offered cover in those days. Before an insurance company fire engine would tackle your blaze however, they had to be sure that you were one of their subscribers and the way they did this was to look to see if there was a firemark attached to the wall of your home. Originally these were lead crests bearing the name of the company and your policy number but many of them must have melted in the heat of the conflagration and later ones were made of copper, tin or zinc and occasionally of terracotta or porcelain. Those which have survived in situ are jealously guarded by the house owners and there is a great interest in collecting them.

Scottish, Commercial Fire and Life Insurance, copper, oval, raised figure of Caledonia. (Phillips) $316 £220

Liverpool Fire Office, lead, liver bird and torse raised on circular section, 'Liverpool' raised on panel below and impressed with policy no. 426. (Phillips) $1,152 £800

Aberdeen Fire and Life Insurance Co., stamped lead, oval, raised arms of the city with motto 'Bon Accord'. (Phillips) $2,160 £1,500

Albion Fire and Life Insurance, cast iron, circular, raised 'Albion Fire Office', with raised border, issued circa 1810-28. (Phillips) $316 £220

Westminster Insurance, lead, open portcullis with Prince of Wales' feathers above, policy no. 20867 on panel below. (Phillips) $504 £350

West of Scotland Insurance, 1823-38, stamped lead, circular, raised crown in centre. (Phillips) $316 £220

North British Insurance, copper, St. Andrew and saltire cross raised in centre, 'North British' raised on panel below. (Phillips) $288 £200

Dundee Assurance, lead, raised arms of the city, impressed policy no. 3294. (Phillips) $1,152 £800

East Kent and Canterbury Economic Fire Assurance, 1824-28, tinned iron, oval. (Phillips) $374 £260

Hampshire and South of England Insurance, 1841-47, copper, rose and crown raised on centre. (Phillips) $273 £190

Eagle Insurance, stamped lead, raised with eagle standing on rock, 'Safety' raised on panel below. (Phillips) $1,180 £820

Edinburgh Friendly Assurance, heavy lead, policy no. 1805 pierced through panel below. (Phillips) $1,584 £1,100

The General Insurance Company of Ireland, lead, rectangular, raised phoenix, torse and borders, policy no. 2036 on panel below. (Phillips) $1,152 £800

London Assurance, lead, seated figure of Britannia with shield, spear and harp, 'London' raised on panel below, issued cira 1805-07. (Phillips) $604 £420

Bristol Crown Fire Office, lead, crown raised in high relief, 'Bristol' raised on panel below. (Phillips) $489 £340

Rare lead firemark of the Suffolk & General Country Amicable Insurance Office, Bury & Ipswich, 6½in. wide. $1,400 £800

Oval firemark for the Royal Irish Assurance Co., dated 1823. (Phillips) $4,375 £2,500

Irish firemark for the Saint Patrick Insurance Co., 1824. $2,100 £1,200

A Norwich General firemark, Policy No. 7522, 1799-1802, made of lead. (James Norwich Auctions) $248 £160

Lead firemark of the Union Assurance Society, London, (1714-1907), 7½in. wide, very rare. $1,400 £800

Rare lead firemark of the Kent Fire Insurance Company, Maidstone, with horse in relief, 6½in. wide. $1,000 £600

Hercules Fire Insurance, cast iron, 'Hercules Fire Office' raised on ornate shield. (Phillips) $288 £200

Royal Exchange Assurance, lead, raised Royal Exchange building, policy no. 570 on panel below, issued circa 1721. (Phillips) $6,336 £4,400

Berkshire, Gloucestershire and Provincial Life and Fire Assurance, 1824-31, copper, castle raised on oval. (Phillips) $230 £160

FISHING REELS

The most popular pastime today is fishing and therefore it is not surprising that there is a great interest in collecting angling artefacts. One of the most accessible, easy to store and display fishing items are reels and some collectors have as many as 500 different types. The best and earliest ones are made of brass and may be produced either by Mallochs of Perth or Hardy's of Alnwick who can claim to make the Rolls Royce of fishing reels, the Silex Rex, a level wind reel that is guaranteed not to get tangled. One of these can change hands today for around £1000.

Other interesting angling-related collectables include rods, flies, fly wallets, creels, gaffs, nets, stuffed fish, permits and, of course, specialist literature on the subject, from 'The Compleat Angler' onwards.

A Hardy Bros. Ltd. 'Fortuna' alloy sea reel with 'ship's wheel' tension nut and double handle, 7in. diam. $610 £350

A Hardy Bros. Ltd. 'St. George' multiplying alloy fly reel with ebonite handle. $175 £100

A Watson, Inverness, brass reel, with horn handle and smooth brass foot, 3½in. diam. $90 £50

A Hardy Bros. 1896 pattern all brass 'Perfect' reel with ivorine handle, 4¼in. diam. $875 £500

A Malloch's Patent spinning reel with horn handle, 4¼in. diam. $130 £75

A Hardy Bros. Ltd. large alloy sea-fishing reel with 'ship's wheel' tension nut, 9in. diam. $800 £450

A Hardy Bros. Ltd. The 'Perfect' alloy reel with ivorine handle and smooth brass foot, 4in. diam.
$260 £150

A Dreadnought Casting Reel Co. Ltd. alloy reel with ivorine handle brass check-nut, 3¼in. diam. **$90 £50**

A Hardy Bros. Ltd. 'St. George' multiplying alloy reel with ebonite handle and ribbed brass foot. **$260 £150**

A Hardy Bros. Ltd. The 'Longstone' alloy reel with ebonised wooden handles, 4¼in. diam. **$130 £75**

A Hardy Fortuna 7in. centre-pin sea reel, fitted with dual ebonite handles and brass star drag. **$350 £200**

An A. C. Farlowe & Co. Ltd. brass faced alloy reel with ebonite handle, 4.3/8in. diam. **$260 £150**

A Hardy Bros. Ltd. 'Sea Silex' alloy reel with smooth brass foot, ebonite handles and ivorine check handle, 7in. diam. **$435 £250**

A Hardy Bros. Ltd. The 'Perfect' alloy reel with ebonite handle, 4¼in. diam. **$300 £175**

A Hardy Bros. Ltd. 'Silex' No. 2 alloy spinning reel with ivorine handles, 4½in. diam. **$130 £75**

A Hardy Bros. Ltd. The 'Perfect' alloy reel with ebonite handle, 3.7/8in. diam. $130 £75

Brass salmon reel with ivory handle and ventilated drum, by Broddell of Belfast, circa 1900, 4¼in. diam. $175 £100

A Hardy Bros. Ltd. 'St. George' multiplying alloy fly reel, 3¾in. diam. $700 £400

A Hardy Bros. Ltd. The 'St. George' alloy reel with ivorine handle, 3¾in. diam. $130 £75

A Victorian gilt brass reel with ivory handle, with spring and cog mechanism, 3in. $3,500 £2,000

A brass reel with foliate engraved band to the front plate, horn handle, 4in. diam. $130 £75

The 'H.J.S.' multiplying reel, blacked alloy with grooved alloy foot and nickel-plated thumb bar, 2.1/8in. diam. $435 £250

A Julius Vom Hofe salmon fly reel, circa 1896, 4½in. diam. $260 £150

A Hardy Bros. all brass 'Perfect' reel with horn handle, smooth foot and oval logo, 2.3/8in. diam. $700 £400

FLAMBE

Flambe is the name given to a streaky, flame like glaze of a deep blood red colour that was devised at the Doulton factory and made its first public appearance to vast acclaim at the St Louis Exhibition of 1904. The technique was discovered by a chemist called Bernard Moore who worked at Doulton's around the end of the 19th century and his glaze was used to stunning effect by artists like Charles Nokes whose flambe elephants are high in collectors' lists of desirables. Flambe is produced by mixing copper oxide and other minerals and allowing fixed amounts of oxygen to enter the kiln at various stages of firing, It is a time consuming and costly business because mistakes were very possible but the trouble proved to be worthwhile because it became so popular with Doulton's customers. Flambe glazes are still being produced.

A Royal Doulton flambe ashtray with elephant heads on the corners, by Moore, 3½in. wide. $190 £110

Pig Dish, 2½in. high x 4½in. long, silver mounted, circa 1927. $525 £300

Two foxes, curled asleep, Model 15, 4in. long. $210 £120

Royal Doulton flambe jardiniere decorated with a desert scene. $490 £280

Monkey, dunce's cap, HN972, 5½in. high. $525 £300

The Dragon, A Royal Doulton flambe figure, 2085, introduced 1973, 7½in. high. $330 £190

Pigeons, two fantail, Model 46, 3¾in. high. $350 £200

Pomegranate, 2¾in. high. $260 £150

A Royal Doulton flambe model of a bulldog, 14.2cm. high. $1,750 £1,000

FUCHI KASHIRA

The Japanese sword is a full-scale work of art, and its accoutrements, such as fuchi kashira (the pommels at the top and bottom of the hilt) are collector's items in their own right. Often these were made and signed by specialist craftsmen and are richly decorated with mythological figures, animals, birds, etc.

Generally speaking, value increases with age and the quality of workmanship. Older ones have often been handed down from father to son as treasured heirlooms, intimately bound up with the family.

A shibuichi migakiji fuchi-kashira, signed Hidekatsu, early 19th century. (Christie's) $880 £550

A 19th century shakudo nanakoji fuchi-kashira, inscribed Ishiguro Masa-yoshi. (Christie's) $968 £605

A 19th century fuchi-kashira, silver takazogan, inscribed Omori Eishu. (Christie's) $2,195 £1,372

A shakudo nanakoji fuchi-kashira, signed Kondo Mitsuyasu, circa 1800. (Christie's) $1,091 £682

An 18th century shakudo nanakoji gilt rimmed in fuchi-kashira, Soten style. (Christie's) $704 £440

A shibuichi fuchi-kashira, decorated with carp among gilt water-weeds, signed Tomohisa, Mito School, circa 1800. (Christie's) $844 £528

Early 19th century copper fuchi-kashira depicting Raiden among clouds on the kashira, unsigned. (Christie's) $440 £275

A shakudo nanakoji fuchi-kashira, iroe takazogan, reed warblers on branches of blossoming plum, signed Ganshoshi Nagatsune and kao. (Christie's) $739 £462

A 19th century shakudo migakiji fuchi-kashira decorated with Gentoku, signed Yasumasa. (Christie's) $563 £352

A shakudo migakiji fuchi-kashira decorated in taka-zogan with ants and their eggs, 19th century. (Christie's) $563 £352

A 19th century shakudo nanakoji fuchi-kashira, unsigned. depicting a cuckoo in flight. (Christie's) $563 £352

151

GALLE

Perhaps the leading Art Nouveau glass maker was Emile Galle (1846-1904) who also made a great name as a designer of furniture, ceramics and jewellery. Along with his father, he worked at Nancy where he established his glass factory in 1874, turning out a vast number of lamps, vases and tableware decorated with his characteristic flowing designs of foliage, flowers, birds or female figures. He developed his own techniques for making and decorating glass but he was also much influenced by Japanese styles. He exhibited at several Paris Expositions to great acclaim. All his pieces were signed, even the ones made by his collaborators, and he influenced several other glassmakers including the Daum brothers. The Galle factory continued in operation after his death but finally closed in 1931.

A Galle oviform single-handled ewer, the silver mount modelled with stylised flowers, signed, 10¼in. high. (Christie's) $1,066 £820

A Galle double overlay carved blowout vase, the amber glass overlaid with fruiting vines, 27.5cm. high. (Christie's) $7,078 £4,950

An Emile Galle fruitwood and marquetry table a deux plateaux, 52.5cm. wide. (Christie's) $858 £561

A Galle cameo baluster vase, the amber and milky white glass overlaid in purple, carved with fuschia, 16cm. high. (Christie's) $902 £550

A Galle flask-shaped scent bottle, the neck with a gilt band, rim chip, 12.5cm. high. (Christie's) $570 £396

A Galle double overlay cameo glass lamp, circa 1900, 32.4cm. high. (Christie's) $10,962 £7,560

A Galle carved and acid etched double-overlay landscape vase, 29cm. high. (Christie's) $8,659 £5,280

A Galle carved and acid-etched clock, 13cm. high. (Christie's) $4,089 £2,860

An artistic Galle 'verrerie parlante' vase, engraved Galle expos 1900, 41.5cm. high. (Christie's) $75,504 £52,800

An enamelled glass jug with stopper, by Galle, decorated with enamelled hearts and a dwarf playing a violin, 20cm. high. (Christie's) $633 £440

A Galle blowout lamp, varying shades of red on an amber ground, signed, circa 1900, 44.5cm. high. (Christie's) $59,508 £41,040

A tall Galle cameo table lamp, the domed shade and stem overlaid with claret-coloured glass, 63.5cm. high. (Christie's) $12,584 £8,800

A Galle marqueterie de verre vase, bun foot with body shaped like a crocus bloom, circa 1900, 35cm. high. (Christie's) $13,311 £9,180

A Galle faience bowl of squat dimpled bulbous shape, 1890's, 14cm. $435 £250

A Galle mahogany and marquetry two-tier etagere, signed in the marquetry Galle, 59.3cm. wide. (Christie's) $2,662 £1,836

GINGER BEER BOTTLES

In rubbish dumps all over the country old ginger beer bottles can be found and some of them are worth as much as £75 each. The ones collectors seek are made of stoneware usually by manufacturers Price or Doulton and often they have very attractive lettering. Galtee More is the name of a certain patent bottle which had the corks held in place by a metal pin through the neck and they are fairly rare because they were only produced between 1900 and 1918. On the other hand they were made in every part of the country so there is always a chance of one turning up even in the most remote places. Ordinary ginger beer bottles are coloured white, light or dark brown but real rarities have blue or green shoulders and they're the ones that are worth most money.

'Old Style Brewed Ginger Beer' bottle by W. Carter, Oswestry, honey colour with black printing. $18 £10

W. Carter, Oswestry, 'Old Style Ginger Beer', in honey coloured bottle with black printing. $18 £10

Honeynecked Ginger Beer bottle from A. H. Nash, Market Harboro', Chemist. $18 £10

Galtee More bottle from E. Cox & Sons, Reading and Newbury, Mineral Water Manufacturers. $18 £10

Ginger Beer bottle from T. Weaver, Reading, honeyneck with white base. $20 £12

Galtee More honey coloured Ginger Beer bottle, by Jones Bros., Oxford and Reading. $45 £25

GINGER BEER BOTTLES

Galtee More Ginger Beer, by E. Line & Co., Reading. $25 £15

Ginger Beer bottle from Austins, Birmingham, with ginger root in the design. $18 £10

Wallingford Brewery Ltd. Ginger Beer bottle.$18 £10

'Old Style Ginger Beer' bottle from M. P. O'Brien Universal Providing Stores, Edenderry, honey colour with black printing. $14 £8

Ginger Beer brewed and bottled by Yates Bros., honeyneck with white body. $20 £12

Galtee More Ginger Beer bottle from Wallingford Brewery Ltd. $18 £10

Galtee Patent Ginger Beer bottle of honey colour impressed Lewis Evans, Dolgelly, Wales. $18 £10

Galtee More honeyneck Ginger Beer bottle from The Reading Mineral Water Co. with the lion trade mark. $18 £10

A rare honeyneck Ginger Beer bottle by Joseph Gidman, Mineral Water Works, Knutsford.$130 £75

GOLDSCHEIDER

It was in 1886 that Friedrich Goldscheider founded his factory in Vienna. After his death in 1897, production continued there under the direction of his widow and brother Alois, until, in 1920, the business was taken over by his two sons Marcel and Walter. In 1927, however, Marcel broke away to form the Vereinigte Ateliers fur Kunst und Keramik.

While such things as vases were produced, the factory is best known for the figures and wall masks which epitomised the Art Nouveau and perhaps even more, the Art Deco styles. The favourite subject was the female form and face, with dress and hairstyles faithfully reflecting those of the period. Dancers abound, in every sense, and, in the more exotic of these, the Egyptian influence is once more in evidence.

A Goldscheider pottery bust of a young woman in the Art Deco style, signed F. Donatello, 23½in. high. (Outhwaite & Litherland) $504 £350

A Goldscheider Art Deco globular lamp base, decorated in white, orange, black and blue with banding, 25cm. high. (Phillips) $243 £180

A Goldscheider terracotta figure of a blackamoor, 23½in. high. (Graves, Son & Pilcher) $1,856 £1,600

A Goldscheider pottery mask of a girl looking down, Made in Austria, circa 1925, 23cm. high. (Christie's) $473 £324

A Goldscheider pottery figure of a woman wearing a beaded costume, on a black oval base, 18in. high. (Christie's) $2,108 £1,700

A Goldscheider tin-glazed earthenware wall mask, Wien, Made in Austria, inscribed 8874, 36cm. high. (Christie's) $811 £495

GOLDSCHEIDER

A Goldscheider pottery figure modelled as a naked young lady holding a fan, and trailing a shawl behind, 13¾in. high. (Christie's) $514 £350

A pair of Goldscheider pottery figures of a young girl and a young man, made in Austria, 15in. high. (Christie's) $528 £400

A Goldscheider pottery figure of a dancing girl, designed by Lorenzl, 16in. high. (Christie's) $1,057 £682

A Goldscheider pottery figure, modelled as a sailor holding a girl, 30cm. high. (Christie's) $537 £330

A Goldscheider pottery 'Negro' wall mask, 26.5cm. high. (Phillips) $228 £150

An Art Nouveau Goldscheider pottery figure, modelled as a girl wearing long flowing robes, designed by E. Tell, 65cm. high. (Phillips) $691 £480

'Butterfly Girl', a Goldscheider figure after a model by Lorenzl, 7in. high. (Christie's) $634 £420

A Goldscheider pottery double face wall plaque, the two females in profile, 12in. high. (Christie's) $596 £385

A Goldscheider pottery group after a model by Lorenzl, of a flamenco dancer and a guitar player, 17in. high. (Christie's) $893 £580

GOLFING BOOKS

Next to playing the game, golfing enthusiasts enjoy reading about it. For over 200 years there has been a steady output of books about golf and some of them fetch amazing prices when they come up for auction. The Victorians were keen authors about sport and the golfing books they produced are fairly easy to find. Many of them relate to the Royal and Ancient Course at St Andrews and the famous characters who played there. Books with anecdotes about players of the past or, even better, written by them, fetch premium prices. If they are in good condition and well illustrated, they can go easily for four figures. However, the real rarities are golfing books from the 18th century and one of the most unusual is a little paperback leaflet containing a poem called ''The Golf'' written in 1743 by a poet called Mathison. A first edition copy sold a few years ago for £17000. The demand for golfing books comes from all over the world with the Americans and the Japanese being particularly keen.

Hints on Golf, by Horace Hutchinson, 1891. $140 £80

The Crail Golfing Society, 1786—1936, Being the History of an Eighteenth Century Golf Club in the East Neuk of Fife, by James Gordon Dow, 1936. $700 £400

Taylor on Golf, 1902. $125 £70

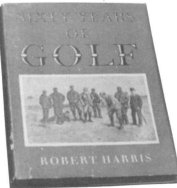

The Soul of Golf, by P. A. Vaile, 1898. $130 £75

Sixty Years of Golf, by Robert Harris, 1953. $105 £60

The World of Golf, by Gorden Smith, published by The Isthmian Library, 1898. $210 £120

GOLFING BOOKS

On The Links, Golfing Stories by Various Hands, Edinburgh, David Douglas, 1889. $525 £300

Some Essays on Golf Course Architecture, by H. S. Colt and C. H. Alison, 1920. $800 £450

Golfing, by W. & R. Chambers, 1887. $350 £200

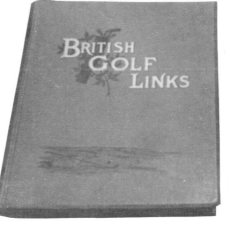

F. G. Tait, A Record, by J. L. Low, 1900. $130 £75

British Golf Links, by Hutchinson, 1897. $875 £500

'The New Book of Golf', edited by Horace G. Hutchinson, 1912. $210 £125

MacHamlet 'Hys Handycap' or 'As You Swipe It', by Paul Triefus, illustrated by Sidney Rogerson, 1922.$90 £50

The Golf Book of East Lothian, by Kerr, 1896. $1,600 £900

A Golfing Idyll, by Flint, 1897. $350 £200

GOSS COTTAGES

The famous Goss factory which started producing china in 1858 started a very popular line in attractive little cottages modelled on the homes of famous people in 1893 and continued making them till 1929. Among the 51 different types they sold were copies of Anne Hathaway's cottage at Stratford on Avon and Robert Burns' home at Alloway.

The cottages were often pastille burners and they sold well because they made attractive and cheap souvenirs. Today they are among the most desirable items in the vast Goss range for collectors who specialise in the products of that enterprising company. The cottages are usually marked with the name W. H. Goss and a goshawk with wings outstretched.

Miss Ellen Terry's Farm near Tenterden in Kent, 70mm. long. $540   £310

Sulgrave Manor, Northamptonshire, 125mm. long. $1,925 £1,100

Old Market House at Ledbury, 68mm. long. $500 £290

Manx Cottage Nightlight, Isle of Man, 122 mm. long. $280 £160

Shakespeare's Cottage, Stratford-on-Avon, 65mm. long. $130 £75

Wordsworth's home, Dove Cottage, 102mm. long. $700 £400

GOSS COTTAGES

The Goss Oven, orange chimney version, 75mm. long. $375 £215

The Feathers Hotel, Ledbury, 114mm. long. $1,400   £800

Isaac Walton's Birthplace, Shallowford, 86mm. long. $610 £350

Portman Lodge, Bournemouth, open door version, 84mm. long. $610 £350

Ann Hathaway's Cottage, Shottery, 50mm. long. $125 £70

St Nicholas Chapel, Lantern Hill, Ilfracombe, 74mm. high. $280 £160

Thomas Hardy's Birthplace, Dorchester, 100mm. long. $610   £350

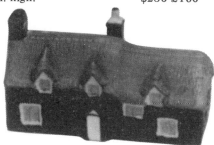

Old Maids Cottage, Lee, Devon, 73mm. long. $210 £120

GOSS COTTAGES

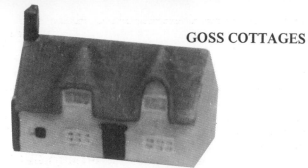

The Old Thatched Cottage, Poole, 68mm. long. $700 £400

Charles Dickens' house, Gads Hill, near Rochester. $225 £130

Southampton Tudor House, 83mm. long. $500 £285

First and Last House in England, with annexe, 140mm. long. $1,300 £750

St Catherine's Chapel, Abbotsbury, 87mm. long. $735 £420

John Knox's House at Edinburgh, 102mm. high. $650 £375

Shakespeare's Birthplace, 40mm. long (Late version). $80 £45

Christchurch, Old Court House, 76mm. long. $570 £325

GRUEBY

The Grueby Faience Co was formed in 1897 by William H Grueby in East Boston, MA, initially manufacturing tiles, Della-Robbia style plaques and vases. From 1898 matt glazes of opaque enamel were used in shades of blue, brown, yellow and sometimes red. The most characteristic of these, however is dark green with a veined effect. Vases were hand thrown, some plain, others decorated with geometrical patterns or plant forms in low relief. From 1904 glazed paperweights were made in scarab form. Grueby art pottery usually bears the artist's signature incised and often **GRUEBY POTTERY BOSTON USA** impressed in a circle surrounding lotus blossom motif. Grueby Faience was declared bankrupt in 1908 and though a new company was formed for architectural ware, vase production had ceased entirely by 1913. The tile manufacture was sold in 1919, and finally ceased operation around 1930.

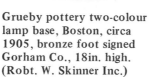

Grueby pottery butterscotch glazed vase, artist's initials W.P. for Wilamina Post, dated 3/12/06, 9in. diam. (Robt. W. Skinner Inc.) $6,500 £3,513

Grueby pottery two-colour lamp base, Boston, circa 1905, bronze foot signed Gorham Co., 18in. high. (Robt. W. Skinner Inc.) $11,750 £8,217

A two-colour Grueby pottery vase, artist's initials A.L. for Annie Lingley, circa 1905, 8¼in. diam. (Robt. W. Skinner Inc.) $3,300 £1,783

A Grueby two-colour pottery vase, circa 1905, 13in. high. (Robt. W. Skinner Inc.) $5,200 £3,611

Late 19th century Grueby Faience Co. bust of 'Laughing Boy', based on a statue by Donatello, 11in. high. (Robt. W. Skinner Inc.) $1,800 £972

Early 20th century Grueby pottery two-colour vase, Mass., 10¼in. high. (Robt. W. Skinner Inc.) $3,000 £1,785

GUINESS BOTTLES

In the last century publicans and hotel keepers bought their Guinness direct from the brewery in large casks and bottled it themselves. Often they bought the bottles in bulk from a large pottery but occasionally they were made locally and bore the name of the hostelry from which the Guinness was to be sold. Today these bottles turn up on rubbish dumps and can make fascinating collections. Early ones date from around the beginning of the 19th century and are usually a creamy white colour. Many were made by the Stephen Green Pottery of Lambeth which pre-dated Doulton. Some were marked "glass lined" which meant they were not porous. It is interesting to find bottles in which the word Guinness is mis-spelt — sometimes it came out as "guineas". An interesting collection can be built up in bottles stamped wih the name of retailers from different parts of Britain and Ireland.

London Stout, 'The Very First Quality', Imperial Half-Pint. $85 £50

Stoneware stout bottle impressed 'London Porter'. $35 £20

Reid's Imperial Stout by J. H. Dewar, Wine Merchant, Glasgow. $50 £30

Guinness' Dublin Stout by J. H. Dewar, Wine Merchant, Glasgow.
          $50 £30

Guiness's XX Stout by James O'Hanrahan, Commercil Hotel, Graigue.
          $85 £50

Bottle impressed 'Roy's Alloa East India Palfitte by Stephen Greens, Lambeth', 'Glass Lined Inside'.
          $260 £150

GUINESS BOTTLES

A very rare bottle impressed 'Guinness'XX from George Gordon, Strabane'. $260 £150

Darcy's XXX Invalid Stout by John Fitzgerald, Newcastle on Tyne. $50 £30

Stout bottle by Henry Burton, Darlington.
$85 £50

Bottle impressed 'Browning Pale Ale Lewes by Stephen Greens, Lambeth,' 'Glass Lined Inside'.　　$260 £150

Stoneware stout bottle, incised 'Guineas, Dublin Porter'.　　$50 £30

Nourishing Stout by O. Bewsher's, Wine & Spirit Merchant, Carlisle.
$50 £30

Guiness's Extra Stout by W. Armstrong, Brunswick Hotel, South Shields.　　$50 £30

Oatmeal Stout by Jas. Rose & Co., Caistor, Lincoln.　　$50 £30

The A.I. Dublin Stout bottled only by W. Davidson, Hudson St., Tyne Dock.　$50 £30

G. W. R. JIGSAWS

Founded in 1835, the highly successful Great Western Railway produced a wealth of publicity material including a range of jigsaw puzzles launched in the 1920's. The first were monotone creations of about 150 pieces, which sold for 2/6. Later puzzles were larger and in colour. Made of wood, they were manufactured by the well-known Chad Valley firm. The most valuable is the Chad Valley card jigsaw given to GWR employees at Swindon, which could be worth £1,000.

'Oxford', two tone sepia puzzle of 150 pieces, 10¾ x 6¾in., 1924. $55 £30

'Stratford upon Avon', Harvard House, Series 2, 400 pieces, 1933. $45 £25

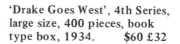

'Drake Goes West', 4th Series, large size, 400 pieces, book type box, 1934. $60 £32

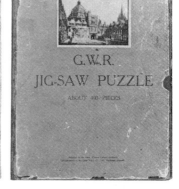

'Brazenose College, Oxford', Series 2, 400 pieces, sleeve box, 1933. $45 £26

'King George V', sleeve type box, 200 pieces, 1933. $75 £42

'Vikings Landing at St Ives', Series 3, 375 pieces, 12½ x 7½in., 1930. $50 £28

'Henley Bridge', 4th Series standard size puzzle of 200 pieces, 9¼ x 6½in. opening tab book box. $45 £25

HAIR CLIPS

Hair clips or combs were first produced in great numbers in the early 19th century, with the revival of Classical taste. They were often set with paste jewels or inlaid with small silver dots (piqué) or more elaborate gold and silver "posé" inlay. Prince Albert's death in 1861 created a fashion for black clips and combs. Later, silver combs, often with flowing Art Nouveau designs, became popular, while after 1900 erinoid combs were all the rage. A simulated tortoiseshell, this was made by mixing sour milk and formaldehyde!

1950's brown plastic hair clip. $1.50 £1

1950's plastic hair clip with eight imitation pearls. $3.50 £2

Edwardian enamel hair clip. $25 £15

Art Deco red and black plastic hair clip. $35 £20

Edwardian enamel butterfly hair clip. $60 £35

1950's red plastic hair clip. $1.50 £1

Early 19th century bone hair clip. $12 £7

A German horn comb, surmounted by panels of green plique-a-jour enamels amid tendrils set with marcasites, 8.5cm. wide. (Phillips) $136 £95

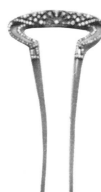

Edwardian folding hair clip inset with diamonettes. $30 £18

Art Deco hair comb set with brilliants. $5 £3

Tortoiseshell hair clip inset with brilliants, circa 1912. $9 £5

An elaborate Edwardian tortoiseshell hair clip. $18 £10

Edwardian diamonte hair clip mounted in silver. $35 £20

Edwardian mother of pearl hair clip. $9 £5

167

HANDBAGS

People have carried some sort of bag or container ever since there has been money to put in it. These have changed radically through the ages, from the medieval 'budget' for carrying documents through 17th century drawstring purses to 19th century reticules, and have increasingly become a fashion accessory as well as a functional necessity. This century has seen a revolution in bag interiors – from the 1920's they have been fitted with mirrors, internal purses, etc. while in the 50's plastics became popular.

1940's simulated leather handbag complete with matching purse and notelette. $20 £12

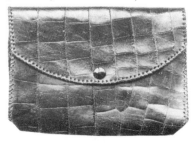

1950's soft leather evening bag with simulated tortoise-shell fittings. $9 £5

1950's handbag in simulated skin, after a design by James Florsheim of London. $18 £10

Satin lined 'Dolly' evening bag, circa 1912. $18 £10

Early 1960's wet look handbag by Ackery. $14 £8

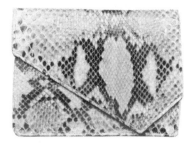

1930's suede lined, snake skin evening bag. $50 £30

Tortoiseshell fitted, embroidered evening bag, circa 1916. $18 £10

1940's brown coloured crocodile bag with leather stitching. $20 £12

1930's cotton, cloth covered, evening bag inset, with brilliants. $18 £10

British made Art Deco style green leather evening bag with chrome fittings. $18 £10

168

HANS COPER

Hans Coper (1920-1981) trained as an engineer in his native Germany, but fled to England in the late '30's. During the war, he met another refugee, Lucie Rie, and went to work in her studio. They started making ceramic buttons, then graduated to domestic ware and in the evenings Coper could experiment with his own designs.

His biggest 'break' came when Basil Spence commissioned two candlesticks from him for Coventry Cathedral.

An early small stoneware bowl by Hans Coper, with undulating rim, circa 1955, 14cm. diam. (Christie's) $7,920 £4,950

A stoneware goblet vase, by Hans Coper, circa 1952, 15.2cm. high. (Christie's) $5,505 £3,850

A bottle vase by Hans Coper, oviform body with short cylindrical neck, circa 1958, impressed HC seal, 65.2cm. high, (Christie's) $23,760 £13,200

A waisted cylindrical stoneware vase by Hans Coper, impressed HC seal, circa 1957, 18.6cm. high. (Christie's) $2,112 £1,320

A stoneware black bulbous bottle, by Hans Coper, circa 1965, 14.7cm. high. (Christie's) $8,651 £6,050

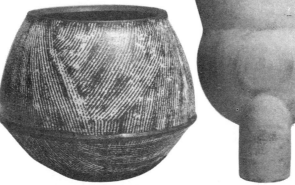

A stoneware spherical vase, by Hans Coper, with horizontal flange, 1951, 19cm. high. (Christie's) $11,566 £7,560

A monumental stoneware 'thistle' vase, by Hans Coper, circa 1965, 57.4cm. high. (Christie's) $44,044 £30,800

169

HARDSTONE

This heading covers natural stone such as agate, malachite, lapis lazuli, rock crystal etc which is either carved or turned on a lathe. Eastern examples from all periods are available, often very finely carved, and these can fetch from a few hundred to several thousand pounds, depending on quality and rarity. European carvers, too, worked in the medium. Hardstone carvings can form a very beautiful and worthwhile collection.

One of a pair of Chinese hardstone flowering trees in lacquer jardinieres, 16½in. high. (Christie's) $702 £495

A 19th century reddish-brown agate bust of a male carved in the antique manner, 3½in. high.(Christie's) $388 £270

A fine pair of gilt metal and malachite candlesticks with vase-shaped nozzles, 6¾in. high. (Christie's) $2,755 £1,650

A smoked crystal figure of a hawk, perched on a rocky outcrop, 9in. high. (Lawrence Fine Art) $303 £209

A rock crystal relief plaque depicting the life of Christ, in the Gothic style, 5¼ x 3½in., mounted in a leather case. (Christie's) $1,430 £817

A Chinese 20th century carved agate Foo dog in tones of smoky brown, grey and white, 5.3/8in. high. (Robt. W. Skinner Inc.) $650 £445

A Hepple & Co. malachite fish pattern jug, 7in. high. (Anderson & Garland) $106 £60

One of a pair of heavily carved malachite groups of predatory birds, late Qing Dynasty, 20.5cm. high. (Christie's) $1,140 £864

An 18th/19th century lapis lazuli mountain of slender slightly concave cross-section, 26cm. wide. (Christie's) $3,706 £2,808

A large malachite vase formed as an irregular upright tree trunk issuing from rockwork, late Qing Dynasty, 26cm. high. (Christie's) $683 £518

A malachite flattened baluster vase and cover, late Qing Dynasty, 12cm. high. (Christie's) $285 £216

One of a pair of rock crystal and gilt metal pricket candlesticks, mid 19th century, 11in. high. (Christie's) $3,436 £2,420

A chalcedony agate group carved as a lady standing holding a scroll, another beside her, late Qing Dynasty, 23cm. high. (Christie's) $498 £378

A green hardstone stele carved with Guanyin astride a caparisonned lion, late Qing Dynasty, 62cm. high. (Christie's) $1,853 £1,404

A carnelian agate group of two lady Immortals, late Qing Dynasty, 16.5cm. high. (Christie's) $455 £345

A rock crystal vase and cover, the high domed cover with a plain globe finial, late Qing Dynasty, 23.5cm. high. (Christie's) $855 £648

HAT PINS

The fashion for large hats, lavishly and top heavily decorated with fruit, flowers and feathers, during the last few decades of the 19th century made it difficult for the wearers to secure their hats to their heads. As a result long, steel hat pins became an essential item in a lady's toilette. They were sold in pairs or in sets of three or four and ranged in size from five to twelve inches long. Some looked so dangerous that they were regarded as offensive weapons and, in America, anyone possessing a hat pin longer than nine inches had to acquire a licence. The hat pin quickly became an item of decoration as well as being very useful. They were made of steel and tipped with gold, silver, glass or semi precious stones. The decorations devised on them were butterflies, teddy bears, thistles, flowers, birds, shells or clusters of jewels and some were hinged to give a close fit to the head. In the early 1920's women began to shingle their hair and wear tiny hats, so that the hat pin suffered a decline in popularity and those made after that date were of inferior quality.

Citrine glass thistle surrounded by silver thistle leaves, hallmark ALLD (Adie & Lovekin) Birmingham 1912. $32 £24

Silver metal decorated sphere. $10 £6

Cut steel abstract design. $33 £19

Silver and enamel dog rose, excellent condition. $45 £26

Large, attractive head in silver metal, mistletoe design, set with clear brilliants. $38 £22

Portrait in pressed foil, hand coloured and lacquered, in a brass rim. $52 £30

Green faceted glass surrounded by 24 clear, claw set brilliants, brass mounted. $32 £18

Gilt Isle of Man emblem in blue enamel surrounded by mother-of-pearl and set in brass. $35 £20

Coiled silver wire and faceted amethyst glass, hallmarked FB, Chester, 1908.
$32 £18

Coloured glass flowers applied to a white glass background, set in brass. $21 £12

Carved bone dog rose. $38 £22

Silver fylfot, or swastika which, before becoming a Nazi emblem, was an Oriental symbol of good luck, swivel mount. $26 £15

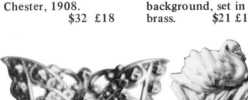

Stamped silver metal butterfly with swivel head. $28 £16

Rare silver swan in bullrushes. $65 £38

Hand painted miniature (less than ½in. diameter) of a dog – probably the hat pin owner's pet. $30 £17

Charles Horner entwined hearts in silver, hallmarked Chester 1908. $38 £22

Wafer of pink glass decorated on both sides with an Egyptian sphinx motif in brass. $65 £38

Imitation pearl in base metal mount. $5 £3

Exquisitely executed enamelled hat pin, with two circles of green enamel, one of white decorated with tiny pink roses and a large central rose, superb condition, 1½in. diam. $80 £45

Silver acorn, unmarked. $18 £10

Small, unmarked gold sphere. $32 £18

Pewter stag-beetle circa 1918. $60 £35

9ct. gold set with an amethyst in each side, 1905. $60 £35

Fine hand-painted porcelain, early 20th century. $60 £35

Plastic Art Deco ram's horn. $35 £20

Large Art Deco hat pin head in black plastic with a painted tulip. $25 £14

Base metal mount set with grey and white mother-of-pearl and a small central brilliant, swivel head. $12 £7

Two-part stamping, silver sword, hallmarked WD, Birmingham 1908. $38 £22

Unusual large and fine silver bear, 1911. $60 £35

Silver metal butterfly with pale blue and green painted wings. Body set with clear brilliants. ·$35 £20

Carved ivory hat pin in the form of a dragon, circa 1890. $60 £35

Silver "Tennis Racquet" hat pin, 1912. $55 £30

HELMETS

Historians now say that the legend about Viking warriors wearing horned helmets is a myth but it is certain that protective helmets for the face and head have been worn by warriors since earliest times and finely wrought helmets and face masks turn up in Greek burial sites and on old Roman camps. The workmanship was of top quality and it is obvious that helmet making was a highly regarded skill. Helmets treasured by collectors range from Cromwellian troopers' helmets to the wartime tin hats worn by air raid wardens. There is a huge range from which to choose and some people can be lucky enough to find one in the trenches of the land fought over during the First World War or on the site of a bygone battle — particularly Border reivers' helmets. Some of the most impressive and elaborate are those made with face guards and manufactured by skilled German helmet makers or by Turkish or Persian manufacturers. The Germans were particularly good at making fearsome masks that struck fear in the hearts of opponents.

A Prussian Infantryman's ersatz (pressed felt) pickelhaube of The 87th Infantry Regt. (Wallis & Wallis) $432 £270

A closed cuirassier's Savoyard type burgonet with raised comb and pointed peak. (Christie's) $1,909 £1,155

An early 17th century pikeman's pot helmet, formed in two pieces with engraved line decoration and brass rivets. (Wallis & Wallis) $455 £260

A Prussian NCO's lance cap of The 1st Guard Uhlan Regt. (Wallis & Wallis) $1,040 £650

HELMETS

An officer's 1855 pattern shako bearing gilt plate of the 82nd Regiment with VR cypher on the gilt ball, upper lining missing. (Christie's) $728 £400

An interesting WW1 steel helmet in the form of a tropical helmet, khaki painted overall. (Wallis & Wallis) $100 £55

A good other ranks helmet of the 1st Dragoon Guards, brass skull and fittings, brass and white metal helmet plate, red horse hair plume. (Phillips) $810 £500

A Prussian M.1915 Ersatz (Pressed Felt) O.R's Pickelhaube of a Pioneer Battalion. (Wallis & Wallis) $245 £140

A good Spanish Officers shako, fawn cloth, leather peak and headband, simulated leather top. (Wallis & Wallis) $380 £210

A Hesse M. 1915 Infantryman's Pickelhaube, grey painted helmet plate and mounts leather lining and chinstrap. (Wallis & Wallis) $260 £150

Queen's Own Cameron Highlanders: officer's feather bonnet by W. Cater, Pall Mall. (Christie's) $584 £352

A well made modern copy of an English close helmet from a Greenwich armour, of good form and weight. (Wallis & Wallis) $500 £280

A Cabasset circa 1600, formed in one piece with 'pear stalk' finial, plain narrow brim. (Wallis & Wallis) $230 £130

HELMETS

A large round black hat with pale drab cotton cover bearing a large elaborate badge in wire embroidery of the Bersaglieri. (Christie's)
$127 £70

An English civil war period pikeman's 'pot', made in two pieces with sunken edges and steel rivetted borders. (Wallis & Wallis)
$800 £460

An Italian black velvet fez by Unione Militare, Roma with an embroidered badge surmounted by Fasces. (Christie's)
$218 £120

An officer's bearskin cap of the Royal Welsh Fusiliers with fine white metal mounted gilt grenade. (Christie's)
$475 £260

A Bavarian M.1915 Uhlan ORs Tschapska, grey painted helmet plate and mounts. (Wallis & Wallis)
$315 £180

5th (Northumberland Fusiliers): officer's bearskin cap with regimental gilt grenade, inside is marked H.W. Archer, Esq., 5th Fusiliers. (Christie's)
$639 £385

A very rare helmet of an experimental pattern for French Dragoon regiments circa 1900, bearing manufacturer's stamp: B. Franck et ses fils, Aubervilliers. (Christie's)
$728 £400

An interesting composite close helmet made up for the Pisan Bridge Festival, the skull from a very rare Milanese armet circa 1440-1450. (Wallis & Wallis)
$2,750 £1,500

A Rifles officer's Astrakhan busby, a tunic with scarlet facings and a composite pouch-belt with a whistle, chin-boss and badge. (Christie's)
$435 £240

HORN

Horn was used by primitive people for making simple utensils and it continues to be used as a cheap, everyday material. Treated horn was and is used for the manufacture of spoons, combs, shoehorns, snuff boxes and drinking vessels. Rough, unpolished and untreated horn, especially the horns of stags, is used for making the legs of chairs or tables, for chandeliers and for the hilts of knives or other cutlery. Stags' heads, complete with their horns, are also used for wall decorations in some homes.

Early horn items from the 16th and 17th centuries are not surprisingly the most highly regarded by collectors and spoons with whistles in their shafts are among the favourite items. Powder horns are also sought after because they can be used as wall decorations and sometimes are finely carved or stamped with coats of arms. Some horn items are bizarre but the more unusual they are, the more desirable they will be.

Victorian horn and brass gong. (British Antique Exporters) $101 £75

Late 19th century Victorian steer horn armchair, upholstered in maroon velvet, America. (Robt. W. Skinner Inc.) $1,300 £909

A late 18th century Scottish horn snuff mull carved with the profile of the Old Pretender, 4¼in. high. (Christie's) $466 £324

A 17th century rhinoceros horn libation cup, the handle pierced and carved as groups of chilong, 17cm. wide. (Christie's) $8,651 £6,050

Part of a set of twelve Victorian silver mounted horn beakers, maker's initials H.W.D., London, 1877, together with a horn claret jug, 11½in. high. (Christie's) $1,346 £880

A Bohemian carved staghorn powder flask decorated with three deer moving through a forest, with silver mounts. (Bermondsey) $1,200 £800

ICONS

An icon is an image or portrait figure, generally one of the sacred personages of the Eastern Church. The subjects are usually Christ, the Virgin, the saints or scenes of religious life and they are always rendered in flat painting in tempera on wood or in very low relief. Sometimes haloes are applied in gold and icons may be studded with precious stones. These religious paintings have been produced by monks of the Orthodox Church since early times and the work was often regarded as an offering towards the discipline of a life of contemplation. Icons are usually set in a flat frame and are often quite small for they were intended to be carried from place to place. The frames themselves can be of great beauty and are often made of precious metal and sometimes also jewelled. An icon set in a triple frame and opening like a screen is called a triptych. They can often be seen set up as objects of worship on church altars. Some icons are of exquisite workmanship and are extremely valuable, especially Russian ones dating from between the 10th and 17th centuries.

A 19th century icon of The Mother of God 'Helper of Those Who Are Lost', 53.5 x 45cm. $1,267 £880

A 19th century Palekh School icon, depicting St. Roman in a wooded landscape, by Ovchinnikov, 17.5 x 11cm. (Phillips) $2,934 £1,800

The Hodigitria Mother of God, inscribed 'through the hand of Nicholas Lamboudi of Sparta', 15th century, 67 x 47.5cm.
$28,512 £19,800

A Russian icon: The Mother of God Vladimirskaya, Moscow 1861, maker's mark cyrillic I.A., 31 x 27cm. (Lawrence Fine Art)
$1,337 £715

Early 17th century icon of St. Onouphrios The Great, signed by E. Lambardos, 55.5 x 36.5cm.
$60,192 £41,800

The Kazan Mother of God, maker's mark of I. A. Alexceev, Moscow, 1908-17, 27.3 x 22.7cm.
$1,267 £880

A 19th century icon of The Kazan Mother of God, 31 x 26.4cm. $760 £528

An icon of Christ Pantocrator, maker's mark of F.V., Moscow 1830, 32 x 27cm. $1,980 £1,375

The Virgin Hodigitria, Cretan, 1480-1520, 40.5 x 32.5cm. $7,268 £5,060

The Mother of God of the Burning Bush, bearing fake assay marks for Moscow, 1908-1917, 71 x 57cm. $5,702 £3,960

Saint Sergei of Radonejh, maker's mark S.G., Moscow 1908-26, 31 x 27cm. $1,029 £715

An icon of the 'Six Days' (Shestodnev), 19th century, 53 x 44cm. $1,663 £1,155

An icon of Christ Pantocrator, maker's mark E.U., Moscow, 1899-1908, 22.5 x 17.8cm. $712 £495

A 19th century Russian icon of St. Nicholas the Miracle Worker, maker's mark for N. Dubrovin over 1830, 12½ x 10¾in. (Robt. W. Skinner Inc.) $300 £243

Saint Nicholas, probably Byzantine, early 15th century, shown bust length, 36.5 x 27.5cm. $4,118 £2,860

INHALERS

In the days before drugs and antibiotics, people suffering from chest troubles and nasal congestion found much relief from inhaling the warm fumes of various potions and infusions. Patients sat with a towel over their head and sniffed up the fumes of medicines like Friar's Balsam from a special inhaler. Some of those inhalers were specially made by the chemist who prepared the medicine and many of them were very attractive, painted over with flower prints or other pretty transfers. They were made of ceramic and came in different shapes and sizes, ranging from little ones for people travelling to larger ones that could hold up to two pints of fluid. Fumes were breathed up from inside the inhaler through a series of tubes. Some of the tubes were set at right angles to the container while others ran straight up from the top. Most inhalers however were bulbous in shape with an outlet at the back and a mouthpiece in a cork. Firms like Maw's and Dr Nelson's went on producing inhalers till the 1930's when they were superceded by drug cures for chest infections.

Hockins 'Acme' inhaler in white with grey leaves and orange flowers decorating the shoulders. $88 £50

D. R. Nelson's inhaler of bulbous design in white, distributed by Boots.
$18 $10

The 'Hygienic' inhaler, attractively veined in blue, distributed by Boots.
$53 £30

The Household inhaler by Ayrton & Saunders, with the intake moulded into the container. $44 £25

The Simplex inhaler in white, over printed with black lettering. $70 £40

The Oxford inhaler, an attractive jar with sepia lettering. $105 £60

INHALERS

The Boval inhaler, an attractively shaped jar decorated in sepia with bluebells and daisies.
$105 £60

A small travelling inhaler with sepia printed floral decoration.
$25 £15

The Universal inhaler by Bourne, Johnson & Latimer of London, in white mottled in lavendar.
$70 £40

The Saunders Family Inhaler of bulbous shape in white with blue lettering.
$70 £40

The Double Valve inhaler, with the mouthpiece situated in the cork, and blue leaf decoration.
$105 £60

Wallich's Improved Inhaler by Burroughs & Wellcome of unusual jug shape, complete with handle.
$70 £40

Savers Popular Inhaler with a white ground marbled in pink.
$88 £50

Maws Vel-fin Hygienic Inhaler with the mouthpiece incorporated in the lid.
$53 £30

A rare version of the Universal inhaler with an all-over light blue colouring veined in black.
$105 £60

INROS

Japanese artistry is shown at its finest in the making of tiny things like netsuke and inros. Inros are slim, rectangular lacquered boxes which were used by men for carrying their family seal, any medicine they needed and their tobacco. These boxes were worn hanging from the belt beside the sword and they were in general use between the 16th and 19th centuries. Most inros were made in three or five sections which slotted neatly together. Cords were threaded through the sides of the box and each cord was secured in place by a bead called the ojime. The knot between the inro and the belt was kept in place by a netsuke, carved in wood or ivory and always in delightful shapes — monkeys, old men, wrestlers, deer, fish — made with wonderful skill and humour.

A 19th century four-case inro with a spherical red glass ojime and a manju netsuke. (Christie's) $6,292 £4,400

Late 18th/early 19th century four-case nashiji inro, unsigned. (Christie's)
$4,114 £2,420

A 19th century small Roiro two-case inro of fluted fan-shaped form, unsigned. (Christie's) $755 £528

A 19th century four-case Roiro inro with fundame compartments, signed Koma Kyuhaku saku. (Christie's)
$4,719 £3,300

A 19th century bamboo Kodansu inro, signed Toyo and Kao, with a bone ojime attached. (Christie's)
$2,516 £1,760

A 19th century four-case inro decorated in gold taka-makie and inlaid with coral, amber, metal and other materials, 7.2cm. long. (Christie's) $2,431 £1,430

183

Late 19th century four-case roironuri inro, 8.5cm. high, with an attached ojime with fish, squid and seaweed in Hiramakie. (Christie's)
$3,520 £2,200

A 19th century three-case Kinji inro, signed Tatsuke Takamasu. (Christie's)
$4,114 £2,420

A 19th century four-case inro, signed Nikkosai, 8.5cm. long. (Christie's) $3,366 £1,980

Late 19th century lozenge-shaped inro, signed on a mother-of-pearl tablet Yasuyuki, 9cm. long. (Christie's) $5,610 £3,300

A 19th century five-case roironuri inro, 10cm. high, with an attached agate ojime. (Christie's) $5,632 £3,520

Early 19th century five-case fundame inro, signed Kaji-kawa saku with red tsuba seal, 9.2cm. high, and an ivory ojime of a monkey. (Christie's) $1,230 £770

A 19th century three-case inro, signed Tojo saku, with an attached coral ojime, 7cm. long. (Christie's)
$13,090 £7,700

Early 19th century three-case circular inro, signed Kanshosai, with a silvered-metal ojime, 8.3cm. diam. (Christie's) $3,179 £1,870

A 19th century five-case inro, signed Jokasai, with an attached soft metal ojime, 9.4cm. long. (Christie's) $7,106 £4,180

IVORY

Ivory comes from the tusks of the elephant, the hippopotamus or the walrus and it has always been highly prized because it is an ideal material for carving. Different animal tusks provide different colours and qualities of ivory and that of the African elephant is most desirable because it is whiter than the ivory from the tusks of Indian elephants which has a yellowish tinge. The desirability of African Ivory has meant that elephants have had to be protected but smugglers are systematically destroying the herds that used to roam the Continent.

In past times however there was no proscription against the taking of ivory and some magnificent pieces can be found in the shape of figures, boxes, knife handles, combs, buttons, fan sticks, umbrella handles, toilet articles. Sailors on long sea voyages used to spend their spare time carving walrus' horns with intricate patterns and their work is called scrimshaw. Ivory inlaid with designs in precious metals is called Shibayama after a Japanese family who excelled at the work. Unsuspecting buyers are often offered to fake pieces of ivory because plastic can be made to look almost authentic but one test is infallible – plastic melts and ivory does not so a hot needle pressed against the base of a piece will prove authenticity immediately.

A Napoleonic prisoner-of-war period bone-ivory games box, raised on four cabriole legs, 8½in. wide. (Christie's) $1,386 £825

Pair of 19th century carved ivory figures of a swain and his lass, 14cm. high. (Phillips)
$1,793 £1,100

Late 19th century stained ivory group of four children playing beside a drum, 21cm. high. (Christie's) $2,618 £1,540

A 19th century German miniature ivory tankard with silvered metal mounts, 10.5cm. high. (Christie's) $3,674 £2,200

Late 18th century ivory Kitsune mask, 3.5cm. high. (Christie's) $345 £187

A 19th century carved ivory bust of a bishop in the Gothic style, on silver metal base with lion supports at each corner, 16cm. high. (Phillips) $896 £550

Late 19th century ivory carving of a farmer holding a birdcage, 33cm. high. (Christie's) $2,640 £1,650

An 18th century ivory workbox of octagonal form, 22.5cm. wide. (Phillips) $684 £420

Late 19th century ivory carving of a hunter, signed Kozan saku, 22cm. high. (Christie's) $792 £495

A pair of curved ivory elephant tusks on ebonised bases, 6ft. high, overall. (Prudential Fine Art) $2,788 £1,700

Late 19th century boxwood, rootwood and ivory group of doves attending their young, signed Mitsuhiro, 49cm. high. (Christie's) $18,700 £11,000

An ivory carving of a sennin, eyes inset in dark horn, stylised seal mark, 20.5cm. high. (Christie's) $935 £550

A 19th century ivory okimono of a farmer with a fox and a hare, dressed as humans, 6cm. high. (Christie's) $748 £440

A 19th century ivory mask of a Buaku, signed Ryuraku, 3.8cm. high, (age cracks). (Christie's) $566 £306

A 19th century German carved ivory lidded tankard with caryatid handle, 13¾in. high. (Capes Dunn) $8,055 £4,500

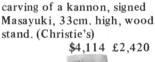

Late 19th century ivory carving of a scholar, signed Akira, 26cm. high. (Christie's) $704 £440

A pair of Chinese 19th century ivory handscreens with ivory handles hung with ornaments and silk tassels, 13½in. long, contained in a fitted brocade case. (Christie's) $1,870 £1,068

Late 19th century ivory carving of a kannon, signed Masayuki, 33cm. high, wood stand. (Christie's) $4,114 £2,420

A 19th century Dieppe ivory tazza, by E. Blard, 17.5cm. high. (Christie's) $2,204 £1,320

A 19th century Japanese ivory group on wood stand, signed, 8¾in. high. (Capes Dunn) $841 £470

A 19th century Japanese ivory tusk vase, 12in. high, with a lobed wooden base and wood stand, 23in. high overall. (Capes Dunn) $501 £280

JADE

Jade comes in three different types — jadeite which is white with a purple tint or more commonly emerald green. Jadeite is the finest jade that can be found. Nephrite, also green but not so vivid, is a type of jade that has been worked since ancient times and chromoelite is so very dark green that it looks almost black. Jade is mined in Burma, India, Turkestan, Siberia, New Zealand, Silesia and Alaska but strangely not in China although jade is a material highly prized by Chinese people. They imported it from very early times and carved it into a large variety of beautiful objects. It is soft and easy to work and Chinese jade carvers have been perhaps the most skilled in the world. The beauty and intricacy of their work has never been surpassed.

A Mogul dark celadon jade ewer of oval octafoil cross-section, 17th/18th century, 15.5cm. high. (Christie's) $7,840 £5,940

An early celadon and russet jade burial cicada, Han Dynasty or earlier, 5cm. wide. (Christie's) $570 £432

A celadon lobed hexafoil dish, Northern Song Dynasty, 17.4cm. diam. (Christie's) $8,553 £6,480

A pale celadon jade model of two mythical birds feeding from a branch of peaches, 6¾in. wide, on wood stand. (Christie's) $3,480 £2,400

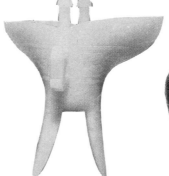

A pale celadon jade tripod libation vessel carved with a single bracket handle, Qianlong seal mark, 13.4cm. high. (Christie's) $6,032 £4,104

A jade figure of a crouching Buddhistic lion, probably Han/Six Dynasties, 6.8cm. wide. (Christie's) $1,140 £864

A pale celadon jade figure of a recumbent horse, Yuan Dynasty, 4.6cm. long. (Christie's) $2,143 £1,458

A jade figure of a recumbent horse, Tang/Song Dynasty, 6.5cm. long. (Christie's) $1,140 £864

A celadon jade brush washer modelled as a pressed hollowed melon, 3in. wide. (Christie's) $986 £680

An 18th century flecked celadon and russet jade box and cover, 8cm. wide, with fitted box. (Christie's) $641 £486

A pale celadon and brown jade vase, 17th/18th century, 12.5cm. high, with wood stand. (Christie's) $7,128 £5,400

An early celadon jade circular disc, bi, Han Dynasty, 10.7cm. diam., in fitted box.(Christie's) $3,564 £2,700

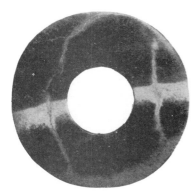

An archaic jade pierced circular disc, bi, Zhou Dynasty, 16cm. diam. (Christie's) $1,111 £756

A Longquan celadon yanyan vase, early 14th century, 26.5cm. high. (Christie's) $3,991 £3,024

A small Longquan celadon jarlet and lotus-moulded cover, 13th/14th century, 7.5cm. high. (Christie's) $1,568 £1,188

JEWELLERY

Of all the artefacts we have inherited from antiquity perhaps jewellery is in greatest supply, thanks to our ancient forebears' obliging custom of burying their dead in company with their valuables! In fact, the durability of precious metals and stones means that plenty of examples exist from all periods.

Jewellery is essentially a fashion accessory and, leaving aside the intrinsic value of the materials, fashion still to a degree dictates what fetches top sums at any time.

To hedge against such vicissitudes, the golden rule when collecting should always be to buy the best you can afford, such as base gold and silver rather than base metal. Very interesting collections can, however, be made out of more unusual items, such as jet, amber, hair brooches or mourning rings. There are possibilities for all tastes and pockets.

Three-stone ring with a total of 3¼ct. claw set in white metal. (Peter Wilson)
$2,961 £2,100

Sapphire and diamond ear-clips, 'Yard', the oval sapphires weighing approx. 5ct. (Robt. W. Skinner Inc.)
$5,000 £3,472

Gold stickpin, set with a large realistically rendered gold 'fly'. (Robt. W. Skinner Inc.)
$250 £173

Art Deco diamond bow pin, pave-set with 105 diamonds weighing approx. 3.00ct. and highlighted by calibre cut onyx. (Robt. W. Skinner Inc.)
$3,600 £2,500

A gold, diamond and plique-a-jour pendant fashioned as a seagull in flight, 7.5cm. wide, probably French. (Phillips)
$576 £400

A Theodor Fahrner enamelled bar brooch, the ends set with coral beads, 5.2cm. long, stamped TF monogram and indistinct 925. (Phillips)
$360 £250

An Arts & Crafts brooch, possibly Birmingham Guild of Handicrafts, 4cm. diam. (Phillips) $108 £75

A George Hunt enamelled and gemset locket pendant of oval shape, inside is a lock of hair, 8.5cm. long. (Phillips)
$1,008 £700

An enamelled and garnet set 'Gothic' brooch, based on a design by A. W. N. Pugin, 4.5cm. across. (Phillips)
$504 £350

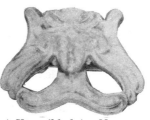

A Tiffany & Co. two-colour gold, sapphire and moonstone oval brooch, 3.3cm. across. (Phillips) $1,008 £700

A sunray brooch, centring an opal with diamond set cluster and rays, gold set, in Goldsmiths & Silver-smiths case. (Woolley & Wallis) $1,490 £1,000

A Kerr gilded Art Nouveau brooch, 6.5cm. across, stamped with maker's mark, Sterling and 1702. (Phillips) $432 £300

A German 'Egyptianesque' plique-a-jour brooch, formed as a scarab, 11cm. wide. (Phillipo) $547 £380

A Liberty & Co. gold sapphire and moonstone pendant, probably designed by A. Gaskin, 5cm. long, 15ct. (Phillips) $547 £380

Antique gold and diamond brooch, French hallmarks, designed as a French poodle. (Robt. W. Skinner Inc.) $1,000 £694

Enamelled diamond ring on an 18ct. gold band, English hallmark. (Robt. W. Skinner Inc.) $800 £555

A silver brooch, stamped Georg Jensen 300 and with London import marks for 1965. (Christie's) $117 £82

14ct. gold and diamond ring, the centre oval gold plaque with tiny raised 'fly' encircled in a frame of diamonds. (Robt. W. Skinner Inc.) $850 £590

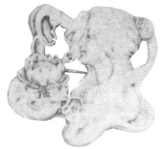

Cultured pearl and diamond necklace, 'Cartier', a double strand of 86, 9mm. pearls, the diamonds weighing approx. 2.20ct. (Robt. W. Skinner Inc.) $7,000 £4,861

Art Deco emerald and diamond ring, diamonds weighing a total of approx. 2ct. (Robt. W. Skinner Inc.) $1,100 £763

An Unger Brothers Art Nouveau brooch, 5.5cm. across, stamped 925 Sterling fine. (Phillips) $360 £250

A plique-a-jour pin with fresh-water pearls, probably French, circa 1910, marked 800, 1½ in. long. (Robt. W. Skinner Inc.) $200 £119

9ct. gold and plique-a-jour Art Nouveau wing brooch in Egyptian style, 4¼ in. wide, maker's mark HL conjoined. (Capes Dunn) $547 £306

A Russian diamond, sapphire, ruby and plique-a-jour enamel moth brooch, St. Petersburg maker's mark JV. (Lawrence Fine Art) $16,661 £8,910

An early George III moss agate and garnet ring on a gold shank with memorial inscription and dated 1765. (Lawrence Fine Art) $514 £275

A 19th century sapphire and diamond frog brooch, set in silver and gold. (Dreweatt Neate) $6,358 £3,400

An emerald and diamond cluster ring, in a basket mount on a plain gold shank. (Lawrence Fine Art) $1,357 £726

An oval diamond set gold mounted shell cameo brooch, 1¾ in. high. (Christie's) $2,860 £1,634

Zuni silver and turquoise bracelet, openwork silver cuff, 3¼ in. diam. (Robt. W. Skinner Inc.) $650 £365

A 19th century oval gold mounted onyx cameo pendant brooch, the frame set with pearls and with black enamel ropework, 2½ in. high. (Christie's) $1,650 £942

An old cut diamond and pearl three stone ring, centre stone approx. 1.65ct. (Dreweatt Neate) $3,459 £1,850

A Murrle Bennett gold wirework oval brooch, with opal matrix and four seed pearls, stamped MB monogram and 15ct. on the pin, circa 1900. (Christie's) $336 £220

A diamond bracelet composed of 17 graduated stones in a half-hoop gold setting. (Morphets) $2,537 £1,450

A diamond solitaire ring, the stone weighing 4.23ct, claw set on an 18ct gold shank. (Lawrence Fine Art)
$7,816 £4,180

An opal and diamond bangle with nine oval cabochon opals divided by pairs of old cut diamonds on a hinged 15ct. gold band. (Lawrence Fine Art)
$1,604 £858

A diamond set bound scroll double dress clip set in white gold, combining to form a brooch with white metal conversion. (Dreweatt Neate)
$2,150 £1,150

A 15ct. gold and enamelled ceremonial coat-of-arms pendant, made by Spencer of London. (Dreweatt Neate)
$299 £160

Victorian gold, diamond and turquoise ring. (Hobbs & Chambers) $464 £290

A 19th century large sapphire cluster ring set in silver and gold with leaf pierced scrolling shoulders. (Dreweatt Neate) $1,271 £680

A 19th century oval gold mounted shell cameo brooch, probably Italian, 2½in. high. (Christie's) $1,650 £942

Zuni silver and turquoise bracelet, large single stone carved in the form of a leaf, 3in. diam. (Robt. W. Skinner Inc.) $375 £210

A gold mounted pink coral carved brooch, the openwork scrolling foliage frame set with four small diamonds, 2¼in. high. (Christie's) $1,760 £1,005

An 18ct. gold bracelet set with eight sapphires alternating with seven diamonds. (Worsfolds)
$504 £300

A double trapezoid shaped amethyst brooch bordered by small rose cut diamonds, calibre jet and seed pearls. (Dreweatt Neate) $897 £480

A diamond and half pearl ring, all claw set on a gold shank. (Lawrence Fine Art) $678 £363

JUST WILLIAM BOOKS

Richmal Crompton's 'William' books have delighted children now for over 60 years, since the first was published in 1922. Surprisingly, first editions of later books can be worth more than the earlier ones. Most were illustrated by Thomas Henry, who, on his death, was succeeded by Henry Ford. Ford illustrated just three before the death of the authoress in 1968. The last book, published posthumously, was 'William the Lawless' and could be worth £300 in mint condition.

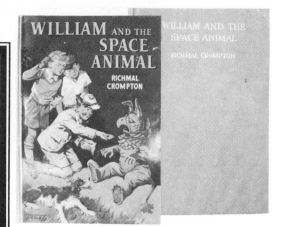

William and the Space Animal', 1st edition, 1956, complete with dust wrapper. $175 £100

'William – In Trouble, Troubles Never Come Singly!' 23rd impression, 1951. $18 £10

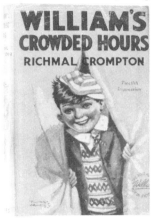

'William's Crowded Hours', 12th impression, first issued November 1941. $20 £12

'William Again', 27th edition, October 1941. $18 £10

'William The Explorer', 1st edition, 1960. $130 £75

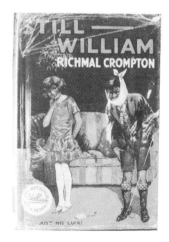

'Still — William, Just His Luck', 26th impression, 1935. $20 £12

'William The Rebel', 16th edition, 1954. $20 £12

KEYS

Keys come in a variety of sizes from tiny little silver ones used for lady's jewel boxes to huge metal monsters that used to turn in prison gates. The earliest keys were only slivers of metal and some Chinese locks can be found in which the mechanism is worked by inserting a strip of brass into a hole in a padlock. Keys were usually made of steel, iron or brass though some were made in gilded iron or pinchbeck. Old ones which are found still united with their original locks are rare. They come in a large variety of designs — some plain and functional but others more decorative with the handles shaped as bows or hearts and decorated with birds, cupids or heraldic motifs. Modern keys are of little interest to collectors but anything from the Victorian period or earlier is a potential collectable. If a key comes with a history or a note of where it was used and when, so much the better.

17th century steel key with geometric motif, 5½in. long. $130 £75

A 15th/16th century Venetian key, 6in. long. $175 £100

Late 17th century French Renaissance key, the bow cut as two stylised dolphins, 6in. long. $385 £220

An all steel patent safe key, 3in. long, 'Climax Detector Birmingham'. $60 £35

Italian 18th century iron casket key, 4¼in. long. $5,750 £3,300

Late 17th/18th century South German steel lock and key, 16.5 x 9.2cm. $2,128 £1,650

Early 18th century French iron masterpiece lantern key, 5¾in. long. $4,600 £2,640

An extremely well made flintlock key pistol in the French style of circa 1640, 11in. long. $875 £500

A small 18th century cut steel key, 4in. long. $18 £10

An 18th century cut steel key with a comb end, 5½in. long. $260 £150

KINGSWARE

The pottery flasks once extensively produced for holding whisky were made of Kingsware. Some of them are still being made today but the heyday was in the early 20th century when firms like John Dewar and Son, Bulloch Lade, Greenlees and Watson and the Hudson's Bay Company bought hundreds and thousands of Kingsware jars for the retailing of their products. The production of this sort of pottery began at Burslem in 1899 and colour slips of subdued greens, yellows and reddish browns were applied to the interior of plaster moulds in which designs were impressed. Finally another brown slip was poured over the colours to give a deep and soft effect to the embossed design. The resultant glaze was usually a dark treacle brown though a paler yellow called Kingsway yellow glaze was also found and it is more unusual.

The Alchemist, A Royal Doulton Kingsware clock, 7½in. high, circa 1913. $560 £320

Huntsman, a Royal Doulton Kingsware loving cup, issued 1932, 8in. high. $210 £120

Royal Doulton Kingsware whisky flask in the form of Tony Weller, 3½in. high. $350 £200

Royal Doulton Kingsware single-handled jug depicting a golfer and his caddie. $385 £220

Pair of Royal Doulton Kingsware candlesticks, a hunting scene in low relief, circa 1912, 11in. high. $385 £220

George V Coronation, a Kingsware jug with silver hallmarked rim, circa 1911, 6¾in. high. $315 £180

KINGSWARE

Bill Sykes, a miniature Royal Doulton Kingsware loving cup with silver hallmarked rim, circa 1907, 2½in. high.$60 £35

One of the Forty, a Royal Doulton Kingsware ashtray, designed by H. Tittensor, circa 1921, 3¾in. high. $455 £260

Pied Piper, a Royal Doulton Kingsware teapot, with silver mounts, circa 1905.$150 £85

Squire, a Kingsware Toby jug, hallmarked silver rim, 6½in. high. $435   £250

A Royal Doulton Kingsware jardiniere decorated with seagulls, circa 1910, 5½in. high, 9in. wide. $165   £95

The Crown, a Kingsware George VI commemorative flask, made for Dewar's Whisky, 1,000 issued 1937, 6in. high. $315 £180

Sydney Harbour, A Royal Doulton triangular Kingsware flask, Dewar's Scotch Whisky, 6½in. high, circa 1914.$490 £280

Ben Jonson, a Kingsware flask made for Dewar's Scotch Whisky, issued 1909, 7in. high. $125   £70

The Leather Bottle, a Royal Doulton Kingsware flask, circa 1918, 6¼in. high, 6in. long. $455 £260

LACQUER

Lacquering dates from around 400 BC, and involved applying up to 40 coats of resin from the Eastern lac tree, each rubbed to achieve a smooth surface. It was applied mainly to previously treated wooden surfaces, but it can also be used on metal, papier mache etc. Lacquerwork became very popular in the 1920's, with such craftsmen as Dunand, Gray and Printz providing beautiful lacquered furniture. Though black is the predominant colour, greens, ochres and yellows can be obtained.

Late 18th/early 19th century lacquer Chinese style fan (uchiwa), 43.7cm. long. (Christie's) $3,436 £2,420

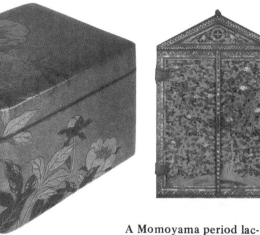

A red lacquer altar vase carved with eight Buddhist emblems, Qianlong seal mark and of the period, 24.5cm. high. (Christie's) $865 £605

A Gyobu silver rimmed tebako decorated in gold takamakie with flowering peonies, circa 1800, 27.5 x 22.5 x 16.5cm. (Christie's) $6,996 £4,400

A Momoyama period lacquer Christian shrine (seigan), 49.3cm. high. (Christie's) $101,088 £70,200

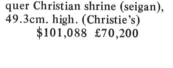

Late 17th century Export lacquer cabinet, 74cm. high, with a fitted 18th century English japanned wood stand, 80cm. high. (Christie's) $6,121 £3,850

A set of three mid Victorian black and gilt japanned papiermache oval trays, the largest 31in. wide. (Christie's) $1,861 £1,320

A 19th century Chinese lacquered panel, 33 x 25in. (Dreweatts) $1,680 £1,000

An early 19th century Japanese black and gold lacquer jardiniere, 20½in. diam. (Christie's)
$2,674 £1,870

A Korean inlaid black lacquer hinged rectangular box and cover, 17th/18th century, 21.8cm. wide. (Christie's)
$2,381 £1,598

An 18th century Chinese 4½in. circular red lacquer box. (Parsons, Welch & Cowell)
$73 £44

A 16th century inlaid black lacquer four-tiered box and cover, 27cm. high. (Christie's) $1,142 £767

A 19th century silver rimmed fundame tebako, fitted wood box, 24.2 x 19.1 x 12cm. (Christie's) $11,368 £7,150

A red and yellow lacquer six-tiered square box and cover, Ming Dynasty, 28.2cm. high. (Christie's) $2,381 £1,598

Early 19th century Chinese Export lacquer picnic box, 15in. wide. (Christie's)
$708 £440

A black and gold lacquer tray decorated with chinoiserie figures in a landscape, 30in. wide. (Christie's)
$2,675 £1,760

One of a pair of 19th century Japanese lacquer picnic baskets, 52cm. high. (Phillips)
$1,453 £950

LALIQUE

The master of Art Nouveau glass and jewellery making was Rene Lalique (1860-1945). He started his career as a jeweller, using enamel and inlaid glass paste in his lovely creations which expressed the essential forms of Art Nouveau. In 1908 he opened a glass factory at Combs near Paris and turned out large quantities of moulded, pressed and engraved glass. He was especially interested in the technique of sand blasting which he used to create a look of opalescence. In the beginning he was a follower of Emile Galle but later he developed his own style and his greatest success stemmed from the elegant perfume bottles he created from the firm of Coty. He also made table glass, vases and frosted glass figures for car bonnets. The designs with which he embossed his pieces were elegant flowing representations of flowers, birds, fish, animals and female figures. Lalique signed every piece from his factory but after his death the initial R. was omitted from the signature.

'Camargue', a Lalique frosted glass vase, moulded with horses in amber stained cartouches, 28.5cm. high. (Christie's) $4,561 £3,190

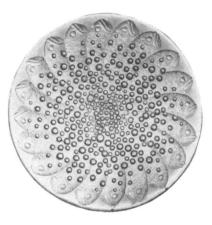

A large Lalique circular, blue opalescent dish, moulded on the underside with carp among bubbles, 35cm. diam. (Christie's) $1,188 £825

A Lalique clear and frosted glass presse-papier, the plaque intaglio moulded with the figure of St. Christopher carrying the infant Christ, 4½in. high. (Christie's)
$712 £440

'Oran', a large Lalique opalescent glass vase moulded in relief with flowerheads and foliage, 26cm. high. (Christie's)
$7,216 £4,400

An Art Deco cocktail bar trolley, the bar handle flanked by two inset clear and satin glass panels by Lalique, 88cm. wide. (Christie's)
$9,914 £6,480

A Lalique table lamp, the clear satin finished glass with amber staining, 27.1cm. high. (Christie's) $3,775 £2,640

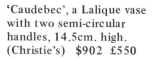

'Caudebec', a Lalique vase with two semi-circular handles, 14.5cm. high. (Christie's) $902 £550

'Cote d'Azur Pullman Express', a Lalique figure, the clear satin finished glass moulded as a naked maiden, 16.8cm. high. (Christie's) $4,404 £3,080

Lalique amber glass shell duck ashtray, 2¾in. high. (Reeds Rains) $186 £120

'Martins Pecheurs', a black Lalique vase, with impressed signature R. Lalique, 23.5cm. high. (Christie's) $8,659 £5,280

A Lalique square-shaped clock, Inseparables, the clear and opalescent glass decorated with budgerigars, 11cm. high. (Christie's) $1,584 £1,100

A Lalique vase, the satin finished glass moulded with marguerites, highlighted with amber staining, 20.5cm. high. (Christie's) $902 £550

'Bacchantes', a Lalique opalescent glass vase moulded in relief with naked female dancing figures, 24.5cm. high. (Christie's) $13,530 £8,250

A Lalique glass inkwell. (Hobbs Parker) $1,890 £1,125

'Rampillon', an opalescent Lalique vase, 12.6cm. high. (Christie's) $613 £374

LEACH

The master of English pottery is Bernard Leach who transformed the style and techniques of his native art potters. He spent much time in Japan in his youth and was greatly influenced by the master potters at work there in the early years of the 20th century. In 1920 he opened his own studio at St Ives in Cornwall and began making pots of simple shapes and with marbled slip decoration in the Japanese tradition. A school of young potters gathered around him and his influence is still obvious today. Leach pots are among the most desirable and sell for astonishing prices. Because they are so fluid and elegant in appearance, they can be copied with varying degrees of success. One clever maker of Leach-forgeries was discovered a few years ago producing his pieces in a prison art studio. Leach always signed his pieces with his initials B L inside a rectangle or painted onto the base. Products of his St Ives pottery were marked with an S and an I crossed and enclosed in a circle or square.

A large stoneware globular vase by Janet Leach, covered in a mottled olive-green ash glaze, circa 1980, 29.4cm. high. (Christie's) $281 £176

A tall stoneware jug by Bernard Leach, with incised strap handle, circa 1970, 27cm. high. (Christie's) $880 £550

A stoneware oviform jar by John Leach, with everted rim decorated in wax-resist, 30.5cm. high. (Christie's) $352 £220

A large stoneware 'fish' vase by Bernard Leach, circa 1970, 37.5cm. high. (Christie's) $9,680 £6,050

A pair of early slip decorated earthenware dishes attributed to Bernard Leach, circa 1935, 19.5cm. diam. (Christie's) $1,056 £660

A Yingqing porcelain slender oviform vase, by Bernard Leach, circa 1969, 36cm. high. (Christie's) $1,598 £1,045

LIBERTY

Arthur Lazenby Liberty was the archetypical Victorian entrepreneur. Starting life as an assistant in a London emporium, he rose to be the manager of a firm called Farmer and Rogers which sold Oriental imports to the rapidly increasing clientele of customers in search of beautiful things for their homes. Recognising the magnitude of the new market, Liberty took a chance and opened his own shop in Regent Street in 1875. Within five years it had proved to be a huge success and it is still thriving on its original site. His success was due to the fact that he had a discriminating taste and knew exactly what his customers wanted to buy. He pioneered the avant garde style and commissioned young artists to produce his merchandise — furniture, fabrics, pottery, silver, pewter and jewellery. Many of the great names of the Art Nouveau, Art Deco and Arts and Crafts movement owed their beginnings to Liberty. They include Alexander Knox who designed pewter and silverware, especially the 1899 Cymric and 1902 Tudric ware, Rex Silver and Jessie Marion King as well as a host of others.

A Moorcroft pottery dark pink glazed box and cover, designed for Liberty & Co., 3¾in. high. (Christie's) $422 £264

An ivory and silver cigar holder on six flattened ball feet, by Tiffany & Co., N.Y., 1881, 6½in. high. (Christie's) $5,280 £3,694

A Liberty & Co. walnut 'Thebes' stool, the square seat strung with brown hide. (Christie's) $1,267 £880

A Liberty pewter and enamel table clock designed by Archibald Knox, circa 1900, 14.2cm. high. (Christie's) $1,879 £1,296

A Liberty pewter and Clutha glass dish on stand, designed by A. Knox, 6½in. high. (Christie's) $589 £418

A Liberty silver coffee pot, designed by A. Knox, Birmingham, hallmarks for 1906, 21.6cm. high. (Christie's) $673 £440

LOUIS WAIN POSTCARDS

Louis Wain (1860-1939) is best known for his illustrations of cats, usually displaying human characteristics. Several hundred of his postcard designs have been identified, and they were used by many publishers. His most famous series is probably the 'Amewsing Write-away' series. In later life Wain became mentally ill, though he continued to work, and his designs became increasingly bizarre. Condition is vital, and cards are generally worth less if the front is written on.

'Off for the Holidays in Style and Comfort', a rare plain black advertising card illustrated by Louis Wain. $60 £35

'Bill Sykes', Tuck oilette card by Louis Wain. $38 £22

'I wish you showers of Good Luck', by the Alphalsa Publishing Co. Ltd. $25 £15

'My word that must have been a German mouse', Tuck's oilette card by Louis Wain. $28 £16

'With best wishes for a Happy Christmas', card with plain back. $25 £15

'Artists in Black and White', calendar postcard No. 5803 by Raphael Tuck. $30 £18

'At Last', 'We Shell', Tuck's oilette card 8819. $30 £18

LOVING CUPS

Loving cups usually had two handles and were meant to be given as gifts to mark important events like marriages or betrothals. There were also decorative jugs which were used for the same purpose. In 1930 however the ingenious Charles J. Noke who worked at the Doulton Pottery realised the potential of the symbolism and attractive appearance of loving cups and jugs and started producing them in limited editions to be given as keepsakes and mementoes.

He used slip cast relief jugs which had been made in Staffordshire for many years but decorated them in bright colours and with new themes.

The first one produced was the Master of Foxhounds Presentation Jug which was painted by William Grace and in which the theme of the decoration was continued around the handle. The Regency Coach Jug followed and every year another was introduced into the market including the Dickens Dream Jug, the Shakespeare Jug and Robin Hood and His Merry Men. No more than 1000 of any jug was ever made and each one was numbered and sold with a certificate of authenticity. Some jugs were made to commemorate special historical events like George Washington's Birthday or coronations. Cecil Noke made a loving cup to mark Queen Elizabeth's crowning in 1953 and in 1977 Richard Johnson produced another range of 250 jugs to mark her Silver Jubilee.

The Wandering Minstrel Loving Cup designed by C. J. Noke & H. Fenton, 5½in. high, issued 1934 in a limited edition of 600. $350 £200

George Washington Bicentenary jug designed by C. J. Noke & H. Fenton, 10¾in. high, issued 1932 in a limited edition of 1000, colour variation on handle. $4,375 £2,500

The Village Blacksmith jug designed by C. J. Noke, 7¾in. high, issued 1936 in a limited edition of 600. $525 £300

The Apothecary Loving Cup designed by C. J. Noke & H. Fenton, 6in. high, issued 1934 in a limited edition of 600.
$480 £275

Treasure Island jug designed by C. J. Noke & H. Fenton, 7½in. high, issued 1934 in a limited edition of 600.$610 £350

William Wordsworth Loving Cup designed by C. J. Noke, 6½in. high, issued 1933 unlimited.
$560 £320

Master of Foxhounds presentation jug designed by C. J. Noke, 13in. high, issued 1930 in a limited edition of 500. $525 £300

Dickens Dream jug designed by C. J. Noke, 10½in. high, issued 1933 in a limited edition of 1000. $610 £350

George Washington Bicentenary jug designed by C. J. Noke & H. Fenton, 10¾in. high, issued 1932 in a limited edition of 1000, variation of handle style.
$2,200 £1,250

Tower of London jug designed by C. J. Noke & H. Fenton, 9½in. high, issued 1933 in a limited edition of 500. $610 £350.

Captain Cook Loving Cup designed by C. J. Noke & H. Fenton, 9½in. high, issued 1933 in a limited edition of 350. $1 400 £800

Sir Francis Drake jug designed by C. J. Noke & H. Fenton, 10½in. high, issued 1933 in a limited edition of 500.$610 £350

MAPS

Maps make big money. There is a large body of collectors interested in maps alone and the older they are the better as Hereford Cathedral's Mappa Mundi has recently proved. The most desirable early maps are those which are illustrated with drawings, sketches and written descriptions and later maps are hiked up in price if they include vignettes, especially coloured ones. Maps by such giants as Ortelius, Janson, Valk and Sanson do not normally come the way of ordinary collectors but people like to find and display maps of their own areas and map makers Speed or Blaeu fetch good prices because theirs are usually among the earliest maps of rural parts of Britain.

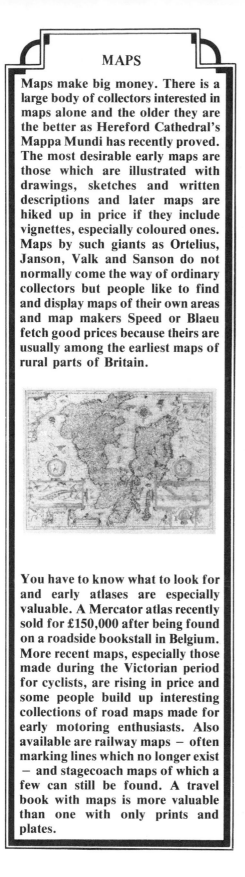

You have to know what to look for and early atlases are especially valuable. A Mercator atlas recently sold for £150,000 after being found on a roadside bookstall in Belgium. More recent maps, especially those made during the Victorian period for cyclists, are rising in price and some people build up interesting collections of road maps made for early motoring enthusiasts. Also available are railway maps — often marking lines which no longer exist — and stagecoach maps of which a few can still be found. A travel book with maps is more valuable than one with only prints and plates.

John Speede 'The Countie Pallatine of Lancaster', hand coloured engraved map with English text on the reverse, circa 1676, 15 x 20in. (Capes, Dunn & Co.) $268 £150

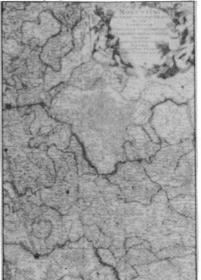

Nicolaus Visscher, 'Atlas Minor sive totius orbis terrarum', 36 hand coloured double page engraved maps, Amsterdam, after 1705. $8,750 £5,000

Crutchley's County Map of Hereford for Cyclists, muslin bound, 1930's. (Border Bygones) $30 £18

Louis Renard: Atlas de la Navigation et du Commerce, 28 charts, Amsterdam 1715. (Phillips) $7,520 £4,700

Bartholomew's Tourist's Map of England & Wales, mounted on cloth. $7 £4

Mattheus Seutter: Atlas of the World, 62 hand-coloured maps, folio, Augsberg, circa 1740. (Phillips) $2,560 £1,600

Burrow's Pointer Guide Map of Gloucester, with cloth indexer. $7 £4

Camden (W.): Britannia, engraved title, 57 maps, and 8 plates of coins, London, folios, 1610. (Phillips) $2,793 £1,900

Ordnance Survey map, sheet 32/48, 1950. $5 £3

J. Gardner — A Pocket Guide to the English Traveller, 100 copper plates, oblong 8vo, 1719. (Woolley & Wallis) $994 £650

Great Western Railway Map of Stations, Hotels and Halts. $50 £30

Irish Railway Commission, Atlas to accompany 2d Report of the Railway Commissioners Ireland 1838. $595 £462

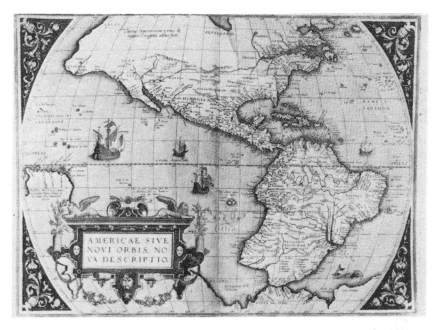

Abraham Ortelius, 'Theatrum Orbis Terrarum', 112 double page maps, Anvers, C. Plantin, 1584. $26,250 £15,000

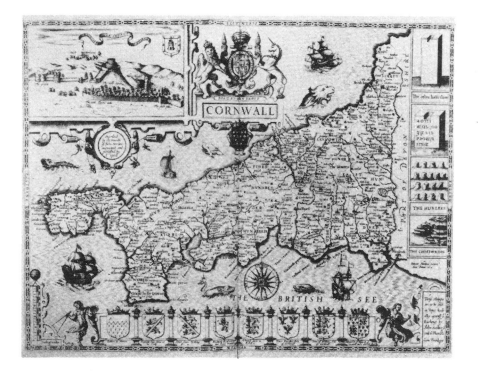

John Speed, 'The Theatre of the Empire of Great Britaine', 2nd Edition, 64 double page maps of 67, 1614. $17,500 £10,000

MARTINWARE

Classic Martinware is not to everyone's taste because some of the figures have a sinister and leering appearance but it is their originality which marks them out for collectors. Three brothers, Robert, Walter and Edwin Martin started their potting career by working for Doulton's at Southall but in time they decided to open their own studio and became the first of the truly original art potters. A fourth brother, Charles, opened a shop at Holborn to sell the things his brothers made and they soon became a vogue. The Martin brothers are best known today for the leering, knowing eyed birds that look like a cross between a crow and a vulture. These were modelled by the eldest brother Robert while Walter prepared the clay and made the attractive vases which were another of their trademarks. The youngest brother Edwin was responsible for the fancy decoration and some of the glazes used on Martinware are exquisite. The brothers also produced candlesticks, jugs, clock cases and goblets. Their style was so distinctive that death and old age forced closure on their factory in 1914.

A Martin Bros stoneware spherical vase, London Southall, 1892, 9in. high. (Christie's) $472 £350

A Martinware stoneware gourd vase, the oviform body incised and cross hatched at the neck with green, 9½in. high. (Christie's) $547 £380

A Martinware stoneware single handled jug, the incised decoration in shades of brown, green and blue on a cream ground, 8¾in. high. (Christie's) $316 £220

A Martin Bros. stoneware model of a bird, 36cm. high, the head only dated 1898. (Phillips) $4,896 £3,400

A Martin Bros. stoneware grotesque, double face jug with strap handle, 1897, 22.8cm. high. (Christie's) $1,879 £1,296

A Martin Bros. stoneware jug painted with fish and sea monsters on mottled blue ground, 10¼in. high, London and Southall 1897. (Reeds Rains) $1,085 £700

A large Martin Bros. stoneware jardiniere of tapering
cylindrical shape, 32cm. high.
(Christie's) $960 £600

A Martin Bros. stoneware
jug, the bulbous body sug-
gesting a sea-creature,
21.8cm. high. (Christie's)
$626 £432

A Martin Brothers stoneware
'Gourd' vase, 17.5cm. high,
signed 'Martin Bros., London
& Southall', dated '2-1910.
(Phillips) $222 £120

A Martin Bros. stoneware
grotesque double-face jug,
London and Southall G
1897, 17.3cm. high.
(Christie's) $594 £410

A Martin Bros. stoneware bird
with detachable head, 9¾in.
high, London and Southall,
1902. (Reeds Rains)
$6,975 £4,500

A Martinware gourd single-
handled lobed pottery jug,
London Southall, circa
1900, 10in. high. (Chris-
tie's) $513 £380

A Martin Brothers stoneware
vase with incised decoration
of flowering lilies and a
dragon-fly, London & Southall 18.7.84, 20.5cm. high.
(Christie's) $551 £378

A Martin Bros stoneware two-
handled spirit flask, 9½in.
high, London and Southall,
1901. (Reeds Rains)
$1,085 £700

A Martin Bros. oviform single-
handled pottery jug, in an
uneven grey glaze with deeper
brown patches, 9¼in. high.
(Christie's) $250 £190

MASONIC ITEMS

Part of the mystique of masonry lies in its secrecy and exotic regalia. Some very valuable collections have been built up and perhaps the finest of all is the Museum of the Grand Lodge in London. Because Freemasonry is universal, pieces can be found in unlikely places all over the world. They include paintings, books, items of regalia, jewels, glassware, furniture and even postal items. Because there are many degrees of Freemasonry, each with its special jewels and regalia, the field is vast. Freemasons have always been fond of displaying hints about their membership and Napoleon owned a snuff box which had a secret compartment. When opened it showed the symbol of the Royal Arch. Though the movement was proscribed during Napoleon's lifetime, it is thought he was a secret member of the Brotherhood.

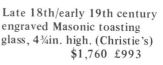

A gold openface Masonic watch, with nickel 19-jewel movement, signed Dudley Watch Co., Lancaster, Pa., 45mm. diam. (Christie's) $1,650 £1,008

An albumen Civil War print, 3¼ x 4¼in., showing four soldiers and chaplain, all wearing Masonic aprons. (Robt. W. Skinner Inc.) $55 £45

Late 18th/early 19th century engraved Masonic toasting glass, 4¾in. high. (Christie's) $1,760 £993

One of a pair of mahogany, Mason's open armchairs, with hinged foot rests, possibly Irish. (Christie's) $3,537 £2,700

A Swiss silver Masonic keyless lever watch, the triangular case with mother-of-pearl dial, 60mm. high. (Phillips) $1,428 £850

A Victorian Arts & Crafts carved walnut Masonic secretaire, 4ft.2in. wide. (Capes, Dunn & Co.) $864 £600

MASONIC ITEMS

A Wedgwood Masonic handled jug, white ground, cobalt-blue neck and gilded rim, circa 1935, 7in. high. (Giles Haywood) $65 £40

An Irish gold and silver gilt oblong Masonic snuff box, the base inscribed Dublin, 1819, maker's initials E.(?), 3½in. long. (Christie's) $1,772 £1,188

A Masonic eagle historical pint flask, golden amber, White Glass Works, 1820-40. (Robt. W. Skinner Inc.) $275 £193

Menu for ladies night at the Masonic Hall, West Bromwich, 1928. $35 £20

Late 19th century brass door knocker with Masonic emblems. $50 £30

A large late 19th century brass trivet with Masonic emblems. $130 £75

Hallmarked silver founders medal, Wallshale Lodge, 1931. $35 £20

MATCH STRIKERS

Before matchboxes came into general use, little containers were designed for the holding of matches with strikers on their sides. They were made of wood, bone, glass, papier mache, Tunbridge ware, enamel, stone or china and the striker was always a roughened surface on one side. Many were made by the German firm Conte and Boehme who also made 'fairings' and the strikers were cheap to buy. Many were inscribed with advertising slogans by brewers or mineral water manufacturers and given away by enterprising firms to their customers. Others were printed with lines from funny or suggestive music hall songs of the time. Match strikers went out of use about the time of the First World War but they can be found in jumble sales and junk shops and are generally quite cheap to buy although an example in good condition with an unusual slogan can fetch around £30.

'Mountain Dew' whisky by Robertson Sanderson & Co., Leith, circa 1882. $50 £30

Striker with old 'Good Luck' symbol by Royal Doulton, circa 1905. $70   £40

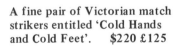

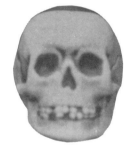

Stoneware match striker and holder made for Worthingtons, 4in. high, circa 1900. $80 £45

A fine pair of Victorian match strikers entitled 'Cold Hands and Cold Feet'. $220 £125

Porcelain skull match striker, circa 1900. $80 £45

Late 19th century German match holder and striker featuring a boy with his dog.
$80 £45

A Doulton Lambeth stoneware ashtray match holder, 'Queen Anne's Mansion'. $50 £30

German cupid match striker and holder, circa 1890. $60 £35

'Gentleman in Khaki' striker made by McIntyre, circa 1890. $70 £40

German fairing match striker, circa 1890. $85 £50

Ship's striker with hallmarked silver decoration London 1889. $105 £60

German match striker 'Penny Please, Sir?', circa 1890. $130 £75

Cheerful late 19th century Oriental looking gentleman combined striker/spillholder/ashtray. $70 £40

China match striker figurine of a young girl, circa 1890. $85 £50

Match holder and striker advertising 'Sir Edward Lee's Old Scotch Whisky', with the slogan 'As supplied to the House of Commons'. $70 £40

German match striker in the form of an elephant, circa 1890. $60 £35

Doulton Lambeth stoneware match holder and striker for John Dewar & Sons. $70 £40

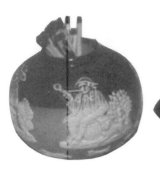

Doulton's of Lambeth match striker with impressed date, 1885. $60 £35

Royal Doulton Dewar's White Label whisky striker/ashtray, circa 1905. $70 £40

Doulton of Lambeth striker with impressed mark, 1918. $70 £40

Taylors' 'Stone Ginger Beer' match striker made by Wiedekind & Co., circa 1890. $45 £25

German fairing match striker 'Match Sir', circa 1890. $130 £75

Cantrell & Cochrane's Ginger Ale, Club Soda striker, circa 1895. $90 £50

Rosbach Table Waters striker made by Wardle of England, circa 1890. $45 £25

'Camwal' Waters combined striker and ashtray, circa 1900. $50 £30

Match striker for use on a card table showing Diamonds, Hearts, Spades and Clubs on each of the four sides, circa 1895. $70 £40

Commemorative striker for the Coronation of Edward VII, 1902. $60 £35

Wedgwood jasper ware striker, circa 1900. $70 £40

Floral design striker by Taylor Tunncliff, circa 1900. $50 £30

Dunville's striker made by Richard Patterson, circa 1890. $45 £25

German fairing match striker featuring a girl with her dog, circa 1890. $90 £50

Greer's O.V.H. whisky match striker made by Fieldings, circa 1895. $50 £30

'A match for any man', made in Devon, circa 1930. $25 £15

A stoneware match striker made for Bass, 'Bottled Bass', 3½in. high, circa 1919. $80 £45

Wright & Greig's Premier Old Scotch striker, circa 1885. $45 £25

MEDALS

Since Roman times medals were cast to honour heroes and mark special events. Examples of the medal makers' art fetch enormous prices, and collectors prize medals for their beauty and also their portability and ease of display. Most families treasure a medal or two, mementoes of grandfather's stint in the trenches in the First World War but generally speaking these are unlikely ever to be worth much because they were issued in their millions. However special awards for gallantry are valuable and Victoria Crosses or medals belonging to a famous personality fetch premium prices. Some collectors confine their search to medals for specific battles or campaigns — the Crimean War or the Dardanelles for example. Medal fakers' work frequently turns up because of escalating prices but can be spotted because the rims are usually narrower. A field of interest for new collectors are modern medals and several skilled artists are specialising in the work.

Three: Army of India, 1 bar Ava, (Ensign, 13th Foot), Sutlej for Ferozeshuhur, no bar (Capt. 62 Regt.), Indian Mutiny, 2 bars Relief of Lucknow, (Lieut. Col. C. W. Sibley, 64th Regt. (Wallis & Wallis) $1,200 £750

Pair: Sutleg for Moodkee with 3 bars, 31st Regt; Punjab 2 bars, Joseph Coles, 10th Foot. (Wallis & Wallis) $416 £260

The Orders and medals of Rear Admiral R. J. Prendergast, comprising Order of the Bath, Knight Commander (mil.) set of neck badge and breast star in silver gilt and enamels and neck badge in HM silver (1918), also group of five. (Wallis & Wallis) $1,440 £900

C.G.M. (Victorian), engraved to Danl. Drady, Pte. R.M.L.I. HMS Cleopatra, not his original medal. (James Norwich Auctions) $138 £85

Group of four to Pte. T. Sheen 1/KRRC, Indian General Service 2 bars, Samana 1891, Hazara 1891, Indian General Service 1 bar, Relief of Chitral 1895, Queen's S. Africa 5 bars, King's S. Africa 2 bars. (James Norwich Auctions) $320 £200

M.G.S. 1793-1814, 3 bars: Busaco, Albuhera, Badajoz, to Thomas Bradley, 7th Foot. (James Norwich Auctions) $391 £240

N.G.S. 1793, 1 bar Spartan 3rd May 1810, Henry Bourne. (Wallis & Wallis) $480 £300

Pair: 29th Ft. Sutlej (Feroz. in exergue), 1 bar Sobra'on Punjab, 2 bars Chilianwala, Goojerat, to Serjt. Timothy Dunne. (James Norwich Auctions) $330 £200

M.G.S. 1793, 1 bar Chateauguay (Sak Sotaontion, Warrior). (Wallis & Wallis) $1,560 £975

I.G.S. 1895, 3 bars: Relief of Chitral, Punjab Frontier, Tirah, to 3372 Pte. J. Henderson, 1st Bn. Gordon Highlanders. (James Norwich Auctions) $179 £110

Three: Canadian General Service, 1 bar Fenian Raid 1866, L.S. & G.C., Victorian issue, (935 Cr. Sergt. N. Lanc. R.), Vol. Force L.S., Edward VII, (1st Vol. Bn. L.N. Lancs. Regt.). (Wallis & Wallis) $288 £180

Afghanistan 1878-80 4 bars, Peiwar Kotal, Charasia, Kabul, Kandahar, to Driver W. Gibson 1/C. R.H.A. (James Norwich Auctions) $206 £125

MEDALS

M.G.S. 1793-1814, 1 bar Egypt, to R. Baird, 42nd Foot. (James Norwich Auctions) $407 £250

Pair: Royal Household Faithful Service medal, Victorian issue, Jubilee 1887, in silver. (Wallis & Wallis) $416 £260

Waterloo, Serjt. John Gray, 1st Batt. 79th Regt. Foot, slightly damaged silver(?) clip, 17mm. split ring suspender. (James Norwich Auctions) $635 £390

Crimea 1854, 2 clasps, Balaklava, Inkermann, to George Adams, 1st Royal Dragoons. (James Norwich Auctions) $391 £240

Pair: 78th Highlanders, India General Service, 1 bar Persia. Indian Mutiny, 2 bars Defence of Lucknow, to F. Brownswood. (James Norwich Auctions) $330 £200

Waterloo 1815, Lieut. W. F. Fortescue, 1st Bn. 27th Regt. Foot. (Wallis & Wallis) $1,296 £810

A Nazi S.S. 12 Year service award, silver swastika with ribbon woven with silver thread, S.S. runes. (Wallis & Wallis) $280 £170

Pair: G.S.M. 1962, 1 bar N. Ireland, South Atlantic medal with rosette, together with an H.M.S. Ambuscade cap tally. (Wallis & Wallis) $272 £170

Baden: Order of the Zahringen lion, 5th class badge, in silver, glass and enamels. (Wallis & Wallis) $156 £95

MEDALS

Waterloo, John Galley, 2nd Britt. 30th Reg. Foot, steel clip, thin 22mm. split ring suspender. (James Norwich Auctions) $293 £180

Indian Mutiny, 1 bar Lucknow, to Geo. Hawkings, 84th Regt. Another, 2 bars Defence of Lucknow, Lucknow, renamed 374 Pte. F. Paterson, 78th Highlanders. (James Norwich Auctions) $179 £110

M.G.S. 1793-1814, 3 bars: Busaco, Salamanca, Pyrenees, to Patrick Farrall, 11th Foot. (James Norwich Auctions) $391 £240

M.G.S. 1793-1814, 4 bars: Roleia, Vimiera, Talavera, Albuhera, to Samuel Bannister, 29th Foot. (James Norwich Auctions) $619 £380

Pair of Colour Sergt. John Burgess 97th Foot (later 2nd Batt. R. West Kents), Distinguished Conduct Medal, Crimea, 1 bar Sebastopol. (James Norwich Auctions) $586 £360

I.G.S. 1895, 1 bar, Defence of Chitral 1895, to 1577 Naik Sham Sing, 14th Bengal Infantry. (James Norwich Auctions) $1,426 £875

M.G.S. 1793-1814, 7 bars: Talavera, Barrose, Vittoria, Pyrenees, Nivelle, Nive, Orthes, to R. Walsh, Serjt. 87th Foot. (James Norwich Auctions) $912 £560

Pair of F. Frost, 9th Lancers: Punjab 2 bars; Indian Mutiny, 3 bars. (James Norwich Auctions) $619 £380

M.G.S. 1793-1814, 4 bars: Albuhera, Ciudad Rodrigo, Salamanca, Toulouse, to E. Morgan, 23rd Foot. (James Norwich Auctions) $423 £260

MEDICAL ITEMS

From the comparative safety of the twentieth century, we can look back with a certain morbid fascination and even glee at some of the seeming instruments of torture used by the medical and dental professions of the past. There is an abiding interest in such items and some of them are very finely made and beautifully cased. Apothecary boxes are particularly fascinating and can be quite readily found. Often cased in mahogany, they usually contained a secret compartment for poisons and opiates.

A Pascal's apparatus, unsigned, 14in. wide, with three different shaped glass vessels mounted in brass collars to fit the limb. (Christie's) $811 £495

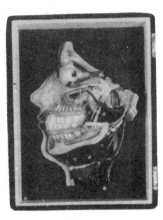

A wax model of the human head showing the nerves, arteries, veins and muscles, in an ebonised and glazed case, 9¾in. high, by Lehrmittelwerke, Berlin. (Christie's) $302 £198

A 19th century bone saw and three dental elevators. (Christie's) $153 £93

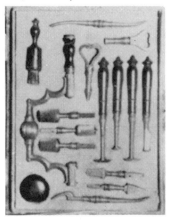

An 18th century set of surgeon's instruments, engraved Ambulance de S M. L'Empereur. (Christie's) $9,882 £8,100

A 19th century single cupping set by J. Laundy, with lacquered brass syringe and shaped glass cup, the case 5in. wide. (Christie's) $422 £264

A hydraulic tourniquet on octagonal mahogany base, circa 1830, 54cm. high. (Christie's) $605 £422

An apothecary's chest, the mahogany case with recessed brass carrying handle, 10¾in. wide. (Lawrence Fine Art) $771 £638

MEDICAL ITEMS

A late 18th century pocket dental scaling kit, with mirror in a shagreen case, 2¼in. wide. (Christie's) $286 £176

A 19th century cupping set by Weiss, London, with two glass cups in plush lined fitted case, 5½in. long. (Christie's) $432 £264

A Rein & Son 'London Dome' silver plated hearing trumpet, English, circa 1865, 6¾in. long. $430 £374

Late 19th century sectional model of the eye, the plaster body decorated in colours and with glass lenses, 6¾in. high. (Christie's) $541 £330

A 19th century mahogany domestic medicine chest by Fischer & Toller, 9½in. wide. (Christie's) $1,232 £770

Pajot's midwifery forceps, signed Charriere a Paris, late 19th century, 34cm. long. (Christie's) $286 £199

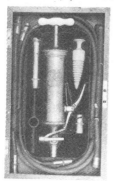

Mid 19th century S. Maw, Son & Thompson enema or stomach pump apparatus, English, 12½ x 7½in. $202 £176

A 19th century amputation saw by Weiss, with anti-clog teeth and ebony handle, 15½in. long. (Christie's) $144 £88

An 18th century decorated baluster two-handled 'leech' jar with cover, approx. 14in. tall. (J. M. Welch & Son) $2,584 £1,700

MEISSEN

From its inception in 1710, the Meissen pottery produced wares that were sought after by the aristocracy of Europe. The pottery was situated in Meissen, Saxony, and its work was distinguished by sheer elegance and romanticism because pieces were trimmed with posies and bouquets of miniature flowers, realistic looking and exquisitely modelled. During the Napoleonic Wars the demand for Meissen dropped off but in 1849 H.G. Kuhn was appointed Director and the company's fortunes took an upturn. He introduced new models and re-issued 18th century models which had not lost their appeal. The most popular pieces were children and mythological flower bedecked goddesses produced between 1860 and 1890. After 1870 figures of soldiers and people in contemporary costume also appeared. The Meissen mark is a device of crossed swords with dates in some cases. Between 1924 and 1934, a dot was placed between the blades of the swords. Since inception, Meissen fakes have been circulating and some are stamped with the crossed swords.

A large Meissen group of Count Bruhl's tailor on a goat, blue crossed swords and incised numeral marks, circa 1880, 43cm. high. (Christie's) $4,041 £2,420

A Meissen small cylindrical tankard by Johann G. Horoldt, circa 1728, 10.5cm. high. (Christie's) $28,336 £17,600

A Meissen kinderbuste, blue crossed swords and incised numeral marks, circa 1880, 25cm. high. (Christie's) $918 £550

A Meissen figure of the Courtesan from the Cries of London series, modelled by J. J. Kandler and P. J. Reinicke, circa 1754, 14cm. high. (Christie's) $2,851 £1,760

Pair of Meissen Hausmalerei teacups and saucers painted by F. F. Meyer von Pressnitz, circa 1740. (Christie's) $4,958 £3,080

A Meissen yellow ground quatrefoil coffee-pot and domed cover, blue crossed swords mark, gilder's mark M. to both pieces, circa 1742, 23cm. high. (Christie's) $11,313 £6,050

A Meissen figure of Dr. Boloardo modelled by J. J. Kandler, circa 1742, 18.5cm. high. (Christie's) $8,553 £5,280

A Meissen KPM baluster teapot and domed cover, painted by P. E. Schindler, circa 1724, 15cm. wide. (Christie's) $12,474 £7,700

A Meissen figure of a tailor from the series of craftsmen modelled by J. J. Kandler, circa 1753, 23.5cm. high. (Christie's) $2,656 £1,650

A Meissen hunting group, blue crossed swords marks and incised X to base, circa 1755, 16cm. high. (Christie's) $1,603 £990

A Meissen deckelpokal, blue crossed swords mark to the base, and gilder's mark c to both pieces, circa 1725, 18cm. high. (Christie's) $13,282 £8,250

A Meissen group of a Mother and Children modelled by J. J. Kandler and P. Reinicke, circa 1740, 23.5cm. high. (Christie's) $2,673 £1,650

A Meissen tea caddy with domed shoulder, circa 1755, 10.5cm. high. (Christie's) $623 £385

A Meissen crinoline group of the gout sufferer modelled by J. J. Kandler, circa 1742, 19.5cm. wide. (Christie's) $9,740 £6,050

A Meissen cylindrical pomade pot and domed cover, painted in the manner of Gottfried Klinger, circa 1745, 15cm. high. (Christie's) $2,851 £1,760

MICRO MOSAICS

The art of the mosaic is an ancient one dating back to Classical times and beyond. Though one tends to think of mosaics being mostly of marble, they can be of metal or even of glass. Wonderful glass mosaics were produced in Imperial Russia and by Austrian glass makers in the last century. As their name suggests, micro mosaics are miniature forms of these panels, designed either as simple picture panels, or perhaps incorporated onto a box lid. As with most miniatures, the effect is very fine and delicate.

A micro-mosaic panel of the Colosseum, signed G. Rinaldi, 59 x 77cm. (Phillips) $34,230 £21,000

Early 19th century circular Roman micro-mosaic decorated in the style of Rafaelli with a finch, the box 3in. diam. (Christie's) $1,730 £1,210

A 19th century Roman micro-mosaic panel decorated in bright colours with a bunch of flowers, approx. 8in. long. (Christie's) $5,505 £3,850

A circular tortoiseshell snuff box with detachable cover, the mosaic circa 1820, 2¾in. diam. (Christie's) $1,487 £880

A Roman micro-mosaic panel decorated with Pliny's Doves of Venus, circa 1840, 2.5/8in. long. (Christie's) $1,337 £935

A circular Roman micro-mosaic of a pannier brimming with flowers, circa 1830, the box 2¾in. diam. (Christie's) $2,674 £1,870

A 19th century Roman rectangular mosaic panel, decorated with a view of the Piazza del Popolo in Rome, 2¾in. long. (Christie's) $1,573 £1,100

MILITARY BADGES

Since many regiments of the British Army no longer exist, the collecting of military badges has taken on a new impetus. Throughout the history of a regiment, badges were changed in many ways — different numerals, materials and even designs appeared and collectors usually try to build up a complete record. Sometimes collections start because a previous member of the family served in a special regiment and kept his badge for sentimental reasons. The most frequent souvenir was the cap badge which has a prong, a slide or two metal loops to be fastened by a split pin. Cap badges were kept because they were usually larger than badges worn on the collar. Old Army Lists provide a mass of information for anyone researching a regiment's history and there are specialist auction houses like Wallis and Wallis of Lewes, Sussex, where badges can be sought out.

An Imperial Turkish Empire Air Force pilot's badge. (Wallis & Wallis) $495 £300

The Royal Guelphic Order, Knight Commander's Civil neck badge in gold, HM 1815, and enamels. (Wallis & Wallis) $1,520 £950

An NCO's helmet plate of The Ayrshire Yeomanry. (Wallis & Wallis) $240 £150

An officer's silver (not HM) Maltese Cross shako plate of The 6th Lancashire Rifle Vols. (Wallis & Wallis) $112 £68

A Victorian officer's silvered and gilt shoulder belt plate of The 3rd Bn., The Black Watch (Royal Highlanders). (Wallis & Wallis) $198 £120

A Victorian other rank's white metal helmet plate of The Volunteer Medical Staff Corps. (Wallis & Wallis) $99 £60

A silver cap badge of The Bedfordshire & Hertfordshire Regt., HM B'ham 1932. (Wallis & Wallis) $113 £69

An Imperial German World War I Zeppelin crew badge (Army). (Wallis & Wallis) $470 £285

A silver cap badge of The Duke of Cornwall's Light Infantry, HM B'ham 1899. (Wallis & Wallis) $74 £45

An officer's full-dress grenade badge of The Royal Dublin Fusiliers. (Wallis & Wallis) $231 £140

A cast brass badge of 602 (City of Glasgow) Bomber Squadron. (Wallis & Wallis) $96 £60

An other rank's white metal glengarry of The 7th Vol. Bn. The Argyll & Sutherland Highlanders. (Wallis & Wallis) $25 £16

An officer's gilt and silvered 1878 pattern helmet plate of The 88th (Connaught Rangers) Regt. (Wallis & Wallis) $222 £135

A pre-1855 officer's gilt and silver plated copper shoulder belt plate of The 1st Devon Militia. (Wallis & Wallis) $396 £240

A cast silvered pouch belt plate of The Canada Rifles. (Wallis & Wallis) $128 £80

An other rank's white metal shako badge of The 74th (Highlanders). (Wallis & Wallis) $112 £70

A sterling silver cap badge of The 17th (Duke of Cambridge's) Lancers. (Wallis & Wallis) $140 £85

An Elizabeth II silver cap badge of The Green Jackets Brigade, HM B'ham 1958. (Wallis & Wallis) $49 £30

An Imperial German U-boat badge (as issued 1910), silvered finish. (Wallis & Wallis) $206 £125

Order of the Bath, Civil Division, Knight Commander's breast star, circa 1900, in silver with gold and enamel centre, in Garrard's case of issue. (Wallis & Wallis) $224 £140

A Victorian officer's gilt silvered and enamel fur cap grenade badge of The Royal Fusiliers. (Wallis & Wallis) $173 £105

Order of the Garter breast star in silver and enamels, 85mm. diam., mid Victorian period. (Wallis & Wallis) $3,200 £2,000

An officer's gilt and silvered shoulder belt plate of The Gordon Highlanders. (Wallis & Wallis) $165 £100

An officer's silvered Rifle Brigade pouch belt badge. (Wallis & Wallis) $107 £65

MINERAL WATER BOTTLES

The rubbish of the past, idly thrown onto tips, now yields some of the most interesting finds for collectors — old mineral water bottles. There were more than 1000 patents recorded for different closures for these bottles and some of them were very ingenious. As well as the patented closures there were many other variations which were unrecorded. The great thrill of bottle hunting is to see how many different closures can be found. Nearly every town had its own mineral water works which sold its wares in specially marked bottles. Some of them were clear glass, others opaque or blue and the company names often sounded splendid — especially the Mona Mineral Water Company of Douglas, Isle of Man. A Mona bottle today is worth around £1000.

Mitchells Patent (1878). A bulbous cavity at the top of the aqua coloured bottle retains a long glass stopper.
$350   £200

Edwards Patent (1874). Internal annular projection to retain a glass marble near the base of the bottle, 9in. high.
$140 £80

Caley's Patent Codd. Standard Codd Patent neck and seal, on a shuttlecock shaped bottle, aqua coloured, 9in. high.
$435 £250

Barrett & Elers Hybrid, Round-ended aqua coloured bottle with a long wooden stick stop per, 9½in. high. $260 £150

Billows Patent. Aqua coloured, cylindrical bottle, with one flat side which has a groove near its base, 7½in. high.
$525   £300

Chapman's Patent Hybrid. Round ended, aqua coloured bottle with a round rubber ball to close bottle, 8½in. high. $175 £100

MINERAL WATER BOTTLES

Stone Codd. Brown stoneware standard Codd shape, 8½in. high, embossed Cooper's, Mineral Waters, Hanley.
$1,750 £1,000

Codd's Patent Dumpy (1872). Round glass stopper, Codd-type seal, dumpy seltzer shaped, aqua coloured bottle, 6in. high.
$260 £150

Edwards Patent (1874). Flat-bottomed Hamilton, aqua coloured bottle with wired metal cap, 9½in. high.
$875 £500

Connor's Patent (1897). Two bulbous cavities in neck to retain a pear-shaped glass stopper, 9in. high. $350 £200

Adams & Barrett Patent (1868). A blob topped aqua coloured bottle with double shoulder, 7½in. high. $130 £75

Sutcliff's Patent. Scalloping in shoulders to retain a Sutcliffe & Fewings glass stopper, 8½in. high. $100 £55

Aylesbury Patent (1875). The stopper consists of two India-rubber discs on a spindle, 9¼in. high. $175 £100

A Rylands Patent Codd. Cavity back and front to retain an elongated glass stopper, Codd-type seal, 9¼in. high. $305 £175

Waugh's Patent (1875). Round rubber ball, round shoulders and blob top, deep aqua coloured, 8¾in. high. $130 £75

MINTON

Thomas Minton was born in 1765 and apprenticed at the Caughley Porcelain Works where he was trained in the art of engraving copper plates for underglaze-blue printed designs. In 1793 he opened his own pottery at Stoke on Trent and his earliest products were earthenwares. A favourite design was Nankeen Temple in the style of the Chinese imports which were flooding into England. Porcelain was added to his output around 1797 and his original china ware pattern book has survived. Minton produced Parian ware, vases in the Sevres style, tableware, tiles, decorated panels and garden ornaments in terracotta and majolica. Many famous artists worked for Minton including T. Allen, who painted vases; T. Kirkby whose speciality was flowers and fruit; H. Mitchell, painter of animals and R. Pilsbury who also painted flowers. Tiles by Walter Crane, Moyr-Smith and E.J. Poynter were much sought after in the Art Nouveau period as were the vases decorated by L.V. Solon.

A Minton Pilgrim vase, painted probably by A. Boullemier after W. S. Coleman, 20cm. high, date code possibly 1873. (Phillips) $434 £260

A Minton majolica-ware teapot and cover in the form of a Chinese actor holding a mask, 14cm. high, impressed Mintons, model no. 1838, date code for 1874. (Phillips) $660 £400

One of a pair of Minton majolica vases, twelve-sided oviform shape, date code for 1859 on one vase, 29cm. high. (Christie's) $918 £550

A Minton majolica barrel-shaped garden seat in the Oriental taste, date code for 1873, 50cm. high. (Christie's) $871 £528

A Minton majolica cheese dish and cover with reclining bull finial, 29cm. high. (Christie's) $1,285 £770

A Minton majolica figure of a partially draped putto holding a lyre-shaped viol seated on a conch-shell, impressed Minton 1539 and with date code for 1870, 46.5cm. high. (Christie's) $3,674 £2,200

MINTON

A Minton pink-ground cabinet cup and saucer, circa 1825. (Christie's) $272 £165

A pair of Minton 'Dresden Scroll' vases and pierced covers in neo-rococo style, 29cm. high. (Phillips) $2,101 £1,100

A Mintons Kensington Gore pottery moon flask, 34.2cm. high. (Phillips) $555 £300

One of a pair of Minton porcelain dessert plates, one with swallow in flight, signed Leroy, the other with a bird perched on fuchsia branch, 9½in. diam. (Dacre, Son & Hartley) $2,062 £1,250

A massive Minton 'majolica' peacock after the model by P. Comolera, circa 1875, 153cm. high. (Christie's) $30,800 £17,600

A Minton porcelain dessert plate, the central pate-sur-pate panel signed L. Solon, circa 1880, 9¼in. wide. (Dacre, Son & Hartley) $495 £300

A Minton white and celadon glazed centrepiece modelled as three putti holding a basket, circa 1868, 26cm. high. (Christie's) $731 £418

A pair of Minton candlestick figures, both in richly decorated costumes and with flowered and striped designs, 22cm. high. (Phillips) $2,769 £1,450

A Minton 'majolica' garden seat modelled as a crouching monkey, circa 1870, 47cm. high. (Christie's) $12,512 £7,150

MIRRORS

The earliest mirrors, examples of which have survived in Egyptian tombs, were hand held discs of polished metal and it was not till 1507 that Venetian glassmakers at Murano acquired a monopoly for making mirrors of plain glass backed by an amalgam of mercury and tin. These mirrors tended to distort and spot because the backing soon flaked off but a century later a technique of backing glass with mercury and tinfoil was adopted in England and a factory was started which exported mirrors all over Europe.

When the Duke of Buckingham opened another glass factory at Vauxhall that could make mirrors of large size, a new vogue began and rich people all wanted large mirrors to decorate their homes. They hung them between windows and over chimney pieces and some of them were embellished with beautifully carved frames while others had fine pictures superimposed on top of them. In the 18th century it became the fashion for ladies to give up peering at themselves in tiny hand mirrors and have larger ones on their dressing tables. Swing dressing mirrors and cheval mirrors were produced in large numbers. Each succeeding fashion in furnishing had its equivalent style of mirror ranging from Chippendale gilded pine to Victorian gilt gesso frames and the beaten bronze of the Arts and Crafts period.

A George II walnut and parcel gilt mirror, 52 x 26½in. (Christie's)
$21,714 £15,400

A Dutch marquetry toilet mirror, the solid cylinder enclosing a fitted interior, 21½in. wide. (Christie's)
$3,190 £2,200

A Regency mahogany cheval mirror, the plain frame on reeded uprights, 70½in. high, 32in. wide. (Christie's) $1,156 £756

A Regency carved giltwood and gesso convex girandole, 1.03m. x 59cm. (Phillips)
$3,168 £2,200

A George III giltwood mirror with later oval plate in a tied, out-scrolled rush frame, 39 x 26½in. (Christie's) $6,940 £4,536

A Regency carved giltwood convex mirror with ribband tied laurel leaf surround, 1.31m. x 78cm. (Phillips)
$15,120 £10,500

MIRRORS

An early George III giltwood mirror with later plate, 33½ x 21¼in. (Christie's)
$8,530 £6,050

A Regency satinwood large toilet mirror with oval swing frame, lacking plate, 25½in. wide. (Christie's) $495 £324

One of a pair of giltwood mirrors in the rococo style with cartouche-shaped plates, 35 x 21in. (Christie's) $1,022 £715

A giltwood mirror with rectangular plate in shaped frame, 45½ x 35½in. (Christie's) $4,998 £3,520

A Chippendale carved giltwood oval marginal wall mirror with contemporary plate and bird crestings, 1.06m. high. (Phillips)
$7,200 £5,000

A George II silver gilt dressing table mirror, by Edward Feline, 1750, 23¾in. high, 62oz. (Christie's)
$25,168 £17,600

A giltwood mirror with later arched shaped bevelled plate with mirrored slip, 54 x 33in. (Christie's)
$2,343 £1,650

A Lalique hand mirror, 'Deux Chevres', 16.20cm. diam., in original fitted case. (Phillips)
$1,152 £800

One of a pair of Regency giltwood pier glasses with rectangular plates in leaf moulded frames, 98 x 52½in. (Christie's) $13,959 £9,900

MODEL ENGINES

Model engines represent a labour of love par excellence. Manufactured by craftsmen, they are usually the product of hundreds or even thousands of hours of painstaking and dedicated work, and this must be remembered when they quite often sell for thousands of pounds. They are usually in perfect condition and working order, for they were built not as children's toys, but for adults who would love and treasure them as much as their makers.

A well presented approx. 1.20 scale model of the Weatherhill Pit Winding Engine of 1833, built by W. K. Walsam, Hayes, 19 x 14½in. (Christie's) $918 £600

A model Stuart triple expansion vertical reversing marine engine built by G. B. Houghton, Rochester, 7 x 8¾in. (Christie's) $994 £650

An unusual model of a steam driven 19th century twin bore Deep Well Engine House and Pump, built by R. J. Sare, Northleach, 16½ x 18½in. (Christie's) $306 £200

An early 19th century small full size single cylinder six pillar beam engine, 31 x 34in. (Christie's) $1,377 £900

An exhibition standard model of the three cylinder compound surface condensing vertical reversing marine engine, fitted to S.S. 'Servia', and modelled by T. Lowe, 1907, 14½ x 12½in. (Christie's) $6,120 £4,000

MODEL ENGINES

An early 19th century model of a single cylinder table engine, possibly by Murdock, 15½ x 10in. (Christie's) $1,377 £900

An exhibition standard model of the three cylinder compound surface condensing vertical reversing marine engine fitted to the Cunard Liner S.S. 'Servia' and modelled by Thos. Lowe, 1907, 14½ x 12½in. (Christie's) $5,075 £3,500

A fine contemporary late 19th century small, full size, single cylinder horizontal mill engine, measurements overall 18 x 25in. (Christie's) $968 £650

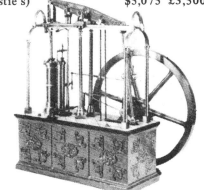

A contemporary early 19th century brass and wrought iron single cylinder six pillar beam engine, built by Chadburn Bros., Sheffield, 19 x 19¼in. (Christie's) $3,060 £2,000

A well presented model single cylinder vertical reversing stationary engine, built from Clarkson castings, 17½ x 9¾in. (Christie's) $1,071 £700

Late 19th century model of the three cylinder compound vertical surface condensing mill engine 'Asia', 16¼ x 13¼in. (Christie's) $2,907 £1,900

An early 20th century model single cylinder surface condensing 'A' frame beam engine, 19½ x 24in. (Christie's) $2,465 £1,700

An early 20th century single cylinder horizontal mill engine, complete with mahogany lagged brass bound cylinder, 2½ x 3in. (Onslow's) $397 £260

A detailed steam driven model of a Bengali Die Mixing plant, built by A. Sare, Northleach, measurements overall 18½ x 24in. (Christie's) $1,043 £700

A Stuart Major Beam engine, cylinder, 2¼ x 4in., on wood stand in glazed case. (Onslow's) $780 £510

A finely engineered and well presented model 'M E', centre pillar beam engine, built by K. R. F. Kenworthy, measurements overall 13 x 17½in. (Christie's) $1,192 £800

A model of an early 20th century twin cylinder horizontal mill engine, complete with mahogany lagged copper bound cylinders, 2½ x 5in. (Onslow's) $734 £480

MODEL SHIPS

During the Napoleonic Wars French prisoners earned money for extra food by various handicrafts and some of the most beautiful were the model ships which they made and sold to local people from stalls set up at the roadsides. The ships were crafted from left over bones, string and straw and embellished with scraps of wood, ivory or metal. Some of them were truly works of art and very accurate models of 100 gun warships like the ones the prisoners had sailed on during hostilities. Examples which have survived are valued at many thousands of pounds. Model ship making has always been a hobby practised by old sailors, some of whom were extremely skilled and managed to imbue their models with their own love of the sea and the ships that sailed on it. Collectors are especially fond of ships under glass and especially of ships in bottles, some of which make it impossible to imagine how they were ever put inside their glass containers.

A 1:100 scale model of a Trouville trawler of circa 1866, built by M. Deveral, Folkestone, 6 x 6½in. (Christie's) $336 £220

Late 19th century possibly builder's model of the fully rigged model of a yawl believed to be the 'Constance' of 1885, built for C. W. Prescott-Westcar by A. Payne & Sons, Southampton and designed by Dixon Kemp, 28 x 35¾in. (Christie's) $6,120 £4,000

A finely carved 'Dieppe' ivory model three masted man-of-war with spars and rigging, full suit of carved ivory sails, mounted on wood with two ship's boats, 7 x 9in. (Christie's)
$994 £650

An exhibition standard 1:75 scale fully planked and rigged model of the French 60 gun man-of-war 'Le Protecteur' of circa 1760, built by P. M. di Gragnano, Naples, 31 x 38in. (Christie's)
$7,650 £5,000

A 20th century American model of the
extreme clippership 'Cutty Sark', on a
walnut base, fitted in a glass case. (Christie's)
$1,320 £964

A contemporary early 19th century French
prisoner of war bone and horn model man of
war reputed to be the French ship of the line
'Redoubtable' of 74 guns, 20½ x 26¾in.
(Christie's) $11,600 £8,000

Late 18th century prisoner-of-war carved
ivory ship, with rigging and thirty-four gun
ports, Europe, 13½in. long. (Robt. W.
Skinner Inc.) $800 £583

A planked and rigged model of a Royal Naval
Cutter built by I. H. Wilkie, Sleaford, 36 x
42in. (Christie's) $507 £350

A fully planked and rigged model of a 72-gun
man-o'-war, built by P. Rumsey, Bosham,
26 x 37in. (Christie's) $2,772 £1,650

Early 19th century prisoner-of-war bone
model of a ship-of-the-line, 7¾in. long.
(Christie's) $3,190 £2,328

A 20th century American model of a fishing schooner, 'Kearsar', fitted in a glass case, 33½in. long. (Christie's) $935 £682

Late 19th century carved and painted model of the 'William Tapscot', in a glass and mahogany case, 38in. long. (Christie's) $1,540 £995

A detailed ¼in.:1ft. model of a twelve gun brig of circa 1840 built to the plans of H. A. Underhill by M. J. Gebhard, Tottenham, 36 x 47in. (Christie's) $4,350 £3,000

A 19th century carved bone model of a frigate, probably French, 16½in. long. (Christie's) $3,080 £2,248

An early 19th century French prisoner-of-war bone model of a ship-of-the-line, 8½in. long. (Christie's) $2,530 £1,846

Early 19th century prisoner-of-war bone model of a First Class ship-of-the-line, 21in. long. (Christie's) $9,900 £7,226

MODELS

The difference between models and toys is that toys were usually mass produced while models were the individual work of a skilled craftsman. They were usually done as an adult hobby and were not intended as a toy. High prices are paid for miniature working models of steam and traction engines which were often powered by methylated spirits and were marvels of miniaturisation, shining with brass. The German toy makers Bing, Carette and Marklin produced a specialised line of working models of steam trains. Other models were made of moated castles, dolls houses, Noah's Arks complete with animals or Victorian shops, some complete with their scaled down wares. Butchers' shops had ribs of beef, tiled counters and rose cheeked butchers in boaters and striped aprons. One very specialised type of model were the miniature sailing ships made out of pieces of bone by French prisoners of war during the conflict with Napoleon. Models are usually very expensive which is only to be expected considering the hours of work that must have gone into them.

A 1½in. scale model of a spirit-fired Shand-Mason horsedrawn fire engine of 1894. (Phillips) $1,176 £800

A well engineered 3in. scale model of a Suffolk Dredging tractor, built by C. E. Thorn, 27 x 30in. (Christie's) $705 £480

An early 20th century wood model of the 1860 horse-drawn goods wagon owned by Carter Paterson & Co, London and Suburban Express Carriers, 17in. long. (Onslow's) $489 £320

A well engineered 2in. scale model of an Aveling and Porter twin crank compound two speed, four shaft Road Roller, 19½ x 35in. (Christie's) $3,987 £2,600

A finely engineered model twin cylinder compound undertype stationary steam engine built to the designs of A. H. Greenly, by P. C. Kidner, London, 14½ x 24½in. (Christie's) $2,295 £1,500

An approx. 4in. scale Foden type twin cylinder overtype two speed steam lorry, built by A. Groves, Watford, 1937 and restored by M. Williams at the British Engineerium, Hove, 1983, 36½ x 88in. (Christie's) $7,650 £5,000

A 2in. scale model of a single cylinder three shaft two speed Davey-Paxman general purpose agricultural traction engine built by A. R. Dyer & Sons, Wantage, 23½ x 38in. (Christie's) $2,610 £1,800

A 1½in. scale model of a Burrell single crank compound two speed three shaft general purpose agricultural traction engine, built by J. B. Harris, Solihull, 15½ x 25in. (Christie's) $3,190 £2,200

An exhibition standard 2in. scale model of the Burrell 5 n.h.p. double crank compound two speed three shaft 'Gold Medal' tractor, engine No. 3846, Registration No. AD7782 'Poussnouk-nouk', built from works drawings by P. Penn-Sayers, Laughton, 19¾ x 27¼in. (Christie's) $10,875 £7,500

An exhibition standard 3in. scale model of the Savage horse-drawn Electric Light Engine No. 357, built by C. J. Goulding, Newport, 27 x 47in. (Christie's) $4,284 £2,800

MODELS

A scale model of a Ferguson TE20 tractor and plough, 15¾in. long overall. (Lawrence Fine Art) $421 £285

An ingenious and well presented model steam driven Stone Sawing Plant, built by R. J. Sare, Northleach, 13½ x 24½in. (Christie's) $489 £320

An exhibition standard 2in. scale model of a Burrell 5 N.H.P. double crank compound three shaft, two speed Showman's Road Locomotive, 20 x 30½in. (Christie's)
$8,415 £5,500

A finely engineered, exhibition standard 1in. scale model of the single cylinder two speed four shaft general purpose agricultural traction engine 'Doreen', built to the designs of 'Minnie', by H. A. Taylor, 1980, 11½ x 18in. (Christie's)
$1,617 £1,100

An exhibition standard 1½in. scale model of the Allchin single cylinder two-speed four-shaft General Purpose Traction Engine (Royal Chester'. (Onslow's) $2,295 £1,500

A 4½in. scale model of a Burrell single cylinder, two-speed, three-shaft general purpose traction engine, built by Lion Engineering Co., 1971, length of engine 68in. (Onslow's) $6,120 £4,000

MOORCROFT POTTERY

A pottery designer called William Moorcroft decided to go into business for himself in 1913 after James Macintyre and Co., the firm which he had worked for over a period of 15 years, decided to discontinue pottery making. He established his pottery at Cobridge, near Stoke on Trent and was able to hire many of his former colleagues to help him turn out distinctive looking domestic pottery and tableware which enjoys great popularity with collectors today. His products were all signed W. Moorcroft in green until 1920 and thereafter the signature appeared in blue together with the impressed mark Moorcroft or Moorcroft Burslem.

A Wm. Moorcroft pottery circular plaque, trailed and enamelled with anemonies in red and yellows on a yellow ground with blue centre. (Biddle & Webb)
$631 £410

A Moorcroft pottery ovi-form vase made for Liberty & Co., in the Toadstool pattern, 10in. high, signed in green. (Christie's)
$1,029 £715

A Moorcroft two-handled box and cover, decorated in the 'Claremont' pattern, 6½in. high. (Christie's)
$691 £480

A ginger jar and cover, by Walter Moorcroft, factory mark and potter to the Queen, circa 1945, 11in. high. (Peter Wilson) $528 £300

A Moorcroft MacIntyre Florian ware four-piece teaset, in shades of blue and white, teapot, 4½in. high. (Christie's) $387 £242

One of a pair of Moorcroft Art pottery vases, painted with red and ochre poppies, 10½in. high. (Biddle & Webb) $662 £460

MOTORBIKES

The first steam-powered bicycle was realised by S. H. Roper in the U.S. in the 1860's, but the true forerunner of the modern motorbike was Daimler's 1885 bicycle, powered by an Otto 4-stroke engine. By 1914 over 100,000 motorbikes were registered in the U.K. alone. The heyday of the European and U.S. bike was in the interwar years when many classic models were developed by companies such as Harley Davidson. After the war, Western production declined.

1921 B.S.A. 986 c.c. Solo motorcycle, Frame No. 1296, Engine No. 1268, twin cylinder. (Christie's) $1,550 £1,100

1931 BSA Single-Cylinder OHV Solo motorcycle, Reg. No. RJ 3145. (Christie's)
$612 £400

1922 Ariel Sports 3½ h.p. Solo motorcycle, Reg. No. CJ 5030, Frame No. 932311690. (Christie's) $2,448 £1,600

1939 Brough-Superior 1150 Vee-Twin Solo motorcycle, Reg. No. FXW 184, Frame No. M 82119, Engine No. LTZ G 652105. (Christie's) $3,672 £2,400

1909 Premier Vee Twin 499 c.c. Solo motorcycle, Reg. No. 1910 DG, Frame No. 5238, Engine No. B40. (Christie's) $3,978 £2,600

1913 Rover 496 c.c. Solo motorcycle, Reg. No. FH 1332, Frame No. 31538. (Christie's)
$3,978 £2,600

1924 AJS 350 c.c. 'Big Port' Solo motorcycle, Reg. No. DD 9758, Frame No. H80593, Engine No. 41910. (Christie's) $1,683 £1,100

246

1932 BSA 350 c.c. 'Twin Port' Solo motorcycle, Reg. No. FO 2861, Frame No. Z43096, Engine No. Z53385. (Christie's) $918 £600

1919 Calthorpe 2¾ h.p. Solo motorcycle, Reg. No. OE 1152, Frame No. A301, Engine No. Y708. (Christie's) $2,295 £1,500

1931 Dunelt Monarch 350 c.c. Solo motorcycle, Reg. No. VE 7835, Frame No. 8717, Engine No. 555. (Christie's) $1,071 £700

1933 Norton Racing International 500 c.c. Solo motorcycle, Reg. No. AFC 310, Frame No. 40-50946, Engine No. 2433. (Christie's) $5,145 £3,500

1924 BSA 4¼ h.p. motorcycle combination, Reg. No. TC 8454, Frame No. 7323, Engine No. 9006. (Christie's) $3,825 £2,500

1972 BSA Gold Star Trials motorcycle, Reg. No. NUY 842K, Frame No. HE 15507, Engine No. HE 15507. (Christie's) $765 £500

1924/5 Indian Scout Vee Twin Solo motorcycle, Reg. No. XW 1903, Frame No. 55Y078, Engine No. 55Y078. (Christie's) $3,366 £2,200

1939 Norton International Solo motorcycle, unregistered, Engine No. D1122926. (Christie's) $3,978 £2,600

MUSICAL BOXES

The earliest musical boxes were made by clockmakers in the 18th century and they were mostly very small — so small in fact that many of them were placed in the handles of walking sticks, in watches or tiny boxes like snuff boxes. They were novelties which, when opened, played only one tune.

The first large sized musical box which was capable of providing a range of music was the work of David le Coultre in the early 19th century and it was a clockwork mechanism powered by a coiled spring which caused a cylinder studded with steel pins to rotate. The pins struck against a steel comb with teeth of different lengths and a range of notes were created. The musical boxes were set to play a small selection of popular tunes of the day. Some of the more exotic musical boxes also had drums, flutes, whistles or castanets built into them to add variety to their music. The mechanism was often encased in boxes of fine woods and inside the lids were pasted sheets of paper detailing the tunes available. In some boxes coloured models of butterflies were set on the strings inside the box and they vibrated their wings when the tunes were played.

An interchangeable cylinder mandolin musical box on table with six eight-air cylinders, 47in. wide overall, the cylinders 11in. (Christie's) $6,160 £4,000

A Celestina twenty-note organette in gilt stencilled walnut case, with fourteen rolls and nineteen new rolls. (Christie's)
$1,336 £825

A clockwork barrel-organ, by Flight & Robson, 66½in. wide, the barrels 35 x 8in. diam., and a discus electric suction unit. (Christie's) $8,470 £5,500

A musical box playing 12 airs, tune sheet and inlaid lid, 26in. wide, the cylinder 14in. (Christie's) $4,633 £2,860

A Britannia 'smoker's cabinet' upright 9in. disc musical box in walnut case, 26½in. high, with fourteen discs. (Christie's) $2,494 £1,540

A musical box, by Baker-Troll, playing eight airs accompanied by drum, castanet and six-engraved bells, 23½in. wide. (Christie's) $3,080 £2,000

A Harmonia 16¼in. disc musical box with single comb movement and walnut veneered case, 23in. wide, with ten discs. (Christie's) $1,782 £1,100

An Amourette organette in the form of a chalet, with seventeen discs, 14in. wide, the discs 9in. (Christie's) $801 £495

A 14in. Stella disc musical box with twin-comb movement in walnut case with disc storage drawer, and 13 discs. (Christie's) $1,736 £1,400

A key-wind forte piano musical box, by Nicole Freres, No. 39788, playing twelve airs, 22in. wide, the cylinder 13 x 3¼in. diam. (Christie's) $2,618 £1,700

A bells and drum in view cylinder music box, by B. A. Bremond, circa 1875, box 21in. long. (Christie's) $2,530 £1,546

A musical box by Ducommun Girod, playing eight operatic and other airs, in bevelled corner case, 23¾in. wide, the cylinder 13in. (Christie's) $1,692 £1,045

MUSICAL INSTRUMENTS

The need to make music appeared very early in primitive man who thumped away on a drum or blew a simple flute but by the time of the Pharoahs there were some very sophisticated musical instruments including the long golden horns which were found in the tomb of Tutankhamun and which can still be blown to produce a clear note. Percussion, stringed and wind instruments like the serpent, the sackbut, the dulcimer and the cornet were treasured by their owners through the ages and a few have survived today though the earliest and rarest of them are usually in museums or special collections like the one maintained by Edinburgh University in St Cecilia's Hall. Early pianos and harpsichords are especially valuable but perhaps the most cherished of all are early stringed instruments like violins and cellos. Stradivarius and Guarneri violins change hands for very large sums of money.

A classical carved mahogany pianoforte, by James L. Hewitt & Co., Boston, 1820-30, 67in. wide. (Christie's)   **$1,650 £1,145**

A spinet shaped pianoforte by John C. Hancock, 1779, in a crossbanded mahogany case with figured walnut interior. (Christie's) **$16,720 £10,450**

An English grand pianoforte, by John Broadwood, in mahogany case with sycamore interior on trestle stand, 88 x 38in. (Christie's) **$5,702 £3,960**

An important Steinway parlour concert grand piano, circa 1904, 91in. long, together with a duet stool, 44in. long. (Christie's) **$66,000 £37,714**

A George III mahogany square piano with ivory keyboard, enamel plaque inscribed 'Longman, Clementi & Comp'y, London, New Patent', 5ft.5in. wide. (Woolley & Wallis) $936 £650

A Classical Revival mahogany inlaid piano-forte, Boston, circa 1825, 72½in. long. (Robt. W. Skinner Inc.) $3,400 £2,125

A Carillon of twenty-five hemispherical metal bells (glockenspiel), by H. Godden, circa 1810, overall height with stand 55in. (Phillips) $835 £500

A double-manual harpsichord, by Jacob Kirckman, 1761, 91½ x 37in. (Christie's) $123,200 £77,000

A portable table harmonium in an oak case, by Metzler & Co., circa 1845, 23¼in. wide. (Phillips) $384 £230

An English single manual harpsichord, by Jacob Kirckman, in a mahogany case, 87 x 37in. (Christie's) $24,564 £15,400

Mid 17th century Venetian guitar, School of Sellas, length of back 46.6cm., in case.
$8,140 £5,500

A brass slide trumpet by J. A. Kohler, London, circa 1850, in case. $1,221 £826

Early 19th century four or six-keyed ebony flute by Cusson, Valenciennes, in mahogany case.
$814 £550

A French pedal harp by Holtzmann, Paris, 5ft.4in. high, circa 1780. $1,302 £880

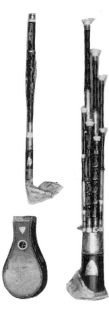

An Irish harp by John Egan, Dublin, 34¾in. high, circa 1825, in case.
$1,628 £1,100

A presentation set of Union pipes by Robt. Reid, North Shields, 1830.
$5,860 £3,960

A treble viola converted from a Pardessus De Viole, length of body, 34.3cm., in case.
$1,139 £770

A cased pair of five-keyed cocuswood flutes by Monzani & Co., London, circa 1815, in mahogany case. $1,709 £1,155

MUSTARD POTS

Mustard was used as a seasoning for food from pre-Tudor times but the possession of special mustard pots was rare before the end of the 18th century. The earliest pots were of silver made in a drum shape with flowing scroll designs engraved on them.

The late 18th century silversmith Hester Bateman made some very fine ones shaped like vases. Victorian mustard pots were always much larger than the 18th century examples and some are so large that they doubled as marmalade pots. They are the ones which sell for the highest prices.

Bardolph, a Royal Doulton Kingsware mustard pot with silver hallmarked rim, circa 1904, 3in. high. $75 £45

A mustard pot by Eliza Simmance, the handle and body with incised blue leaves, 1875, 2¼in. high. $130 £75

A George III mustard pot, by Samuel Wheatley, 1816, 9.2cm. high. (Lawrence Fine Art) $534 £286

A French mustard pot with clear glass liner, Paris, circa 1825, 3.5oz. (Phillips) $367 £210

Pair of Staffordshire enamel mustard pots with gilt metal mounts, on three pad feet, circa 1770, probably Birmingham, each 5½in. high. (Christie's) $5,443 £3,780

A C. R. Ashbee silver mustard pot, set with six turquoise cabochons, London hallmarks for 1900, 8cm. high. (Christie's) $1,313 £864

NAPOLEONIC MEMORABILIA

Few figures in history have captured the public imagination like Napoleon, and this is reflected in the wealth of related material that exists in countless different media. Busts and statuettes are prime examples and many documents signed by or relating to the great man are also extant, while his likeness, or sometimes only his famous tricorne, adorn everything from paperweights to carriage clocks and coach panels. Value therefore depends on the rarity or intrinsic value of the piece rather than simply upon his presence!

A rectangular metal mounted frame with oval miniatures of Napoleon and Josephine, signed Derval, 7½in. long. (Christie's) $1,082 £660

A 19th century ivory rotunda with stepped roof and fluted columns framing a statuette of Napoleon, 7in. high, 5½in. diam. (Christie's)
$7,576 £4,620

Napoleon I: Letter signed 'Napoleon', to the Archduke Charles, Compiegne, 24 March 1810, one page, sm. 4to, mounted beside a color printed engraving of Napoleon's head. (Christie's) $3,427 £2,090

A 19th century brass carriage clock with enamel dial and statuette of Napoleon, 8in. high. (Christie's) $721 £440

After Vauthier: Notables de a France revolutionaire, by E. Bovinet, engravings, 400 x 273mm. (Christie's)
$1,082 £660

A Continental biscuit porcelain equestrian group of Napoleon crossing the Alps after the painting by David, mid 19th century, 8in. wide, 10½in. high. (Christie's)
$2,164 £1,320

Napoleon I: Document signed 'Napol', one page, large folio, printed heading the crest, Moscow, 12 October 1812. (Christie's) $1,353 £825

A 19th century French bronze bust of Napoleon The First, after Ambrogio Colombo, 32cm. high. (Christie's) $998   £605

A 19th century bronze, ormolu and verde antico paperweight mounted with a trophy of Napoleon's hat, sword and scroll, 6in. wide. (Christie's) $1,984   £1,210

A bronze bust of Napoleon, signed 'Noel Ruffier', 11½in. high. (Christie's)
$1,443   £880

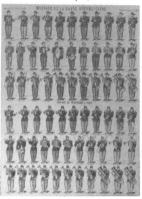

After Robert Lefevre: Joseph Napoleon, Roi de Naples et de Sicile, by L. C. Rouolle, colored mixed method engraving, 436 x 324mm. (Christie's) $396 £242

A 19th century French bronze statue of Napoleon on Horseback, on rouge marble base, 61cm. high. (Christie's) $2,755 £1,650

Pellerin & Co., Publishers: Genie; Musique de la Garde Republicane; Fanfare de Dragons; Hussards; Chasseurs; and Musique de Hussards, colored engravings, 373 x 265mm. (Christie's) $144   £88

After Cornillet: Napoleon au Palais des Tuileries; and Napoleon assis, after F. Flameng, 304 x 210mm. (Christie's)
$505   £308

A 19th century bronze group of Napoleon and a French soldier, 6½in. wide, 7in. high. (Christie's) $631   £385

A 19th century bronze bust of Napoleon signed 'Noel R', on spreading verde antico marble plinth, 6½in. high. (Christie's) $216 £132

A 19th century French bronze bust of Napoleon, inscribed on the reverse J. Berthoz, 24cm. high. (Christie's) $689 £418

An Empire scarlet morocco leather despatch box with brass hasp backplate, clips and angles, 27in. wide. (Christie's) $7,216 £4,400

A Continental biscuit porcelain bust inscribed 'Napoleon I', 16½in. high. (Christie's) $2,886 £1,760

After Jean Baptiste Isabey: Napoleon a Malmaison, by C. L. Lingee and J. Godefroy, mixed method engraving, 637 x 433mm. (Christie's)
$505 £308

A bronze equestrian statue of Napoleon issuing instructions from a galloping horse, on a breccia marble base, 10in. wide, 11½in. high. (Christie's)
$631 £385

An Empire ormolu toilet mirror, with inscription '. . . taken by a Sergeant of the 11th Lt. Dragoons from Napoleon's Carriage dressing case . . .', 12 x 8in. (Christie's)
$1,102 £660

A 19th century bronze bust of Napoleon, signed 'Linedon' on verde antico marble plinth, 18½in. high. (Christie's)
$1,713 £1,045

A 19th century ormolu and porphyry encrier, the pen-tray centered by a bust of the Emperor with initial N below, 14½in. wide. (Christie's)
$2,886 £1,760

A 19th century French bronze figure of Napoleon, the base inscribed Vela. F. 1867, and on the reverse F. Barbedienne, 28cm. high. (Christie's) $1,361 £825

NAPOLEONIC MEMORABILIA

An Empire ormolu mounted mahogany fauteuil de bureau with revolving circular seat covered in ochre leather, 21½in. diam. (Christie's) $99,220   £60,500

Early 19th century circular tortoiseshell box, the cover painted with Napoleon on horseback, 3in. diam. (Christie's) $541 £330

A trooper's helmet of the French Cuirassiers (Second Empire) with chin-chain, mane and tuft, 18in. high. (Christie's) $1,804 £1,100

A 19th century bronze bust of Napoleon as First Consul, 36cm. high. (Christie's) $635 £385

Napoleon I: Document signed 'Nap', granting a pardon to Jean-Marie Merle, who had been sentened to 5 years hard labour in 1805 for desertion, one page, oblong folio, 395 x 505mm.. (Christie's) $1,984 £1,210

An ivory statuette of Frederick the Great on eight-sided base carved with relief portraits of ladies, 7¼in. high. (Christie's) $4,690 £2,860

Napoleon I: Endorsement signed 'N', 26 May, 1813, one page, folio, printed heading of Ministere de la Guerre, Bureau de la Gendarmerie. (Christie's) $631 £385

One of two early 19th century French shallow circular boxes, possibly Grenoble, 3½in. diam. (Christie's) $270 £165

Early 19th century marquetry coach panel inlaid in shaded woods with Napoleon on horseback, 27¾ x 19½in. (Christie's) $1,262 £770

NAUTICAL ITEMS

Anyone with sea fever does not have to hunt very hard to find collectables relating to their chief interest. There are ships' models, paintings of full rigged ships usually breasting the waves in heavy weather, nautical instruments of superb quality and precision ranging from sextants to astrolabes and telescopes, scrimshaw carved by sailors on long voyages, ships' figureheads, wheels and cabin fittings, ships' lamps, nautical furniture like sea chests with heavy brass handles inset in the drawers and fittings like ships' decanters with heavy bases which prevented them being toppled over in rough seas. It is even possible to collect items of naval uniform or, for the stay-at-home sailor, books about ships and the sea or postcards of distant places.

A copper and brass diver's helmet, date 8.29.41, with clamp screws, valves, plate glass windows and guards, 20in. high. (Christie's) $2,032 £1,210

A late 19th century ship's brass plaque, enamelled with H.M.S. Centurion Comm^{n} 1895-98, 14in. diam. (Christie's) $258 £154

A mid 19th century wall salt box, inlaid with different woods, back inlaid with a sailing ship. (Woolley & Wallis) $429 £260

A sextant by Lilley & Son, London, in wooden case. (Greenslade & Co.) $551 £310

A copper and brass masthead lamp with spirit lamp and moulded glass lens, 23½in. high, and another lamp labelled Toplight. (Christie's) $332 £198

A Millville steel die sailing boat mantel ornament, attributed to Michael Kane, 5½in. high. (Christie's) $1,210 £691

NAUTICAL ITEMS

A two-day marine chronometer, the 4in. dial signed Kelvin Bottomley & Baird Ltd., Glasgow, and numbered 9550, in a brass bound mahogany box. (Phillips) $1,567 £950

A Cary brass sextant with gold scale, numbered 3856, 11¾ x 11¼in. (Lawrence Fine Art) $1,929 £1,595

A small cricular brass sextant, signed Thos. Harris & Son, London. (Greenslade & Co.) $267 £150

A 16th/17th century Italian ship's drycard compass, 11cm. diam. (Phillips) $6,200 £4,000

A small one-day marine chronometer by John Roger Arnold, the dial 64mm. diam. (Christie's) $3,732 £2,592

Early 20th century brass sextant by H. G. Blair & Co., 6½in. radius, with two telescopes.$350 £242

Mid 19th century English ship's wheel with ten turned mahogany spokes, 68cm. diam.$1,116 £770

Early 20th century Kelvin & White Ltd. ship's binnacle, 53in. high, together with a Brown Brother's ship's wheel, circa 1920. $1,515 £1,045

An early marine chronometer by John Arnold & Son, with 4½in. circular silvered dial, in mahogany box. (Phillips) $11,600 £8,000

259

NAUTICAL ITEMS

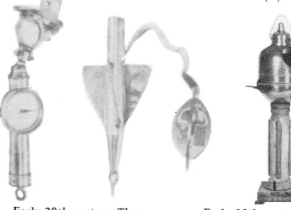

A 19th century anodised brass Troughton & Simms double frame sextant, the index arm with 8in. radius. (Phillips) $806 £520

An early 19th century cast iron ship's bulwark swivel cannon, 22in., bore 1in., with turned reinforces, swollen muzzle and curved iron tiller for aiming. (Wallis & Wallis) $518 £360

A small brass sextant of T-frame style signed Berge, London, in fitted shaped mahogany case, circa 1800. (Reeds Rains) $1,944 £1,350

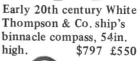

A Kelvin & Hughes Ltd. ship's binnacle compass, English, circa 1940, 53in. high. $860 £748

Early 20th century Thos. Walker 'Harpoon' depth finder, English, 6½in. long. $239 £165

Early 20th century White Thompson & Co. ship's binnacle compass, 54in. high. $797 £550

A two-day marine chronometer, the silvered dial signed James Muirhead, Glasgow, No. 2169, 100mm. diam. of dial. (Christie's) $7,668 £5,400

An Italian brass ship's pedestal telegraph with enamelled dial, lever and pointer, two lamps and chain drive, 42in. high. (Christie's) $1,108 £660

A mariner's brass astrolable, the scale divided from $0°$ to $90°$, with rising loop handle, 23.5cm. diam. (Christie's) $1,430 £986

NETSUKE

The traditional Japanese kimono had no pockets so any possessions had to be carried around in little purses or boxes swinging from the belt, which was a sash called the obi. The cords which attached the purses to the obi were held in place by a netsuke (pronounced netsky). The simplest netsuke were wooden toggles but adroit Japanese craftsmen soon seized the opportunity of turning the toggle into an object of beauty by carving it into the shape of birds, animals, flowers or people. It became a matter of pride to own a fine netsuke and by the end of the 18th century the elaboration of the carving reached a peak with many famous artists specialising in netsuke alone.

Netsuke were made out of wood, ivory, bone, rhino, buffalo or stag horn, jade, jet, turtle shell, amber or more rarely metal. The subjects were innumerable ranging from characters in Japanese folk tales and representations of traditional craftsmen to eroticism which was a popular subject.

A large number of the over 3000 craftsmen known to have made netsuke lived around Osaka, Nagoya, Kyoto and Edo but the popularity of their wares declined after 1868 when Japan was opened up to the West and foreign style clothes with pockets began being worn. The popularity of netsuke with tourists however meant a rebirth in the craft and vast numbers of them — though of inferior quality to earlier netsuke — have been exported to America and Europe or sold to visitors in Japan itself.

Early 19th century lacquered wood netsuke of Tososei, unsigned, 6.3cm. high. (Christie's)
$1,580 £935

An ivory netsuke of a seated kirin, signed Yoshimasa, circa 1800, 10.5cm. high. (Christie's)
$44,616 £26,400

An 18th century ivory netsuke of a dog and awabi shell, signed Tomotada, 3.5cm. high. (Christie's)
$12,083 £7,150

An ivory netsuke of a Daruma doll, signed Mitsuhiro and kao (1810-75), 4cm. high. (Christie's)
$4,089 £2,420

A 19th century ivory netsuke of Songoku the magical monkey, signed Mitsuhiro, 5.2cm. high. (Christie's)
$13,013 £7,700

An 18th century ivory netsuke of an Amagatsu doll, signed Masanao (of Kyoto), 5.5cm. high. (Christie's)
$48,334 £28,600

261

A 20th century ivory netsuke, Boyasha Sonjiro, signed Nasatoshi, 5cm. high. (Christie's) $6,692 £3,960

An ivory netsuke of a grazing deer, unsigned, circa 1800, 6.2cm. high. (Christie's) $4,833 £2,860

An 18th century ivory netsuke of Shoki and Oni, unsigned, 7.7cm. high. (Christie's) $2,974 £1,760

A 19th century cloudy amber netsuke of Fukurokuju, 6.3cm. high. (Christie's) $1,301 £770

Early 18th century wood netsuke of a bitch and puppies, signed Matsuda Sukenaga, 6.8cm. long. (Christie's) $1,673 £990

A boxwood netsuke of Daruma, signed Sansho (1871-1936), 4.3cm. high. (Christie's) $7,807 £4,620

A 19th century boxwood netsuke of a large snake holding a rat in its jaws, signed Masanori, 5cm. wide. (Christie's) $2,992 £1,870

Late 18th century wood netsuke of Roshi seated on a mule (seal netsuke), 7cm. high. (Christie's) $1,766 £1,045

An ivory seal netsuke carved as a well-known foreigner who came to Nagasaki, signed Mitsumasa, circa 1880, 4.8cm. high. (Christie's) $792 £495

A 19th century Hirado ware
netsuke of Gama Sennin,
impressed signature Masakazu,
8.1cm. high. (Christie's)
$1,022 £605

An 18th century ivory netsuke of a grazing horse,
unsigned, 7cm. high.
(Christie's) $3,346 £1,980

A 20th century ivory
netsuke of Ryujin, signed
Masatoshi, 9.2cm. high.
(Christie's) $6,506 £3,850

A 19th century metal
netsuke of a Kendo mask,
signed Nagayasu saku,
3.8cm. high. (Christie's)
$3,718 £2,200

Early 19th century wood
netsuke of an ostler trying
to shoe a horse, 4.8cm.
long. (Christie's)
$2,416 £1,430

A 20th century stag-antler
netsuke of an owl, signed
Masatoshi, 4.5cm. high.
(Christie's) $5,948 £3,520

A wood netsuke of a dog
with one foot on a clam shell,
Kyoto School, circa 1780,
3.4cm. high. (Christie's)
$1,936 £1,210

Late 18th century ivory
netsuke of Moso and bamboo
shoot, signed Awataguchi,
8.4cm. high. (Christie's)
$5,205 £3,080

A 19th century wood netsuke
of three human skulls, signed
Yoshiharu, 5.3cm. wide.
(Christie's) $2,602 £1,540

OINTMENT POTS

In the days when medicine was less advanced than it is today, sick people were prepared to try almost anything to become well and newspapers were full of advertisements promising miraculous cures if such and such a medicine or ointment was used. Quack medicine dealers made fortunes with their potions and the bottles and jars which can be found in rubbish dumps today make fascinating collections. Often they carried labels listing the cures they would effect and the claims were astonishing. The ingredients contained in the ointments were not listed because they were often ineffectual or, at worst, harmful. When legislation was passed making it necessary for ingredients to be listed — and even later when advertising claims had to be upheld — the day of the spurious patent medicine was over. Some early ointments were sold in attractive jars ranging from Delft ones of the 16th century to glazed pottery ones of the Victorians. They are cheap to buy and easy to display as well as being interesting and colourful.

'Professor" Holloway's Ointment was sold world-wide because of brilliant promotion. (Over £26,000 per annum was spent on advertising in 1850). Holloway became very rich and a great philanthropist with an estate valued at 15 million pounds on his death in 1883.　　Non pictorial pots　　$12 £7　　　　Pictorial pots　　　　$5 £3

The propriety ointment with the longest history — Singleton's Eye Ointment, on sale from late 1700's until 1949, was based on a recipe 'invented' by Dr. Thomas Johnson in 1596. The pots contained a thin layer of ointment, covered by parchment and later foil, which was designed to be held against the eye. Early pots were bulky with a large pedestal foot and unglazed examples are extremely rare. From 1780-1825 they were signed Fulgham, from 1826-1858 they were signed Green, then reverted to Singleton.
　　　　Early examples　　　　$45 £25　　　19th & 20th examples $2 £1

Brown's Herbal ointment, later Nature's, inscribed 'In all pulmonary complaints, soreness of the chest and lungs, sore throat, neuralgia, rheumatism, croup in children, severe pains in the stomach, spinal diseases, epilepsy or fits, affections of the heart and liver, for corrupt sores of long standing such as ulcers and tumours of a scrofulous character'. Hence 'cure-alls'.
　　　Small 1¾in. high.　　$9　£5　　　　Large 2¾in. high.　　$25 £15

OINTMENT POTS

Pinkish tin glaze ointment pot, possibly 17th century, 1.1/8in. tall. $80 £45

An early bluish glaze ointment pot with dark blue decoration, circa 1730. $125 £70

Mrs. Croft's Ointment, West Hanley, near Chesterfield. $25 £15

Sturton's Poor Man's Cerate, Peterborough. $55 £30

Bluish grey glaze ointment pot, circa 1730, 1.5/8in. high. $45 £25

The Egyptian Salve, Wolverhampton, based on a recipe first recorded in the Ebers Papyrus in 1500 B.C., 1½in. high. $14 £8

Tibbald's Blood Tonic pot, Taunton, complete with its advert, 1¼in. high. $45 £25

'Poor Man's Friend', sold by Beach & Barnicott, Bridport, circa 1840, 1¾in. high. $25 £15

Boots 'Confection of Senna' pot with attractive fern decoration, 3¼in. high. $18 £10

Clarke's Miraculous Salve, Lincoln, 'For the Cure of ...', 1½in. high. $7 £4

Waller & Son, bluish tin glaze pot, Guildford, Surrey, late 18th century. $260 £150

Machin's Infallible Pearl Ointment, Dudley. $35 £20

265

Cook's Carbolic Jelly, Nottingham, 1.1/8in. high. $70 £40

Small bluish glaze pot with dark blue decoration, circa 1700. $155 £90

Handall's Celebrated Ointment, Plymouth. $45 £25

Sands' Ointment, 1½in. high. $60 £35

An early bluish glaze pot with dark blue decoration, circa 1780. $95 £55

Grandfather's Ointment. $55 £30

Clarke's Miraculous Salve 'Best Application For . . . , 2.5/8in. high. $14 £8

'Poor Man's Friend', by Dr. Giles Roberts, on sale from late 1700's, to early 1900's, 1.5/16in. high, by courtesy of Bridport Museum. $70 £40

Moonseed Ointment, The Great Household Remedy, Swindon, 2in. high.$45 £25

No Name Ointment, Birmingham. $35 £20

'Delescot', bluish tin glaze pot, Duke St., London, 1749. $260 £150

Isola 'The Bishop's Balm', 1¼in. high. $140 £80

PAPERWEIGHTS

Glass paperweights as we know them today were made in France and Venice during the middle years of the 19th century and were bought by the rich as elegant additions to the writing boxes of the period and to adorn the tops of writing desks. Three French firms were reckoned to produce the best paperweights in the world and they were Baccarat, Clichy and St Louis.

Several other companies, like Bacchus and Sons and the Boston and Sandwich Glass Co in England and America followed the fashion and started making paperweights but their fame was never as great as that of their French rivals.

The basic idea of a paperweight was a heavy glass dome in which was enclosed a design made from multi coloured glass rods. These were worked to create flowers, fruit, dragonflies, frogs, birds, nymphs or kaleidoscopic patterns and some very famous artists as well as the masters like Baccarat tried their hands at paperweight making. They include Daum, Lalique and Almeric Walter. Most good paperweights were signed by the artist but this was often done with such cunning, incorporating initials in the design for example, that the signature is often hard to spot.

Top quality paperweights from Baccarat or others of that class are very expensive but collections can be made of lesser priced examples including the cheap and cheerful snowstorm paperweights or tourist souvenirs produced during Victorian times showing views of esplanades in various seaside towns.

A Baccarat faceted blue-flash patterned millefiori weight, 8cm. diam. (Christie's)
$3,080 £1,760

A Baccarat faceted green-ground sulphide huntsman weight, 8.5cm. diam. (Christie's)
$1,760 £1,005

A St Louis orange dahlia weight on a star-cut base, 6.8cm. diam. (Christie's)
$19,800 £11,314

A Clichy 'barber's pole' chequer paperweight, the spaced canes with a central pink rose, 6.8cm. diam. (Phillips) $1,623 £850

A New England blown pear weight, 3¼in. diam. (Christie's) $1,320 £754

A Baccarat garlanded sulphide weight, the crystallo-ceramie portrait of Sir Walter Raleigh in profile, 2¾in. diam. (Christie's) $990 £565

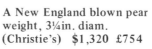

A Mount Washington magnum pink dahlia weight, 4¼in. diam. (Christie's) $28,600 £16,342

A St. Lous faceted upright bouquet weight on a star-cut base, 3.1/8in. diam. (Christie's) $2,530 £1,445

A Baccarat pink clematis-bud weight on a star-cut base, 3¼in. diam. (Christie's) $1,980 £1,131

A Baccarat snake weight, 3in. diam. (Christie's) $9,350 £5,342

A Millville rose pedestal weight, the flower with numerous dark red petals, 3½in. high. (Christie's) $880 £502

A St. Louis concentric mille-fiori mushroom weight, on a star-cut base, 3.7/8in. diam. (Christie's) $1,650 £942

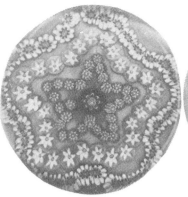

A Baccarat millefiori paper-weight, one cane dated B. 1847, 7.5cm. diam. (Phillips) $1,135 £680

A Clichy pink-ground patterned concentric millefiori weight, 3.1/8in. diam. (Christie's) $2,420 £1,382

A Mount Washington magnum pink rose weight, 4in. diam. (Christie's) $4,400 £2,514

A French (unknown factory) strawberry weight, 3.1/8in. diam. (Christie's) $3,850 £2,200

An Almaric Walter pate-de-verre paperweight designed by H. Berge, 8cm. high. (Christie's) $15,334 £9,350

A St. Louis double clematis paperweight, the two rows of pink striated petals with yellow match-head stamen, on a green leafy stalk, 6.4cm. diam. (Phillips) $764 £400

A Baccarat patterned mille-fiori white carpet-ground weight, 3in. diam. (Christie's) $6,050 £3,457

A St. Louis blue dahlia weight on a star-cut base, 2¾in. diam. (Christie's) $1,650 £942

A Clichy triple-colour swirl paperweight, 7.4cm. diam. (Phillips) $1,536 £920

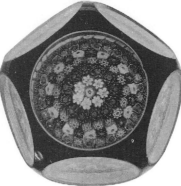

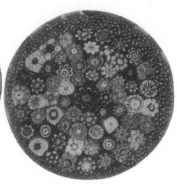

A St. Louis purple dahlia weight on a star-cut base, 2¾in. diam. (Christie's) $2,860 £1,634

A Clichy faceted pink double-overlay concentric millefiori mushroom weight on a straw-berry-cut base, 3.1/8in. diam. (Christie's) $5,500 £3,142

A Clichy close concentric millefiori weight, 2.1/8in. diam. (Christie's) $3,520 £2,011

A Sandwich blue poinsettia weight, the pale-blue flower with twelve petals, 2½in. diam. (Christie's) $550 £314

An Almaric Walter pate-de-verre paperweight, the blue glass moulded as a bird, 12cm. high. (Christie's) $902 £550

A Baccarat garlanded butterfly weight, on a star-cut base, 3.1/8in. diam. (Christie's) $2,420 £1,382

A St. Louis concentric mille-fiori paperweight, one cane dated SL 1848, 6.8cm. diam. (Phillips) $2,254 £1,350

A Gillinder flower weight, 2.7/8in. diam. (Christie's) $935 £534

A St. Louis amber flash gar-landed sulphide weight, the portrait of the young Victoria in profile, 2½in. diam. (Christie's) $1,430 £817

PARIAN

Parian is slightly translucent, silky textured, matt white porcelain which looks a little like marble but which can be moulded to produce figures and reproductions of sculpture. Most of the porcelain manufacturers produced lines in Parian ware and these ranged from Wedgwood to Belleek. It was particularly effective in making small figures of Greek goddesses.

It first appeared about 1840 when two firms, Minton and Copeland and Garrett recognised the possibility of making Parian statuary and this idea was also adopted by Wedgwood in 1848. They all turned out slightly less than lifesize models of Classical figures and sold them as adornments for modern homes where they were used as decorations in conservatories and halls. Later, when the technique of manufacture was refined, Parian was used for the manufacture of tableware and ornaments.

A large Parian group entitled 'Detected', signed R.J. Morris, 41cm. high. (Dee & Atkinson) $284 £160

Coloured Parian bust of The Beautiful Duchess, who was Georgiana, Duchess of Devonshire. (Goss & Crested China Ltd.) $2,250 £1,250

A Sam Alcock & Co Parian seated portrait figure of Wellington with joined hands and crossed legs, 28cm. high. (Phillips) $498 £300

A Copeland Parian group, entitled 'Go To Sleep', impressed Art Union of London, J. Durham Sc 1862, 26in. high overall. (Anderson & Garland) $525 £370

Kirk Braddon Cross in brown washed parian. $140 £82 Unusually, the white parian example is more valuable. (Goss & Crested China Ltd) $325 £185

Parian bust of Lord Palmerston on socle base and fluted column, 335mm. high. (Goss & Crested China Ltd.) $270 £150

A Parian bust of Wellington wearing military uniform, 14in. high. (Christie's) $234 £180

A Minton Parian group of Ariadne and the Panther on rectangular base, year cypher for 1867, 13.7in. high. (Woolley & Wallis) $390 £300

A Goss Parian bust of Queen Victoria, for Mortlock's of Oxford Street, 236mm. high. (Phillips) $400 £225

A coloured Parian group modelled as a young girl on rockwork, entitled 'You can't read', 12¼in. high, possibly by Robinson & Leadbetter. (Christie's) $222 £150

A Parian standing female figure, probably Belleek but unmarked, 36.5cm. high. (Lawrence Fine Art) $159 £110

One of a pair of glazed Parian figure brackets, allegorical figures in rock-like niches, 9½in. high. (Capes, Dunn & Co.) $163 £110

A Minton parian figure of Dorothea, after John Bell, 13¾in. high, registration tablet for 1872. (Parsons, Welch & Cowell) $323 £210

A Parian figural group of sleeping children 'Le Nid', circa 1875, signed 'Croisy', 15in. high. (Robt. W. Skinner Inc.) $750 £418

An 18th century French biscuit group modelled as a bearded god attended by two cupids, 40cm. high. (Christie's) $1,069 £660

PATCH BOXES

Up until the 19th century smallpox was a scourge that attacked all classes of society and even if patients were fortunate enough to survive an attack, they were often left with pock marked faces. To conceal the scars, fashionable women in the 18th century began wearing tiny patches, either round or shaped like hearts and stars, on their faces. The fashion proved to be so becoming that even women who were not victims of smallpox took to wearing patches. The little patches themselves were kept in special boxes made of papier mache, silver or painted enamel from Battersea, Bilston, Birmingham or South Staffordshire where they were manufactured by fusing glass onto copper and painting the decoration on by hand. The box was then fired at a very high temperature. After the disappearance of patches from a well to do lady's toilette, the boxes continued to be used for snuff, nutmeg or to hold little sponges soaked in aromatic vinegar which was used like smelling salts.

A Staffordshire portrait patch box, the lid with 'Marquis of Wellington', circa 1813, 4cm.
$525   £300

Early 19th century oval Staffordshire patch box, 3.5cm.
$435 £250

A Staffordshire patch box of oval form, lid mirror lined, 4cm. $1,300 £750

A South Staffordshire oval enamel patch box, transfer-printed and painted on the cover with Bristol Hot Wells, circa 1800, 1¾in. long. (Christie's) $544 £330

A Staffordshire small oval combined patchbox and nutmeg grater, with gilt metal mounts, circa 1765, 1.7/8in. long. (Christie's)
$629 £440

Late 18th century oval Staffordshire patch box, the lid printed with a view of Buckingham Palace, 4cm.
$525 £300

A Bilston enamel combined bonbonniere and patch box, 5cm. high. (Lawrence Fine Art) $1,116 £770

A George III enamel patch box, South Staffordshire, circa 1770, 1.5/8in. wide. (Christie's) $2,420 £1,382

A Bilston patch box of circular form, circa 1775, 1¾in. diam., slight damage.
$1,010 £902

273

PHONOGRAPHS

The first phonograph was invented in America in 1876 by Thomas Alva Edison and ten years later the gramophone was patented by Emile Berliner. Originally Berliner's machine played zinc coated rubber discs and the sound was very jerky because it was hand cranked. However 1900 the clockwork mechanism was more sophisticated and the first shellac discs had appeared. Most of the machines on sale then had large horns usually made of brass but occasionally of papier mache or painted tin which looked very pretty. Machines produced by firms like The Gramophone Co, G and T, or H. M. V. had attractive names like Aeolian, Vocalion, Deccalion and Oranoca. It was fashionable to have a gramophone in the parlour and soon, to make the machines merge more with household furniture, the horns were removed and gramophones were encased in neat cabinets with the loudspeakers inside. As well as old gramophones and phonographs, collectors also look for gramophone needles, record cleaners and needle sharpeners.

An Edison Fireside phonograph, Model A No. 25426, the K reproducer, crane and 36 two-minute and four-minute wax cylinders in cartons. (Christie's) $748 £462

An Edison Diamond disc phonograph in walnut case of Louis XV design, 50in. high, and 46 Edison discs. (Christie's) $1,188 £900

An Edison Home phonograph, Model A No. H104435, with B reproducer, crane 42in. long, and 25 cylinders. (Christie's) $693 £450

An Edison Amerola 1A phonograph, No. SM 950 in mahogany case with two-minute and four-minute traversing mandrel mechanism, 49in. high. (Christie's) $1,782 £1,100

An early Edison electric phonograph mechanism, in oak case with glass cover, with rear part of a Bettini carrier arm (lacks Edison carrier arm, Bettini reproducer and horn). (Christie's) $1,960 £1,210

An Edison Fireside phonograph, Model A No. 31916, now with Diamond B reproducer, Model R and Model K reproducers with adapter ring. (Christie's) $646 £420

PHONOGRAPHS

An Edison Bell 'Commercial' electric phonograph, No. 21164, the motor in oak base with accessories drawer. (Christie's) $1,336 £825

An Edison Home phonograph, early Model A, with automatic reproducer, and modern brass witch's hat horn. (Christie's) $427 £264

An Edison concert phonograph with Bettini spider diaphragm, American, circa 1902. $2,059 £1,430

An Edison Diamond Disc phonograph, Chippendale Laboratory Model (C19) No. SM 106640, 51½in. high, with nineteen discs. (Christie's) $748 £462

An Edison spring motor phonograph with Bettini Type D reproducer, American, circa 1903. $1,552 £1,078

An Edison Fireside combination type phonograph, Model B No. 89443, with four minute gearing. (Onslows) $700 £470

An Edison Red Gem phonograph, Model D No. 316478D, with K combination reproducer, maroon fireside octagonal horn and crane. (Onslows) $491 £330

An Edison Standard phonograph, Model C No. 660275, with combination gear and Bettini reproducer. (Onslows) $357 £240

An Edison Triumph phonograph, Model A No. 45259, in 'New Style' green oak case, with 14in. witch's hat horn. (Christie's) $770 £500

PIANOLA ROLLS

Pianola rolls could be made either by a special machine attached to a piano (thus recording an actual performance) or they could be produced mechanically. Most early examples are of classical or religious music, but the ones to look out for are those of swing or honky-tonk music produced in the 1920's. The wrappings of pianola rolls are often very elaborate and ornate, and when you consider that these can often still be picked up for a pound or two, we're talking real value for money.

Harrods Ltd., 'Badinage', by Victor Herbert, 1911. $9 £5

Keith Prowse & Co., 'I'm bringing a red, red rose', from 'Whoopee', by W. Donaldson, duty stamp, 1916. $10 £6

Universal music Roll, 'Gliding', a fox trot by P. L. Grant, 1900. $12 £7

The Boston Music Co. Ltd., 'The Rosery', by Nevin, with duty stamp, 1895. $5 £3

The Brixton Music Roll Exchange 'Italian Concerto'. $5 £3

Meloto, 'Pleasant Memories', by Godiana, 1902. $5 £3

Aeolian Company Ltd., 'Hearts and Flowers', 1898. $3.50 £2

The British Autoplayer Company Ltd., 'Valse Caprice', 1890. $7 £4

Meloto Song Roll 'I know a lovely garden', played by Cyril Westbury, 1899. $5 £3

Aeolian Company Ltd., 'Oh Mr Rubinstein', 1898. $3.50 £2

PICTURE FRAMES

Picture frames can often be more valuable than the picture they enclose. Prices as high as £5000 can be paid for carved and gilded frames dating from the time of Louis XIV and for Italian 18th century "Salvator Rosa" frames. Dutch tortoiseshell frames of the 17th century are in the same price bracket. Old frames are snapped up by collectors who want elegant mounts for their paintings and drawings. Frames which might have been sold for firewood a few years ago are today soaring into the four figure bracket. Among the favourites are heavy gilt Victorian frames, bamboo and cane frames (providing they are old) and frames made of unusual woods like maple or burr elm which were fairly common in Victorian times. Padded velvet frames that were used to mount watercolour paintings of flowers are very popular provided they are not too faded or threadbare. Smaller frames are also making high prices. These include Victorian, Art Nouveau and Art Deco silver photograph frames. It is important to make sure that the silver is not worn away by over-enthusiastic cleaning.

An embossed and pierced shaped silver photograph frame, London, 1900, 8in. high. (Dacre, Son & Hartley)
$270 £180

A WMF plated figural easel-backed mirror, stamped maker's marks, 37cm. high. (Phillips) $870 £580

One of a pair of early George III white painted and gilded picture frames attributed to Wm. Vile and John Cobb, 75 x 59in. (Christie's)
$40,176 £32,400

A Liberty silver and enamel picture frame, designed by Archibald Knox, with Birmingham hallmarks for 1904, 21.2cm. high. (Christie's) $5,909 £3,888

An Art Nouveau silver photograph frame, stamped maker's marks W.N. and Chester hallmarks for 1903, 22.3cm. high. (Christie's) $450 £300

One of a pair of carved and pierced sandalwood picture frames with Japanese folded silk and paper pictures, 19½ x 14in. (Edgar Horn)
$310 £250

An Art Nouveau silver picture frame, 35cm. high, marked WN and for Chester 1903. (Phillips) $518 £360

A Wm. Hutton & Sons Arts & Crafts silver picture frame, London hallmarks for 1903, 20cm. high. (Christie's) $2,272 £1,485

A Wm. Hutton & Sons Arts & Crafts silver picture frame, London hallmarks for 1903, 20cm. high. (Christie's) $2,187 £1,430

An Edwardian Art Nouveau silver and enamel photograph frame, Wm. Hutton & Sons Ltd., London, 1904, 10.25in. high, also an Elkington & Co. vase, Birmingham, 1906. (Reeds Rains) $1,162 £750

A Liberty & Co. silver and enamelled picture frame, 19 x 14.50cm., with Art Nouveau hinged support, hallmarked L. & Co., Birmingham, 1899. (Phillips) $2,664 £1,850

An Art Nouveau photograph frame, maker's marks W.N. and Chester hallmarks for 1903, 31cm. high. (Christie's) $3,048 £1,870

A Ramsden & Carr silver picture frame, with London hallmarks for 1900, 15.5cm. high. (Christie's) $1,425 £950

An Art Nouveau silver picture frame, 28cm. high, marked SB, Birmingham, 1903. (Phillips) $374 £260

A late Victorian oblong photograph frame, by Wm. Comyns, London, 1904, 6¾in. high. (Christie's) $230 £160

PISTOLS

Because of the laws against possessing offensive weapons it is best to check with the police before keeping any old firearms. However pistols make splendid room decorations and some very old weapons can still be bought. Flintlock and percussion weapons are the earliest and most straightforward from a legal point of view but any with pinfire mechanisms can be regarded as firearms still and police advice must be taken over them. When buying old pistols it is essential to look for weapons in good condition with no missing or replaced parts. The names of the makers which are most highly regarded are Nock, Manton, Egg, Kuchenreuter and Lepage. Remember that pairs of pistols, especially if boxed and complete with accessories, are far more valuable than single examples and can in fact be worth three times as much.

A steel barrelled flintlock blunderbuss pistol circa 1820, 12in. overall, swamped barrel 7in. with B'ham proofs and stamped 'London' at breech, trade quality flat lock with swan neck cock and unbridled frizzen. (Wallis & Wallis) $820 £450

A 40-bore all-metal Scottish percussion dress belt pistol, circa 1850, 9½in., 3 stage barrel, 6in., silvered metal stock, ram's horn butt, button trigger, pricker to butt, steel ramrod, sprung steel belt hook and stock profusely engraved overall. (Wallis & Wallis) $1,980 £1,200

A 22-bore Prussian model 1850 percussion Cavalry trooper's pistol, 15in., barrel 8¾in., halfstocked, regulation brass mounts, steel lanyard ring, side-plate and backstrap. (Wallis & Wallis) $660 £400

A 16-bore New Land pattern flintlock holster pistol, 15in., browned barrel 9in., Tower proved, fullstocked, stepped lockplate, regulation brass mounts, swivel ramrod and stock struck with inspector's marks. (Wallis & Wallis) $792 £480

A 14-bore miquelet flintlock Spanish belt pistol, by Toronto, circa 1800, 10in., half octagonal barrel 5½in., fullstocked, brass furniture with applied silver foil bosses to buttcap, trigger guard bow and escutcheon. (Wallis & Wallis) $726 £440

PISTOLS

A 6-shot 54-bore single action T. K. Baker's patent transitional percussion revolver, No. 2120, 11in., half octagonal barrel 5½in., Birmingham proved, sliding side safety catch and two-piece polished wooden grips. (Wallis & Wallis) $346 £210

A 5-shot .31in. Budding bronze framed and barrelled 3rd model hand rotated percussion pepperbox revolver, 8in., fluted cylinder 3¾in. (Wallis & Wallis)
$1,650 £1,000

A 14-bore Continental m. 1820 percussion Cavalry trooper's pistol, 14½in., barrel 8in., fullstocked, lock arsenal converted from flintlock, regulation brass mounts, steel swivel ramrod and backstrap. (Wallis & Wallis) $396 £240

A 22-bore flintlock duelling pistol, by H. Nock, circa 1800, 14½in. overall, octagonal barrel 9in., plain flat stepped lock with swan-neck cock and roller on frizzen spring, plain walnut fullstock and rounded butt. (Wallis & Wallis) $693 £420

A plain flintlock boxlock pocket pistol by Wogdon & Barton, circa 1800, 6¼in. overall, turn-off barrel 2in., London proved, top thumb safety, rainproof pan, hidden trigger, plain walnut slab butt. (Wallis & Wallis)
$313 £190

An 18 bore all steel Scottish flintlock belt pistol, circa 1780, 12½in., barrel 8in., threequarter stocked, horizontally acting scear, 'ram's horn' butt, elaborately pierced and engraved belt hook. (Wallis & Wallis)
$640 £350

A Belgian 54-bore pill-lock boxlock sidehammer pocket pistol, circa 1830, 6½in. overall, turn-off damascus barrel 2½in., Liege proved, scroll engraved frame, long-nosed hammer with vent, hidden trigger and fluted walnut butt. (Wallis & Wallis)
$330 £200

PISTOLS

A 22-bore model 1850 Prussian percussion Cavalry holster pistol, 15in., round cannon mouth, comb sighted, barrel with octagonal breech 8¾in., and raised groove rearsight. (Wallis & Wallis) $1,815 £1,100

A 16-bore William IV flintlock Cavalry pistol, 15in., barrel 9in., Enfield proved, fullstocked, regulation brass mounts, trigger guard engraved 'D.Y.C. 69'. (Wallis & Wallis) $1,089 £660

A 6-shot 65-bore Devisme patent single action enclosed hammer percussion revolver, No. 884, 13in., blued octagonal barrel 6¼in., with two-piece chequered walnut grips. (Wallis & Wallis) $1,237 £750

A 20-bore flintlock duelling pistol, by Brander & Potts, circa 1800, 14in. overall, octagonal barrel 9in. with London proofs. (Wallis & Wallis) $495 £300

A 16 bore flintlock belt pistol circa 1815, 9½in. octagonal barrel 5in. stamped Watt Inverness, full-stocked, foliate engraved lock with roller bearing frizzen spring. (Wallis & Wallis) $545 £300

A 20-bore Cossack nielloed silver mounted miquelet flintlock holster pistol, 17¼in., barrel 11½in., with traces of a little foliate chiselling, fullstocked, lock with maker's stamp to bridle, ribbed frizzen face. (Wallis & Wallis) $948 £575

A 6-shot 62-bore self-cocking W. J. Harvey's First Model transitional percussion revolver, No. 3617, 12¼in., octagonal barrel 5½in., Birmingham proved. (Wallis & Wallis) $594 £360

PLAYING CARDS

Playing cards have been in use for many centuries and they were sufficiently popular in Florence in the 14th century for a decree to be issued prohibiting their use. The standard design of cards as we know them today originated in Rouen during the 15th century and since then the four different suits of thirteen cards each have been fairly universal at least in Europe. However the suit signs of hearts, diamonds, spades and clubs are not universal even inside Europe for they are only used by the English and the French while Germanic countries use hearts, leaves, dumbbells and acorns and Italians prefer cups, swords, coins and sticks. Outwith Europe, Indian playing cards are circular and can have between eight and twenty suits with 12 cards in each while Chinese cards are long and narrow like book marks. The Japanese play with small pieces of board called Mekuri Fuda. From the beginning of the 17th century in England playing games with cards became a national passion and there was a considerable amount of heavy gambling. Queen Anne's government was forced to impose a tax of sixpence on every pack of cards in an effort to discourage the gambling mania but the tax was little deterrent. Playing cards make fascinating subjects for collection. The earliest cards that most collectors can hope to find date from the 17th century and the range thereafter is very wide indeed with highest prices being paid for "non standard" decks. Age is not a guarantee of value because many old packs sell for modest sums while unusual modern packs, especially ones with notable connections like the cards produced for the Kennedy presidential campaign in 1963, can be very expensive.

Marlborough's Victories — 52 engraved cards each with scene relating to War of the Spanish Succession, Christopher Blanchard, circa 1708. $5,250 £3,000

A complete set of fifty-two playing cards, illuminated on pasteboard, each card made up of four layers of paper pasted together, South Flanders possibly Lille, circa 1470-85. $175,000 £99,000

Musical Pack, 32 lithographed cards, each with a section of a dance tune in the lower half and miniature card or court figure in the upper half, Germany, circa 1860. $600 £350

Italy — 18th century 'Cucu'
deck 38/38.　　$525 £300

Educational cards, complete
set of 52 wood cut cards, each
with decorative border of
flowers, circa 1680.$2,625 £1,500

Iran — Persian 'Asnas' deck,
circa 1860, 25/25, hand painted
and lacquered.　　$490 £280

France — Standard Marseille
Tarot, circa 1850, 78/78, by
N. Conver.　　$435 £250

Austria — 'The Residenz — whist
number 147', by Piatnik of
Vienna, circa 1910.　　$85 £50

England — Biblical education
cards by J. Wallis, circa 1800.
$175 £100

Russian Alphabet Cards
complete set of 28 with
illustrations of street sellers,
Moscow, circa 1830.
$2,625 £1,500

France — 'Cartes a Rire', trans-
formation pack attributed to
Baron Louis Atthalin 1819.
$1,660 £950

England — A deck to honour
the marriage of The Duke of
Edinburgh published by De
Larue 1874.　　$350 £200

POLYPHONES

About the same time as gramophones and phonographs were beginning to appear, Paul Lochmann invented his polyphone which was a development of the musical box. He founded the Symphonion Company Leipzig in 1885 and, together with Gustav Brachausen, started producing the machines. In 1894 Brachausen emigrated to America where he began manufacturing polyphones at his Regina Company in New Jersey. Like music boxes, the sound from polyphones was produced by projecting metal pegs in a disc pinging against the teeth of a metal comb. The disc was set in such a way that when it was revolved it reproduced the music of operas or songs from music halls. Polyphones came in a variety of sizes, the smaller ones had discs which were about eight inches in diameter and were intended to be played in the home while machines with 24 inch discs were for public performance.

A 15.5/8in. Polyphon in panelled walnut case with double combs and forty-seven discs in circular wood box. (Christie's)
$2,304 £1,600

An 11.7/8in. Symphonion disc musical box with twin comb movement in rococo simulated case, with 15 discs. (Christie's)
$1,364 £1,100

A 9½in. Symphonium disc musical box with 'Sublime Harmony' combs, with one disc. (Christie's)
$1,069 £660

A 19.1/8in. upright Symphonion disc musical box with 'Sublime Harmony' combs, and six discs. (Christie's) $2,448 £1,700

A 15.5/8in. table polyphone with twin combs and 17 discs. (Christie's)
$2,316 £1,430

A 24.5/8in. upright Polyphon with coin mechanism and drawer, in glazed walnut case, 46in. high, with twenty-seven discs. (Christie's) $8,019 £4,950

POMANDERS

Pomanders are really first cousins to vinaigrettes and, like them, date from the time when personal hygiene and laundry care were not all they are now. The most basic pomander was probably an orange stuck with cloves, but like most other Good Ideas, they became more and more sophisticated, coming complete with hook, made from such attractive materials as silver and ceramics, and beautifully decorated. It's interesting to note that they are enjoying quite a revival today!

A silver pomander with eight compartments, circa 1700, 2in. high. (Christie's)
$4,452 £2,420

Early 18th century German silver pear-shaped pomander in three threaded sections, 2.5/8in. high. (Christie's)
$798 £484

A German spherical pomander, 6.4cm. high, 17th century, 80gr. $2,200 £1,250

Early 18th century German silver pomander with entwined foliage stem, 2in. high. (Christie's) $272 £165

Early 18th century silver gilt pomander of threaded acorn shape, 2½in. high. (Christie's) $1,052 £638

A silver gilt pomander, the six-hinged segments engraved with flowers and foliate sprays, circa 1600, probably German, 1¾in. high. (Christie's)
$4,950 £2,750

Early 18th century German silver pear-shaped pomander with perforated interior, 2½in. high. (Christie's)
$816 £495

PORTRAIT MINIATURES

Before the invention of the camera people gave their loved ones portraits of themselves painted in miniature as remembrances. With the development of the Empire, when many young men went abroad, the trade of the miniaturist expanded greatly for the travellers wanted to take pictures of loved ones with them. One of the finest miniaturists was Nicholas Hilliard who worked at the time of Queen Elizabeth I, but his clientele was confined to the very rich and well born. Later, the practice of having a miniature done spread to the emergent middle class and watering places like Bath, Tunbridge Wells or Cheltenham supported colonies of miniaturists. Many of them were women but the most famous were Richard Cosway, Henry Spicer, Horace Hone, Richard Crosse, Ozias Humphrey, Jeremiah Meyer, Charles Bestland and George Engleheart. The best miniatures were painted with watercolour on ivory which gave a flesh like glow to the skin and an opaque colour to the clothes.

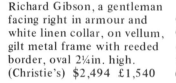

Richard Gibson, a gentleman facing right in armour and white linen collar, on vellum, gilt metal frame with reeded border, oval 2¼in. high. (Christie's) $2,494 £1,540

Captain and Mrs. Wm. Croome, by G. Engleheart, both signed and dated 1811 and 1812, later gold frames, ovals, 3¼in. high. (Christie's)　　　$8,316 £4,620

Thomas Flatman, a nobleman called John Maitland, 2nd Earl and Duke of Lauderdale, on vellum, signed with initial, oval 2.1/8in. high. (Christie's) $7,128 £4,400

John Smart, a miniature of Peter Johnston, signed with initials and dated 1803, gold frame, oval 3½in. high. (Christie's) $10,692 £6,600

Aldani, a miniature of a gentleman seated on a stone wall, signed, gilt metal frame, rectangular 3.1/8in. high. (Christie's) $1,782 £1,100

William Grimaldi, a portrait of a child seated beside a tree with a blue finch on his hand, signed, gold frame, oval 2¾in. high. (Christie's) $6,237 £3,850

PORTRAIT MINIATURES

Andrew Plimer, an officer in scarlet uniform with blue facings and silver lace, gold frame, oval 3in. (Christie's) $3,207 £1,980

John Smart, a miniature of Miss Elizabeth Cottingham of County Clare, signed and dated 1777, gold frame, oval 2in. high. (Christie's) $10,335 £6,380

James Green, a gentleman possibly the Rt. Hon. Edward Ellice, gold frame, oval 3.1/8in. high. (Christie's) $981 £606

Philip Jean, a gentleman in blue coat with gold buttons, gold frame, oval 2.5/8in. high. (Christie's) $715 £440

David Des Granges, a miniature of a lady in black dress with lace border and white lace collar, on vellum, oval 2.3/8in. high. (Christie's) $8,019 £4,950

Studio of Richard Gibson, a gentleman believed to be Sir John Germaine, on vellum, oval 3.1/8in. high. (Christie's) $1,782 £1,100

George Place, a miniature of an officer of the Weymouth Vol. Artillery, gilt metal frame, oval 4¾in. high. (Christie's) $5,346 £3,300

John Smart, Jane Palmer in ermine-bordered pale blue surcoat, signed with initials and dated 1777, gold frame, oval 1¾in. high. (Christie's) $7,128 £4,400

John Comerford, Capt. James Hughes in the blue uniform of The 18th Dragoons (Hussars), signed and dated 1807, oval 3in. high. (Christie's) $2,138 £1,320

PORTRAIT MINIATURES

Gernard Lens, a gentleman facing right in beige coat, signed with gold monogram, gilt metal mounts, rectangular wood frame, oval 2.7/8in. high. (Christie's) $1,069 £660˙

James Peale, a lady in white shawl and bonnet, signed with initials and dated 1800, oval 3in. high. (Christie's) $1,960 £1,210

Thomas Flatman, a self-portrait, on vellum, signed and dated 1678, gold frame, oval 2½in. high. (Christie's) $10,335 £6,380

George Engleheart, a miniature of Capt. John Cummings in the uniform of The 8th Dragoons, signed and dated 1806, oval 3½in. high. (Christie's) $6,237 £3,850

George Engleheart, a lady in decollete white dress with frilled border, gold frame, oval 2.7/8in. high. (Christie's) $5,346 £3,300

John Cox Dillman Engleheart, a gentleman in dark blue coat with gold buttons, signed on the reverse and dated 1814, oval 2.5/8in. high. (Christie's) $980 £605

Philip Jean, a gentleman in blue coat with gold buttons, gold frame with plaited hair reverse, oval 2¾in. high. (Christie's) $1,336 £825

Attributed to Pierre Chasselat, a lady seated on a bench in a landscape, set in the lid of a tortoiseshell box with gold rims, 2.5/8in. diam. (Christie's) $3,920 £2,420

John Cox Dillman Engleheart, a gentleman in black coat and waistcoat, gold frame, oval 2.7/8in. high. (Christie's) $534 £330

POT LIDS

In the 19th century one of the most common containers for a myriad different items ranging from hair dressing to anchovy paste was a circular shallow ceramic pot with a loose fitting lid that rested on a slight lip around the top of the pot. One of the most prolific manufacturers of these pots was F. & R. Pratt and Co of Fenton in Staffordshire. They made pots for more than 300 different outlets and the manufacturers who bought their wares filled the pots with such diverse things as ointment or jam. The way their wares were distinguished for the public was by brightly coloured lids which were transfer printed and designed to catch the eye. It is those lids that collectors seek out today. The most popular designs ranged from portraits of Queen Victoria and other popular heroes of the day to pretty landscapes or rural scenes. Pot lid collectors look for them in rubbish dumps and the value is dictated by the condition and rarity of the lid.

A Gay Dog. (Phillips) $1,914 £1,100

The Kingfisher, early issue, the reverse stamped '6' or '9'. (Phillips) $1,653 £950

Bears Reading Newspapers. (Phillips) $3,654 £2,100

Pegwell Bay, S. Banger, Shrimp Sauce Manufacturer. (Phillips) $522 £300

Sebastopol. (Phillips) $191 £110

Exhibition Buildings 1851, large, figures omitted, white surround. (Phillips) $1,740 £1,000

A Prattware pot lid depicting Wellington seated, 5in. diam. $220 £125

Medium small lid depicting bear hunting. $1,000 £600

A Prattware pot lid depicting Strathfieldsay, 5in. diam. $150 £85

A pot lid, 'England's Pride', black background and beaded border, 4¼in. diam. $275 £150

Belle Vue Tavern (with cart). (Phillips) $1,218 £700

Victorian pot lid titled 'The Fair', 4in. diam. $65 £40

Pot lid 'Our Home', one of only two known examples. $4,500 £2,600

The 'Garden Terrace', a medium small lid. $525 £300

Small pot lid with purple lined border, 'The Bride'. $435 £250

A large pot lid with marbled border, 'The Late Duke of Wellington'. $210 £125

A medium pot lid with chain border 'Embarking for the East'. $175 £100

A medium pot lid with laurel leaf border, 'The Allied Generals'. $250 £120

A large pot lid with double line border and title, 'Napirima Trinidad'. $260 £150

Pot lid by Mayer Bros., circa 1850, 12.7cm. diam. $4,750 £2,700

A pot lid, 'The Buffalo Hunt'. $1,750 £1,000

POWDER FLASKS

In the days of muskets and barrel loading guns, men carried their gunpowder in flasks attached to their belts. One of the most common materials for those flasks was horn which could be elaborately engraved and decorated with foliage or scrolls. One of these horn flasks today can cost several hundreds of pounds but less valuable are flasks of metal like the ones made by Batty, Hawkins, Ames, Dixon or the American Flask and Cap Company. They were turned out in large numbers and are still fairly plentiful. Most were decorated in some way; a few were fluted while others carried carved coats of arms, basket weave patterns or engraved battle scenes. Old Colonial powder horns were often decorated by the owners themselves and carved with personal mottos and devices.

A good embossed copper powder flask (R. 355) 8in., graduated nozzle stamped G. & J. W. Hawksley. (Wallis & Wallis) $90 £55

A powder horn circa 1800, brass circular base plate engraved with the device of the Percy Tenantry, 13½in. long. (Wallis & Wallis) $135 £80

An embossed copper powder flask (R.535), 8in. embossed with panel of geometric and foliate ornament, patent brass top stamped James Dixon & Sons. (Wallis & Wallis) $87 £50

An 18th century Persian all steel powder flask, of swollen boat or swan form. (Wallis & Wallis) $107 £65

A good scarce Japanese cow horn powder flask, 5½in. very well made and polished, turned ivory spout and collar emanate from fluted horn tehenkanemono. (Wallis & Wallis) $160 £95

An engraved rifle horn with carved horntip powder measure, Midwest, dated 1843, in cartouche, 4½in. long. (Robt. W. Skinner Inc.) $1,200 £714

A good 18th/19th century Transylvanian stag horn powder flask, 6in. decorated overall with geometric devices. (Wallis & Wallis) $175 £100

A brass mounted Continental lanthorn powder flask, fixed baluster turned nozzle swivels on knuckle joint for cut off. (Wallis & Wallis) $150 £90

A 17th/18th century Persian Circassian walnut powder flask, 6in., sprung steel lever charger with shaped top. (Wallis & Wallis) $400 £240

PRAMS

The first prams were made for the children of royalty in the early 18th century and were designed like little carts to be drawn by tiny ponies, donkeys or sometimes goats. Many of them were manufactured out of wicker work and were very elaborate. The general public did not take to baby carriages until the 1840's when a three wheeled version with iron tyres appeared. It was still of the variety that had to be pulled and not pushed. Four wheeled, pushable bassinettes made their appearance in the 1890's and after that nursemaids pushing babies in the parks became a common sight. Funnily enough in the early days of prams the authorities regarded them as road vehicles but this was later relaxed.

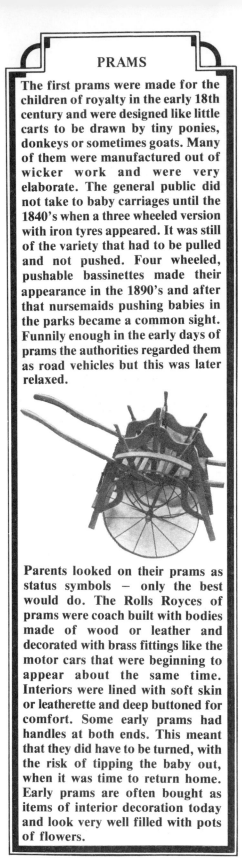

Parents looked on their prams as status symbols — only the best would do. The Rolls Royces of prams were coach built with bodies made of wood or leather and decorated with brass fittings like the motor cars that were beginning to appear about the same time. Interiors were lined with soft skin or leatherette and deep buttoned for comfort. Some early prams had handles at both ends. This meant that they did have to be turned, with the risk of tipping the baby out, when it was time to return home. Early prams are often bought as items of interior decoration today and look very well filled with pots of flowers.

Doll's pram with scroll and lattice wicker-work body, 30in. long. $140 £80

A wicker and bentwood baby carriage, labelled Whitney, raised on wooden wheels, America, circa 1895, 55in. long. (Robt. W. Skinner Inc.) $300 £232

A 19th century child's perambulator with button upholstered leatherette interior, carved American walnut body, 47 x 54in. (Lawrence Fine Arts) $696 £385

An early Star Manufacturing Co. round-head pram with leather trim and porcelain handle.
$435 £250

A metal bodied Leeway pram with plastic interior. $100 £60

A rare T. Trotmans patent 1854 folding pram with carpet back seating and wood and brass wheels. $700 £400

A baby carriage with maker's name plate attached, A. Mitchell, Margate, height to hood 31in. (Worsfolds) $537 £320

1950's Royal' pram with plywood body.
$80 £45

Wooden bodied doll's pram with vinyl interior and fabric hood. $70 £40

1920's Acme pram with wooden body and 'C' springs, reg. no. 465485.   **$140 £80**

1950's doll's pram with tin body and fabric hood.   **$70 £40**

Wooden 'mail cart' pram with carved sides, leather hood and brass trim.   **$525 £300**

A rare Bassinett two handled double pram with painted leather body, circa 1860. **$435 £250**

1930's German wickerwork pram with alloy wheel arches and bumpers.   **$100 £60**

Tri-ang doll's pram with metal body and plastic and fabric hood, 1960's. **$50 £30**

PREISS FIGURES

Art Deco found one of its most vivid expressions in the bronze and ivory, or chryselephantine, figures of F. Preiss. Virtually nothing is known about Preiss, save that he was probably born in Vienna, his forename may be Friedrich and he flourished in the late 20's and 30's. His work was closely copied by one Professor Otto Poerzl, working out of Coburg, so closely copied in fact that there is speculation that they may be one and the same.

Preiss modelled classical and modern nudes — and the Olympic figures, lithe and vibrant, glorifying the body beautiful and so much in tune with the spirit of the 1936 Olympics and the Nazi preoccupation with the physical prowess of the Aryan master race that suspicion has abounded that Preiss was an adherent of the movement.

What is in no doubt is that the present popularity of Preiss figures has meant that they fetch phenomenal sums at auction. A negative effect is the appearance of very clever reproductions — caveat emptor!

A painted bronze and ivory figure, 'Hoop Girl', 20.50cm. high, inscribed F. Preiss. (Phillips) $1,872 £1,300

Kneeling girl with clock, a bronze and ivory figure cast after a model by F. Preiss, 54.4cm. high. (Christie's) $14,071 £8,580

Art Deco bronze and ivory figurine of a young woman on a jetty holding a canoe paddle. (Biddle & Webb) $3,586 £2,200

Mandolin Player, a bronze and ivory figure cast and carved from a model by F. Preiss, signed, 59cm. high. (Christie's) $31,395 £20,520

'Bat Dancer', a bronze and ivory figure cast and carved from a model by F. Preiss, 23.5cm. high. (Christie's) $5,412 £3,300

Flute Player, a bronze and ivory figure cast and carved from a model by F. Preiss, 48.5cm. high. (Christie's) $28,090 £18,360

PREISS FIGURES

'Torch Dancer', a bronze and ivory figure cast and carved from a model by F. Preiss, 41.5cm. high. (Christie's) $6,314 £3,850

'Con Brio', a bronze and ivory figure cast and carved from a model by F. Preiss, 29cm. high. (Christie's) $9,020 £5,500

A painted bronze and ivory figure, 'Champagne Dancer', 41.50cm. high, inscribed on bronze F. Preiss. (Phillips) $3,600 £2,500

'Sunshade Girl', a gilt bronze and ivory figure cast and carved from a model by F. Preiss, 20.2cm. high. (Christie's) $2,035 £1,404

An Art Deco green onyx mantel clock with ivory figures carved after a model by F. Preiss, 25.2cm. high. (Christie's) $2,349 £1,620

A painted bronze and ivory figure, 'Sonny Boy', 20.50cm. high, inscribed F. Preiss. (Phillips) $2,160 £1,500

'Russian Dancer', a bronze and ivory figure cast and carved after a model by F. Preiss, 32.4cm. high. (Christie's) $5,051 £3,080

An Art Deco bronze and ivory figurine of a young bather reclining on a large rock. (Biddle & Webb) $7,498 £4,600

'Nude', an ivory figure carved after a model by F. Preiss, on a green marble base, 43.9cm. high. (Christie's) $12,528 £8,640

PRINTS

Any impression made in ink by a hard block or plate on paper can be called a print. The block may be of wood, metal or stone. Sometimes a print is referred to as an engraving which is the impression produced by an engraved block or plate. When a print is marked "by so and so after someone else" it means that the print maker has copied another artist's designs. Original prints are conceived and executed by the same artist. Prints that sometimes confuse buyers are those produced by photo-mechanical processes and many were given away by art magazines in the early part of the 20th century. Some modern prints were also reproduced by photographic methods. Most good prints were produced in limited editions and they were numbered and signed by the artist. Old Master prints are among the most desirable but prints by artists like Picasso, Chagall, Warhol or Hockney also demand large sums. On a more moderate level seek out the work of print makers Le Blond, Baxter, Icart, Cruickshank and Blampied.

Jacob Kramer: Vorticist Figure, lithograph, circa 1920, on laid paper, 417 x 252mm. (Christie's) $2,402 £1,430

Marc Chagall: Now the King loved Science and Geometry, Plate X from Four Tales from the Arabian Nights, lithograph printed in colours, 1948, 380 x 286mm. (Christie's) $27,621 £17,050

Theodore Alexandre Steinlen: Motocycles Comiot, lithograph printed in colours, 1899, on two joined sheets of thin tan wove paper, 1,885 x 1,280mm. (Christie's) $13,365 £8,250

Paul Delvaux: La Reine de Saba, screenprint in colours, 1982, on Arches, 596 x 431mm. (Christie's) $1,336 £825

Erich Heckel: Mannerbildnis, woodcut printed in black, olive-green, brown and blue, 1919, second state of three, 463 x 327mm. (Christie's) $92,664 £57,200

Marc Chagall: Femme de l'Artiste, lithograph printed in colours, 1971, on Arches, 649 x 503mm. (Christie's) $33,858 £20,900

Yoshijuro Urishibawa: Paeonies and Fresias, one of four wood-cuts printed in colours, circa 1910, 303 x 201mm. and smaller. (Christie's)
$2,032 £1,210

Albrecht Durer: St. Jerome in his Study, engraving, water-mark Three Balls (?), 245 x 189mm. (Christie's)
$5,913 £3,520

Henry Moore: Reclining Figures and Reclining Mother and Child, lithograph printed in colours, 1971 and 1974, 299 x 239mm. (Christie's) $1,386 £825

Pierre-Auguste Renoir: La Danse a la Campagne, Deuxieme Planche, soft-ground etching, circa 1890, on wove paper, 220 x 135mm. (Christie's)
$8,553 £5,280

Henry Moore: Girl Seated At Desk VII, lithograph printed in colours, 1974, on J. Green wove paper, 242 x 175mm. (Christie's) $1,570 £935

Dame Elisabeth Frink: Geoffrey Chaucer, etching illustrating Chaucer's Canterbury Tales, Leslie Waddington Prints Ltd., London, 1972, 588 x 694mm. (Christie's) $702 £418

David Hockney: Black Tulips, lithograph, 1980, signed, dated and numbered 80/100, publi-shed by Waddington, 112 x 76cm. (Phillips) $5,670 £3,500

Laura Knight: At The Fair, aquatint, signed in pencil, mount-stained, taped to front mount, 26 x 21cm. (Phillips) $486 £300

Andy Warhol: Hand-coloured Flower, lithograph, signed with initials, 102 x 68cm. (Phillips) $1,944 £1,200

Henry Moore: Three reclining Figures on Pedestals, lithograph printed in colours, 1966, on Arches, signed and dated in pencil, 312 x 263mm. (Christie's) $2,656 £1,540

Jacques Villon: L'Italienne, after A. Modigliani, aquatint printed in colours, circa 1927, on wove paper, signed, 497 x 309mm. (Christie's)
$6,771 £4,180

David Hockney: Rue de Seine, etching, 1971, on J. Green mould-made wove paper, numbered 92/150, 537 x 435mm. (Christie's)
$8,019 £4,950

Three, Les Maitres de l'Affiche, Volumes I-V, Imprimerie Chaix, Paris 1896-1900, sheet 403 x 315mm. (Christie's) $21,384 £13,200

David Hockney: Potted Daffodils, lithograph, 1980, signed, dated and numbered 81/95 in pencil, 112 x 76cm. (Phillips) $5,670 £3,500

Shuho Yamakawa, oban tate-e, okubi-e of a young woman, signed, entitled Yukimoyoi, dated 1927, 38.5 x 26.5cm. (Christie's) $1,108 £693

Marc Chagall: Cirque avec Clowne-jaune, lithograph printed in colours, 1967, on Arches, numbered 83/150, 675 x 496mm. (Christie's)
$7,484 £4,620

RACKETANA

Primitive bat and ball games date from earliest times, but unlike real tennis which goes back at least to medieval times, lawn tennis, table tennis, badminton and squash did not emerge as formalised sports until the second half of the nineteenth century.

Modern lawn tennis rackets date from around 1880 and were nearly always strung with gut, though experiments were made with a vellum face. Vellum battledores from the early game of battledore and shuttlecock (which developed into badminton in the 1860's or 1870's) can sometimes be found, but the shuttlecocks are very rare indeed.

These battledores were often cut down for table tennis in the 1890's until John Jaques & Son produced their own under the registered title "Ping-Pong"—representing the "ping" on the table and the "pong" on the hollow battledore. Wooden bats, with a variety of coverings or none at all, first appeared around 1900.

Original ink drawing found in a family album and dated 1901. $45 £25

Box of Gardiner's lawn tennis balls (unused), 1920's. $85 £50

Table tennis battledore with single vellum sheet in bamboo frame, circa 1900, made by J. R. Mally. $85 £50

De Luxe 'Ping-Pong or Gossima' set in wooden box, by J. Jaques & Son, circa 1900. $350 £200

A pair of very rare table tennis battledores with single vellum sheet in bamboo frame, circa 1900. $175 £100

(The Gurney Collection)

Huge shuttlecock, made in India circa 1840, and designed for the game of battledore and shuttlecock in the garden. $210 £125

Table tennis bat, circa 1900, delicately cut out in fretwork. $85 £50

Miniature battledore and shuttlecock set, the battledores faced with vellum and only 8in. overall. $130 £75

Very large vellum battledore, 23in. overall, for the game of battledore and shuttlecock, circa 1890. $130 £75

Silver-mounted table tennis bat with high quality Art Nouveau decoration and hallmarked for Birmingham, 1901. $610 £350

Very fine label for a French table tennis set, showing a tournament scene, circa 1900. $210 £125

Tinted 1920's photograph by H. Jetter, showing an unusual backhand. $70 £40

(The Gurney Collection)

Very high quality lawn tennis racket by Slazenger, circa 1895 and showing the flat-topped head characteristic of the period. $350 £200

Handsome multiple press in solid mahogany and with brass fittings, circa 1910. $175 £100

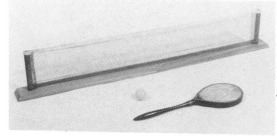

1930's lop sided real tennis racket. $130 £75

Squash racket by T. H. Prosser & Sons, circa 1900. $175 £100

Unusual free-standing table tennis net produced by Grays of Cambridge, circa 1900, with the idea of avoiding damage to the edge of the table. $50 £30

Miniature lawn tennis game made in Germany, circa 1900. $85 £50

An early 20th century lawn tennis racket. $85 £50

A 1930's 'Vitiv' badminton racket with decorations characteristic of the period. $50 £30

THE GAME OF POUCH BALL
AN IMPROVED TABLE TENNIS.

The only known surviving example of Pouch Ball, an American variant of table tennis, circa 1900. $350 £200

(The Gurney Collection)

Fine 'fish-tail' lawn tennis racket, circa 1920.
$175 £100

Badminton racket made in India, circa 1885.
$175 £100

Miniature 19th century racket, for tennis-on-a-table. $130 £75

Late 19th century vellum battledore for the game of battledore and shuttlecock. $70 £40

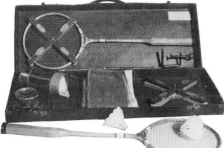

Unusual 1930's table badminton set with miniature rackets strung with silk. $85 £50

Victorian table tennis set with a fine illustration of domestic play. $175 £100

Very rare American badminton racket with steel shaft and head and wire stringing, circa 1925.
$175 £100

Late nineteenth century vellum battledore for the game of battledore and shuttlecock.
$105 £60

'Ping-Pong — The Great Tennis Game for the Table', by Parker Bros., Salem, U.S.A., circa 1900. $350 £200

(The Gurney Collection)

RATTLES

Rattles have been made for several different purposes although the most common one was for the amusement of small babies. Otherwise American Indians used rattles in their religious ceremonial and wooden rattles were used to frighten birds on 19th century farms and later by football fans in cheering on their side.

Babies' rattles were originally dried gourds with a few seeds rattling inside but in the 18th and 19th centuries it became the custom to present a new born child with a silver rattle as a gift. Georgian ones were usually quite plain but Victorian rattles were often ornamented with elves, rabbits or symbols of good luck. Some rattles had bells and whistles attached to them and more commonly they were found with teething rings. These rings were made of ivory or coral which were thought to contain health preserving properties. Though silver was the most common medium, rattles of ivory, wood and later of celluloid can be found.

17th century child's rattle bearing the Edinburgh date letter for 1681.
$2,200 £1,250

Northwest Coast polychrome wood rattle, cedar, carved in two sections and joined with square metal nails, 11¼in. long. (Robt. W. Skinner Inc.) $350 £196

Sterling silver baby rattle with sliding monkey, Birmingham, circa 1905, 6½in. long. $560 £320

A 19th century beech-wood rattle for bird scaring, 10½in. long. $130 £75

A goldwashed silver and coral rattle whistle, hall-marked Birmingham, 1862, 6in. long. (Robt. W. Skinner Inc.) $290 £235

A 20th century baby's plated rattle. $18 £10

Northwest coast polychromed carved wood raven rattle, carved in two sections, 12¼in. long. (Robt. W. Skinner Inc.) $4,000 £2,777

A French Christening set, post 1838, guarantee, with maker's mark of Veyrant, 8.8oz. of weighable silver. (Lawrence Fine Arts) $510 £352

RAZORS

Whenever some new invention makes an aspect of everyday life obsolete, another possible field for collecting is created. The safety razor and then the electric razor spelt the death of "cut throat" razors which are now sought out by collectors. Everyday plain black and white handled razors are too common to be worth more than a pound each but there are pearl handled ones to be found and they make around £20 if they have Sheffield steel blades. Silver handled razors and silver on ivory are even more desirable. Collectors look for uncracked pre-1800 razors with straight handles; German razor sets and imitation ivory sets which are cheaper to buy than real ivory sets which are often made in Sheffield.

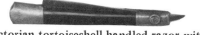

Victorian tortoiseshell handled razor with silver mounts. $35 £20

Mid 19th century razor with chequered ivory handle. $140 £80

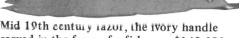

Mid 19th century razor, the ivory handle carved in the form of a fish. $140 £80

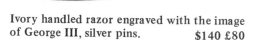

Ivory handled razor engraved with the image of George III, silver pins. $140 £80

Mid 19th century razor with silver inlaid tortoiseshell handle. $35 £20

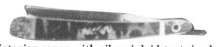

Victorian razor with silver inlaid tortoiseshell handle. $35 £20

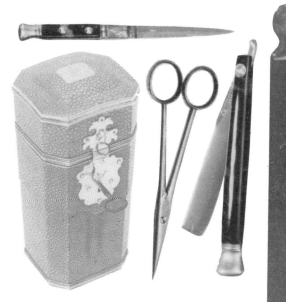

A superb mid 18th century solid tortoiseshell set contained in a silver mounted fish skin case. $1,400 £800

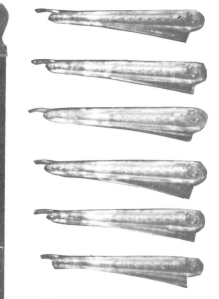

A possibly unique set of six razors with silver gilt handles, by Paul Storr, with matching strap, 1834. $2,600 £1,500

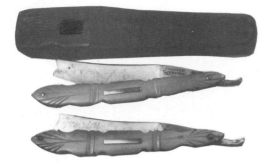

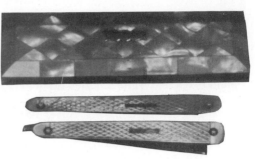

Pair of late 18th century razors by Johnson, with pressed horn handles. $50 £30

A pair of chequer carved pearl handled razors with solid gold pins, contained in a mother-of-pearl case, by I. H. Farthing, circa 1805. $305 £175

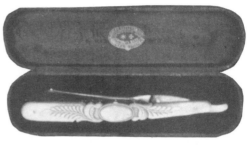

Pair of mid 19th century razors with embossed silver handles. $175 £100

Mid 19th century pearl handled razor, in its velvet lined case. $85 £50

A rare sailor's twin-bladed razor, with penwork handle, engraved 'Plymouth'. $175 £100

Mid 19th century razor with inlaid black horn handle. $25 £15

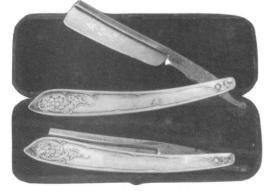

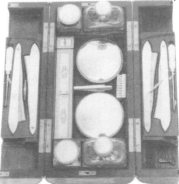

A pair of Swedish steel razors marked Dannemora Gjutstahl, with silver handles, contained in a black leather case, 1874. $150 £85

A good late 18th century French mahogany case necessaire de voyage in silver gilt with solid pearl handles including razors, moustache combs, toothbrush and tongue scraper. $4,725 £2,700

RIFLES

Gunsmiths through the ages have been more than mere craftsmen, they were artists as well. Guns are never just 'made' they are 'built' and the work that goes into them is time consuming and exacting. It is rare for a good gunsmith to be able to produce more than five weapons a year. When sporting guns come up for sale, the magic name J. Purdey and Sons means that a big price will be paid. Guns need not be old to be valuable and a modern gunsmith like David McKay Brown can see their guns change hands for five figure prices. The desire to own a good gun is not confined to any one nation or part of the world. It is very much an international rich man's obsession. The first long barrel guns were simply brass or iron tubes with stocks of wood and they came into general use in the 15th century. The German invention of the wheel lock in 1517 gave the world the rifle. After that the flint lock and the wheel lock rifle were invented and the double barrelled shotgun made its first appearance in 1784. By the mid 19th century England had become the centre of the gun making world, a position it still holds.

Some collectors specialise in unusual old guns like the ones made by Robert Murden during the English Civil War or the guns used by cowboys in the Wild West. Some of them come complete with their romantic history. One of the most attractive guns is the dragon carbine, also from the Civil War period, which had bellied muzzles and flat sided butts with dragons carved along them. It was from those guns that the word "dragoon" appeared.

A Greene's patent 28-bore breech loading Maynard's tape primed percussion carbine. (Wallis & Wallis) $1,815 £1,100

A .450in. Westley Richards 'monkey-tail' breech loading percussion sporting rifle. (Wallis & Wallis) $792 £480

A 40-bore Austrian percussion sporting rifle, by W. Leithner of Ischl, circa 1850. (Wallis & Wallis) $1,773 £1,075

A 9-shot 36-bore P. W. Porter's patent vertically revolving turret percussion rifle. (Wallis & Wallis) $2,640 £1,600

A 30-bore Hall's patent American breech loading military flintlock Harper's Ferry rifled, dated 1837. (Wallis & Wallis) $1,980 £1,200

A matchlock gun with oak butt and stock, brass match-holder, spring, lock-plate, trigger and guard, the octagonal iron barrel signed Goshu Hino Yoshihisa saku, barrel length 77.8cm. (Christie's) $792 £495

An interesting Irish military style flintlock blunderbuss by Pattison of Dublin circa 1800, 34in., flared steel barrel 18in. stamped on octagonal breech 'Pattison Dublin', fullstocked, military style lock with throat-hole cock. (Wallis & Wallis) $700 £400

A 16-bore Austrian military flintlock carbine, 30in., barrel 14½in., two-third length stock, regulation steel mounts, finger scrolls to trigger guard, carved cheekpiece, steel ramrod and lanyard rings to extended side-plate. (Wallis & Wallis) $495 £300

A good .22in. LR Remington semi-auto take-down Model 24 rifle No. 101927, 45½in. overall including blued 7in. Parker Hale sound moderation, blued barrel 21in. with Remington address and Browning patent 1916, blued telescopic sight stamped with Winchester address. (Wallis & Wallis) $315 £180

A U.S. .30in. M1-A1 semi-automatic carbine with folding skeleton stock for airborne troops, 36in. overall, barrel 18in., number 370180, the action stamped 'InlandDiv', with sling swivels and webbing sling. (Wallis & Wallis) $455 £260

A French 11mm. Gras Model 1874 bolt action single shot military rifle 46¼in. overall, barrel 28in., number 18015, the frame stamped 'Manufacture d'Armes St.Etienne Mle 1874'. (Wallis & Wallis) $160 £90

An unusual 19th century 16 bore all steel wheelock sporting gun in the Romantic Style, 43in., barrel 27in. with tubular rearsight chiselled as a dragon, openwork pierced steel butt of foliate design, stock engraved overall with foliage. (Wallis & Wallis) $875 £500

A 6.5mm. Steyr Model 1899 bolt-actionbox magazine sporting rifle, 47in. overall, barrel 26in., number 8493 on trigger guard, the barrel engraved 'Charles Lancaster, 151 New Bond St. London, W.' (Wallis & Wallis) $115 £65

A .303in. B.S.A. Long Lee Enfield Military pattern bolt action rifle, 49½in. overall, barrel 30in., number G0725/1236, sliding and adjustable aperture rearsights, bayonet lug on fore end cap, sling swivels with leather sling. (Wallis & Wallis) $165 £95

A 6.5mm. Mannlicher Schoenauer M. 1903 bolt-action short sporting rifle, 38½in. overall, barrel 18in. number 2145, double set triggers single folding rearsight, the frame marked 'Oesterr. Waffenfabr. Ges. Steyr'. (Wallis & Wallis) $315 £180

A 24 bore Austrian rifled flintlock sporting carbine circa 1770, 34in., swamped octagonal barrel 19½in. with fixed sights, flattened lock, un-bridled frizzen, brass furniture, carved wooden trigger guard with brass inlay. (Wallis & Wallis) $875 £500

An attractive Indian flintlock rifle, circa 1830, 57in. damascus twist barrel with swollen muzzle, gold inlaid scrolls and foliage at breech and muzzle, fullstocked, English lock with Frenchstyle cock. (Wallis & Wallis) $840 £480

ROOKWOOD

The Rookwood Pottery was established in Cincinnati in 1880 by M L Nichols. After initially producing utility earthenware the company gradually developed a distinctive style in art pottery. Early techniques included impressed geometrical motifs, transfer printing and relief designs, and an initial tendency to Japanese motifs was succeeded by the naturalistic representation of plants and animals. 1883 saw the introduction of an atomiser to apply underglaze grounds in blended brown, orange, yellow and green and this, together with barbotine decoration, usually flowers, became characteristic of Rookwood Standard ware. In 1901 matt glazes were introduced, used with painted or relief decorations, and, following this, the manufacture of architectural wares such as plaques, wall panels and house tiles began. The pottery continued in operation until it was declared bankrupt in 1941.

A Rookwood silver overlay vase, impressed artist's monogram SS, 12.5cm. high. (Christie's) $792 £550

One of a pair of Rookwood stoneware bookends, modelled as sphinx holding books, light brown glaze, 18cm. high. (Christie's) $190 £132

A Rookwood pottery standard glaze pillow vase, 1889, artist's initials ARV for Albert R. Valentien, 14in. high. (Robt. W. Skinner Inc.) $1,000 £595

A Rookwood pottery vase with sterling silver overlay, circa 1899, signed by J. Zettel, 8½in. high. (Robt. W. Skinner Inc.)
              $2,300 £1,597

A Rookwood pottery scenic vellum loving cup, initialled by Frederick Rothebusch, 1908, 7¼in. high. (Robt. W. Skinner Inc.) $1,000 £625

A Rookwood standard glaze pottery Indian portrait vase, decorated by Grace Young, date cypher for 1905, 30.5cm. high. (Christie's) $4,620 £3,000

ROYAL DUX

The Royal Dux Factory was started by E. Eichler in Dux, Bohemia, in 1860 and had an immediate success with its beautifully made portrait busts and ornate vases. Much of its output was exported to America and Australia where it enjoyed huge popularity.

Today's collectors are particularly fond of the elegant nymphs which were fashioned to drape themselves seductively around bowls or curved picture frames. Royal Dux porcelain is unglazed and its distinctive mark is its soft pastel tones of beige, pink and green. It is marked with an embossed pink triangle stamped Royal Dux Bohemia or E. for the initial of the proprietor in an oval surmounted by Royal Dux Bohemia.

A Royal Dux group of two figures in classical dress on oval base with red triangle mark no. 1980, 16½in. high. (Prudential Fine Art) $439 £230

Pair of Royal Dux figurines, flower girl carrying flower basket and boy with apron carrying basket, signed F. Otto, pink triangle to base. (Giles Haywood) $574 £350

A Royal Dux porcelain group of classical figures, the boy in wolf-skin, and girl wearing a gown, 26in. high. (Dacre, Son & Hartley) $1,094 £760

A Royal Dux bust, the young Art Nouveau maiden gazing to the left, raised pink triangle mark, 20in. high. (Christie's) $943 £660

Pair of Royal Dux figurines, signed F. Otto, pink triangle to base, 17in. high. (Giles Haywood) $574 £350

A Royal Dux pottery toilette mirror, depicting an Art Nouveau maiden. (Phillips) $1,091 £620

ROYAL DUX

A Royal Dux porcelain group of a lion, lioness and dead gazelle on rustic base, 19in. wide, no. 1600. (Dacre, Son & Hartley) $260 £250

Royal Dux 'Austria' Art Nouveau vase having fold-over leaf top, 14in. high. (Giles Haywood) $124 £65

A fine Royal Dux group of a classical Grecian horseman with his charges, 43cm. high, circa 1900. $625 £500

A Royal Dux gilt porcelain figure of a girl bather seated on a rock, 19in. high. (Dacre, Son & Hartley) $450 £360

A Royal Dux porcelain figure group of a Dutch farm boy and girl, 30.5cm. high. (H. Spencer & Sons) $275 £220

A large Royal Dux figure of a peasant boy leaning on a wooden pitcher, 59cm. high. $468 £375

Large Royal Dux group with camel and Bedouin seated on its back, 19¾in. high. (Reeds Rains) $835 £580

An Art Nouveau Royal Dux figural vase modelled as a tree trunk with a maiden climbing around the side, 46cm. high. (Phillips) $364 £270

A Royal Dux Art Nouveau conch shell group with three water nymphs in relief, 17½in. high. (Reeds Rains) $676 £470

ROYALTY BOOKS

The public fascination with the Royal Family that started during the reign of Victoria meant there has been a rush of books about royalty and a year does not pass without at least one new publication appearing. Some of the best known are the books written about the little Princesses Elizabeth and Margaret Rose by their governess Crawfie. She alienated herself from the Royal Family for writing them but made a fortune and collectors today seek out copies of her anodyne outpourings. Also popular with collectors are the many books of photographs of the Royal Family and editions of Queen Victoria's own journals, some of which are illustrated by her drawings. Books range from sweetly sentimental about the Queen Mother to the more critical in which are included the many books written about the Duke of Windsor and Mrs Simpson. Each eminent member of the Royal Family is always recorded in at least one weighty biography and there have been many about Edward VII who provided his biographers with a considerable amount of incident and colour.

King Albert's Book, 1914, published for the Daily Telegraph Belgian Fund. $25 £15

The Prince of Wales Book published for St Dunstans, 1920. $9 £5

The Queen's Book of the Red Cross, 1939. $10 £6

The Queen's Gift Book, in aid of the Queen Mary Convalescent Auxiliary Hospitals. $25 £15

V.R.I. Her Life and Empire, published 1904. $18 £10

The Princess Elizabeth Gift Book, in aid of the Princess Elizabeth of York Hospital for Children. $20 £12

The Coronation of Her Majesty
Queen Elizabeth II approved
souvenir programme. $3.50 £2

His Majesty The King
1910-1935, published by
Associated Newspapers Ltd.
$12 £7

The Prince of Wales Eastern
Book published by Hodder
& Stoughton, 1922. $14 £8

Approved souvenir programme
of the wedding of The Princess
Margaret and Mr Antony
Armstrong-Jones. $3.50 £2

Our King and Queen and the
Royal Princesses, published by
Odhams. $5 £3

The First Family, a diary of
the Royal Year by L. A.
Nickolls, 1950. $5 £3

The Queen's Christmas Carol,
1905, published on behalf of
Queen Alexandra's Fund for
the Unemployed. $20 £12

Silver Wedding of George VI
and Queen Elizabeth. $7 £4

Princess Mary's Gift Book, in
aid of the Queen's Work for
Women Fund. $25 £15

Edward the Eighth — Our King. $18 £10

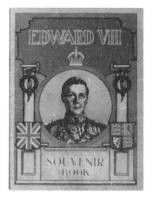

Edward VIII, Souvenir Book.
$5 £3

Souvenir programme of the Coronation of King George VI and Queen Elizabeth, 1937.
$3.50 £2

The Illustrated London News, Elizabeth II's Coronation, 1953. $7 £4

King George's Jubilee Trust, Official Programme of the Jubilee Procession. $5 £3

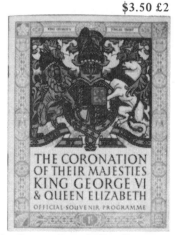

The Coronation of King George VI and Queen Elizabeth, published by Associated Newspapers, $9 £5

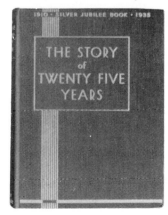

The Story of Twenty-Five Years, Silver Jubilee Book, 1935. $10 £6

Queen Victoria — A Personal Sketch by Mrs Oliphant, 1900.
$10 £6

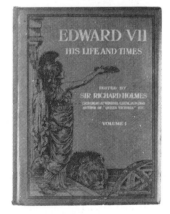

Edward VII, His Life and Times, edited by Sir Richard Holmes, two volumes. $35 £20

RUSKIN POTTERY

The Ruskin Pottery of West Smethwick, near Birmingham, was started by William Howson Taylor in 1898 and thrived until his death in 1935. He named his pottery after John Ruskin, who he much admired, and it was famous for the beautiful afterglaze on earthenware which Taylor was able to produce. Unfortunately only he knew the secret of those glazes and before he died he destroyed his worknotes. The products of the Ruskin Pottery are very varied ranging from bowls, vases and eggcups to hatpins. Various marks were employed usually incorporating the name Taylor or Ruskin and a device of a pair of scissors which was scratched or painted on the base. Some pieces were dated.

A Ruskin high-fired transmutation glazed vase, 1911, 38cm. high. (Christie's)
$594 £410

A Ruskin flambe vase, mallet-shaped with blue and red speckled glaze, 1909, 17.4cm. high. (Christie's)
$236 £162

A large Ruskin high fired transmutation glaze vase and matching circular stepped stand, England, circa 1930, 36cm. high including stand. (Christie's)
$346 £237

A Ruskin high fired shaped cylindrical vase, 1925, 23.6cm. high. (Christie's)
$600 £400

A large Ruskin low-fired crystalline glaze vase of swollen cylindrical shape, England, 1926, 41.5cm. high. (Christie's)
$283 £194

A Ruskin high fired transmutation glaze vase, England, 1933, 21cm. high. (Christie's)
$283 £194

SAMPLERS

From the early 18th century young girls of leisured families were set to make a sampler when they were around ten years old as a sort of "apprentice piece" to show their developing skill as needlewomen. The samplers were designed to display the various stitches which the girl could execute and they were laid out in stylised form incorporating the letters of the alphabet, the maker's name and age, sometimes the place where it was made and a stitched representation of the owner's home. Occasionally lines from hymns or edifying mottos were also included. Samplers have a refreshing simplicity and appeal and are often treasured as relics of a particular family. The custom of making samplers ended around the time of the First World War though in recent years needlework sampler kits are being produced again.

Late 18th century framed needlework sampler, by Charlotte Richardson 13 years, Dec. 1786, American, 17 x 20in. (Robt. W. Skinner Inc.) $1,500 £937

A needlework sampler 'Susannah Styles finished this work in the 10 years of her age 1800', worked in silk yarns on wool ground, 13in. square. (Robt. W. Skinner Inc.) $1,000 £595

Sampler with alphabet verse and figures of plants and birds, dated 1824, 17 x 13in. (Lots Road Chelsea Auction Galleries) $501 £300

A needlework sampler by Mary Ann Cash, 1801, the linen ground worked in coloured silks, 37 x 30cm. (Phillips) $356 £200

A 17th century needlwork sampler by Anna Stone, the linen ground worked in pink, green and blue silk threads, 41 x 19cm. (Phillips) $1,176 £700

Needlework sampler, 'Betsey Stevens, her sampler wrought in 10th year of her age AD 1796', silk yarns on linen, 15 x 16in. (Robt. W. Skinner Inc.) $3,000 £1,685

317

Needlework sampler, silk yarns worked on ivory linen ground fabric, by 'Harriatt Shoveller, 1799', England, 12½ x 17in. (Robt. W. Skinner Inc.) $1,600 £1,118

Framed needlework pictorial sampler, inscribed 'Harroit Hoyle, Aged 21, 1834', 24 x 24in. (Robt. W. Skinner Inc.) $2,200 £1,538

Needlework spot sampler, Germany, 1759, vivid polychrome silk yarns on natural linen fabric, 12 x 21½in. (Robt. W. Skinner Inc.) $2,500 £1,748

Needlework sampler, 'Sally Butman her work in the 11th year of her age, 1801', Marblehead, Mass., 10.3/8 x 12½in. (Robt. W. Skinner Inc.) $15,000 £10,489

Needlework sampler, England, dated 1826, silk yarns in a variety of stitches on natural linen ground, 13 x 15½in. (Robt. W. Skinner Inc.) $700 £489

A needlework picture, by Mary Fentun, dated 1789, 21¼ x 16½in. (Christie's) $2,860 £2,001

An early 19th century needlework sampler by S. Parker, aged 14 years 1817, 37 x 32cm. (Phillips) $862 £560

An early 19th century needlework sampler, by Elizabeth Campling, aged 12 years, the linen ground embroidered in silks, 31.5 x 34.5cm. (Phillips) $338 £220

A nicely worked needlework sampler, by Sarah Iesson, the linen ground embroidered in silks, 33 x 21cm. (Phillips) $708 £460

Late 18th century needlework sampler, worked in silk yarns of gold, light blue, red, brown, ivory and black on natural linen, 7 x 10½in. (Robt. W. Skinner Inc.) $3,300 £2,307

A needlework sampler worked in silk yarns on natural coloured linen, 'Susanah Cadmore, 1805', 12½ x 13¼in. (Robt. W. Skinner Inc.) $500 £349

A sampler 'Wrought by Harriot Wethrell May Aged 10 years, Plymouth Massachusetts, June 10th 1830', 16¼ x 16½in. (Robt. W. Skinner Inc.) $1,900 £1,130

Late 18th century Spanish needlework sampler with silk embroidered stylised floral and geometric designs, 15½ x 18½in. (Robt. W. Skinner Inc.) $300 £209

A needlework family record, silk yarns in shades of blue, green, pale peach, ivory and black on natural linen ground fabric, 18¼ x 14½in. (Robt. W. Skinner Inc.) $900 £629

A needlwork sampler, by 'Sarah Pell, Febrery 21, 1830', wool yarns on white wool fabric, 12½ x 16in. (Robt. W. Skinner Inc.) $850 £594

An early 19th century needlework sampler by Elizabeth Bushby, March 6, aged 10 years, 1822, 45 x 42cm. (Phillips) $523 £340

Framed needlework pictorial verse sampler, by Eliza. A. Machett, New York, March 22, 1828, 16½ x 16in. (Robt. W. Skinner Inc.) $500 £333

Needlework sampler, by 'Elizabeth Tonnecliff, her work done in 1791', silk yarns, 16 x 20¼in. (Robt. W. Skinner Inc.) $8,700 £6,083

SARDINE DISHES

In Victorian and Edwardian times people sat down to large afternoon teas and one of their favourite snacks was tinned sardines. Refined families did not like the idea of a vulgar tin appearing on their tea table so they devised the practice of having the maid put the sardine tin in a pretty box which was specially made for the purpose. The boxes were manufactured by most major British potteries and in large numbers in Czechoslovakia. They were sometimes decorated with flowers or fruit but most commonly with fish. Though most of the boxes were made of pottery with pottery lids some were made of porcelain or cut glass and a few had silver lids. Fine examples of sardine boxes from Spode or Minton can fetch as much as £450 today.

 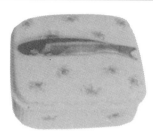 

Pottery bamboo design sardine box with woven pattern on lid, made in Alloa, Scotland by Waverley. $125 £70

Fluted porcelain sardine box decorated with violets and gilding with a finely painted fish. $115 £65

Gilded porcelain sardine box with water weed pattern, English, unmarked. $105 £60

Cut glass sardine box with silver plated stand and lid, unmarked. $175 £100

Czechoslovakian porcelain sardine box with a green marbleized effect and a good painted fish. $280 £160

English porcelain sardine box with a finely painted fish with red fins, complete with silver plated stand and fork. $245 £140

Apricot glaze sardine box marked Flos Maron, with pierced silver plated stand. $245 £140

Fluted white porcelain sardine box with a finely painted fish, marked with an eagle, on plated stand. $435 £250

Gilded pottery sardine box with woven sides and decorated lid embellished with water lilies and reeds, unmarked, probably English. $125 £70

SCRIMSHAW

This strange word is thought to be derived from a surname — perhaps of a particularly artistic sailor — because it is a general term applied to the works of art or handicrafts made by seamen on long voyages. The most common application of scrimshaw was fine engraving on bone or ivory which was done by sailors in 19th century whaling ships. They used whale's teeth or whalebone as their medium and some of their art work was very skilled. They darkened the incised detail with black ink or soot. The usual subjects chosen for illustration were life at sea or depictions of Eskimo life, fishing and trapping, which they witnessed on their voyages. A few scrimshaw pieces have erotic carvings. Scrimshaw work either stands on its own or is incorporated into gongs, inkstands and boxes.

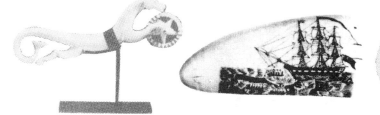

A rare Unicorn Crimper made of scrimshaw. $18,000 £12,675

Mid 19th century finely engraved whale's tooth scrimshaw, 6in. long. $785 £450

A mid 19th century scrimshaw decorated panbone, 10in. wide. $1,000 £600

Mid 19th century scrimshawed whale's tooth, English, 16cm. long. $350 £200

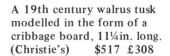

A 19th century walrus tusk modelled in the form of a cribbage board, 11¼in. long. (Christie's) $517 £308

Mid 19th century English whale's tooth scrimshaw, 5½in. high. $455 £260

Pair of 19th century American whale's tooth scrimshaw, 6in. high. $1,250 £725

American 19th century engraved scrimshaw whale's tooth, 6½in. long. (Christie's) $575 £330

An unusual pair of scrimshawed whale's teeth, circa 1840, 8in. high. $1,200 £700

SEALS

Seals were used for closing letters and were symbols of authenticity, like a personal signature because they nearly always incorporated the owner's initials or family crest. They could be worn hanging from a watch chain or as a ring. Larger seals were kept in a writing desk. These desk seals from the 17th and 18th centuries were shaped like mushrooms with wooden handles and a carved silver seal set in the end of the stem. More sophisticated examples were slimmed down and had the handles decorated with semi-precious or precious stones.

A Tiffany sterling silver sealing wax set, N.Y., circa 1891-1902, 8½in. sq., wt.approx. 20 troy oz. (Robt. W. Skinner Inc.)
$800 £432

Fob seals were great favourites with the well-to-do business men from the Victorian and Edwardian eras. They were made of gold, silver or silver gilt, had ornate handles and were sometimes studded with gems. A cluster of fob seals was the mark of a great nob in the mid 18th century.

Seals are still worn as signet rings and have been used for that purpose since Roman times. Designs are very varied. As well as coats of arms or initials, there are self portraits, pictures of favourite deities in the case of the Romans, or symbols of clubs and affiliations. A large number of Masonic signet rings can be found.

A gold mounted bloodstone table seal, the stem formed as a hand, 1830, 3.5/8in. high. (Christie's)
$1,982 £1,296

A two-colour gold and hardstone articulated triple desk seal by Faberge, St. Petersburg, 1908-17, 9.1cm.
$5,224 £3,603

A 19th century Swiss gold musical seal with chased foliage handle. (Christie's)
$1,573 £1,100

An early 19th century English three-colour gold fob seal, 5.3cm. $652 £450

A gold desk seal with handle modelled in ivory as a hand clasping a baton with bloodstone or cornelian seal ends, circa 1830, 2¾in. long. (Christie's) $2,557 £1,728

A two-colour gold and amethyst table seal, the citrine matrix with crest and initials, circa 1830, 2¾in. high. (Christie's)
$1,900 £1,242

Mid 18th century English gold fob seal, with pierced scroll handle, 2.7cm.
$261 £180

Early 19th century Swiss gold musical fob seal with central winder, 4.2cm. high.
$870 £600

Late 18th century English gold double-sided swivel fob seal of oval form, 5.3cm.
$652 £450

Early 19th century English gold fob seal of large size, oval with reeded and fluted mount, 5cm.
$696 £480

Early 19th century Swiss gold and enamel musical fob seal, 4.2cm.
$1,174 £810

An English gold fob seal of oblong form, with plain foiled citrine matrix, 4cm., circa 1835.
$369 £255

Early 19th century English gold fob seal with plain oblong bloodstone matrix, 3.8cm.
$478 £380

A gold double-sided swivel fob seal with scrolled wire-work mount in the form of two serpents, 5cm., circa 1810.
$1,654 £1,141

An English gold fob seal with armorial-engraved oblong citrine matrix, 4.1cm., circa 1835.
$435 £300

SERIES WARE

Standard pottery shapes decorated with designs on a specific theme were 'series ware' which was produced in large numbers by the Doulton Potteries on the suggestion of Charles J. Noke who joined the company in 1889. He realised the sales potential of attractive eye catching designs on a special theme which could be printed on a great variety of pots. In order to keep up public interest and encourage collecting Doulton changed the theme every year until 1939. Designs were transfer printed onto refined earthenware or bone china and hand-coloured which gave the technique the name of "print and tint". The first series issued was "Isthmian Pilgrims" of 1909; the Dickens series; "Gleaners and Gypsies" and "Under the Greenwood Tree".

Robert Burns portrait plaque with his cottage in the background, 10¼in. diam. $50 £28

Oliver Twist jug designed by C. J. Noke, depicting 'Fagin and Bumble', D5617. $115 £65

A Royal Doulton Cecil Aldin Series ware jardiniere, the decoration from the 'Old English Scenes', 18cm. high. $300 £170

Royal Doulton two-handled vase, designed by Charles Crombie, depicting two golfers and a caddie, 8in. high. $395 £225

'Nightwatchman', a Series ware jug by C. J. Noke, 8½in. high, D1198, 1903. $65 £38

A Jacobean jug 'Ye Old Belle' depicting a serving wench and two cavaliers, 6½in. high. $75 £42

Old Moreton Hall Series teapot, 4½in. high, circa 1915, depicting Queen Elizabeth I outside. $95 £55

Early Motoring Series titled 'Deaf', 10½in. diam., circa 1906. $125 £70

'Gallant Fishers' teapot, by Izaak Walton, 6in. high, circa 1906. $95 £55

Huntsman Series water jug, 11in. high, circa 1906, depicting two huntsmen at the inn. $77 £44

The Gleaners, Series ware sandwich tray. $55 £30

Dickens' ware 'Friar' shape jug depicting 'Poor Joe', 4¾in. high. $50 £28

Gleaners and Gypsies Series vase, 7½in. high, circa 1909, depicting a gypsy and child. $75 £42

Series ware rack plate 'Mother Kangaroo and Toby', 10½in. diam. $18 £10

Oliver Twist tankard in low relief, designed by C. J. Noke, issued 1949-1960. $105 £60

SEVRES

The prestigious Sevres pottery was started at Vincennes by King Louis XV of France in 1756 and from the beginning its products were of exquisite quality and style. In 1876 the factory removed to St Cloud where there is today a fine museum which displays some of the beautiful things made there since the pottery's inception.

Sevres technicians were always eager to experiment with formulae and pastes and they were able to devise a kaolin based paste which closely resembled the ancient and secret Chinese formula. They also produced a silicate paste which made it possible to provide a magnificent range of colours for decoration of the pieces. Some of the very best artists in France worked for Sevres over the years. The sculptor Rodin was one of their modellers and so was A. Leonard who made lovely unglazed figures.

One of two Sevres two-handled feuille-de-choux seaux a bouteille, with painter's marks of Tardy and Tandart, 26cm. wide. (Christie's) $1,837 £1,100

One of a pair of late 19th century Sevres pattern royal blue-ground oviform vases and fixed covers with gilt bronze mounts, 42cm. high. (Christie's) $1,116 £770

A Sevres rose pompadour square tray, blue interlaced L marks enclosing the date letter E for 1757 and painter's mark of Noel, 14.5cm. sq. (Christie's)
$6,492 £3,850

A Sevres bleu nouveau baluster milk jug, blue interlaced L mark enclosing the date letter q for 1769, and painter's mark B, 12cm. high. (Christie's)$613 £432

A pair of Sevres-pattern bleu-celeste ground ormolu mounted baluster vases, circa 1860, 60cm. high. (Christie's)
$3,110 £2,160

A jewelled Sevres cylindrical cup and saucer, gilt interlaced L marks and painter's marks LG of Le Guay, circa 1783. (Christie's) $12,150 £8,100

A Sevres hop-trellis fluted cup and saucer, circa 1765. (Christie's) $475 £330

A Sevres bust of Napoleon as First Consul, dated 1802, 29cm. high. (Christie's) $1,093 £810

Late 19th century Sevres pattern gilt bronze mounted two-handled centrepiece, 27.5cm. wide. (Christie's) $998 £605

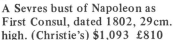

A Sevres hard-paste green-ground soup tureen and cover, gilt interlaced L marks and HP mark of Prevost, circa 1785, 30cm. wide. (Christie's) $1,584   £1,100

A Sevres-pattern porcelain and ormolu mounted mantel clock, imitation interlaced L and initial marks, circa 1880, 61.5cm. high. (Christie's) $3,732   £2,592

A Sevres hard-paste cup and saucer, blue crowned inter-laced L mark enclosing date letter U for 1773. (Christie's) $554 £385

A Sevres ornithological cir-cular sugar bowl and cover, blue interlaced L marks enclosing the date letter U for 1773 and painter's mark of Evans, 11.5cm. high. (Christie's) $766 £540

A Sevres white biscuit group of Le Valet de Chien modelled by Blondeau after Oudry, circa 1776, 30.5cm. long.(Christie's) $1,749 £1,296

A Sevres plate, 23.5cm. diam., LL mark enclosing date letters EE for 1782, painter's marks for Capelle and probably Huny. (Phillips) $6,847 £4,100

SHAKER

This simple, sturdy furniture was produced in the late 18th and early 19th century by the Shaker sect in New England and New York State, originally for use by community members. Later, however, chair-making in particular developed into quite an industry supplying neighbouring towns. The pieces were painted (usually dark red) but undecorated. Most typical items are rocking chairs and slat back chairs designed to be hung on a wall rail. Production declined after 1860.

A Shaker splint sewing basket, probably Enfield, Connecticut, 19th century, 15½in. diam. (Christie's) $880 £539

Early 19th century Shaker pine commode with hinged slant lid opening to reveal a shelf interior, 18in. wide. (Robt. W. Skinner Inc.)
$4,500 £2,678

A Shaker miniature lidded pail with strap handle and two fingers, 2.3/8in. high. (Christie's) $550 £332

A 19th century Shaker cherry hanging cupboard, 24in. wide.
$3,500 £2,000

Shaker maple tilter ladderback sidechair with rush seat, circa 1875, 39½in. high. (Robt. W. Skinner Inc.)
$600 £375

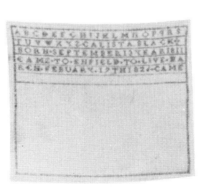

Early 19th century unfinished Shaker needlework sampler on natural linen, 8½ x 10¼in.
$1,300 £750

19th century three-tier Shaker spool rack, 7½in. high.
$1,300 £750

Painted staved wooden cheese/butter box, possibly Shaker, circa 1830, 6½in. diam. (Robt. W. Skinner Inc.) $475 £368

Shaker butternut sewing box, the drawers with ebonised diamond escutcheon and turned ivory pull, New England, circa 1820, 7½in. wide. (Robt. W. Skinner Inc.) $7,750 £5,166

A 19th century oval putty grained Shaker box, America, 5.7/8in. long. (Robt. W. Skinner Inc.) $3,300 £1,964

Shaker birch chest-of-drawers, probably New England, circa 1840, 38½in. wide. (Robt. W. Skinner Inc.) $1,100 £769

A Shaker painted pine and poplar cupboard, possibly N.Y., circa 1830, 28in. wide, 86¾in. high. (Robt. W. Skinner Inc.) $3,500 £2,083

American 19th century Shaker cherry drop-leaf table. $3,500 £2,000

Early 19th century Shaker cherrywood stand, 60cm. high. $13,000 £7,500

Early 19th century Shaker tiger maple and cherry trestle base dining table, Canterbury, New England, 71¼in. wide. (Robt. W. Skinner Inc.) $86,000 £51,190

Early 19th century Shaker pine and maple work table, probably New England, 36in. high. (Robt. W. Skinner Inc.) $2,000 £1,398

SHAVING CREAM POT LIDS

Shaving cream was sold in ceramic pots with decorated lids during the 19th and early 20th centuries. Some of the lids bore the names of famous hotels, distinguished barbers, or chemists like Boots, while others bore pictures of sporting events. Racing or cricket were particular favourites. They were made by the big potteries of the time and the fancier ones usually came from Doulton. The lids sell today for between £5 and £300 each depending on the condition and quality of the decoration. Lids with coloured scenes sell for the most. One or two were printed with recommendations from famous people and several claimed to be used by Prince Albert. The retailing of shaving cream in those attractive pots ended around 1920.

Army & Navy Toilet Club, The United Service Shaving Cream. $45 £25

Violet Shaving Cream, Prepared by C. & J. Montgomery of Belfast, a rare Irish lid. $45 £25

S. Maw, Son & Thompson, Ambrosial Shaving Cream, Perfumed with Almonds, small size. $45 £25

Dale's Almond Shaving Cream, Prepared by John T. Dale, Stirling, Scotland. $45 £25

Erasmic Shaving Cream, lid complete with matching pot. $45 £25

Muire Bouquet Shaving Cream, 'Does not dry on the skin', the French name had sales appeal. $60 £35

Fred Diemer, Superior Shaving Cream, an old lid from the City of London. $30 £18

Henri Freres, Creme D'Amandes, Ambrosial, a French style lid with an attractive trade mark. $60 £35

John Gosnell & Co. Ambrosial Shaving Cream, an early lid. $85 £50

Low, Son & Haydon, Almond
Shaving Cream, Strand, London.
$55 £30

Blondeay & Cie, Premier
Vinolia Shaving Cream for
Sensitive Skins, circa 1920.
$45 £25

Boots Creme D'Amande for
Shaving, probably the most
common shaving cream lid.
$14 £8

Professor Browne's
Luxuriant Shaving Cream,
Fenchurch Street, London.
$45 £25

Carter's Imperial Shaving
Cream, an unusual lid with
white lettering in a black
background. $70 £40

H. Osborne, Cream of
Almonds, Byram Toilet Club,
Huddersfield. $30 £18

Ch. Jaschke's Shaving Cream,
Regent St., London, decorated
with a gold band. $35 £20

Roger & Gallet, Creme de
Savon, a French lid and pot
printed in green. $25 £15

Spratt's Perfect Shaving Cream
a small London lid complete
with directions. $35 £20

F. S. Cleaver's Saponaceous
Shaving Cream, from the
'Inventor of the Celebrated
Honey Soap', London.$70 £40

Creme de Savon, by F. Millot
of Paris, a plain but rare
French lid. $35   £20

Gay & Sons Celebrated
Shaving Cream, London.
$60 £35

SHAVING MUGS

Before electric razors there was a great ritual involved in the act of shaving and men mixed up their lather in big shaving mugs which were often decorated with pictures or inscribed with the owner's name. Most of the mugs were made of pottery but richer people often owned them in silver or porcelain. There were also a few mugs made of brass or copper. Some of the rarer mugs had jutting out lips for water, soap, a brush and the razor and they were called four in ones; there were also three in ones but the majority were simply large mugs like big beakers. French shaving mugs were always taller and thinner than those used in England. Shaving mugs can often be picked up quite cheaply but care should be taken not to buy reproductions. Genuine old mugs feel heavy to the hand and have worn bases. Don't buy mugs that are chipped even if they are old. Among the rarest shaving mugs are crested ones made by the Goss pottery which can sell for around £60 each.

Swan shaped shaving mug with gilt edging, circa 1900. $55 £30

Goss shaving mug with colour transfer of 'The Gibbet Cross, Minehead'. $70 £40

Pearl lustre shaving mug, on four scroll feet, bearing the crest of New Brighton. $35 £40

Large, late 19th century, shaving mug with floral decoration and gilt edging. $45 £25

Tall French shaving mug known as a brush vase with gilt and floral decoration, circa 1890. $70 £40

Large, late 19th century, shaving mug with floral decoration and unusual double handle. $70 £40

Torquay Ware shaving mug in brown and cream bearing the motto 'Better do one thing, Than dream all things!' $55 £30

Three in one shaving mug with a place for water, the soap and a brush, circa 1900. $55 £30

An interesting signed shaving mug, G. Wiegand, with floral decoration. $80 £45

SHAVING MUGS

Victorian shaving mug with hand-painted floral decoration and gilt edging. $70 £40

Large late 19th century bowl shaped shaving mug with floral decoration and shaped handle. $45 £25

Late Victorian shaving mug decorated with floral sprays. $35 £20

Personalised shaving mug in white with gold lettering, 'Thomas Ricks, Maskelyne, Pontypool, 1908'. $85 £50

Late Victorian pewter shaving mug with embossed floral decoration. $95 £55

Souvenir Coronation shaving mug for H.M. King George VI and Queen Elizabeth. $45 £25

Heavy Victorian plain white shaving mug. $35 £20

'Glimpses of the East', a multi-coloured shaving mug, circa 1920's. $45 £25

Late Victorian shaving mug with fine floral decoration and dark blue frieze. $60 £35

Elegantly shaped white shaving mug decorated with pink floral sprays. $35 £20

Elegantly shaped white shaving mug decorated with pink floral sprays. $35 £20

Souvenir Coronation shaving mug for George V and Queen Mary. $45 £25

SHELLS

Among the favourite souvenirs of distant places for travellers in the last century were exotic shells. They treasured the beautiful abalone or mother of pearl shell, the Queen Conch and the magnificent Nautilus. Rare examples like Conus Gloriamarus changed hands for considerable sums even in Victorian times and today will cost a collector several hundred pounds. Some people restrict their collections to only one type of shell and try to find it in various sizes which records its growth development. Victorians were great lovers of all kinds of shells and ladies set mirrors and made shell pictures out of the small, prettily coloured ones found on British beaches. There was also jewellery made of shells. Another type of shell that makes an interesting collection are examples of shell money for shells were used as coinage among tribes in America, Asia, Africa and Australia. The commonest type was the cowrie shell which is abundant in the Indian Ocean and was used as money in Bengal, Western Africa and New Guinea where it was tied in lengths of 40 or 100.

Early 20th century shell art picture frame. $70 £40

Late 19th century Barbadian pair of sailor's Valentine shell pictures, 9in. wide. $717 £495

Early 20th century shell art pin cushion in the form of an anchor. $35 £20

A fine golden cowrie shell from the Fiji Islands. $525 £300

Shell art jewellery box with wooden lining. $50 £30

The infernal harp shell from the Fringing Reef, Mauritius. $260 £150

A Solomon Islands shell ornament, Kap Kap, the tridacna clam shell base with turtle shell disc attached, 11.7cm. diam. (Phillips) $691 £380

A replica of an example of scrimshaw presented to Queen Victoria on the launching of 'The Great Britain', 21.5cm. long. $1,400 £800

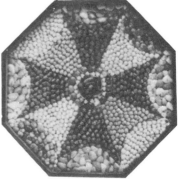

One of three 19th century shell pictures in octagonal wooden frames, 11in. wide. (Lots Road Chelsea Auction Galleries) $480 £300

SHIPS FIGUREHEADS

Ships' figureheads were originally designed to strike terror into the hearts of opponents—imagine the dragon prows of Viking longships materialising through the mists! Later, they adopted a gentler image, often comprising well-endowed female figures and seen rather as good luck mascots, though some fierce-looking birds and animals did perpetuate the aggressive aspect. When ships were broken up, figureheads were often kept for sentimental reasons or transferred to new craft, which is probably why so many survive today.

A 19th century painted and carved pine eagle, possibly taken from the stern of a ship, America, 28in. long. (Robt. W. Skinner Inc.)
$1,900   £1,130

A carved and painted figure of Victory, American, circa 1880, 69½in. high. (Robt. W. Skinner Inc.) $4,000 £2,777

Early 19th century carved and polychrome figurehead, New England, 23in. high. (Robt. W. Skinner Inc.)
$3,500 £1,966

A 19th century English carved oak ship's figurehead, carved in the form of a lion's head, 109cm. high.
$829 £572

A carved and painted ship's head figure, modelled as a partially clad mermaid, 38in. high. (Christie's)
$1,320 £744

A 19th century carved and polychrome allegorical figure, America, 52in. high. (Robt. W. Skinner Inc.) $5,500 £3,089

English 19th century carved and polychromed ship's figurehead, the bearded figure wearing a toga, 188cm. high. $3,509 £2,420

SILHOUETTES

Before the era of photography, if you couldn't afford a portrait, you might sit for a silhouettist. These little black and white likenesses are named after Etienne de Silhouette, a French politician who, it seems, believed in cutting everything down to essentials. They first appeared around 1750, and were done either freehand or by tracing the shadow of a profile on a piece of black paper. Later, more sophisticated techniques developed. The art flourished too among amateurs, and was regarded as quite a drawing-room accomplishment.

Augustin Edouart, a full length group silhouette of the Lambe family, Hogarth frame, 12in. high. (Christie's)
$1,514 £935

A silhouette of a young woman in original gold leaf frame, America, circa 1830, image 7¼ x 5in. (Robt. W. Skinner Inc.)
$3,115 £1,780

A full-length profile of William, 1st Marquess of Lansdowne by Wm. Hamlet the elder, inscribed and dated 1785 on the reverse, 8¾in. rectangular.
$1,730 £990

A full-length profile of Wm. Pitt, by Wm. Wellings, signed and dated 1781, rectangular 10½in.
$4,620 £2,640

A coloured profile of Lieut. Robert Conry by Charles or John Buncombe, circa 1810, oval 3¼in. $805 £460

A lady by J. Thomason, circa 1795, in profile to sinister, painted on plaster, oval 8.6cm. $610 £350

A coloured profile of an officer of the Life Guards called Nunn Davie, by C. Buncombe, circa 1795, oval 4¾in. $1,575 £900

SILHOUETTES

A bronzed profile of a lady by John Field, signed Miers and Field, circa 1810, 5.7cm. oval. **$1,730 £990**

A bronzed profile of an officer of the Light Dragoons called George Baker by John Field, circa 1810, oval 3in. **$1,120 £640**

Miss Mary Ann Lovell as a child, by W. Phelps, 1786, painted on plaster, oval 8.5cm. **$1,640 £935**

A full-length profile of a young lady of the Gosset Family, circa 1780, rect-angular 11½in. **$3,750 £2,145**

A young lady by J. Thomason, in profile to dexter, painted on plaster, circa 1790, oval 8.5cm. **$575 £330**

A full-length profile of John, Earl of St. Vincent, by Wm. Wellings, signed and dated 1783, oval 11¼in. **$5,000 £2,860**

A lady, in profile to dexter, painted on plaster, circa 1795, oval 4in. **$385 £220**

Isaac Taylor III, a family conversation group, silhouette painted on glass, 12.5/8in. high. (Christie's) **$1,540 £880**

A gentleman by J. Thomason, inscribed 1797 on the reverse, oval 12.7cm., with verre eglo-mise border. **$575 £330**

A rectangular silhouette on paper by John Buncombe, of Catherine Reynolds of Newport, circa 1785, 90 x 70mm. (Phillips) $226 £150

A rectangular conversation piece by Wm. Welling, of a husband and wife taking tea, signed and dated 1874, 280 x 380mm. (Phillips) $4,832 £3,200

A gentleman standing full-length profile, by Augustin Edouart, cut-out on card, signed and dated 1836, 10¾in. high. (Christie's) $495 £324

A full-length profile of a family group, by Augustin Edouart, signed and dated 1825, cut-outs on card, 13in. high. (Christie's) $1,573 £1,100

Pair of early 20th century silhouettes, 'The Bull Fighters', by Wilhelm Hunt Diederich, 9½ x 13in. (Robt. W. Skinner Inc.) $450 £315

An oval black silhouette by John Buncombe, of a lady, circa 1800, 95mm. high. (Phillips) $143 £95

Pair of early 19th century bronzed silhouettes by F. Frith, signed and dated 1844, 10½ x 8½in. (Parsons, Welch & Cowell) $512 £320

A gentleman profile to left, by John Miers, on plaster, oval 3½in. high. (Christie's) $131 £86

SIGNED PHOTOGRAPHS

At first glance signed photographs would seem to be an ideal subject for collection. Unless they are really rare and completely authenticated, however, they are unlikely to be worth a great deal. Press offices could have a small army of employees engaged in forging stars' signatures on photographs for avid fans, and now machines exist which can turn out countless numbers of what is apparently the real thing. It is therefore always worthwhile to look for unusual examples and establish provenance.

Louis Bleriot (John Wilson)
$220 £125

Louis Pasteur (John Wilson)
$1,300 £750

Ulysses S. Grant (John Wilson)
$2,100 £1,200

Bernard Law Montgomery
(John Wilson) $130 £75

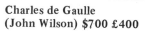

Charles de Gaulle
(John Wilson) $700 £400

Robert Browning (John Wilson)
$1,000 £600

Sir E. H. Shackleton
(John Wilson) $435 £250

Signed photograph of Bernard Law
Montgomery with Eisenhower.
(John Wilson) $210 £120

Robert E. Lee (John Wilson)
$2,100 £1,200

Sir Winston Spencer Churchill,
with Montgomery.
(John Wilson) $2,200 £1,250

Rudyard Kipling (John Wilson) $960 £550

Walt Whitman (John Wilson)
$960 £550

Haakon VII (and family)
(John Wilson) $350 £200

Noel Coward (John Wilson) $150 £85

SNUFF BOTTLES

The Chinese carried their snuff in delicate bottles about two and a half inches high and made of materials like ivory, jade, agate, bronze, porcelain or glass. When they were made of glass they were generally carved out of a solid piece instead of being blown. The snuff bottle was also used in Europe from the 17th century onwards and some of the most precious are in porcelain or carved hardstone. The mark of top quality is a small neck aperture and a large interior, showing the skill of the craftsman who made the bottle.

This is true also of glass bottles, which were usually carved out of a solid piece as opposed to being blown.

Late 18th/early 19th century pink glass snuff bottle, the rim with jewel festoons. (Christie's) $11,797 £7,150

An inside-painted and carved rock crystal snuff bottle, signed Ye Zhongsan and dated 1933. (Christie's) $1,179 £715

An inside-painted rock crystal snuff bottle with flaring sides by Ye Zhongsan, signed and dated 1916. (Christie's) $2,722 £1,650

An enamelled copper European subject snuff bottle of bulbous pear shape, blue enamel Qianlong four-character mark and of the period. (Christie's) $23,595 £14,300

A 19th century embellished copper snuff bottle of flattened baluster form, Qianlong four-character seal mark. (Christie's) $1,542 £935

Mid 19th century famille rose snuff bottle of pilgrim flask form, Qianlong six-character mark. (Christie's) $3,448 £2,090

A conglomerate agate snuff bottle, the stone of varied brown and ochre tones with striations of wood-grain patterns, mid Qing Dynasty. (Christie's) $2,722 £1,650

An inside-painted smoky crystal snuff bottle, probably by Ye Zhongsan, signed and dated 1925. (Christie's) $834 £506

An 18th century chalcedony agate snuff bottle, the surface carved in relief with three carp interlocked with a goldfish. (Christie's) $3,267 £1,980

An important and rare Famille Rose gilt-copper enamel snuff bottle, an oval panel inset with a European lady, 18th/19th century. (Christie's) $36,300 £22,000

A chalcedony agate snuff bottle, Suzhou School, the stone highly translucent. (Christie's) $27,225 £16,500

A 19th century moulded and reticulated porcelain snuff bottle, seal mark. (Christie's) $816 £495

Late 18th/early 19th century chloromelanite snuff bottle, the stone of dark spinach tone with emerald-green mottling. (Christie's) $3,630 £2,200

A 19th century banded agate snuff bottle, the translucent stone with attractive bold opaque ochre, white and brown striations. (Christie's) $635 £383

Late 18th/early 19th century glass overlay snuff bottle, the oviform body with a bubble-glass ground with blue overlay. (Christie's) $1,815 £1,100

A pale apple and emerald-green jade snuff bottle, late Qing Dynasty, wood stand. (Christie's)
$544 £330

Early/mid 19th century embellished pale celadon jade snuff bottle, fitted wood stand. (Christie's)
$1,452 £880

An 18th century glass snuff bottle of spherical shape, probably Beijing workshops. (Christie's) $2,722 £1,650

A coral snuff bottle of ovoid form, carved in relief with a profusion of jars, vases and pots, mid Qing Dynasty. (Christie's) $3,630 £2,200

Late 18th/early 19th century glass overlay snuff bottle, the dense snowstorm ground with blue overlay. (Christie's)
$453 £275

Late 18th/early 19th century shadow agate snuff bottle of ovoid form, the body well hollowed. (Christie's)
$2,178 £1,320

Late 18th/early 19th century shadow agate snuff bottle, well hollowed. (Christie's)
$4,356 £2,640

Early 19th century large white jade snuff bottle, signed Zigang. (Christie's)
$1,270 £770

An inside-painted glass portrait snuff bottle, by Ma Shaoxuan, signed and dated Winter 1909. (Christie's)
$18,150 £11,000

SNUFF BOXES

In past centuries, before the more general smoking of tobacco, all classes of people and both sexes took snuff. It was sold by specialist shops and weighed out on tiny scales. Because it was expensive, customers were anxious not to spill even a grain so they took care to keep their snuff in neat little boxes with tight fitting lids. The boxes were flourished in public every time a pinch of snuff was taken and came to be regarded as a sign of a person's affluence. There were snuff boxes made of gold and silver, tortoiseshell, papier mache, porcelain and enamel ware. Some had gilt interiors and they were nearly all decorated. Many were engraved with their owner's initials, set with semi precious stones or painted with attractive scenes. Some boxes bore pictures of famous castles painted by Nathaniel Mills and they are particularly desirable with collectors today. Sometimes the boxes were divided into two sections for different grades of snuff and a few had watches inset in them.

A small rectangular papier mache lacquer snuff box, the cover with painted portrait bust of Peter the Great, 19th century, 8.5cm. long. (Christie's) $892 £528

A Swiss oval gold and enamel snuff box, the hinged cover painted en grisaille with an allegorical trophy of the sciences, circa 1820, 2.7/8in. long. (Christie's) $8,019 £4,950

A Meissen circular snuff box and cover painted by B. G. Hauer, the interior of the base solid gilt, 1725-30, 7.5cm. diam. (Christie's) $27,604 £19,440

A Swiss oblong gold snuff box champleve enamelled in black, probably by G. L. Malacreda, Geneva, circa 1830, 2¾in. long. (Christie's) $4,752 £2,640

A Meissen rectangular snuff box and cover with contemporary two-colour gold mounts, circa 1750, 8.5cm. wide. (Christie's) $9,968 £7,020

A French oblong gold snuff box, the cover painted on enamel with a portrait of George Annesley, 3in. long. (Christie's) $8,910 £5,500

A mid 19th century Russian niello snuff box with foliate scroll decoration, maker's mark EE, Moscow, circa 1850. (Phillips) $447 £300

A Continental silver and tortoiseshell snuff box, unmarked probably French, circa 1820. (Christie's) $170 £115

An Austro-Hungarian rectangular snuff box, Vienna, 1852, 9cm. long. (Christie's) $125 £85

An early Victorian gilt lined, engine-turned box with applied cast floral thumbpiece, possibly by E. Edwards, London, 1839, 4¾in. long. (Christie's) $666 £450

A George IV rectangular snuff box, maker I.W.G., London, 1828, 3¼in. long. (Woolley & Wallis) $432 £360

A Victorian silver snuff box engraved on the cover with a view of Wricklemarsh, Blackheath, Kent, by Yapp & Woodward, Birmingham, 1845, 4¾in. long.(Christie's) $1,957 £1,350

A George III double section silver snuff box, maker's mark I.A., London, 1814, 3½ x 2½in. (Parsons, Welch & Cowell) $301 £215

A silver mounted stag's horn snuff mull with chained pricker and perforated stopper, circa 1700, 4¾in. wide. (Christie's) $466 £324

An early 18th century oval mounted tortoiseshell snuff box, impressed with a portrait of Queen Anne and signed 'OB' for Obrisset, circa 1710. (Phillips) $294 £200

A Scottish silver mounted cowrie shell snuff box, circa 1810. (Christie's)$162 £110

A Victorian rectangular silver snuff box, maker's mark F.M., Birmingham, 1854, 3½ x 2½in., 4½oz. (Parsons, Welch & Cowell) $287 £205

A French 19th century oblong snuff box, the base and sides nielloed with a chequered effect, 3½in. long. (Christie's) $518 £350

A George IV hunting scene snuff box, by John Jones III, 1824, 8.8cm. long. (Lawrence Fine Art) $814 £550

A late 17th/early 18th century oval tortoiseshell snuff box, the cover inlaid with chinoiserie scene. (Phillips) $176 £120

A French 19th century oblong gilt lined snuff box, the lid finely nielloed with 18th century hunting scene, with house and trees beyond, 3½in. long. (Christie's) $473 £320

An early Victorian castle top snuff box, by N. Mills, Birmingham, 1838, 7.2cm. long. (Lawrence Fine Art) $574 £396

A Victorian table snuff box, by Γ. Clark, Birmingham, 1843, 3¾in. wide, 4½oz. (Woolley & Wallis) $414 £280

A Swiss rectangular gold musical snuff box, circa 1830, 2¾in. long. (Christie's) $9,590 £6,480

A late 17th/early 18th century tortoiseshell snuff box inlaid in silver with a seascape, circa 1700. (Phillips) $323 £220

A George II silver gilt fox mask snuff box, by T. Phipps & E. Robinson, 1807, 3¼in., 3oz. 10dwt. (Christie's) $3,110 £2,160

An Italian rectangular silver gilt mounted hardstone snuff box, by Giacomo Sirletti, Rome, 1811-36, 3½in. long. (Christie's) $4,510 £3,132

George IV silver snuff box, London, 1825, 3¼in. wide, 5oz. (Hobbs & Chambers) $403 £280

A late 18th century Italian silver gilt circular snuff box, Venice, circa 1770, 5.6cm. diam. (Phillips) $372 £250

A Birmingham rectangular silver gilt snuff box, by Joseph Willmore, 1841, 3¾in. long. (Christie's) $1,278 £864

SPORTING STONEWARE

Stoneware is basically earthenware baked at a higher temperature, making it very tough and able to withstand decoration by polishing, staining, cutting into the ware itself or even through the glaze to the body (sgraffiato). Sporting stoneware was produced principally by Doulton, and comprises a range of mugs and jugs with relief figures of famous sportsmen. They were first introduced in 1880 and the figures are the work of John Broad, perhaps the best known being his W. G. Grace jug.

A silver mounted cycling jug and two beakers, circa 1900, the jug 8in. high, the beakers 4¾in. high. $315 £180

A golfing jug, sprigged in white with the panels of 'The Lost Ball', 'Putting' and 'Driving', impressed Lambeth mark, circa 1880, 20cm. high. $490 £280

A waisted mug applied with moulded white figures of a bowler, wicket keeper and a batsman, circa 1900, 6in. high. $210   £120

A cricketing jug, the moulded relief figures against the buff saltglaze ground within stylised floral borders outlined in white slip and coloured in blue and green, circa 1900, 9¼in. high. $300   £170

A silver mounted sporting tyg, circa 1900, 6in. high, the silver rim maker's mark H. W., Sheffield. $280 £160

A cricketer's mug applied with moulded white figures of a bowler, wicket keeper and a batsman, circa 1880, 15.5cm. high. $210 £120

A cricketing tyg, impressed registration mark and dated 1884, 6¼in. high. $420 £240

348

SPORTING STONEWARE

A mug with applied moulded golfing vignettes of 'The Drive', and 'The Lost Ball', circa 1900, 5in. high. $400 £230

A beaker with relief white figures of a shot putter, a runner and a long-jumper, the silver rim hallmarked 1900, 5in. high. $105   £60

A cycling mug with three applied white figures inscribed 'Military', 'Road' and 'Path', circa 1900, 4¾in. high.
$150   £85

A cycling jug with three white vignettes, inscribed 'Military', 'Road' and 'Path', circa 1900, 7¼in. high. $210 £120

A sporting jug with three moulded white vignettes, a man running, men playing football and a man putting the shot, circa 1900, 8in. high. $155 £90

A cricket jug with applied vignettes of a bowler, wicket keeper and a batsman, circa 1900, 7in. high. $280 £160

A rugby football jug with vignettes of two men kicking a ball, a scrummage and two of the men running with a ball, 1883, 7½in. high. $225 £130

A cricket mug with three applied figures of batsmen in high relief, registration mark of 1880, 5¼in. high.
$245 £140

A golfing jug with three applied white vignettes of 'The Lost Ball', 'Putting' and 'Driving', circa 1900, 7¾in. high.
$455   £260

Throughout the ages, stained glass, first produced by the Egyptians, has been one of the loveliest ways of adorning any building. It is interesting to note that, despite modern technology, it has been virtually impossible to improve upon the quality and beauty of medieval cathedral glass, where even the flaws hold the light and enhance the effect.

The Art Deco period saw stained glass translated into modern settings, and the Tiffany lamps of the 20's are among the loveliest examples of this.

Edwardian stained glass window with diamond shape centre, 18in. wide. $55 £30

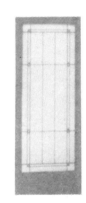

A stained glass panel with scene of mediaeval punishment, 18¾ x 15in. (Capes Dunn & Co.) $2,337 £1,900

One of two early 20th century prairie school-style leaded glass windows, 20½ x 53½in., and five smaller, 18 x 18¾in. (Robt. W. Skinner Inc.) $1,100 £769

A late 19th century leaded stained and coloured glass window, signed W. J. McPherson, Tremont St., Boston, Mass. (Robt. W. Skinner Inc.) $800 £490

Tiffany glass mosaic panel, entitled 'Truth', New York, 1898, 87½ x 44¼in. (Robt. W. Skinner Inc) $10,000 £6,666

Flemish 16th century grisaille and yellow-stained glass roundel, 24.46cm. square. (Sotheby's) $1,425 £990

One of a pair of Gruber leaded glass doors, 1920's, 180cm. wide. (Sotheby's) $3,300 £2,200

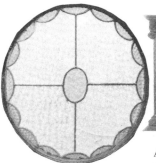

Art Deco style stained glass door roundel, 1930's.

$55 £30

A set of four late 18th or early 19th century English painted glass panels of female allegories of Justice, Faith, Hope and Charity, probably by Thos. Jarvis, after Sir J. Reynolds, each panel 72 x 40cm. (Christie's) $3,490 £2,090

One of a pair of 18th century English oval stained glass armorial panels, 46 x 34.5cm. (Christie's) $734 £440

A large 19th century English stained glass panel showing a lady in Renaissance costume at the prie-dieu, 100 x 55cm. (Christie's) $826 £495

An Art Deco leaded stained glass panel by Jacques Gruber, 70.2cm. wide, 50.3cm. high. (Christie's)
                    $5,772 £3,520

A large rectangular glass panel by John Hutton, sand blasted and wheel engraved with Perseus before the Three Graces, 206.5 x 97cm. (Christie's)
                    $2,706 £1,650

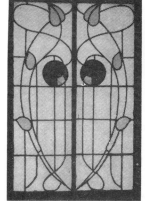

A leaded and stained glass panel by George Walton, after a design by Charles Rennie Mackintosh, 133.6cm. high, 91.4cm. wide. (Christie's) $1,082 £660

A 17th century French rectangular stained glass panel centred with an oval of the martyrdom of St. Stephen, 46.5 x 59cm. (Christie's) $918 £550

A large 19th century English stained glass panel of Mary Queen of Scots, 151 x 80cm. (Christie's) $1,837 £1,100

STANDS

This universal expression covers anything upon which items can be hung, propped, leant or draped. There are umbrella stands, candlestands, reading stands, music stands, plant stands, wig stands, hat stands, coat stands, kettle stands, boot stands, shaving stands... stands for every sort of item you can imagine. The Victorians were great lovers of stands and some of the ones they dreamed up seem to create more clutter than they tidied away. Particularly interesting to collectors are elaborately carved coat and hat stands made in the shape of trees with life size bears trying to climb up. Coats and hats were hung on the tree's branches. More appealing are china umbrella stands, many of them by potteries like Doulton or in Chinese porcelain. Boot stands are often found with scrapers and brushes for cleaning dirty shoes set in at the sides. Music stands were often lyre shaped and very elegant, especially the ones dating from the Georgian period.

An Art Nouveau oak hall stand with circular mirror, stylish hooks and embossed copper panels, 36in. wide. (Lots Road Chelsea Auction Galleries) $567 £350

Regency dark mahogany small fly press with two small drawers to the front, on squat circular feet. (G. A. Key) $875 £500

An Italian walnut pedestal with shaped rectangular top on a bombe support, 50¼in. high. (Christie's) $2,020 £1,210

A Regency brass and rosewood etagere with four rectangular trays, 16½in. wide, 39½in. high. (Christie's) $13,783 £7,700

A cane-sided plant stand, probably Limbert, circa 1910, 23in. high, the top 16in. sq. (Robt. W. Skinner Inc.) $475 £282

A magazine stand with cutouts, Michigan, 1910, 20in. wide. (Robt. W. Skinner Inc.) $700 £416

STANDS

An Edwardian mahogany and inlaid pedestal jardiniere with liner. (J. M. Welch & Son)
$380 £250

A set of George III mahogany library steps with moulded handrail and leather-lined treads, 104in. high. (Christie's)
$6,891 £3,850

A rosewood grained one-drawer poplar stand, American, circa 1830, top 21 x 16in. (Robt. W. Skinner Inc.)
$6,250 £3,720

A black and gold-painted umbrella stand with scrolling foliate sides, 32in. wide. (Christie's) $902 £550

A Regency mahogany teapoy with folding top enclosing a divided interior, 26¾in. wide. (Christie's)
$9,768 £5,280

Early 20th century Mission oak magazine stand with cut out arched sides, 49in. high. (Robt. W. Skinner Inc.)
$500 £312

A Federal tiger maple candlestand, New England, circa 1810, top 17 x 17½in. (Robt. W. Skinner Inc.)
$1,300 £812

A marquetry panelled oak smoking rack, possibly Stickley Bros., Michigan, circa 1910, style no. 264-100, 22in. high, 24in. wide. (Robt. W. Skinner Inc.)
$130 £81

A mid Victorian black and mother-of-pearl japanned papier-mache music stand, 17¾in. diam. (Christie's)
$613 £429

One of a pair of walnut torcheres with lobed tray-tops and hexagonal shaped shafts, 10in. wide, 30½in. high. (Christie's)
$1,156 £756

Painted Tramp art stand with drawers, possibly New York, 1820-40, 17½in. wide. (Robt. W. Skinner Inc.)
$300 £200

Chippendale cherry candle-stand, the shaped top with ovolo corners, circa 1780, 26in. high. (Robt. W. Skinner Inc.)
$2,500 £1,748

A Chippendale style mahogany urn table, 25in. high. (Christie's) $646 £420

An early 18th century Italian carved giltwood stand with a simulated green marble top, 1.10m. high. (Phillips)
$1,200 £800

A George II grained pine pedestal, 53¼in. high. (Christie's)
$10,081 £7,150

Gustav Stickley inlaid tiger maple open music stand, circa 1904, no. 670, signed with Eastwood label, 39in. high. (Robt. W. Skinner Inc.)
$7,250 £5,069

A pair of late 18th century Italian parcel gilt and green painted torcheres, 69½in. high. (Christie's)
$7,810 £5,500

A Victorian mahogany folio stand with brass ratcheted adjustable open slatted slopes, 76cm. high. (Phillips)
$2,550 £1,700

STEVENGRAPHS

The trade name "Stevengraph" was coined by Thomas Stevens, a Coventry silk weaver, about 1863, and he used it to describe the small, multi coloured pictures and bookmarks that he started to produce after a slump in the silk weaving trade around the middle of the 19th century.

He adapted his looms to weave small pieces of silk and found that he could produce eye catching little pictures which found an immediate market. His weavings were used as Christmas, birthday or Valentine cards while others were made into calendars, sashes or badges.

They left Stevens' factory in cardboard mounts with his name and title printed on the front — for example, "Woven in silk by Thomas Stevens, Sole Inventor and Manufacturer."

Stevengraphs were especially popular in America because Stevens was enterprising enough to travel to trade fairs there taking with him some of his looms so that customers could see how the pictures were made.

When buying Stevengraphs care should be taken to see that the mounts are not cut down to fit into a smaller frame. Many of those on the market today have been remounted or the silk has faded, both of which detract from the value. Stevens' pictures depicted a variety of themes from sports and coaching scenes to portraits of famous people or incidents from history like Turpin's Ride to York.

'Are You Ready', Boat Race, original mount, framed and glazed. $130 £75

'A Present From Blackpool', a view of the town and piers. $140 £80

'The Good Old Days', original mount, framed and glazed. $85 £50

'Dick Turpin's Ride To York On His Bonnie Black Bess', original mounts. $85 £50

STEVENGRAPHS

'Her Majesty Queen Alexandra', with the crests of England, Scotland and Ireland below portrait. $70 £40

'Leda' a study of Leda and the swan. $175 £100

'Jake Kilrain', study of notable American boxer. $100 £60

'A Gentleman In Khaki', depicting a wounded soldier with a rifle raised. $60 £35

'The Late Earl Of Beaconsfield', with black and white portrait facing left. $60 £35

'Kitchener of Khartoum', with head and shoulders above a Union Jack. $60 £35

'Ye Peeping Tom of Coventry', with brown window surround. $100 £60

'Sergt. G. H. Bates', the American Standard Bearer. $140 £80

'Her Majesty Queen Victoria', Queen of an Empire on Which the Sun Never Sets. $70 £40

STICKLEY

Gustav Stickley was the eldest of six brothers, including L. & J. G. and G. & A., all of whom were active as U.S. furniture manufacturers in the early 20th century. Gustav trained as a stone-mason, but became best known for his chair designs, mainly in the American Colonial style. The brothers' business relationships were obviously complicated: L. & J. G. left Gustav's factory in 1900 to found their own, then bought it in 1916 following his bankruptcy. The Stickley Manufacturing Co, formed then, is still active today.

An early Gustav Stickley settle with arched slats, 1901-03, 60in. wide. (Robt. W. Skinner Inc.) $27,000 £16,071

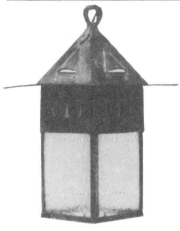

A copper and amber glass lantern, style no. 324, by Gustav Stickley, circa 1906, 15in. high, globe 5¼in. diam. (Robt. W. Skinner Inc.) $7,500 £4,054

A Gustav Stickley round slat-sided waste basket, no. 94, circa 1907, 14in. diam. (Robt. W. Skinner Inc.) $1,200 £714

A Gustav Stickley slat-sided folio stand, no. 551, 1902-03, 40½in. high, 29½in. wide. (Robt. W. Skinner Inc.) $3,000 £1,785

An inlaid oak three-panelled screen, designed by Harvey Ellis for Gustav Stickley, circa 1903-04, 66¾in. high, each panel 20in. wide. (Robt. W. Skinner Inc.) $18,000 £10,714

A Gustav Stickley bent arm spindle Morris chair, circa 1907, with spring cushion seat. (Robt. W. Skinner Inc.) $1,300 £7,738

A Gustav Stickley nine-drawer tall chest, no. 913, circa 1907, 36in. wide, 50in. high. (Robt. W. Skinner Inc.) $4,000 £2,500

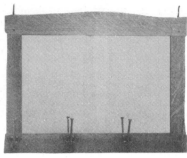

Gustav Stickley oak table lamp with wicker shade, circa 1910, 22in. high, 18in. diam. (Robt. W. Skinner Inc.) $1,100 £769

A Gustav Stickley hall mirror, style no. 66, circa 1905-06, 28in. high, 36in. wide. (Robt. W. Skinner Inc.) $1,200 £714

A leather upholstered dining chair, no. 355, by Gustav Stickley, circa 1910, 33¼in. high. (Robt. W. Skinner Inc.) $950 £513

A Gustav Stickley oak 'Eastwood' chair with original rope support for seat, circa 1902. (Robt. W. Skinner Inc.) $28,000 £16,666

A hammered copper chamberstick, by Gustav Stickley, circa 1913, 9¼in. high. (Robt. W. Skinner Inc.) $700 £378

A Gustav Stickley table with twelve Grueby tiles, 1902-03, 23¾in. wide. (Robt. W. Skinner Inc.) $49,000 £26,486

A Gustav Stickley two-door bookcase with keyed tenons, no. 716, 42½in. high. (Robt. W. Skinner Inc.) $2,500 £1,562

A drink stand, by L. & J. G. Stickley, no. 587, circa 1912, 16in. sq. (Robt. W. Skinner Inc.) $650 £351

A Gustav Stickley slat-sided cube chair, no. 331, circa 1910, 25¼in. wide. (Robt. W. Skinner Inc.) $5,250 £3,125

STONEWARE

Salt glazed stoneware is a very old method of making pottery and there had been workshops producing this sort of ware at Lambeth in South London for many centuries when John Doulton started to work there in 1815. He made salt glazed domestic jars, bottles and barrels in brown with a slip glaze using the the same methods as potters had used since the Middle Ages. John's son Henry realised the potential of stoneware when he followed his father into the business. He expanded the firm's operations into architectural stoneware and then the decorative stoneware which was to make the family fortune. In 1866 he encouraged students from the nearby Lambeth School of Art to come to work in a studio he attached to his pottery and allowed them complete licence to experiment and make everything they wanted. He was fortunate in having as proteges gifted people like the famous Barlow family, Frank Butler, George Tinworth and Eliza Simmance. Their work was shown abroad, particularly at Paris in the 1867 Exhibition, where it created a sensation that put Doulton's name on the international art map.

A mug by Constance E. Redford, the buff ground with white dots and incised blue scrolls, 1882, 5in. high. $130 £75

A pair of candlesticks by Nellie Garbott with incised brown and blue leaves, 1879, 6¾in. high. $455 £260

A large pierced vase by Edith Lupton with three shaped panels painted in pate-sur-pate with wild flowers, 1882, 14in. high. $455 £260

A jug, the dark green elaborate lace ground overlaid with two celadon classical portraits, circa 1888, 7½in. high. $155 £90

A pair of covered vases by Florence Barlow, with upright handles, 1878, 7¾in. high. $560 £320

A handled bottle or spirit decanter by Francis Pope, with incised green leaves, silver hall-marked 1913, 7½in. high. $155 £90

STONEWARE

A bowl by Louisa Davis, the brown ground with incised blue flowers and scrolling, 1878, 7½in. high. $560 £320

A pepper pot by Alice Budden with incised leaves and bead work, 1880, 2½in. high. $125 £70

A tea party with pale green mice seated on brown chairs, by George Tinworth, the hollow oval base inscribed Tea-time Scandal, circa 1885, 3½in. high. $1,660 £950

A jug by Ellen Gathercole decorated in the traditional manner with applied vignettes of sporting scenes, 1882, 8¾in. high. $455 £260

A large pair of vases by Hannah Barlow, each with an incised frieze of wolves and their cubs amongst foliage, 1885, 16½in. high. $910 £520

A model owl with detachable head, the feathers formed by applied motifs in shades of blue, ochre and brown, circa 1880, 8in. high. $490 £280

A tazza by Eliza Simmance, the surface with an incised blue and brown leaf pattern, 1877, 6½in. high. $280 £160

A vase by Eliza S. Banks, with carved panels of blue foliage surrounded by painted white flowers, 1882, 8½in. high. $235 £135

A vase modelled by Eliza Simmance, with yellow apples growing from green branches, 1887, 9½in. high. $455 £260

SWORDS

A sword is one of the most ancient weapons and warriors throughout the ages treasured them above all things. Many warriors were even buried with their swords beside them. A man displayed his status by the sword he carried and in Japanese society, the sword stood for the spirit of the family and was passed down through the generations for hundreds of years. Swords vary from needle thin rapiers to massive two-handed swords that it must have taken superhuman strength to wield. There are elegantly curved scimitars and swords with waved blades and jewelled hilts that were carried by eastern potentates. When an army was vanquished, the victors symbolically took the swords of the defeated and many homes of old military families display those trophies of war from foreign campaigns.

One of the most popular types of sword are Japanese ones taken from prisoners at the end of the last war. Many of those swords have ancient blades signed by the craftsmen who made them and Japanese buyers vie to buy them back when they come up for sale. The rarest examples sell for thousands of pounds each. Swords with elaborately engraved hilts or decorated blades are very sought after and so are swords which were used in wars of the past — Turkish campaigns, the Crimea, the Napoleonic Wars or the American Civil War.

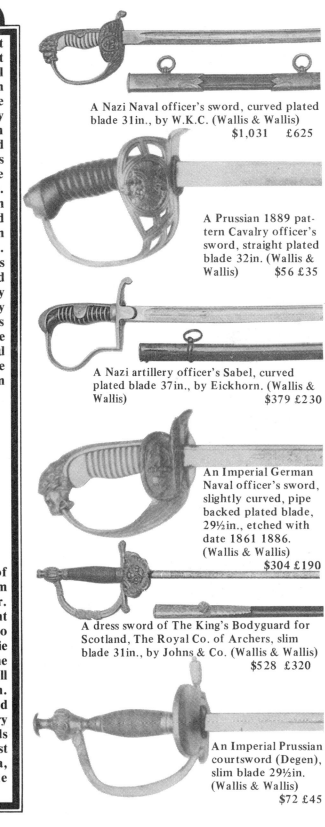

A Nazi Naval officer's sword, curved plated blade 31in., by W.K.C. (Wallis & Wallis) $1,031 £625

A Prussian 1889 pattern Cavalry officer's sword, straight plated blade 32in. (Wallis & Wallis) $56 £35

A Nazi artillery officer's Sabel, curved plated blade 37in., by Eickhorn. (Wallis & Wallis) $379 £230

An Imperial German Naval officer's sword, slightly curved, pipe backed plated blade, 29½in., etched with date 1861 1886. (Wallis & Wallis) $304 £190

A dress sword of The King's Bodyguard for Scotland, The Royal Co. of Archers, slim blade 31in., by Johns & Co. (Wallis & Wallis) $528 £320

An Imperial Prussian courtsword (Degen), slim blade 29½in. (Wallis & Wallis) $72 £45

SWORDS

A Victorian 1821 pattern Light Cavalry officer's sword, slightly curved blade 35in., by Henry Wilkinson, Pall Mall, officer's crest and initials, steel hilt, triple bar guard, silver wire bound fish-skin grip, in its steel scabbard. (Wallis & Wallis) $313 £190

A Saxony Cavalry officer's sword, curved blade 33in., by Ewald Cleff, Solingen, plain steel semi-basket guard, wire bound fish-skin covered grip, in its steel scabbard. (Wallis & Wallis) $128 £80

A Victorian 1854 Levee pattern Coldstream Guards officer's sword, blade 32in. of flattened diamond section, by Henry Wilkinson, Pall Mall, No. 22529, steel hilt, copper wire bound fish-skin covered grip, in its steel scabbard. (Wallis & Wallis) $462 £280

A Prussian 1889 pattern Cavalry trooper's sword, plain, pipe back, clipped back blade 33in., by Weyersberg Kirschbaum, steel guard with marking of The 2nd Guard Dragoon Regt., composition ribbed grip. (Wallis & Wallis) $48 £30

A George V Royal Naval officer's prize sword, blade 31in., by Henry Wilkinson, Pall Mall, No. 59467, retaining all original polish, gilt hilt, folding side-guard, lion's head pommel, bullion dress knot, gilt wire bound white fish-skin covered grip, in its leather scabbard. (Wallis & Wallis) $792 £480

An Imperial German Naval officer's sword, curved blade, 32in., gilt chiselled hilt, large and small folding sideguards, lion's head pommel, wire bound ivorine grip, in its leather scabbard with three gilt mounts. (Wallis & Wallis) $320 £200

SYPHONS

The fashion for taking soda water or seltzer in spirits and wine started in the early 19th century and in order to make sure that the liquid was aerated, it had to be kept under pressure. There were some early patents, both French and English, for soda water bottles and they had wonderful names like Gazateur and Seltzogene. A few were liable to explode and therefore the bottles were encased in basket weave or wire net to prevent shards of glass injuring people. The classic soda syphon shape was devised in the late 19th century and the tops were of tin or pewter. Later they were porcelain lined and chrome plated before the advent of modern plastic tops. A few early syphons had porcelain bodies and some were made of coloured glass – pink, green, blue, yellow, brown or amber.

An early Sparklets wire-bound soda syphon. $18 £10

Blue glass soda syphon inscribed Job. Wragg Ltd., with acid etching on front, dated 1902. $20 £12

Greenock Apothecaries & Lawsons Ltd. soda syphon, circa 1902. $10 £6

Spaco Ltd., blue glass soda syphon with silver plated top. $20 £12

Faceted clear glass syphon by Wrights of Walkery, 31cm. high. $28 £16

One shot, basket covered, Sparklets type syphon, 32cm. high. $14 £8

Amber glass writhened syphon by Parker Bros. of Drighlington, 31cm. high. $45 £25

Table syphon by J. Burgess, 12in. tall. $10 £6

Green glass syphon by the Victoria Wine Co. illustrated with a picture of Queen Victoria, 33cm. high. $28 £16

Early cobalt blue syphon by S. J. Coley of Stroud with patented porcelain top, 30cm. high. $45 £25

Pink faceted glass syphon by Maps, illustrated with a figure of a man, 33cm. high. $30 £18

Job Wragg of Birmingham clear glass syphon illustrated with a picture of the syphon in use in red print, 31cm. high. $18 £10

Sparklet syphon charger used by hotels to refill syphons, 39cm. high. $60 £35

Basket covered Gazateur syphon with a porcelain base, 45cm. high. $90 £50

Yellow glass syphon by L. G. Weeks & Sons of Torrington, 33cm. high. $28 £16

Seltzogene twin bulbed syphon made by D. Fevre, Paris, 45cm. high. $55 £30

TAPESTRIES

Tapestry dates from ancient times, but remained principally an amateur occupation in Europe (with the Bayeux as perhaps the supreme example) until the 14th century, when major centres developed at Arras, Tournai and Brussels in Belgium and the Beauvais and Gobelins factories in France. Medieval tapestries were often used as portable draught screens. From the 16th century such leading painters as Raphael were commissioned to design them.

A 17th century Brussels verdure tapestry, depicting a dog and animal beside a river, framed by trees and foliage, 2.92 x 2.46m. (Phillips) $5,184 £3,600

An 18th century Gobelins tapestry woven in wools and silks with two Chinamen in a landscape, 9ft.6in. x 5ft. 4½in. (Christie's) $9,979 £7,560

Early 18th century Brussels tapestry woven in silk and wool with the family of Darius prostrate before Alexander the Great, 13ft.9in. x 22ft.7in. (Christie's) $6,998 £4,860

Early 18th century Brussels tapestry woven in wool and silk depicting Neptune, 13ft. 10in. x 10ft.4in.(Christie's) $4,665 £3,240

A 16th century Dutch tapestry woven in silks and wools with Christ and the woman caught in adultery, 7ft.10in. x 6ft.7in. (Christie's) $18,662 £12,960

A 17th century Brussels tapestry depicting a boar hunt, 9ft. x 6ft.1in. (Christie's) $5,702 £4,320

Late 16th century Flemish Verdure tapestry woven with various scenes in a forest, 8ft. 5in. x 21ft.11in. (Christie's) $24,883 £17,280

A 17th century Brussels tapestry woven in silks and wools, 10ft.11in. x 10ft.6in. (Christie's) $8,553 £6,480

A 17th century Brussels tapestry woven in well preserved wools and silks, 8ft. x 11ft.2in. (Christie's) $14,256 £10,800

A late 17th century Brussels tapestry in well preserved silks and wools, 9ft.8in. x 7ft.10in. (Christie's) $19,245 £14,580

Mid 18th century Brussels tapestry woven in silk and wool with Jupiter and his eagle receiving thunderbolts from Vulcan, 13ft.1in. x 8ft. 4in. (Christie's)$5,909 £4,104

A 17th century Spanish or Italian tapestry woven in muted colours, 94 x 99in. (Christie's) $6,577 £4,536

An Aubusson tapestry woven with lovers and sheep in a rustic landscape, 7ft.6in. x 4ft.8in. (Christie's) $3,576 £2,484

A 17th century Flemish Verdure tapestry woven with a dog beneath a tree in a pond by a forest clearing with a palace beyond, 8ft.5in. x 9ft.7in. (Christie's) $3,421 £2,376

An 18th century Louis XV Beauvais tapestry from the Tenture des Verdures Fines, woven in silk and wool, 8ft. 7in. x 6ft.1in. (Christie's) $5,702 £4,320

A late 17th century Flemish Verdure tapestry with a shepherd and shepherdess in a forest with their flock, 9ft. 3in. x 8ft.7in. (Christie's) $4,561 £3,456

TAPS

Early Victorian taps were usually made of gunmetal and later of nickel or chrome-plated brass. The modern trend with these is to acid-strip the chrome or nickel and polish and lacquer the brass. They then fetch very good prices. Often these had ceramic insets in the head with the maker's name, or some decoration. The Edwardians sometimes had ceramic levers on silver plate, which are worth seeking out, as are rare Victorian shower taps. Early Art Deco styles too can be very attractive.

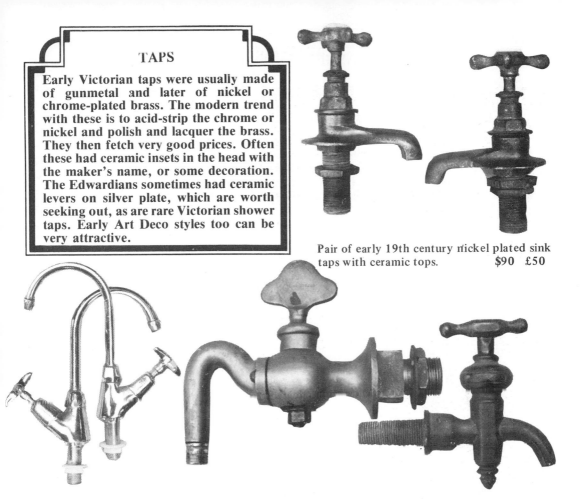

Pair of early 19th century nickel plated sink taps with ceramic tops. $90 £50

Pair of 1960's chromium plated laboratory taps. $35 £20

Late 19th century patent wine tap with clover leaf top. $60 £35

19th century brass twin head wine tap with screw fitting. $70 £40

Pair of Shanks Art Deco chromium plated taps with ceramic tops. $130 £75

A large late 19th century brass hose connector tap. $35 £20

Pair of 1930's plated brass crosshead taps with ceramic tops $50 £30

367

TASSIE MEDALLIONS

There are two famous Tassies — James who lived between 1735-99 and his nephew William who was born in 1777 and died in 1860. Both of them were skilled makers of medallions and the senior Tassie was the man who made the famous copy of the Portland Vase. James Tassie was born at Pollokshaws, Glasgow, and settled in London where he set up a thriving business making cameo portraits of the distinguished people of the day. The cameos were made of decorated glassware with the relief in ceramic paste and the results were astonishingly lifelike. Everybody who was anybody wanted to sit for Tassie. His nephew William succeeded him in the business and was as successful and as skilled as his uncle. There are some excellent examples of Tassie ware in the British Museum.

Hugh, 1st Duke of Northumberland, K.G., signed with a 'T', inscribed and dated 1780, on black ground. (Christie's) $1,230 £702

William Pitt, by Tassie probably after Flaxman, on blue ground. (Christie's) $2,835 £1,620

Major M. Macalister of the Glengarry Fencibles, signed Tassie F, inscribed and dated 1796, on blue ground. (Christie's) $1,510 £864

William, 1st Earl of Mansfield, signed Tassie F, dated 1779, on blue ground. (Christie's) $1,700 £972

Philip Dormer Stanhope, 4th Earl of Chesterfield, by Tassie after Gosset, integral white paste ground. (Christie's) $1,100 £626

Admiral Lord Duncan, signed Tassie F, inscribed and dated 1797, on green ground. (Christie's) $1,410 £810

TAXIDERMY

Stuffed animals and birds are not to everyone's taste but the best examples really deserve to be regarded as works of art. The stuffed animal or bird must be set in a mobile, lifelike manner in a suitable background with details of its natural habitat. Condition is very important because taxidermy specimens are very liable to attack from moths and beetles.

The art of taxidermy thrived during the Victorian period when there was an enormous demand for it. Sportsmen sent fish, foxes, badgers, stags' heads and even the heads of buffalo, lions and tigers for stuffing and mounting. In drawing rooms there were enormous glass cases full of colourful birds perched on flowering trees or set pieces with partridges and pheasants striding through tufts of heather. So great was the demand that most towns had their resident taxidermist and some of them were very skilled indeed. Mostly they put labels at the back of the cases or else signed their work in some way — Peter Spicer of Leamington left a signed pebble on the floor of his cases. Only top quality items in good condition sell for large sums of money today.

Osprey by Grant of Devizes, circa 1880. $435 £250

Grey Squirrel by H. Bryant of Wellingborough, circa 1910. $130 £75

Shelduck by T. E. Gunn of Norwich, circa 1890. $190 £110

(The Enchanted Aviary)

369

3 Bream by J. Cooper of London in bowed case,
1912. $1,650 £650

Green Woodpecker by E. C. Saunders of
Yarmouth, circa 1910. $165 £95

Pheasant (partly white) by J. Gardner of Oxford
Street, London, circa 1880. $165 £95

Badger by J. Gardner of Oxford Street, London,
circa 1880. $260 £150

Cuckoo & Wryneck by T. E. Gunn of Norwich,
circa 1900. $190 £110

Pair of Nightjars with two chicks by J. Cooper of
London, circa 1890. $300 £175

(The Enchanted Aviary)

Otter (taxidermist not known), 1919. $410 £235

Fox by J. Hutchings of Aberystwyth, circa 1900.
$520 £295

African Grey Parrot in oval dome (removed for
the photo) by W. Lowne of Yarmouth, circa
1900. $220 £125

Black-headed Gull by E. C. Saunders of
Yarmouth, circa 1910. $165 £95

Canada Goose by W. Hine of Southport, circa
1920. $520 £295

(The Enchanted Aviary)

TERRACOTTA

Terracotta is a fired clay, principally associated with sculpture, and terracotta figurines were common in Greek and Roman times. The art was revived during the Renaissance, when the Della Robbia family in Venice specialised in enamelled terracotta Madonnas. In the eighteenth century France became a leading centre of production, with such superb craftsmen as Houdon and Pajou (to whom we are indebted for the portrait sculpture of many leading figures of the day) and Clodion, who modelled mythological figures.

A 19th century terracotta garden ornament, probably France, 25½in. diam., 25½in. high. (Robt. W. Skinner Inc.) $750 £520

A late 18th century French terracotta bust of a man wearing The Order of St. Esprit, in the style of Pajou, 20in. high. (Christie's)
$2,811 £1,980

A set of three black glazed terracotta jugs of graduated size, printed in yellow with portraits and vases of enamelled flowers. (Phillips)
$160 £100

A French terracotta bust of an 18th century lady with dressed hair, 16in. high. (Christie's)
$2,505 £1,728

A pair of Regency painted terracotta figures modelled as Chinese ladies, 8½in. and 8in. high. (Christie's)
$366 £280

A French terracotta bust of an 18th century boy, 18in. high. (Christie's)
$3,288 £2,268

A pair of 19th century Continental terracotta figures of a peasant girl and a boy, 90cm. and 91cm. high. (Phillips) $2,700 £1,800

TERRACOTTA

A Cypriot terracotta chariot drawn by two horses, 7th-6th century B.C., 13cm. long. (Phillips) $656 £400

A terracotta figure of Eros, 4th-3rd century B.C., Boetia, 7.5cm. high. (Phillips)
$426 £260

A Cypro-geometric bowl raised on three looped supports, circa 1700 B.C., 15cm. high. (Phillips) $1,230 £750

A 19th century French group of Bacchus and a Bacchante, cast from a model by Clodion, 33cm. high. (Christie's)
$734 £440

A 19th century French terracotta bust of a little girl, attributed to Houdon, 39cm. high. (Christie's)
$1,837 £1,100

A Cypriot terracotta equestrian figure, slight traces of red and black pigment, 7th-6th century B.C., 11.5cm. high. (Phillips) $311 £190

A Cypriot terracotta equestrian figure, 7th-6th century B.C., 15cm. high. (Phillips)
$360 £220

A pair of 19th century French terracotta busts of 'L'Espiegle' and 'Le Printemps', signed J.-Bte-Carpeaux, 48cm. and 55cm. high. (Christie's)
$5,143 £3,080

A terracotta figure of Eros, naked except for a drape across the shoulders, Boetia, 4th-3rd century B.C., 7cm. high. (Phillips) $328 £200

TEXTILES

Textiles are a vast subject and provide a fascinating insight into life down the ages, since they are intimately connected with dress and domestic life. Hair and wool were in use from prehistoric times, while linen, derived from flax, was also an early discovery, declining only when cotton became more widespread. The silks and satins of the East were always sought after—the former being of such importance that the ancient trade route from China to the Mediterranean was known simply as the Silk Road. Today, few textile sales are without rich examples of Oriental cloths.

The subject covers not only the materials themselves, but also the arts connected with them which flourished at various times, such as beadwork, tapestry, needlework, stumpwork, quilting, samplers, embroidery and lace making—the list is endless. Now, of course, the use of synthetic fabrics have greatly extended the textile industry's range, though it remains to be seen whether they will become the collectables of the future.

A 19th century Rescht cover of red worsted decorated with multi-coloured insertions and applique, 2.24 x 1.45m., fringed, lined. (Phillips) $672 £400

A mid 19th century needlework picture by Ann Wright, designed with a tablet showing 'The Given Chap. of Exodus', The Ten Commandments, Moses and Aaron, 46.50 x 31.50cm. (Phillips) $1,596 £950

A rectangular cushion worked with metal thread strapwork and foliage on a green silk velvet ground, 26in. (Christie's) $233 £132

A mid 18th century gros et petit point arched firescreen panel worked in coloured wools with a garden scene of musicians, 87.50 x 67cm. (Phillips) $806 £480

Late 18th century needlework pocketbook, silk yarns worked in a variant of the Queen stitch, probably New England, 4¾ x 4in. (Robt. W. Skinner Inc.) $550 £384

A mid 19th century Japanese fukusa, of blue silk with embroidered, applied and couched silks in pastel shades, 78 x 66cm. (Phillips) $745 £460

TEXTILES

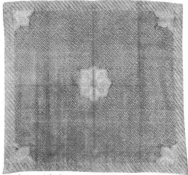

A 19th century patchwork coverlet worked in plain and printed cottons, 2.80 x 2.60m. (Phillips) $291 £180

A late 18th century oval silk-work picture depicting a country lass gathering wheat-sheafs in her apron, 34 x 28cm. (Phillips) $806 £480

A late 18th century Benares cover of red silk gauze woven in gold thread with a central shaped medallion, 1.08 x 1.14m. (Phillips) $297 £180

A 19th century Chinese coverlet of crimson silk, lined and fringed, 2.32 x 2.14m. (Phillips) $288 £160

A shaped panel of 19th century Chinese silk, the blue ground embroidered with coloured silks in pekin knot and satin stitch, 2.08m. high, joined. (Phillips) $648 £400

A late 18th century embroider-ed picture, the ivory silk ground worked mainly in satin stitches, 65 x 70.50cm. (Phillips) $604 £360

A silk embroidered picture, Mass., 1807, worked in silk yarns on ivory silk satin ground fabric, 8 x 8½in. (Robt. W. Skinner Inc.) $2,200 £1,333

A late 19th century Japanese wall hanging of K'o-ssu woven in pastel coloured silks and gold thread, 3.04 x 1.80m. (Phillips) $3,240 £2,000

An Oriental panel, the fuchsia ground worked in coloured silk threads with butterflies, flowers and Oriental figures, 2.60 x 2.40m. (Phillips) $972 £540

TEXTILES

Late 19th century Soumak bag face, S. Caucasus, (minor wear), 1ft.7in. x 1ft.6in. (Robt. W. Skinner Inc.) $650 £433

One of a pair of 17th century needlework stumpwork pictures, England, 5¼ x 4¼in. (Robt. W. Skinner Inc.) $2,300 £1,608

A Chinese needlework picture, the ivory silk ground embroidered in shades of blue, brown, ochre and ivory, 36cm. square. (Phillips) $286 £190

A late 19th century Chinese k'o-ssu picture of fighting warriors on horseback and on foot, with companion, 1m. x 0.25m. (Phillips) $656 £400

Needlework picture, 'Shepherdess of the Alps', N.Y., 1800, 12½ x 15¼in. (Robt. W. Skinner Inc.) $1,800 £1,258

A late 19th century Chinese k'o-ssu cover, the centre worked in pastel silks on a gold thread ground, 1.84 x 1.44m., lined. (Phillips) $1,771 £1,150

Late 18th century silk embroidered picture, New England, 21 x 19in. (Robt. W. Skinner Inc.) $3,500 £2,447

A 17th century Turkish bocha, the linen ground embroidered in shades of red, blue, yellow and green silks, 1.10 x 1.04m. (Phillips) $1,260 £750

An Arts & Crafts linen cover embroidered in red and ivory linen, 1.46 x 1.58m. (Phillips) $453 £300

THIMBLES

Though we know that the Romans used thimbles, early examples are rare and are usually only found in museums. The earliest sort of thimble generally available to collectors dates from the late 18th century. It helps with dating to know that before the middle of the 17th century thimbles were hand punched and the indentations showed irregularity. After that mass production techniques became more common. Most thimbles were made of cheap metals but gold and silver ones do turn up and so do thimbles made of porcelain, ivory, bone, bronze, brass, enamel, wood and leather. Up till the late 19th century thimbles were not hall marked. Condition is all important and if the tops are damaged or perished, this detracts from the value.

Silver and turquoise thimble, circa 1890. $90 £50

Plated thimble with patterned border. $7 £4

Silver 'stone top' thimble, circa 1890. $80 £45

Silver thimble size 6, Chester 1895. $35 £20

Dorcas silver thimble, size 8, circa 1890. $35 £20

Elizabeth II coronation thimble. $175 £100

Great Exhibition 1862 thimble. $350 £200

Dorcas silver thimble, size 5, circa 1890. $35 £20

Plated thimble 'Prestwick'. $30 £18

Cable bottom silver thimble, circa 1870. $90 £50

Silver thimble with leaf border, circa 1890. $50 £30

Albion 'Calf Meal', aluminium thimble. $5 £3

THIMBLES

Plated 'Just a thimble full' measure. $35 £20

French 'stone top' silver thimble, circa 1880. $70 £40

Chelsea thimble in hinged silver filagree case, circa 1700.
$2,600 £1,500

Goss china thimble 'Heckington'. $45 £25

Filagree silver thimble, circa 1800. $525 £300

Meissen thimble decorated in Schwarzlot and gold by I. Preissler.
$7,800 £4,500

Silver thimble containing a bottle, circa 1800. $700 £400

A fine filagree silver thimble, circa 1800.
$525 £300

Coral and silver thimble, circa 1880. $130 £75

French silver thimble with gilt border.
$85 £50

Pewter thimble depicting the 'House of Commons' and 'Big Ben'. $12 £7

Silver thimble, Birmingham 1901.
$70 £40

Patent guard silver thimble. $130 £75

Charles Horner silver thimble. $175 £100

Abel Morrell thimble, circa 1900. $18 £10

Dorcas fern leaf silver thimble, 1890. $25 £15

TICKETS

While railway tickets have long been prized by collectors, this interest is now extending to other sorts, the more unusual, decorative and early the better. Those of potential value include tickets for early pop concerts, while tickets for events where access was limited, such as Cup Finals or Royal Enclosures, are also of interest. Consider the likely value of a cloakroom ticket for the Titanic! Prices have yet to stabilise, but 'ticket collecting' seems set to be popular in the 1990's.

Harry Isaacs 'betting' ticket no. 188.
$2 £1

Bluebell Railway, Observation Coach ticket. $3.50 £2

Welshpool & Llanfair Railway Saloon Coach ticket. $5 £3

Birmingham and Midland Tramways, Ettingshall Railway Station to Fighting Cocks. $5 £3

Entrance ticket to the Paris International Exhibition, 1937. $20 £12

Great Western Railway, Museum Souvenir Ticket. $2 £1

Dartmouth Floating Bridge ticket. $2 £1

Kent & East Sussex Railway return from Tenterden. $2 £1

Birmingham Co-operative Society Laundry ticket, No. 6082. $1 50p

Horsham Show 1955 Exhibitor's ticket. $7 £4

TICKETS

Festiniog Railway special tour ticket, third class. $3.50 £2

Manchester Corporation Car Park ticket, 30th December 1966. $1 50p

Ravenglass Eskdale Railway, Child's Return ticket. $1 50p

St Helens Corporation Transport ticket, advertising windows on reverse. $3.50 £2

Birmingham and Midland Motor Omnibus Co. Bus ticket, advertising bread on reverse. $5 £3

Festiniog Railway ticket for a dog. $7 £4

Flannel Dance ticket, Presteigne, June 21st, 1928, dancing 8—2.30 a.m. $9 £5

Wolverhampton Corporation Tramways ticket, Stow Heath Lane to Railway Station. $10 £6

Mersey Tunnel Toll ticket, dated 13th Oct. 1940. $9 £5

Second Class Season ticket, 1955, between Fawley and Hereford, issued by British Transport Commission. $5 £3

TILES

Dutch tiles were among the finest made in the 16th and 17th centuries and they exported them all over the world. They were often blue and white and the patterns were sometimes copied from Chinese ceramics. Early Dutch tiles were often large, about twelve inches square, and they were often laid on floors or around fireplaces. There is an ancient synagogue in Cochin, South India, with a floor laid entirely in 16th century Dutch blue and white tiles.

In the 19th century tiles became very popular for many different types of decoration and they were not only put around hearths and on floors but set into toilet tables and cupboard tops, built into bathrooms, made into kettle stands and cheese stands or simply framed. Minton's were one of the first companies to start making tiles around 1830 and other ceramic manufacturers followed their lead. Because they were washable and cheerful looking tile-panel pictures were often used in shops, especially butcher's shops or dairies, and in hospitals especially in children's wards where they were made into nursery rhyme pictures. Artists like William de Morgan realised the artistic possibility of the tile and made many beautiful ones based on Persian Iznik designs.

Four of a set of twenty-five late 18th century English tinglaze tiles. (Woolley & Wallis)　　Twenty-five　　$493 £340

A Wedgwood pottery tile picture by W. Nunn, 46 x 77cm.　　$1,310 £750

A set of four Continental ceramic tiles, square, each depicting industrial and artisan subjects in the purist style, 10½in. sq., printed marks, each painted with Cocrah. (Christie's)　　$1,167 £638

TILES

Bristol delft polychrome tile, circa 1760, 13cm. square, slightly chipped. $350 £200

Liverpool delft tile printed in black with a garden scene, circa 1760. $175 £100

A Safavid tile panel with a figure of Sagittarius surrounded by palmettes, 4ft. 1in. x 2ft.10in. (Christie's) $14,877 £10,260

A large early 20th century Doulton decorative tile picture of Little Jack Horner.
$7,000 £4,000

Late 19th century Mettlach tile picture, signed C. Warth, 16¾in. high. $187 £150

A Castelli rectangular plaque painted with Pan being comforted after the musical contest with Apollo seated, circa 1725, 28cm. square. (Christie's) $1,458 £972

A De Morgan tile panel, comprising three tiles, 1882-8, 51 x 20.6cm.
$875 £500

A Doulton terracotta tile picture by George Tinworth, moulded and carved in low relief with Samson, circa 1880, 8½in. x 8½in. $525 £350

TOBACCO JARS

The first criterion for the tobacco jar is that it should not absorb moisture from the tobacco and allow it to dry out. Many early ones were made from lead, and, since this was an easily damaged and reusable material, very few have survived. In the 17th and 18th centuries, lead was superceded by lead or foil-lined wood and later, in the 19th century, by glazed earthenware.

Shapes were many and varied: the larger, barrel shaped jars were most often used by tobacconists to store their stock.

Paddy tobacco jar by Doulton, 5½in. high, issued 1938-41.
$450 £300

Doulton Burslem Morrisian Ware tobacco jar and cover decorated with a band of dancing girls, 5½in. high. $80 £55

A stoneware Martin Bros. bird tobacco jar and cover, dated 1903, 28cm. high. (Christie's) $4,354 £3,456

Royal Doulton Sung tobacco jar and cover of hexagonal form, 6¼in. high, circa 1930.
$225 £150

A waisted jar and cover painted with rings of white flowers, c.m.l. & c., date letter for 1907, 6½in. high. $180 £120

A Foley 'Intarsio' tobacco jar and cover, 14.3cm. high, no. 3458, Rd. no. 364386 (SR). (Phillips) $203 £140

Nightwatchman Series tobacco jar, 5½in. high, circa 1909, by Noke, depicting a watchman carrying a pike. $72 £48

Royal Doulton Kingsware tobacco jar decorated in relief with a gentleman smoking, 8¼in. high. $75 £50

A Liberty & Co. 'Tudric' pewter tobacco box and cover, designed by Archibald Knox, 11.9cm. high. (Christie's) $380 £264

A treen barrel-form tobacco canister, the lift-off cover set with a wine bottle and two glasses, 7in. high. (Christie's) $330 £193

Double Foxes (one curled), a Royal Doulton Kingsware tobacco jar with silver hall-marked rim, circa 1912, 7½in. high. $427 £285

Old Charley tobacco jar by Doulton, 5½in. high, issued 1938-1941. $420 £280

A Martin Bros. stoneware tobacco jar and cover, modelled as a grotesque grinning cat, 1885, 22cm. high. (Christie's) $10,962 £7,560

A tobacco jar and cover, the body with incised brown glazed cows frolicking amongst incised green foliage, r.m. & e., circa 1895, 6½in. high. $240 £160

A Bretby tobacco jar and cover, inscribed 'Nicotiank', 16.5cm. high. (Phillips) $94 £65

A tobacco jar decorated with applied blue and white beads, r.m., impressed date for 1888, 4¼in. high. $27 £18

TOBACCO SILKS

These were issued in the early part of this century by various cigarette companies such as Godfrey Phillips (BDV brand) and Kensitas (Flags series). They can vary from cigarette card size through postcard to cabinet and large size. They were issued with a protective wrapper and this should be still intact — in fact, to be of value, they should really be in mint condition. Smaller ones are usually kept in albums, but the larger sizes, when framed, can make attractive wall decorations.

B.D.V. Cigarettes, Regimental Colours, 14th The Kings Hussars. $5 £3

B.D.V. War Leaders, General Cadorna. $9 £5

B.D.V. Victoria Cross Heroes, Lieut. General Sir Douglas Haig, K.C.B. $10 £6

B.D.V. Celebrities, King of Roumania. $7 £4

War Leaders, B.D.V. Lord Kitchener. $7 £4

B.D.V. Celebrities, Princess Mary. $18 £10

B.D.V. British Admirals, Admiral Sir John R. Jellicoe, 1916. $7 £4

B.D.V. Celebrities, David Lloyd George. $14 £8

B.D.V. War Leaders and Celebrities, the New Coalition Cabinet, Mr Balfour, Admiralty. $7 £4

Old Masters Set 5, Auguste Strobel. $2 £1

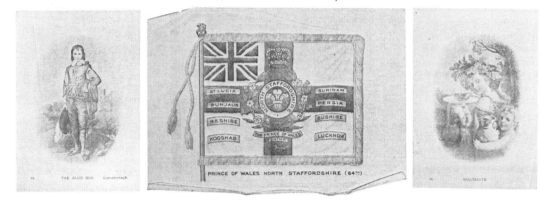

B.D.V. Old Masters, The Blue Boy, cabinet size. $28 £16

B.D.V. Regimental Colours, Prince of Wales, North Staffordshire. $5 £3

B.D.V. Old Masters, Bacchante, cabinet size. $32 £18

Great War Leaders and Warships, B.D.V., Rear Admiral Bernard Currey. $7 £4

Flags series B.D.V., the Allied Flags. $10 £6

B.D.V. Great Leaders and Warships, Admiral Sir George Neville. $7 £4

TOLEWARE

Toleware is essentially painted tin, and is akin to bargeware inasmuch as the original purpose was to make basic, functional items such as coffee pots more decorative. As in so many cases, however, what started as something relatively simple became much more sophisticated. Some toleware items, such as coalscuttles became very florid and ornate and worthy of a place in the most elegant drawing room. These can now fetch many hundreds of pounds at auction.

A 19th century French oval toleware tray, the maroon ground heightened in gilt with foliate and military trophies, 26in. wide. (Christie's) $539 £308

A mid Victorian black and gilt japanned tole purdonium, with shovel, 12½in. wide. (Christie's) $597 £418

A mid Victorian black and gilt japanned tole hubble-bubble, with metal label of Lowe, London, 10½in. high. (Christie's) $346 £242

A Victorian tole workbox, the glazed octangular lid decorated with a winter scene, 19½in. wide. (Christie's) $1,331 £918

Decorated tin coffee pot, possibly Maine, circa 1830, 8½in. high. $875 £500

A Regency black japanned tole coal box on cabochon feet, 24in. wide. (Christie's) $629 £440

Late 19th century American Toleware painted and stencilled chocolate pot, 8½in. high. (Christie's) $1,100 £620

TOY VEHICLES

Every small boy's desire to be 'just like Daddy' probably has something to do with the eternal popularity of these toys. When Daddy drove a horse and cart or even a chariot, son probably had a carved model to play with. Nowadays, however, the car, van and lorry have taken over, and an increasing number of special sales are being devoted to Dinky toys and the like which were new within the lifetime of many of us. Most people probably have one or two models in the attic, but to be worth much they have to be in good condition and, more particularly, should be accompanied by their original box. Originally boxed gift sets of several vehicles can often fetch thousands.

Less classic examples, such as clockwork and battery operated models have their following too, while a child's pedal car, in very poor condition, recently fetched over £1,000!

1931 Ranlite bakelite clockwork Austin car.
$2,600 £1,500

1924 tinplate Rolls Royce biscuit tin.
$2,100 £1,200

1935 Wells tinplate clockwork van. $875 £500

1931 Ranlite bakelite clockwork Singer car.
$2,600 £1,500

(Jock Farquharson)

388

1946 tinplate clockwork made in England.
$435 £250

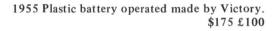

1955 Plastic battery operated made by Victory.
$175 £100

1924 tinplate biscuit tin tram. $435 £250

1947 Chad Valley tinplate clockwork biscuit tin.
$1,050 £600

1946 Minic tinplate clockwork London taxi.
$700 £400

1952 Plastic battery operated made by Victory.
$175 £100

(Jock Farquharson)

1939 Mettoy tinplate clockwork. $210 £120

1910 tinplate biscuit tin bus. $1,400 £800

1936 Wells tinplate clockwork bus. $1,050 £600

1946 Wells tinplate clockwork Milkman.
$140 £80

1938 Dinky tinplate
AA Telephone Box.
$45 £25

1938 Lines Bros. tinplate
clockwork AA man.
$225 £150

1946 tinplate clockwork made in Great Britain.
$435 £250

1931 Ranlite bakelite clockwork Golden Arrow.
$3,500 £2,000

1930 Wells tinplate clockwork truck.
$610 £350

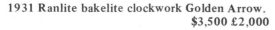

(Jock Farquharson)

TRADE CARDS

Not to be confused with cigarette cards, trade cards were, and still are, given away with confectionery, magazines, tea and many other household goods.

Priced and sold in sets, lower priced cards have little value individually, while more valuable sets would realise a proportionate value for single cards.

Some valuable sets to look out for are: AB & C Gum 'Crazy Disguises' 1970 (24) – £120; D W Allen Ltd 'Bradman's Records' 1931 (32) – £350; Amalgamated Press 'Cricket Stars' 1932 (32) – £175; Baileys Toffee 'War' series 1916 (25)—£200; Barratt & Co 'Felix pictures' (32)—£400; Huntley & Palmer 'Aviation' 1900 (12) – £350; Bouchere's Firm 'War Portraits' 1916 (50)—£1,000; Slade & Bullock 'Cricket' series 1924 (25)—£750.

F.C. Calvert Ltd., Dan Dare, 1954, set of 25. $21 £12

Amalgamated Press, Ships of the World, 1924, set of 24. $55 £30

Nelson Lee Library, Footballers, 1922, set of 15. $32 £18

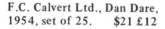

Clevedon Confectionary Ltd., Famous Cricketers, 1962, set of 25. $175 £100

A. & B.C. Gum Ltd., Batman, 1966, set of 55. $55 £30

Primrose Confectionary Co. Ltd., Popeye, 3rd Series, 1962, set of 50. $5 £3

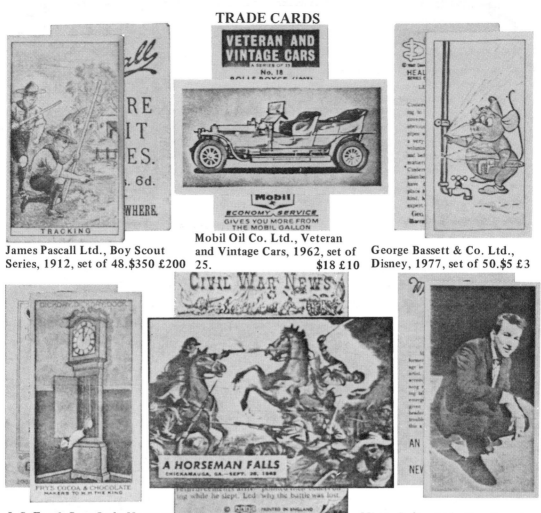

James Pascall Ltd., Boy Scout
Series, 1912, set of 48.$350 £200

Mobil Oil Co. Ltd., Veteran
and Vintage Cars, 1962, set of
25. $18 £10

George Bassett & Co. Ltd.,
Disney, 1977, set of 50.$5 £3

J. S. Fry & Sons Ltd., Nursery
Rhymes, 1917, set of 50.
            $125 £70

A. & B.C. Gum Ltd., Civil War
News, 1965, set of 88. $90 £50

Mister Softee Ltd., Top Twenty
1963, set of 20. $9 £5

William Gossage & Sons Ltd.,
Butterflies and Moths, 1924,
set of 48. $70 £40

J. Sainsbury Ltd., Foreign
Birds, 1924, set of 12. $60 £35

Slade & Bullock Ltd., Modern
Inventions, set of 25, 1925.
                  $220 £125

TRANSPORT

Transport forms an integral part of modern life: our vehicles seem very dear to our hearts, and older examples are a constant source of instant nostalgia for many. Motor museums receive a constant stream of visitors, and while vintage car rallies have been with us for a long time, it is only comparatively recently that the major international auction houses have started holding regular high profile sales devoted solely to transport subjects.

Now, in fact, older cars are becoming the latest status symbol, and a great deal of money which previously went into property is now finding its way into this market. Nor are we talking about vintage cars in the true sense of the word, for 1930's roadsters for example are also fetching huge sums. In recent sales, one or two have cracked the £1 million barrier and this has had the effect of concentrating attention on the market and hoisting up prices right through the range.

1956 Bentley S1 Continental two-door drop-head Coupe, coachwork by Park Ward, Reg. No. PLG 123, Chassis No. BC 77 BG, Engine No. BA 76128 UE 3764. (Christie's)
$94,446 £58,300

1925 Dodge 24 H.P. four-seat tourer, Reg. No. YR 9579, Chassis No. A324590, Engine No. A396282, 3,478 c.c., 23.8 h.p. (Christie's)
$14,256 £8,800

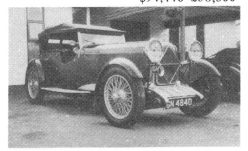

1931 Lagonda 14/60 Low Chassis 2-litre Tourer, Reg. No. GN 4840, Chassis No. OH 9825, Engine No. OH 1574, 1,955 c.c., (Christie's)
$40,172 £26,950

1932 Austin Seven two-door saloon, Reg. No. KJ 5917, Chassis No. 15490, Engine No. M152369, 747 c.c., 7.8 h.p. (Christie's)
$4,455 £2,750

1982 De Lorean DMC 12 Gullwing Sports Coupe, Reg. No. C 441 FKE, Chassis No. 11761, Engine No. 7979, 2,850 c.c., 130 b.h.p. (Christie's)
$21,912 £13,200

1926/1932 Sentinel DG4 steam waggon, Reg. No. OD 1572, Chassis No. 8666, 120 b.h.p. (Christie's)
$42,454 £25,575

1955 Citroen Light 15 four-door saloon, Reg. No. WFX 436, Chassis No. 657720, 1,911 c.c., 56 b.h.p. (Christie's) $8,217 £4,950

1967 Morgan plus four open Sportscar, Reg. No. PUV 316F, Chassis/Engine Nos. not known, engine, Triumph TR4, 2,138 c.c., 104 b.h.p. (Christie's) $5,478 £3,300

1974 Alfa-Romeo 2000 Spider Veloce 2 + 2 open Sportscar, coachwork by Pininfarina, Reg. No. GLT 87N, Chassis No. 247/0730, Engine No. AROS 12/519285, 1,962 c.c., 131 b.h.p. (Christie's) $6,938 £4,180

1957 Ford Thunderbird Sports two-seater with hard and soft tops, Reg. No. KRV 1P, Chassis No. D7FH 302275, 352 cu. ins. (5,769 c.c.), 130 b.h.p. (Christie's) $19,602 £12,100

1935 Bentley 3½-litre four-door Sports saloon, coachwork by Hooper, Reg. No. BLE 714, Chassis No. B40CR, Engine No. U2 BH, 3,669 c.c., 105 b.h.p. (Christie's) $23,166 £14,300

1938 Rolls-Royce Phantom III two-door fixed head Coupe, coachwork by Hooper, Reg. No. 11 DPW, Chassis No. 3CM173, Engine No. P98N, 7,340 c.c., 50.7 h.p. (Christie's) $98,010 £60,500

1930 Austin Seven open two-seater, Reg. No. PG 5934, Chassis No. 105171, Engine No. 105002, 747 cc., 7.8 h.p., right-hand drive. (Christie's) $4,455 £2,750

1957 Mercedes-Benz 300SL two-seat Roadster, Reg. No. CSU 418, Chassis No. 7500143, Engine No. 198042, 2,996 c.c., 215 b.h.p. (Christie's) $76,692 £46,200

1949 Aston Martin DB1 open Sports two-seater, coachwork by Swallow, Reg. No. MKE 836, Chassis No. AMC 49/8, Engine No. LB6B/50/630, 2,580 c.c.. (Christie's) $31,042 £18,700

1932 Mercedes-Benz 170 four-door saloon, Reg. No. GP 6387, Chassis No. U88418, Engine No. 88418, 1,692 c.c., 32 b.h.p. (Christie's) $7,669 £4,620

1937 MG VA four-seat drophead Coupe, coachwork by Tickford, Reg. No. COR 331, Chassis No. VA 0850, Engine No. TPBG 1099, 1,549 c.c., 55 b.h.p. (Christie's) $16,929 £10,450

1930 Rolls-Royce Phantom II Sedanca De Ville, coachwork by Barker, Reg. No. USV 694, Chassis No. 202 GN, Engine No. J65, 7.7-litre, 40/50 h.p. (Christie's) $94,952 £57,200

1937 Mercedes-Benz 540K Supercharged Cabriolet B, coachwork by Daimler-Benz, Sindelfingen, Reg. No. Not registered in U.K., Chassis No. 154119, 5,401 c.c., 115 b.h.p. (Christie's) $182,600 £110,000

1954 Jaguar XK 120 Roadster To Rally Specification, Reg. No. RJH 400, Chassis No. S661165, Engine No. F2111/85, 3,442 c.c., 160 b.h.p. (Christie's) $63,910 £38,500

1956 Bentley S1 four-door Sports saloon, Reg. No. JTL 717, Chassis No. B80 CK, Engine No. BC40, 3,887 c.c. (Christie's) $12,830 £7,920

1952 Aston Martin DB2 two-seat Sports saloon, Reg. No. NGO 655, Chassis No. LML/50/218, 2,580 c.c., 107 b.h.p. in standard tune. (Christie's) $12,474 £7,700

1968 ISO Grifo A3L 2 + 2 Sports Coupe, Not Registered in U.K., Chassis No. 820 202, Engine No. 1067Y0323HT, 5,359 c.c., 350 b.h.p. (Christie's) $17,820 £11,000

1955 Triumph TR2 two-seat Sportscar, Reg. No. RXV 318, Chassis No. TS 7707, Engine No. TS 8003, 1,991 c.c., 90 b.h.p. (Christie's) $7,304 £4,400

1953 Alvis-Healey G-type 3-litre convertible Sports 2/3 seater, Reg. No. NXR 829, Chassis No. G518, Engine No. 25318, 2,993 c.c. (Christie's) $10,956 £6,600

1931 Rolls-Royce 20/25 Doctor's Coupe, coachwork by Windover, Reg. No. GP 5803, Chassis No. GO510, Engine No. D9E, 3.7-litres, 20/25 h.p. (Christie's) $60,588 £37,400

1968 Aston Martin DB6 Superleggera Grand touring four-seater, Reg. No. SKK 714G, Chassis No. DB6L/L001R, Engine No. 400/406, 3,996 c.c., 282 b.h.p. (Christie's) $17,820 £11,000

1953 Jaguar XK120 Special Equipment two-seat Roadster, Reg. No. IRXB 240 (USA), Chassis No. S673307, Engine No. W6896-85, 3,442 c.c., 160 b.h.p. (Christie's) $24,057 £14,850

1963 Chevrolet Corvette Stingray 'Split-Window' Sports Coupe, Reg. No. ABK 747A, Chassis No. 30837S102721, 327 cu. ins. (5,350 c.c.). (Christie's) $28,512 £17,600

1927 Austin Seven four-seat Chummy tourer, Reg. No. WW 753, Chassis No. A4-2041, Engine No. 33977, 747 c.c., 7.8 h.p. (Christie's) $5,346 £3,300

TRAYS

When it became fashionable to drink tea in the afternoon, butlers or maids were required to carry a loaded tea tray into the drawing room every day. In the 18th and early 19th century the trays that were used were more often made of wood and could be the work of a fashionable cabinet maker like Chippendale or Vile who made trays with high lattice work sides out of mahogany. Hepplewhite and Sheraton trays were often made of mahogany too, oval shaped and decorated with a stylised shell in the middle. The handles were often brass scrolls. Victorian trays were far more flights of fancy because they preferred them to be bright and colourful — sometimes made of enamel painted all over with roses, japanned metal or papier mache set with mother of pearl. Returning travellers often brought home engraved trays of brass from India or Burma and in the 1920's tin trays decorated with bold Art Deco designs made their appearance.

A 19th century large papier mache tray with raised rim, 30½ x 22in. (Lawrence Fine Art) $2,472 £1,705

A late 19th century enamelled pub tray Dunville's Whisky. $70 £40

A papier-mache tray of rounded rectangular form, gilt painted with flowering plants on a black ground, 30in. wide., circa 1840 $645 £500

An 19th century oval papier mache tray, centrally decorated after Morland, 30in. wide. (Dreweatts) $1,276 £880

A Regency mahogany two-handled rectangular wine tray, on melon feet, 13½ x 9¾in. (Geering & Colyer) $910 £700

18th century metal tray decorated with a bird, urn and floral displays. $340 £275

A 19th century Japanese black and gold lacquer tray, 23.5in. wide. (Woolley & Wallis) $1,935 £1,500

A mid Victorian black and gilt japanned papier-mache tray of waved and shaped rectangular form, 23¾ x 31in. (Christie's) $2,055 £1,430

1930's oak tray with moulded edge. $14 £8

TRAYS

A Regency scarlet and gold papier-mache tray with everted gallery, 30in. wide. (Christie's) $660 £462

'Coca Cola' advertising tip tray, round, America, circa 1905. (Robt. W. Skinner Inc.) $200 £155

A papier-mache tray fixed to a folding wooden stand, 31½in. (Lawrence Fine Arts) $2,700 £1,540

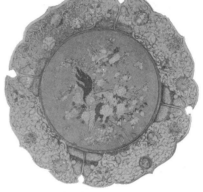

An inlaid waiter with an everted brim, on four cast feet, by Tiffany & Co., 1878-91, 9½in. diam., gross weight 10oz. (Christie's) $19,800 £11,971

'Clysmic' advertising tip tray, oval, copy reads 'Clysmic, King of Table Waters' (Robt. W. Skinner Inc.) $50 £38

Late 19th century silver mounted shibayama inlaid lacquer tray, signed Yasuaki, 24cm. diam. (Christie's) $2,805 £1,650

19th century papier-mache tray, stamped Clay, London, with cricketing scene.(Phillips) $1,300 £750

Victorian mahogany butler's tray on stand, 1860. $260 £150

A painted tray by Duncan Grant, circa 1920, 35.3cm. diam. $875 £500

TREEN

Treen is one of those umbrella words that covers a mutitude of articles. According to the dictionary it means "of a tree" and in common usage it is appled to any article made of wood and turned on a lathe. Usually treen was strictly utilitarian and was used by farmers, tradesfolk, apothecaries and ordinary housewives. The term covers bowls, spoons, goblets, moulds, napkin rings, measures, mortars, egg cups, boot trees and boxes – things that were useful and had to be cheap. Articles in every day use were usually left plain but if they were to be displayed in any way, they were decorated with mother of pearl or other woods, painted or inlaid with ivory. Some pieces were lacquered and inlaid with coloured glass and when they turn up their value is greatly enhanced. Favourite woods for making treen were finely grained hardwoods like yew, sycamore, olivewood and lignum vitae. Many pieces have acquired a satisfying patina after years of use. Not long ago treen could be picked up for next to nothing but today it is avidly collected and 18th century American treen is particularly valuable.

An 18th century mahogany offertory tray in the form of a scallop shell, 8 in. wide.
$435 £250

An early 19th century rosewood letter rack with six fan-shaped divisions, 5 x 9 in.
$350 £200

A Regency rosewood tazza with moulded ring-turned bowl, 10¼ in. wide.
(Christie's) $484 £275

A 16th/17th century elm double sided platter of square form with a salt sinking to each side, 9¾ in. long.
$785 £450

Mid 19th century painted wooden splint basket, probably Pennsylvania, 11 in. wide, 7½ in. high, 8 in. deep. (Christie's)
$825 £544

A 19th century boxwood and fruitwood bucket, probably Dutch, 12 in. high.
(Christie's) $1,339 £1,080

A 17th/18th century lignum vitae two-handled quaich with silver mounted handles, 5½ in. wide. $350 £200

A 19th century mahogany wine tray, with six square divisions, 10¾ in. long.
(Christie's) $605 £354

An 18th century mahogany offertory tray of turned circular form, 12 in. long.
$260 £150

399

An early 19th century
mahogany cheese board, 10in.
diam. $525   £300

Late 17th/early 18th century
lignum vitae loving cup with
plain bowl, 7in. high.
                    $1,000 £600

An 18th/19th century boxwood
table salt, with a boxwood
spoon and pestle, 4in. high.
                    $435 £250

A 19th century mahogany egg
cup stand, 7½in. high.$875 £500

A late 17th century lignum
vitae Montieth, 10in. high,
12in. diam. $7,700 £4,400

A pearwood clothes press with
double arched handle, inscribed
Elizabeth Brayant 1704,
8.7cm. high. $435   £250

An engraved and painted
wood pantry box, New
England, circa 1800/20,
10½in. diam. (Christie's)
        $3,410 £2,351

A George III mahogany
cistern, the vase shaped
body with lead lining, 17in.
diam. (Christie's)
          $2,770 £2,052

An 18th century twelve sided
offertory plate with moulded
border, 11½in. wide.$350 £200

A 19th century snuff jar, 5in. high. $350 £200

A late 18th/early 19th century mahogany artist's palette, 18in. long. $130 £75

A 19th century turned beech-wood dentist's drill tip holder, 5¼in. high. $260 £150

A 19th century lignum vitae inkwell carved in the form of a boxer dog, 5in. high.
                    $1,300 £750

A George III mahogany and brass bound beer barrel, 18½in. high by 23in. wide.
                    $2,800 £1,600

An early 17th century hard wood and ivory caster, 6in. high. $600 £350

A 19th century rosewood and boxwood egg cup stand, 9½in.
                    $1,350 £770

A lignum vitae mortar and boxwood pestle, mortar 6½in., pestle 9½in. $175 £100

A 17th century leather covered oak laundry tally board, 9 x 8in. $830 £475

TROPHIES

Many of the countless trophies issued for everything under the sun have only curiosity value. Even silver trophies are generally valued by their weight as scrap items unless they are by a particular maker or are extremely decorative.

Look out for more unusual trophies, especially for prestige sports. Engraved examples or those with engraved plaques are always interesting, as are those for early sporting events or unusual feats. Valuable or not, they always make a superb display.

A presentation loving cup, by Dominick & Haff, Newark, for J. E. Caldwell & Co., 1895, in original mahogany box, 11½in. high, 82oz. (Christie's) $9,900   £5,985

A 19th century French racing trophy cup, the lower part of the foot electroplate, circa 1870, 38cm. high, weighable silver 115oz. (Phillips)
$2,574   £1,800

The Richmond Race Cup, 1764: a George III silver gilt two-handled cup and cover, designed by Robert Adam; by D. Smith and Robert Sharp, 1764, 19in. high, 142oz. (Christie's)
$106,920 £66,000

A late Victorian neo-classical style two-handled trophy cup, by Charles S. Harris, London, 1899, 15in. high, 81oz. (Woolley & Wallis)
$789 £530

A George III maritime vase-shaped presentation cup and cover, by Robert Salmon, London, 1793, 14in. high, 43 troy oz. (Reeds Rains) $3,550 £2,500

A George IV silver gilt racing trophy cup, by Benjamin Smith, 1824, 34cm. high, 116.5oz. (Phillips)
$3,525 £2,500

The Richmond Race Cup, 1768: a George III silver gilt two-handled cup and cover, by D. Smith and R. Sharp, 1768, 17¼in. high, 112oz.17dwt. (Christie's) $16,929 £10,450

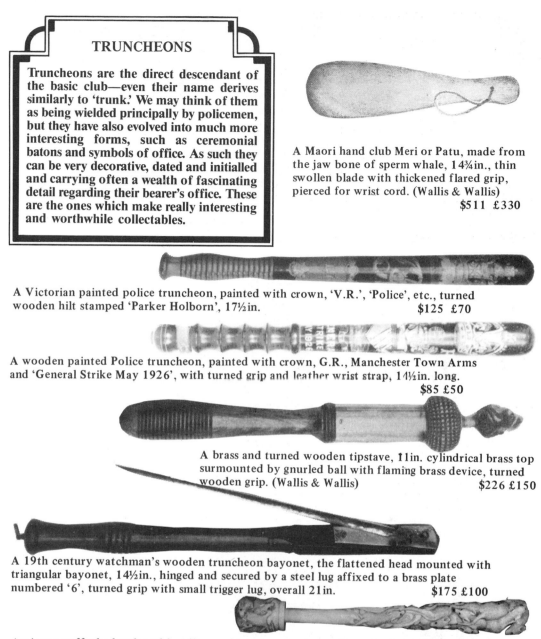

TRUNCHEONS

Truncheons are the direct descendant of the basic club—even their name derives similarly to 'trunk.' We may think of them as being wielded principally by policemen, but they have also evolved into much more interesting forms, such as ceremonial batons and symbols of office. As such they can be very decorative, dated and initialled and carrying often a wealth of fascinating detail regarding their bearer's office. These are the ones which make really interesting and worthwhile collectables.

A Maori hand club Meri or Patu, made from the jaw bone of sperm whale, 14¾in., thin swollen blade with thickened flared grip, pierced for wrist cord. (Wallis & Wallis)
$511 £330

A Victorian painted police truncheon, painted with crown, 'V.R.', 'Police', etc., turned wooden hilt stamped 'Parker Holborn', 17½in. $125 £70

A wooden painted Police truncheon, painted with crown, G.R., Manchester Town Arms and 'General Strike May 1926', with turned grip and leather wrist strap, 14½in. long. $85 £50

A brass and turned wooden tipstave, 11in. cylindrical brass top surmounted by gnurled ball with flaming brass device, turned wooden grip. (Wallis & Wallis) $226 £150

A 19th century watchman's wooden truncheon bayonet, the flattened head mounted with triangular bayonet, 14½in., hinged and secured by a steel lug affixed to a brass plate numbered '6', turned grip with small trigger lug, overall 21in. $175 £100

An ivory staff, the knob and handle carved with swarming and entwined rats, 9¾in. long. (Reeds Rains) $460 £320

A William IV turned wooden tipstave, 13¾in., black painted with gilt and red WR, crowned IV. (Wallis & Wallis) $130 £75

A George IV painted police truncheon of the City of Bath, 14in., painted with town arms, turned wooden grip. $175 £100

TSUBAS

The hand protectors for Japanese swords are called tsubas and, like so many Japanese items, they were objects of beauty and examples of exquisite craftsmanship. Made of iron, brass or copper, and sometimes with gold or silver decorations, they were about two inches across with a wedge shaped hole in the centre for the sword blade. There were also other openings for the sword knife (kogatawa) and skewer (kogai).

The engravings and patterns on tsubas were either inlaid or applied, decorated with gold, silver, cloisonne or Champleve enamel. They depicted landscapes, animals, historical events and stories from Japanese folklore. In early times tsubas were made by swordsmiths but they were later taken over by other craftsmen and artists who turned them into a speciality.

An 18th century iron soten tsuba depicting Kyoyu and Sofu in hikone-bori, 8.3cm. diam. (Christie's) $860 £506

An oval shakudo-nanakoji tsuba decorated in gilt, silver and copper takazogan with seven horses, 7.3cm. (Christie's) $1,320 £825

Mid 18th century circular iron tsuba formed as the madogiri or paulownia and window design in yosukashi and kebori, 8.5cm. (Christie's) $1,760 £1,100

A rounded-square shinchu and sahari tsuba decorated with Taira no Kiyomori seated on an engawa, signed Masanaga, Meiji period, 8.8cm. (Christie's) $1,936 £1,210

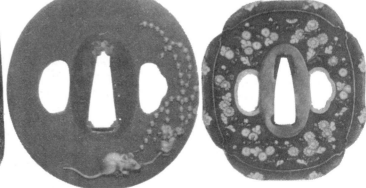

An oval shakudo-nanakoji tsuba decorated in silver and gilt takazogan with three rats and branches of mochi-bana, circa 1800, 6.6cm. (Christie's) $1,215 £715

A mokko-shaped Shakudo Nanako Tsuba decorated with flowers in gilt, the rim with gilt kiri-mon, 7.6cm. (Phillips) $563 £320

A hexagonal copper ishimeji tsuba decorated with a swallow-tail butterfly, signed Mitsumasa, Meiji period, 9.6cm. (Christie's)
$2,464 £1,540

Late 18th century ju-mokko-gata migakiji iron tsuba, Awa Shoami style. (Christie's)
$748 £440

A 19th century sentoku and copper tsuba formed as the eight-headed snake, signed Katsuchika, 8.8cm. (Christie's) $4,576 £2,860

An 18th century gilt rimmed shakudo mokkogata tsuba, unsigned, 7.6cm. (Christie's)
$1,122 £660

An iron tsuba with maple leaves and pine needles in ikizukashi, signed Suruga Takayoshi saku, circa 1850, 7.8cm. diam. (Christie's)
$935 £550

An 18th century mokkogata shakudo-nanakoji tsuba, Mino-Goto style, 7.1cm. (Christie's) $860 £506

An aorigata copper ishimeji tsuba decorated with Emma-o the King of Hell holding a shaku, 9.1cm. (Christie's)
$4,400 £2,750

A 19th century mokkogata iron tsuba, Edo Bushu school, 7.4cm. (Christie's)
$448 £264

A sentoku tsuba with canted corners decorated with a carp in copper takazogan, signed Tenkodo Hidekuni, 1825-91, 9.6cm. (Christie's)
$6,160 £3,850

A 19th century sentoku tsuba formed as a serpent in marubori, signed Nagat-sugu, 8.4cm. (Christie's) $3,344 £2,090

A 19th century iron tsuba with a crayfish in marubori, with gilt hirazogan seal of Munenori, 6.9cm. diam. (Christie's) $860 £506

Late 19th century otafuku-mokko sentoku hari-ishimeji tsuba decorated with two carp, signed Nagamasa. (Christie's) $8,800 £5,500

A shallow mokkogata tsuba decorated with Susano-o no Mikoto attacking the monster Yamata no orochi, Meiji period, 8.9cm. (Christie's) $1,672 £1,045

An iron higo tsuba formed as a blossoming plum tree, circa 1725, 7.8cm. diam. (Christie's) $561 £330

Mid 19th century hakkaku copper tsuba carved as a tree-trunk with an eagle, signed Ryuo (Ittosai). (Christie's) $7,040 £4,400

A large mokkogata iron tsuba, branches of bamboo in taka-bori, Kyo-shoami school, circa 1800, 8.7cm. (Christie's) $486 £286

Late 18th century iron tsuba, signed Bushu ju Masakata, 7.7cm. diam., and another, early Echizen school, 7cm. diam. (Christie's) $561 £330

Late 19th century hari-ishimeji tsuba decorated with Emma-O and a demonic attendant, inscribed Hamano Noriyuki, 9.6cm. (Christie's) $4,928 £3,080

TUNBRIDGEWARE

During the 18th and 19th centuries, Tunbridge Wells was a popular watering place, almost as well attended as Bath. Local craftsmen seized the opportunity of the tourist trade and set about providing small, easily portable souvenirs of the town. Their speciality was what was known as "English mosaic" or Tunbridgeware. They made boxes, trays and toilet articles and decorated them with trimming made out of thin strips of wood veneer in a variety of colours which were set in an arranged pattern and then stuck together to form a block from which sheets could be cut. The decorative veneer was then applied to the boxes or other items to be decorated. The simplest patterns were made up of cube shapes but later veneers became more elaborate and intricate designs of flowers, birds and even landscapes were produced. Tunbridgeware was still being made as late as 1927 when the last firm of manufacturers Boyce, Brown and Kemp ceased production.

A rosewood stationery casket of wedge form with sloping lid, 6½in. wide. $260 £150

A rosewood single division Tunbridgeware tea caddy, 5½in. wide. $260 £150

A miniature Tunbridgeware cabinet with domed top and hinged door, 18cm. wide, 15cm. high. (David Lay) $360 £200

A Tunbridgeware rosewood writing slope, the double hinged top inlaid with a view of an abbey and a panel of roses, 14in. wide. (Christie's) $1,020 £600

A Tunbridgeware lignum vitae rectangular inkstand, the tapering sides with a band of Berlin woolwork flowers, the hinged cover to the top fitted with a pin cushion, 9in. wide. (Christie's) $408 £240

A Tunbridgeware rosewood 'Russell' marquetry travelling writing box, the hinged cover enclosing a velvet lined slope and compartments, 16in. wide. (Christie's) $1,105 £650

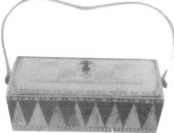

An early 19th century Regency Tunbridgeware work basket and cover with a hinged loop handle, 8¼in. wide. $525 £300

A Tunbridgeware thermometer stand by H. Hollanby, 4½in. high. $175 £100

A Regency period book trough veneered in pollard oak, 12in. long. $1,300 £750

A rosewood jewellery box with mosaic borders and velvet lined interior, 7in. wide. $175 £100

A 19th century inkstand inlaid throughout with floral mosaic, 11in. wide. $525 £300

A domed top rosewood Tunbridge writing box, depicting a ruined castle, 10½in. wide. (Geering & Colyer) $195 £135

A Tunbridgeware rosewood workbox, the gabled cover with cube parquetry inlay, the interior partly fitted with sewing implements, 8¾in. wide. (Christie's) $1,275 £750

A miniature Tunbridgeware chamber candlestick with mahogany base inlaid with an end grain mosaic panel, 1¾in. high. $150 £90

A two-compartment Tunbridge-ware tea caddy, on bun feet. (David Lay) $250 £140

A Tunbridgeware rosewood rectangular table cabinet, the top inlaid with Berlin wool-work flowers, the base with the trade label of T. Barton Late Nye, 8¼in. wide. (Christie's) $646 £380

A Tunbridgeware walnut cigar table, the rectangular top with protruding D-end corners, on a baluster turned support with tripod scroll feet, 14½in. wide. (Christie's) $2,380 £1,400

A Tunbridgeware combined thermometer and compass stand, with stickware top and base 5½in. high; another similar, 4¾in. high; and a thermometer stand of obelisk shape, 7½in. high. (Christie's) Three $1,020 £600

A rosewood Tunbridgeware visiting card tray of rectangular shape, 10¾in. wide. $350 £200

A domed top rosewood ground Tunbridgeware box depicting Eridge Castle, 25cm. wide. (Geering & Colyer) $159 £110

A rosewood Tunbridgeware writing slope, the interior fitted with compartments and inkwells 12¼in. wide. $385 £220

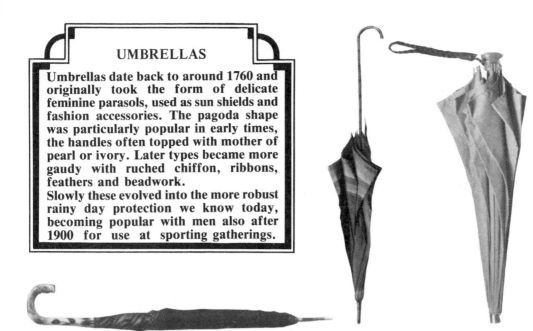

UMBRELLAS

Umbrellas date back to around 1760 and originally took the form of delicate feminine parasols, used as sun shields and fashion accessories. The pagoda shape was particularly popular in early times, the handles often topped with mother of pearl or ivory. Later types became more gaudy with ruched chiffon, ribbons, feathers and beadwork.

Slowly these evolved into the more robust rainy day protection we know today, becoming popular with men also after 1900 for use at sporting gatherings.

Edwardian brass tipped umbrella with florally decorated hawthorn handle, circa 1912. $30 £18

1930's umbrella with brass tipped willow limb. $14 £8

1950's ladies umbrella with thonged hanging cord and plastic handle. $9 £5

1930's Art Deco style umbrella with plastic handle and hanging cord. $9 £5

Edwardian black parasol with ebonised carved bamboo handle. $35 £20

Venetian multi coloured umbrella with wooden handle. $14 £8

Ladies bamboo, walking umbrella with silver plated fittings, circa 1930. $14 £8

UNIFORMS

Uniforms are essentially a means of distinction, and have probably existed in some shape or form since man felt the need to organise himself into one group as opposed to (very often literally) another. These developed further to distinguish the wearer's position within the group, resulting in the many details which make uniforms so fascinating. Often these become collectables in their own right, e.g. cap badges, buttons.

Rarity and condition usually determine value.

An officer's silver mounted shoulder belt and pouch of The 16th (The Queen's) Lancers, HM Birmingham 1890. (Wallis & Wallis) $467 £320

An officer's full dress uniform items of The 10th Royal Hussars, together with metal uniform case. (Christie's) $2,142 £1,400

A yellow Skinner's kurta with plain shoulder chains, a fine pouchbelt and its Skinner's Horse title scroll. (Christie's) $4,500 £3,000

A South Australia Militia Lancers uniform. (Christie's) $5,510 £3,800

Part of an Imperial Russian diplomatic/court uniform. (Christie's) $841 £550

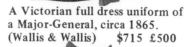

A post 1902 Lt. Colonel's part uniform of The Prince of Wales's Own Royal Wiltshire Yeomanry. (Wallis & Wallis) $666 £450

A Victorian full dress uniform of a Major-General, circa 1865. (Wallis & Wallis) $715 £500

Part of an officer's 88th Connaught Rangers uniform. (Christie's) $7,250 £5,000

A complete post 1902 trooper's full dress blue uniform of the City of London Yeomanry (Rough Riders). (Wallis & Wallis) $792 £600

The Imperial Russian uniform of Count A. Benckendorff, Ambassador to the Court of St James's, together with British Court dress cocked hat. (Christie's) $2,465 £1,700

A good post 1902 Lt. Colonel's full dress scarlet doublet of The Gordon Highlanders, and a pair of tartan trews. (Wallis & Wallis) $365 £200

A pair of East India Company Light Company officer's wings of The 6th (Bengal?) Regt. (Wallis & Wallis) $251 £170

One of a pair of officer's embossed gilt shoulder scales of the Bengal Artillery. (Wallis & Wallis) $293 £180

A Nazi period Field Marshal's epaulette with gold and silver embroidery. (Wallis & Wallis) $125 £85

A Victorian officer's full dress sabretache of The 18th Hussars, the inner flap with trade label of Hawkes & Co., Piccadilly. (Wallis & Wallis) $830 £550

A Prussian officer's full dress sabretache of The 12th Hussars, circa 1890. (Wallis & Wallis) $325 £220

One of a pair of pre 1830 Light Company officer's wings of The 54th (West Norfolk) Regt. (Wallis & Wallis) $296 £200

A fine Black Watch broadsword by Wilkinson Sword Co. Ltd, London with 32½in. blade, an officer's Black Watch full dress doublet, a kilt and Black Watch sporran by Wm. Anderson & Sons Ltd. (Christie's) $1,550 £850

One of a pair of U.S. Army officer's full dress epaulettes, possibly of Civil War period. (Wallis & Wallis) $138 £105

VETERINARY ITEMS

Like medical items for humans, veterinary instruments of the past hold an immediate fascination; many an animal lover will shudder with relief that their pet will no longer be subjected to such horrors. Vets too may be relieved, for many old instruments are fairly primitive, such as a device for dehorning bulls, which weighed all of 28 lbs!

It's interesting to note those which have stood the test of time, and also to note old cures and potions.

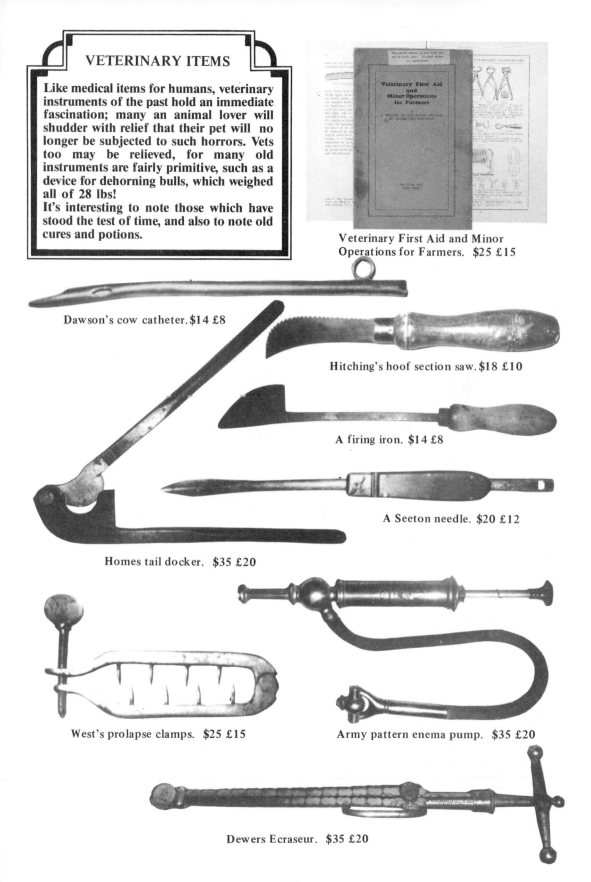

Veterinary First Aid and Minor Operations for Farmers. $25 £15

Dawson's cow catheter. $14 £8

Hitching's hoof section saw. $18 £10

A firing iron. $14 £8

A Seeton needle. $20 £12

Homes tail docker. $35 £20

West's prolapse clamps. $25 £15

Army pattern enema pump. $35 £20

Dewers Ecraseur. $35 £20

VINAIGRETTES

When they ventured abroad Tudor ladies carried pomanders up to their noses to ward off evil smells and prevent them breathing in noxious air. The pomander was often only a dried orange stuck with cloves and the vinaigrette was its more sophisticated descendant and carried by ladies of Victorian times.

They were little boxes made of gold, silver, pinchbeck, glass or porcelain and one side was a pierced grill. Inside was kept a small piece of sponge or wadding soaked in aromatic oils or vinegar which were thought to ward off disease when sniffed and bring back consciousness to swimming heads. In the filthy steets of big cities, a sniff at the vinaigrette must often have been a necessity.

Vinaigrettes were made to look as ornamental as possible and some were studded with precious or semi-precious stones. They could be worn like brooches or chatelaines suspended by a chain while others were carried inside a muff or purse. Vinaigrettes by Nathaniel Mills are particularly desirable especially the ones with embossed views on the lid.

A gold and enamel mounted nephrite vinaigrette, probably 19th century, 3¼in. high. (Christie's) $1,321 £864

A 19th century Chinese Export oblong vinaigrette with engine-turned base, by Khecheong of Canton, circa 1850. (Phillips) $178 £120

A George III articulated fish vinaigrette, 7.25cm. long, by Samuel Pemberton, Birmingham, 1817. (Phillips) $598 £320

An oblong 'castle-top' vinaigrette chased with a view of Litchfield Cathedral, by N. Mills, 1843-4. (Christie's) $1,652 £1,080

VINAIGRETTES

A silver gilt engine turned vinaigrette, by Nathaniel Mills, Birmingham, 1825, 1¾in. long. (Christie's) $580 £352

A William IV vinaigrette, the cover chased in relief with a ruined building, by Taylor & Perry, Birmingham, 1835. (Phillips) $800 £500

A Victorian oblong silver-gilt castle-top vinaigrette, with a view of a large church, Yapp & Woodward, Birmingham 1844. (Christie's) $544 £330

An attractive late Victorian vinaigrette, the cover set with turquoise and incised with a name in Persian script, by William Summers, 1888. (Phillips) $147 £90

A George IV rectangular purse shaped silver vinaigrette, by Clark & Smith, Birmingham, 1824, 1.25in. long. (Woolley & Wallis) $159 £95

A large silver gilt castletop vinaigrette, the hinged cover chased with a view of Warwick Castle, by Nathaniel Mills, Birmingham, 1839, 1¾in. long. (Christie's) $1,452 £880

An early 19th century gold engine-turned rectangular vinaigrette, 3 x 2.2cm unmarked, circa 1830. (Phillips) $935 £500

A Victorian shaped oval gilt-lined vinaigrette, the lid depicting a river scene with tree-lined banks and buildings, Nathaniel Mills, Birmingham 1846, 1½in. (Christie's) $471 £286

A silver gilt vinaigrette, the cover repousse and chased with four pheasants in a wooded landscape, by Ledsam, Vale & Wheeler, Birmingham, 1829, 1¾in. long. (Christie's) $1,089 £660

A parcel gilt vinaigrette, the cover repousse and chased with a man in 17th century dress, by Nathaniel Mills, Birmingham, 1835(?), 1¾in. long. (Christie's) $907 £550

A small oblong gold vinaigrette, the cover with a winged putto holding a butterfly. (Christie's) $1,416 £770

A silver gilt vinaigrette with engine turned sides and base, London, 1829, maker's initials A.D. possibly for Allen Dominy, 1.5/8in. long. (Christie's) $635 £385

An oblong silver gilt castletop vinaigrette chased with a view of Westminster Abbey, by Taylor & Perry, Birmingham, 1839. (Christie's) $712 £540

An oblong silver castletop vinaigrette chased with a view of Abbotsford House, by N. Mills, Birmingham, 1837. (Christie's) $541 £410

A Victorian rectangular vinaigrette, the cover chased with a view of York Minster, by Joseph Willmore, 1842, 4cm. wide. (Christie's) $422 £325

Victorian shaped rectangular vinaigrette, by Yapp & Woodward, 1848, 3.5cm. wide. (Christie's) $195 £150

A silver gilt vinaigrette of scallop shape, by Matthew Linwood, Birmingham, 1802. (Christie's) $398 £302

Silver gilt cushion-shaped vinaigrette, by John Shaw, circa 1810, 3.2cm. wide. (Christie's) $195 £150

An oblong silver gilt vinaigrette with pierced foliage panel on the cover, by J. Bettridge, Birmingham, 1827. (Christie's) $213 £162

An unusual, silver gilt vinaigrette chased as a crown, by Joseph Willmore, Birmingham, 1820, with suspension ring. (Christie's) $1,069 £810

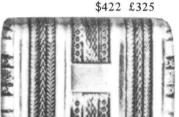

A George III vinaigrette in the form of a purse, by John Shaw, Birmingham 1819, 2.8cm. (Lawrence Fine Art) $172 £132

A large oblong silver castletop vinaigrette chased with St. Paul's Cathedral on matted ground, by N. Mills, Birmingham, 1842, 4.8cm. long. (Christie's) $1,025 £777

A George IV silver gilt rectangular vinaigrette, with maker's marks of T. & S. Pemberton, Birmingham, 1821, 3.4cm. (Lawrence Fine Art) $100 £77

An oblong silver castletop vinaigrette chased with a view of Kenilworth Castle, by Nathaniel Mills, Birmingham, 1839. (Christie's) $455 £345

VIOLINS

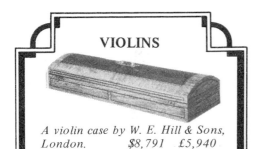

A violin case by W. E. Hill & Sons, London. $8,791 £5,940

The 'cradle' of the modern violin was Cremona in Italy where, in the 16th century Andrea Amati developed the design which became the standard for the instrument we know today. His grandson Nicolo was the family's greatest craftsman. The founders of the other great Cremona violin-making families, Guarneri and Stradivari, studied under him and, with their sons, continued to make outstanding violins, violas and cellos. Violins by these masters will now fetch untold sums at auction, though it is interesting to note that there are more 'Strads' in the U.S. alone than were ever produced by the family!

A viola by Giuseppe Lucci, length of back 16½in., in a case lined in green velvet by Gewa. (Phillips) $3,795 £2,300

A violin by Antonio Capela, 1972, length of back 14in., in shaped case. (Phillips) $198 £120

A violin by William Glenister, 1904, length of back 14. 1/16in., with a bow. (Phillips) $1,567 £950

A violin by Vincenzo Sannino, 1910, length of back 14.1/16in, with a shaped case and cover. (Phillips) $10,725 £6,500

A violin by Joannes Gagliano of Naples, circa 1790, length of back 14in., in case. (Phillips) $9,308 £5,200

A violin by Lorenzo Arcangioli of Florence, circa 1840, length of back 13.7/8in. (Phillips) $6,930 £4,200

A violin by Salomon of Reims, 1746, length of back 14. 13/16in., in an oblong, velvet-lined and fitted case. (Phillips)
$2,970 £1,800

A Florentine violin, circa 1770, bearing the label Lorenzo and Tommaso Carcassi, anno 1773, length of back 14in. (Phillips)
$9,075 £5,500

An English violin, bearing the label of G. Pyne, Maker London, 1888, 14.1/8in. long, with bow. (Phillips)
$2,880 £1,800

A viola, by B. Banks of Salisbury, circa 1770, length of back 15.3/8in., in a shaped and lined velvet case. (Phillips)
$9,308 £5,200

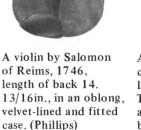

A violin by J. A. Chanot, 1899, length of back 14.1/8in., with a silver mounted bow, in case. (Phillips)
$5,728 £3,200

A violin by Wm. E. Hill & Sons, London, 1904, length of back 14in., in a mahogany case. (Phillips)
$8,055 £4,500

A violoncello by Wm. Forster, London, circa 1784, 29in. long, in wood case. (Phillips)
$6,720 £4,000

A violin by Carolus F. Landulphus, 1766, length of back 13. 15/16in., with a silver mounted bow, in an oak case. (Phillips)
$57,280 £32,000

A Neapolitan violon-
cello, circa 1750,
attributed to G.
Gagliano, 29.7/16in.
long, with a silver
mounted bow and
cover. (Phillips)
$58,800 £35,000

A viola by F.
Gagliano in Naples,
14½in. long, upper
bouts 7.1/8in. long,
lower bouts 9in.
(Phillips)
$17,600 £11,000

A violoncello, circa
1750, of the Tyro-
lesse School, label-
led Carlo Tunon,
1732, 29.3/16in.
long, in wood case.
(Phillips)
$7,056 £4,200

A violin by J. N.
Leclerc, circa 1770,
14in. long, with
two bows, in case.
(Phillips)
$2,520 £1,500

A violin by Alfred
Vincent, dated
1922, 13.14/16in.
long, in a shaped
case, by E. Withers.
(Phillips)
$3,024 £1,800

A violin by Dom
Nicolo Amati of
Bologna, 1714,
14.1/16in. long,
in case. (Phillips)
$15,120 £9,000

A viola, circa 1830,
of the Kennedy
School, 15.5/16in.
long, with two bows,
in an oblong case.
(Phillips)
$2,436 £1,450

A violin attributed
to R. Cuthbert,
1676, 13.7/8in.
long, in case.
(Phillips)
$1,310 £780

WALKING STICKS

From the shepherd's crook to the masher's whangee cane, the walking stick has had a variety of functions and perhaps the least of them was helping to support the halt and the lame. The fashionable man about town in the 17th and 18th centuries always carried his walking stick with him when he went out for a stroll. In old prints dandies can be seen leaning negligently on their sticks and it is obvious that there's nothing wrong with their legs. These fashion accessories were made of cane, rosewood, fruitwood, ebony, ash, ivory, bone, shark's vertebrae or rhinotail. Sometimes the handles were carved from ivory or hardstone or else made of precious materials like gold or silver. From time to time sticks turn up which have a watch, a telescope or a drinking flask attached to them and a few sticks concealed a sword with the slender steel blade attached to the handle and concealed down the middle of the shaft. Often sword sticks were carried by travellers to foreign parts and today they would be regarded as an offensive weapon, making anyone who carried such a stick liable to arrest.

More workaday sticks are those which were country made — often a length of wood cut from a hedge and adroitly carved by a rural artist. The handles of those rough sticks were often carved in the shape of animal heads. Shepherd's crooks were an opportunity for local artistry to be displayed and the handles were cleverly carved from horn. Today in rural districts there are still competitions at fairs to find the best carved crook. Other collectable sticks include comic ones such as were used by music hall comedians, especially the curling blackthorn stick that was one of the trademarks of Harry Lauder and, of course, Charlie Chaplin's cane which recently sold for thousands.

A Kloster Veilsdorf cane handle, formed as a bearded old man, circa 1770, 7.5cm. high.(Christie's)
$810 £540

Late 19th century Uncle Sam animated ivory cane, America, 35in. long. (Robt. W. Skinner Inc.)
$1,400 £833

Top of the handle of a captain's 'going ashore' cane.
$20,000 £11,615

A rare Meissen cane handle in the shape of Joseph Frohlich lying on top of a barrel, 1743, 13.5cm.
$8,750 £5,000

A Bow spirally moulded cane handle of tapering form, circa 1750, 5.5cm. high. (Christie's)
$1,942 £1,110

A French vari-coloured gold and enamel mounted parasol handle, with Paris restricted gold warranty mark in use from 1838, 3¼in. long. (Christie's)$2,877 £1,944

WALKING STICKS

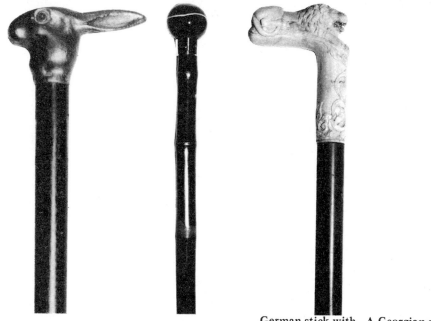

Ebonised shaft cane with a silver gilt handle in the form of a hare's head, 34in. long, dated 1912.
$300 £170

Mid 19th century bamboo shaft walking stick with 'tiger's eye' agate ball handle, 34in. long.
$175 £100

German stick with Malacca shaft and finely carved ivory handle featuring a seated lion, circa 1840. $700 £400

A Georgian walking stick the exterior wrapped in coloured baleen with space for candlestick, candleholder and spills, 35in. long, circa 1830.
$950 £550

Mid 19th century cane with carved horn handle in the form of an elephant with a collar of turquoise, 35in. long. $160 £90

Mid 19th century cane, the carved wood handle in the form of a hand. entwined with a snake, 35in. long. $160 £90

Victorian corkscrew cane with black horn handle and silver collar, bayonet fitting, 34in. long, circa 1880.
$435 £250

Late 19th century silver mounted swordstick with etched blade by Swaine, London, 34in. long, circa 1900. $315 £180

Rare percussion muzzle loading umbrella gun with Birmingham proof stamps, the brolly being ornamental, 35in. long, circa 1840. $1,000 £600

A Malacca shaft walking stick with carved wood dog handle the jaw hinged for holding silk gloves, 34in. long, circa 1870. $160 £90

Japanese cane with Malacca shaft and good ivory handle carved with heads of rats, circa 1860. $525 £300

Victorian lady's cane with silver snipe handle ebonised shaft, 34in. long, circa 1880. $210 £120

Rosewood cane with carved wood walrus head handle with ivory tusks and gilt metal collar, circa 1880, 35in. long. $230 £130

Walking stick with rosewood shaft and carved ivory handle in the form of a horse's head, 34in. long, circa 1865. $600 £350

An early Victorian telescope walking stick the horn screw-off handle fitted with a compass and presentation silver band, 34in. long, circa 1850. $1,000 £600

The 'Ben Akiba' camera cane invented by E. Kronke, Berlin 1903, and manufactured by A. Leh, with 24 exposures and ten spare rolls of film carried in the shaft, 35in. long. $7,000 £4,000

WATCH STANDS

Since man began carrying a watch around 400 years ago there have been stands on which to hang them at night or when they were not being worn but most of the very early ones have long ago disappeared or are in the show cases of museums. The sort of watch stand that most frequently turns up today dates from the 19th century and is a single pillar type made of wood, brass, agate or marble. The better ones had a pivot which allowed the watch to be tilted for more convenient viewing.

More expensive are well head watch stands which consisted of two pillars joined at the top by a bar from which the watch could be suspended. Another two-pillar design had a pivoted holder and sometimes a short central pillar on which there might be a mirror or a cushion. Frequently plain two-pillar stands had a little dish for holding rings, studs and trinkets.

Even more unusual were "triangular prismatic watchstands" which were made of hard wood, often beautifully inlaid, with a small door at the back which gave access to a velvet lined interior. Some of them had front and back panels and the watch was held safely inside when travelling.

Travelling watch stands were made to several designs and often had a souvenir type decoration. Some had hinged lids which were fitted with a stud or hook and the watch could be hung from them so that it nestled in its dished backing. These custom made stands often had locks decorated with ivory, bone or brass.

A mahogany and rosewood watch stand on inverted bun feet, 6½in. high. $175 £100

German porcelain watch holder entitled 'Sedan'. $350 £200

19th century German watch holder entitled 'Gravelotte'. $350 £200

A Doulton Punch and Judy watch stand with a bright blue glaze, circa 1905, 11½in. high. $1,125 £750

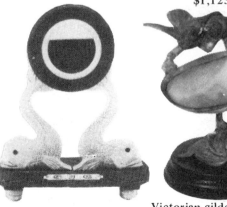

20th century American ebony and ivory watch stand, 6¼in. high. $350 £200

Victorian gilded metal watch stand designed as a mother-of-pearl bird-bath. (Giles Haywood) $98 £60

WATCHES

Watches, as small clocks, first came into use in the early 16th century with Henlein's invention of the mainspring to replace a falling weight as the energy source. These were bulky affairs, often worn on the girdle, but the invention of the balance spring in 1675 converted the watch to a more functional item that could be concealed in the pocket. Through the 17th and 18th centuries much greater accuracy was obtained through the craftsmanship of such masters as Tompion and Graham.

Wristwatches were introduced at the beginning of this century, and in the Great War their advantages to men in uniform made them hugely popular. Between the wars, the attentions of leading jewellers and designers such as Cartier turned the wristwatch into almost an art form. In the late 1960's the first electronic watch appeared, followed by quartz watches, without moving parts, in the 1970's.

Late 19th century 14ct. gold openface calendar watch, Swiss, 50mm. diam. (Christie's) $495 £345

An 18ct. gold openface lever watch, signed Patek Philippe & Co., no. 135231, 45mm. diam. (Christie's)
                    $1,540 £1,074

A 14ct. gold openface lever watch, signed Patek Philippe & Co., Geneva, no. 89566, 50mm. diam. (Christie's)
                    $1,045 £729

An enamelled platinum open-face dress watch, signed Patek Philippe & Co., Geneva, no. 814228, 42mm. diam. (Christie's) $1,210 £844

An enamelled gold openface dress watch of Napoleonic interest, signed Movado, the 18ct. gold case with London import mark 1910, 47mm. diam. (Christie's)
                    $3,080 £1,882

A late 18th century gold and enamel verge watch, the movement signed Gregson A Paris 13123, 50mm. diam. (Phillips) $792 £550

A gold openface chronograph, Swiss, retailed by Tiffany & Co., New York, signed Tiffany, 53mm. diam. (Christie's) $990 £605

A Swiss gold minute repeating grande sonnerie keyless lever clock watch, the cuvette signed for Breguet No. 4722, 57mm. diam. (Phillips) $38,640 £23,000

A Swiss gold openface watch, signed with Patent No. 98234, the 18ct. gold case, London, 1925, 51mm. diam. (Christie's) $935 £571

A small engraved gold pocket chronometer, signed Couvoisier & Comp'e, Chaux-De-Fonds, 46mm. diam. (Christie's) $660 £403

An 18ct. gold openface chronograph, signed Patek Philippe & Co., Geneve, with nickel 23-jewel movement, 48mm. diam. (Christie's) $3,300 £2,016

A floral enamel silver gilt centre seconds watch for the Chinese Market, Swiss, mid 19th century, 57mm. diam. (Christie's) $3,300 £2,016

A platinum openface dress watch, signed Patek Philippe & Co., Geneva, on movement and case, with original box and guarantee certificate, 44mm. diam. (Christie's) $2,640 £1,613

A finely enamelled gold openface dress watch, signed Vacheron & Constantin, 47mm. diam. (Christie's) $3,300 £2,016

A 14ct. rose gold openface dress watch and chain, signed Vacheron & Constantin, Geneve, with 17-jewel nickel lever movement, 42mm. diam. (Christie's) $1,540 £941

Early 19th century silver openface clock watch, Swiss, the cuvette signed Breguet & Fils, the top plate signed Japy, 58mm. diam. (Christie's)
$1,650 £1,008

A gold openface lever watch, signed Paul Ditisheim, La Chaux-De-Fonds, 56mm. diam. (Christie's)
$2,420   £1,479

An 18th century gold pair cased pocket watch, the fusee movement inscribed John Walker, Newcastle upon Tyne 736. (Parsons, Welch & Cowell) $862 £560

An 18ct. gold openface minute-repeating watch, signed Patek Philippe & Cie, 47mm. diam. (Christie's)
$7,150 £4,370

A verge watch, quarter-repeating on two visible bells, the gilt movement signed Georg Schmit, Neustadt, 56mm. diam. (Christie's)
$2,200 £1,344

A silver pair cased verge watch, the movement signed Tho. Tompion, London, 2631, 55mm. diam. (Christie's) $4,240 £2,808

A gilt metal and tortoiseshell pair cased quarter repeating verge watch made for the Turkish market, signed Geo. Prior, London, 62mm. diam. (Phillips) $1,344 £800

A platinum dress watch with integral stand, retailed by Bucherer, Lucerne, 42mm. wide. (Christie's) $990 £605

An enamelled gold convertible cased cylinder watch, signed J. FS. Bautte & Co., Geneve, with gilt cylinder movement jewelled to the third wheel, 36mm. diam. (Christie's) $2,860 £1,748

An 18ct. gold openface
quarter repeating verge watch
with jacquemarts, Swiss, signed
on the cuvette Breguet & Fils,
no. 23592, 55mm. diam.
(Christie's) $2,640 £1,842

An 18ct. gold openface
dress watch, signed Patek
Philippe & Co., Geneva, no.
188192, 42mm. diam.
(Christie's) $880 £614

A two-colour gold openface
dress watch, signed Patek
Philippe & Co., no. 817759,
45mm. diam. (Christie's)
$1,210 £844

An enamelled platinum openface dress watch, signed Patek
Philippe & Co., Geneva, no.
810822, 39mm. diam.
(Christie's) $1,320 £921

A nielloed silver sector watch,
signed Record Watch Co.,
Tramelan, 60mm. wide.
(Christie's) $1,320 £921

A platinum openface dress
watch, signed Patek Philippe
& Co., Geneva, no. 890237,
43mm. diam. (Christie's)
$1,265 £882

An 18ct. gold openface
centre seconds watch, signed
Patek Philippe & Co., Geneva,
no. 185202, 46mm. diam.
(Christie's) $2,200 £1,535

A gold pair cased verge watch,
signed Jams. Hagger, London
200, 54mm. diam.
(Christie's) $3,643 £2,530

A Continental silver pair
cased verge watch, signed
Blanc Pere & Fils, Geneve,
the silver champleve dial
signed P. B., London, 50mm.
diam. (Phillips) $806 £480

WAX MODELS

The Egyptians were already modelling in beeswax and the fluency and adaptability of the medium has appealed to artists down the ages. Wax models are frail, though, and few early examples have survived. Wax miniatures were particularly popular in the 18th and 19th centuries, and notable craftsmen included Percy of Dublin, Isaac Gossett, Mountstephen and Ball-Hughes, who in the 19th century developed his own hardening process.

A pair of Victorian wax reliefs of Queen Victoria and Prince Albert, in mahogany frame, 6 x 8½in. (Christie's) $187 £129

A shoulder-waxed-composition doll, German, circa 1880, 16in. high, right arm loose. $260 £150

A group of late 18th century cream-coloured wax bust-length profile medallions, each 2¼in. high.(Christie's) $622 £432

A shoulder-waxed-composition doll with blonde mohair plaited wig, German, circa 1880, 18in. high. $443 £308

An American 19th century arrangement of various wax fruits on a wooden pedestal base, under a glass dome, 21in. high. (Robt. W. Skinner Inc.) $475 £332

A pair of poured wax portrait dolls, modelled as Edward VII and Queen Alexandra, 21in. high, by Pierotti. (Christie's) $1,837 £1,100

One of a pair of glazed waxed octagonal reliefs of Robt. Adam after Tassie, 6 x 4½in. (Christie's) $1,331 £918

WEATHERVANES

The increasing popularity of old weathervanes with collectors has meant that some have been mysteriously disappearing off the tops of tall buildings and church steeples. They were snatched away by by thieves in helicopters. Before anyone would go to so much trouble, it is obvious that weathervanes mean big money and this is certainly the case, especially in America, where vanes dating from the time of the War of Independence fetch several thousands of dollars.

British weathervanes tend to stick to a few familiar designs — crowing cocks, running horses or witches on broomsticks are the most common — but in America it is possible to find old weathervanes in the form of Red Indians, stage coaches, sailing ships and even butterflies.

A locomotive and tender copper weathervane, America, circa 1882, 61in. long. (Robt. W. Skinner Inc.) $185,000 £115,625

A moulded copper 'North Wind' weathervane, in the form of a cherub's head blowing stylised air, 23in. high, 56½in. long. (Christie's) $18,700 £11,472

'Foxhound' weathervane, L. W. Cushing & Sons, Waltham, Mass., circa 1883, with traces of gold leaf and weathered verdigris surface, 27in. long. (Robt. W. Skinner Inc.) $12,500 £8,741

Late 19th century running horse with jockey weathervane figure, possibly J. L. Mott & Co., circa 1880, America, 16in. long. (Robt. W. Skinner Inc.) $2,000 £1,351

A gilded centaur weathervane, probably A. L. Jewell & Co., Waltham, Mass., circa 1860, 30¼in. high, 40in. long. (Robt. W. Skinner Inc.) $130,000 £81,250

Late 19th century American copper weathervane in the form of a pig, 35in. long. (Christie's) $11,000 £7,586

Sheet copper weathervane, America, late 19th century, silhouette of a cannon, 24in. wide. (Robt. W. Skinner Inc.) $750 £414

Mid 19th century cut out sheet iron banner weathervane, Lafayette, Rhode Island, 50in. long. (Robt. W. Skinner Inc.) $2,500 £1,562

Late 19th century moulded copper and zinc running horse weathervane, 'Smuggler', America, 46in. high, 31in. long. (Robt. W. Skinner Inc.) $1,200 £674

Copper bull weathervane, America, late 19th century, full-bodied figure standing bull, 18½in. high. (Robt. W. Skinner Inc.) $750 £414

Cast iron horse weathervane, Rochester, New Hampshire, late 19th century, full bodied figure of a prancing horse, 36in. wide. (Robt. W. Skinner Inc.) $11,000 £6,077

Mid 19th century moulded copper and zinc leaping stag weathervane, New England, 27in. high, 30in. long. (Robt. W. Skinner Inc.) $5,500 £3,089

A large sheet iron horse weathervane, long. (Christie's) $550 £310

A 19th century moulded copper and zinc trotting horse weathervane, America, 23¼in. high, 34in. long. (Robt. W. Skinner Inc.) $3,400 £1,910

WEATHERVANES

Rare fire hose wagon weathervane, Mass., last quarter 19th century, full-bodied figure of copper horse pulling copper and iron hose wagon. (Robt. W. Skinner. Inc.) $55,000 £30,386

Early 20th century copper train weathervane, America, 60in. long, 12½in. high. (Robt. W. Skinner Inc.) $11,000 £6,547

Sheet iron train weathervane, America, late 19th/early 20th century, silhouette of Locomotive and tender on railroad track, 22in. long. (Robt. W. Skinner Inc.) $650 £359

Late 19th century copper and zinc quill weathervane, New England, with traces of gold leaf, 25½in. high, 24½in. long. (Robt. W. Skinner Inc.) $1,800 £1,011

Late 19th century gilded copper leaping stag weathervane with zinc head, 30in. long, mounted on display stand. (Robt. W. Skinner Inc.) $4,100 £2,440

A trumpeting angel silhouette weathervane, constructed of sheet iron, supported by wrought-iron strapping, New England, circa 1800, 59in. long. (Robt. W. Skinner Inc.) $40,000 £23,809

Mid 19th century copper telescope weathervane, New England, 62in. high, 49in. long. (Robt. W. Skinner Inc.) $4,500 £2,528

Late 19th century copper horse and trainer weathervane, America, traces of gold leaf under yellow ochre paint, 29in. long. (Robt. W. Skinner Inc.) $4,000 £2,380

WEDGWOOD

The Wedgwood Pottery was first established at Burslem in 1759 by Josiah Wedgwood but it moved to Etruria in 1769. It was famed for its green glazed wares, cream coloured wares, black basalt, jasper and cane ware. Parian busts, marketed as Carrara busts, appeared in 1848 and the company also successfully experimented in lithography which gave an imitation of oil painting on pottery. Good quality bone china was produced at Etruria between 1812 and 1829 but after the last date the company concentrated on traditional earthenware until 1878 when the making of bone china recommenced. The advertising at that time said, "We intend to produce articles of the highest quality...". Wedgwood bone china was decorated by some notable artists including Thomas Allen, Therese Lessore, A. and L. Powell and K. Murray. Wedgwood enjoyed great commercial success in the early 20th century with their "Fairyland Lustre". Earthenware production continued at the same time and their transfer printed tiles, majolica ware and pottery decorated with printed landscapes was hugely popular.

A Wedgwood caneware custard cup and cover with rope twist handle, 7.5cm. high. (Phillips) $1,040 £650

A Wedgwood blue and white jasper bulb pot and cover, impressed mark and V, circa 1785, 24cm. high.(Christie's) $1,840 £1,296

A Wedgwood garden seat of rounded hexagonal shape, impressed Wedgwood, 46cm. high. (Christie's) $1,355 £935

A 19th century Wedgwood jasper model of the Portland Vase, 10½in. high. (Reeds Rains) $792 £550

A Wedgwood black basalt encaustic decorated vase, painted in red and enriched in white with a lady and attendants, late 18th century, 24cm. high. (Christie's) $2,217 £1,540

A large Wedgwood black basalt pot pourri vase and cover with loop handles, 12in. high. (Parsons, Welch & Cowell) $784 £490

A Wedgwood majolica-ware 'Kate Greenaway' jardiniere, modelled as a lady's straw bonnet, 16.5cm., impressed Wedgwood and moulded registration mark. (Phillips) $379 £230

A Wedgwood blue and white jasper cylindrical teapot and cover, circa 1790, 10.5cm. high. (Christie's) $847 £550

A Wedgwood three-colour jasper dice-pattern cylindrical jardiniere, 9cm. high, and a stand, circa 1790. (Christie's) $1,439 £935

A Wedgwood caneware oviform jug and cover, 22cm. high, and a saucer dish, circa 1815. (Christie's) $931 £605

Pair of Wedgwood black basalt encaustic decorated oviform two-handled vases and one cover, circa 1800, 37.5cm. high. (Christie's) $5,702 £3,960

A Wedgwood vase designed by Keith Murray, 16.5cm. high. (Christie's) $121 £86

A rare and important Wedgwood Sydney Cove medallion, titled below Etruria 1789, the reverse impressed, 5.7cm. overall diam. (Phillips) $27,600 £15,000

An Art Deco Wedgwood animal figure, modelled as a fallow deer, designed by J. Skeaping, 21.5cm. high. (Phillips) $230 £160

A Wedgwood Fairyland lustre black-ground small globular jar and cover, circa 1925, 8.5cm. high. (Christie's) $2,359 £1,430

WEMYSS

Wemyss Ware is the most distinctive product of the Scottish potteries. Its trademarks are free flowing designs on white of roses, cherries and apples. The pottery of Robert Heron & Sons was based at Kirkcaldy in Fife and its fame really began when a young Bohemian decorator called Karl Nekola joined the staff in 1883. He became Art Director and by the time he died in 1915 he had made Wemyss Ware famous. The name was taken from nearby Wemyss Castle, the home of the Grosvenor family who did much to popularise the pottery with their upper class friends in London. Thomas Goode and Co, the Mayfair china shop, became the sole outlet for Wemyss Ware in London and sent up special orders for individual customers. Nekola trained other artists and also his own two sons in the work of ceramic decoration and though no pieces were signed, it is possible to identify different artists by their style. Wemyss was produced in a vast range of shapes and sizes from buttons to garden seats and the washstand sets were particularly well designed, especially the squat jug with its generous mouth.

A Robert Heron & Son Wemyss ware pink pig, 18in. long. (Woolley & Wallis)
$261 £180

A Wemyss heart shaped inkstand, painted overall with black cockerels, 15cm., 1920's.
$210 £120

A late Wemyss model of a pig of small size, the body painted in green with scattered shamrock, 16cm. high. (Phillips)
$1,566 £820

A Robt. Heron & Son Wemyss ware carp tureen and cover, modelled by Karel Nekola, circa 1900, 18½in. long.
$6,300 £3,600

A Wemyss vase of diamond section, circa 1900, 22in. high.
$500 £285

Large Wemyss ware 'plicta' pig, painted with flower sprays, circa 1930, 15in. long.
$1,750 £1,000

WINE GLASSES

The rapid growth of Venice and Bohemia as glass making centres during the time of the Renaissance meant that metal goblets were replaced by wine glasses on the tables of the rich. This fashion spread down to the rest of society and glass makers vied to produce more original and beautiful wine glasses and goblets. They were often cut in fantastic designs, beautifully engraved and mounted in silver. During the time of the Jacobite Rebellions in Britain, the affiliation of a household was depicted in its wineglasses. If they were Jacobites, the glasses were engraved with entwining roses or cryptic messages and with them men toasted "the King over the water". Bohemian glass was always regarded as very valuable because of the glowing colours. Victorian householders especially loved those heavily carved, gleaming red goblets. At the beginning of the next century however glasses became lighter and later many skilled glass engravers were at work especially men like Rex Whistler. In the Art Deco period and during the Jazz Age, glasses took on a new angular shape.

A 'Lynn' opaque twist wine glass on a conical foot, circa 1770, 14.5cm. high. (Christie's) $826 £462

An opaque twist champagne glass, the double ogee bowl with everted rim, circa 1765, 18cm. high. (Christie's) $1,476 £825

A baluster toastmaster's glass on a conical firing foot, 13.5cm. high. (Phillips) $217 £130

Late 18th/early 19th century green pedestal stemmed wine flute, 15.5cm. high. (Christie's) $1,986 £1,100

A faceted stemmed portrait wine glass, by David Wolff, The Hague, 1780-85, 15.8cm. high. (Christie's) $6,946 £5,184

A dark green tinted wine glass with ribbed cup-shaped bowl, circa 1765, 12.5cm. high. (Christie's)$950 £660

An engraved airtwist wine glass of Jacobite significance, circa 1750, 14.5cm. high. (Christie's) $466 £324

A colour twist wine glass with bell bowl, circa 1760, 16.5cm. high. (Christie's) $1,088 £756

A colour twist wine glass with bell bowl, circa 1760, 17cm. high. (Christie's) $1,056 £734

An engraved mixed twist ale flute, the flared funnel bowl with a hop-spray and two ears of barley, circa 1760, 18cm. high. (Christie's) $434 £302

An armorial light baluster wine glass, the funnel bowl engraved with the arms of Schieland, circa 1760, 18.2cm. high. (Christie's) $1,399 £972

An incised twist wine glass, the bell bowl with honey-comb-moulded lower part, circa 1760, 17.5cm. high. (Christie's) $372 £259

A canary twist wine glass with pan-topped funnel bowl, circa 1760, 14.5cm. high. (Christie's) $3,732 £2,592

An opaque twist deceptive cordial glass with thick-walled ogee bowl, circa 1770, 14cm. high. (Christie's) $652 £453

A composite stemmed wine glass of drawn trumpet shape, circa 1750, 18cm. high. (Christie's) $185 £129

An engraved colour twist wine glass of Jacobite significance, the rounded bowl with a rosebud, circa 1765, 13cm. high. (Christie's) $652 £453

A composite stemmed wine glass of drawn trumpet shape, the stem filled with airtwist spirals set into a beaded inverted baluster section, circa 1750, 17.5cm. high. (Christie's) $247 £172

A 'Lynn' opaque twist wine glass with horizontally ribbed ogee bowl, circa 1775, 14cm. high. (Christie's) $496 £345

A Jacobite airtwist wine glass, the stem with a twisted air core entwined by spiral threads, circa 1750, 14.5cm. high. (Christie's) $434 £302

An opaque twist ale or ratafia glass, the slender funnel bowl with hammered flutes, circa 1765, 18cm. high. (Christie's) $434 £302

A baluster wine glass, the bell bowl with a small tear to the solid lower part, circa 1715, 14cm. high. (Christie's) $403 £280

A Williamite baluster wine glass with trumpet-shaped bowl, 18th century, 17.5cm. high. (Christie's) $2,021 £1,404

A colour twist wine glass with generous bell bowl, circa 1760, 17.5cm. high. (Christie's) $1,866 £1,296

A light baluster dated betrothal wine glass by the monogrammist ICL, 1753, 19.7cm. high. (Christie's) $2,894 £2,160

WOOD. RALPH

The Wood family of Burslem are famous to collectors because of their high quality pottery figures made by two, if not by three, generations of Ralph Woods. Ralph Wood Senior, who died in 1772, and his brother Aaron developed an individual style for their productions which they passed onto their respective sons. Ralph's son, also named Ralph lived betwen 1748 and 1795, and worked as a potter of model figures in Burslem with his cousin Enoch (died 1840). Their products were particularly noted for delicate colouring. Ralph Wood III succeeded his father Ralph but died at the early age of 27 in 1801. Some earthenware figures that bear the name mark Ra Wood may have been his handiwork as may also be porcelain examples. Enoch Wood started his own factory in 1784 and in 1790 went into partnership with James Caldwell, making tableware marked Wood & Caldwell which was shipped to America in vast quantities.

A Ralph Wood Toby jug of conventional type, circa 1770, 25.5cm. high. (Christie's) $2,692 £1,870

A Ralph Wood figure of a recumbent ram, on an oval green rockwork base moulded with foliage, circa 1770, 18.5cm. wide. (Christie's) $3,801 £2,640

A Ralph Wood group of the Vicar and Moses of conventional type, circa 1770, 21.5cm. high. (Christie's) $643 £453

A Staffordshire creamware group of St. George and the Dragon of conventional Ralph Wood type, circa 1780, 28.5cm. high. (Christie's) $3,630 £2,200

A pair of Staffordshire figures of a gardener and companion of Ralph Wood type, circa 1780, 19.5cm. high. (Christie's) $4,356 £2,640

A Ralph Wood Bacchus mask jug, circa 1775, 23.5cm. high.(Christie's) $545 £410

WORCESTER

Porcelain has been produced in the city of Worcester from 1751 to the present day. The first period up till 1774 is called the Dr Wall period when soft paste porcelain was made at Warmstry House on the banks of the Severn. In 1783 Thomas Flight purchased the works, and well designed and decorated porcelain as well as many blue and white pieces were produced. They made dessert ware and comports in glazed porcelain supported by Parian figures and their Limoges ware was exhibited at the Paris International Exhibition of 1855. In 1862 the company was renamed the Worcester Royal Porcelain Company with Richard William Binns as Art Director and Edward Phillips in charge of production. Their products were of very high quality, and the firm is best known for the heavily jewelled decoration of the table services and for the high quality painting and gilding. They also produced figures in ivory paste with bright glazes and enamelled decorations. The birds made by Dorothy Doughty are especially famous.

A Royal Worcester 'ivory' mermaid and nautilus centre-piece, decorated by Callow-hill, circa 1878. (Christie's) $1,399 £972

A Worcester plate from The Duke of Gloucester Service, gold crescent mark, circa 1775, 22.5cm. diam. (Christie's) $23,595 £14,300

Royal Worcester vase and cover painted by Ricketts, 11in. high. (Reeds Rains) $713 £460

A Worcester, Flight, Barr & Barr, urn-shaped two-handled vase and cover, circa 1820, 46cm. high. (Christie's) $2,376 £1,650

A Worcester blue and white bottle and a basin transfer-printed with The Pinecone and Foliage pattern, circa 1775, bottle 22cm. high, basin 27.5cm. diam. (Christie's) $1,439 £935

A Royal Worcester reticulated oviform vase by George Owen, pattern no. 1969, gilt marks and date code for 1912, 17cm. high. (Christie's) $2,799 £1,944

A large 'bow' vase, signed John Stinton, 30.5cm. high, shape no. 1428, date code for 1908. (Phillips)
$4,342 £2,600

A pair of Royal Worcester figures modelled as a lady and gentleman, 14in. high, circa 1887. (Christie's)
$1,480 £1,000

A Grainger's Worcester pedestal ewer with a painted scene of swans, signed indistinctly, 10in. high. (Hetheringtons Nationwide)
$858 £520

An ovoid vase, the body well painted with two Highland cattle, signed H. Stinton, 21cm. high, shape no. 1762, date code for 1910. (Phillips)
$1,107 £580

Royal Worcester Hadley-style footed vase, designed as a jardiniere, 1906, 5in. high. (Giles Haywood)
$458 £240

A Royal Worcester porcelain jug (ice tusk), circa 1884, approx. 12in. tall. (G. A. Key)
$548 £310

Worcester porcelain jug, the blush ivory ground with hand-painted floral sprigs, circa 1902, 7in. high. (G. A. Key)
$346 £210

One of a pair of Grainger Worcester mugs with single spur handles, titled below painted panels, 'Drawing Cover' and 'The Death', 11.5cm. high. (Phillips)
$12,606 £6,600

A Dr. Wall Worcester quart mug with strap handle, circa 1770, 6.1/8in. high. (Robt. W. Skinner Inc.)
$275 £163

Index

A. E. L. 63
Aberdeen Fire and Life Ins. Co 144
Account of the First Aerial Voyage, An 53
Ackery 168
Adams & Barrett Patent 231
Adams, George 53
Advancement of the Art of Navigation, The 53
Aeolian Co. Ltd. 276
Aerial Derby, The 10
Aeriel Sports 246
Aeronautical 9, 10
Air Ministry 10
Akira 187
Albion Fire and Life Ins. 144
Albums 11
Alcock, Sam & Co. 271
Aldani 286
Alexceev, I. A. 179
Alfa-Romeo 394
Almaric Walter 269, 270
Alphalsa Publishing Co. Ltd 204
Alvar 73
Alvis-Healey 396
Amadio, J. 41
Amalgamated Press 391
Amati, Dom Nicolo 419
American Indianware 12-14
Anchovy Pot Lids 15, 16
Anderson, Wm. & Sons Ltd. 412
Andy Cap 30
Angell, Joseph 82
Arapaho 12
Arcangioli, Lorenzo 417
Archer 65
Argy-Rousseau, Gabriel 127
Argyll & Sutherland Highlanders, The 228
Armour 17-19
Armstrong, W. 165
Army & Navy Toilet Club 330
Arnold, John & Son 259
Art Nouveau Postcards 23, 24
Art Pottery 20-22
Ashbee, C. R. 112, 253
Associated Newspapers Ltd. 314, 315
Aston Martin 395, 396
Atthalin, Baron Louis 283
Austin 388, 389, 393, 394, 396
Austins 155
Australian Touring Side, 1964 106
Autographs 25, 26
Automatons 27-29
Aveling and Porter 242
Avon Bottles 30
Awataguchi 263
Aylesbury Patent 231
Ayrshire Yeomanry, The 227
Ayrton & Saunders 181

B.D.V. 385, 386
B.S.A. 246, 247
Babbage, C. 26
Baccarat 267-270
Bacheller, Irving 55
Baden Powell Items 31, 32
Bairnsfatherware 33-35
Baker, T. K. 280
Baker-Troll 249
Bank of England 36-38
Bank of New Zealand 37
Bank of Portugal 36
Bank of South Australia 38
Banknotes 36-39
Banks, B. 418
Banks, Eliza S. 360
Banque Industrielle de Chine 38
Barbadian 334
Barbedienne, F. 256

Barclays Bank 38
Barlow, Florence 21, 359
Barlow, Hannah 360
Barometers 40-42
Barrett & Elers Hybrid 230
Barrett, W. S. 10
Bartholomew's Tourist's Map 208
Barton, T. 408
Barye, Antoine Louis 59
Baskerville, John 53
Baskett, J. 54
Bass 217
Bassett, George & Co. Ltd 392
Bateman, Peter, Anne and William 111
Batman 391
Bautte, J. FS. & Co. 426
Bayley & Blew 57
Beach & Barnicott 265
Beadwork Bags 43
Beard, Ethel 20
Becquerel A. 60
Bedfordshire & Herts Regt., The 228
Beijing 344
Belgian Congo 39
Belleek 44, 45, 272
Bells 46
Bengal Artillery 412
Bengali Die Mixing Plant 238
Bentley 393-395
Burge 260, 269
Bergenbier 141
Berks., Gloucs. and Prov. Assurance 146
Berlin Woodwork 47, 48
Berthoz, J. 256
Bettridge, J. 416
Bewsher's Wine & Spirit 165
Bible, The 53, 54
Bicycles 49, 50
Biggles Books 51
Billows Patent 230
Birmingham & Midland Motor Omnibus 380
Birmingham & Midland Tramways 379
Birmingham Co-op Society 379
Bishop's Balm, The 266
Black Watch, The 227, 412
Blackmar, Abby 55
Blackpool Aviation 10
Blair, H. G. & Co. 259
Blanc Pere & Fils 427
Blanchard, Christopher 282
Blard, E. 187
Blazuiere, P. 58
Bleriot, Louis 339
Blondeay & Cie 331
Blue Racing Car 29
Bluebell Railway 379
Bohm, Hermann 129
Bolviller 84
Bond, Wm. & Sons 87
Bontems 27
Book of Common Prayer 53
Book of Psalms 55
Books 52-55
Boots 181, 265, 331
Boss Clock 9
Boston Music Co. Ltd. 276
Bouillon Oxo 141
Boullemier, A. 232
Bourne, Johnson & Latimer 182
Bovinet, E. 254
Bovril 141
Boxes 56-58
Boyd, George 115
Bradbury, J. 39
Brander & Potts 281
Brard, M. 99
Brayant, Elizabeth 400

Brayshaws 134
Breguet & Fils 426, 427
Breguet 425
Bremond, B. A. 249
Brenet, A. 9
Bridges, R. 55
Bristol Crown Fire Office 145
British Autoplayer Co. Ltd. 276
British Empire Exhibition 35
British Engineerium 243
British Golf Links 159
British Guiana 39
British Municipal Council 39
British Thompson Houston Co. Ltd. 107
British Transport Commission 380
Brixton Music Roll Exchange 276
Broad, John 97
Broadwood, John 250
Brockhampton Press 51
Bronze 59-61
Brooklands Aero-Club 10
Brough-Superior 246
Brown Bros. 259
Brown's Herbal Ointment 264
Browne, Professor 331
Brownie Wirless Co. 107
Browning, R. 55, 340
Brunelleschi 24
Bryant, H. 369
Bte-Carpeaux, J. 373
Bucherer 426
Budden, Alice 360
Buncombe, Charles 336
Buncombe, John 336, 338
Burgess J. 363
Burgess's 15, 16
Burns, Robert 324
Burroughs & Wellcome 182
Burrow's Pointer Guide Map 208
Burton, Henry 165
Bushby, Elizabeth 319
Bushu ju Masakata 406
Butman, Sally 318
Butter Stamps 62
Butterton, Mary 21

C.S. & F.S. 80
Cadmore, Susanah 319
Calder, Horatio H. 45
Callowhill 439
Calthorpe 247
Calvert, F. C. Ltd. 391
Camden, W. 208
Campling, Elizabeth 318
Canada Rifles, The 228
Canterbury Cricket Week, The 106
Cantrell & Cochrane's Ginger Ale 216
Capela, Antonio 417
Car Mascots 63-65
Carcassi, Tommaso 418
Card Cases 66
Carlile, John Jr. 72
Carriage Clocks 84
Carter Paterson & Co. 242
Carter's Imperial 331
Carter, W. 154
Caruso, Enrico 26
Carved Stone 67, 68
Carved Wood 69-71
Cary 42
Cash, Mary Ann 317
Cayley-Robinson, W. 56
Central Bank 37
Chad Valley 120, 166, 389
Chadbum & Son 40
Chadbum Bros. 237
Chagall, Marc 297, 299
Chairs 72-74

Chamber, W. & R. 159
Chanot, J. A. 418
Chapman's Patent Hybrid 230
Charriere 223
Chasselat, Pierre 288
Chaudet, Denis-Antoine 60
Chelsea 75, 76
Chevrolet Corvette 396
Cheyenne 12
Chiparus Figures 77, 78
Christchurch, Old Court House 162
Churchill, Sir Winston Spencer 25, 341
Cibber 67
Cigarette Cases79-81
Citroen 394
City of London Yeomanry 411
Claret Jugs 82
Clark & Smith 415
Clark, F. 347
Clarke's Miraculous Salve 265, 266
Clarkson 237
Cleaver, F. S. 331
Cleff, Edward 362
Clevedon Confectionary Ltd. 391
Clichy 268-270
Clocks Bracket 83
Clodion 372
Cloisonne 92, 93
Coal Boxes 94
Cobb, John 277
Cobden-Sanderson 53
Cochiti 14
Codd Patent 230, 231
Cold Hands and Cold Feet 214
Coldstream Guards 362
Coley, S. J. 364
Colinet, C. J. Roberte 59
Collector, The 55
Colman, Sir Jeremiah 106
Colonial Mfg. Co. 87
Colt, H. S. and Alison, C. H. 159
Combe, William 52
Comerford, John 287
Commemorative China 95-97
Comolera, P. 233
Complete Angler, The
Connaught Rangers 228, 411
Connor's Patent 231
Conran, Terence 74
Constance 239
Conte and Boehme 135, 214
Conversation Pieces 98-101
Cook's Carbolic Jelly 266
Cookson, Issac 111
Cooper, J. 370
Copeland 271
Coq Nain 63
Cordier, Charles-Henri-Joseph 60, 61
Corkscrews 102-104
Corti, A 42
Couvoisier & Comp'e 425
Coward, Noel 341
Cox, E. & Sons 154
Crail Golfing Soc., The 158
Craven 141
Crichton, Alex. 82
Cricketana 105, 106
Cricketers' Almanack 106
Croft's Ointment 265
Crombie, Charles 324
Crompton, Richmal 194
Cross & Blackwell 16
Crowell, A. Elmer 114
Cruikshank Anti-Hanging Note 36
Crutchley's County Map 207
Crystal Sets 107
Culuval Roberts 132
Curry Super Low Loss, The 107
Cushing, L. W. & Sons 429
Cusson 252
Cuthbert, R. 419
Cutty Sark 240

Dale, John T. 330
Dali, Salvador, 108
Dalou, Aime-Jules 60
Dangerfield Printing Co., The 10
Daniell, W. and Ayton, R. 54
Darlington, Harrison 90
Dartmouth Floating Bridge 379
Darwin, Charles 25
Daum 108, 109
Davidson, W. 165
Davis, Louisa 360
De Lorean 393
De Morgan 118
de Gaulle, Charles 339
de Soete, P. 64, 65
Dean & Son 51
Decanter Labels 110, 111
Decanters 112, 113
Decoys 114, 115
Deep Well Engine House and Pump 236
Delft 116, 117
Delvaux, Paul 297
Denecheau 60
Dennis, Ada 22
Derval 254
Des Granges, David 287
Desmo 63, 64
Deveral, M. 239
Devon and Cornwall Banking Co. 39
Devon Militia 228
Dewar's Scotch Whisky 197
Dewar's White Label 216
Dewar, J. H. 164
Dewar, John & Sons 215
Dickens, Charles 26, 55, 162
Diederich, Wilhelm Hunt 338
Diemer, Fred 330
Dinky 390
Disney, Walt 26
Ditisheim, Paul 426
Dixon, James & Son 291
Dodge 393
Dodwell, E. 55
Dolls 119-122
Dolls Houses 123. 124
Dominy, Allen 415
Donaldson, W. 276
Donatello, F. 156
Donzel 139
Doorstops 125
Douglas, David 159
Doulton 20, 21, 96, 97, 214-216, 382-384,
   423
Doves Press 53
Dow, James Gordon 158
Doyle, Jack 26
Dragonfly 63
Dragoon Guards 176
Dramatic Romances and Lyrics 55
Dreadnought Casting Reel Co. 148
Dresser, Dr. C. 112
Dring and Fage 42
Drinking Sets 126, 127
Drouot, E. 61
Droz, Jacquet 28
Dry Fly Entomology 54
Du Chesne, Claudius 83
Dubrovin, N. 180
Dudley Watch Co. 212
Dudson 32
Duesbury, Wm. 75
Duke of Cornwall's Light , The 228
Dummy Teat, The 65
Dundee Insurance 145
Dunelt Monarch 247
Durer, Albrecht 298
Duret 59
Dursley-Pedersen 49
Dyer, A. R. & Sons 243

Eagle Insurance 145
East India Co. 412
East Kent and Conterbury Fire 145

Eastlake, Sir Charles 26
Eaton, Arthur 22
Edinburgh Firendly Assurance 145
Edison 274, 275
Edmondson, W. 68
Edo Bushu 405
Edouart, Augustin 336, 338
Edwards Patent 230, 231
Edwards, E. 346
Edwards, Sydenham 53
Egan, John 252
Egyptian Salve, The 265
Elegance 30
Eliot, T. S. 54
Elkington & Co. 82
Ellis, Harvey 357
Employment Exchange 9
Enamel 128, 129
Engleheart, G. 286, 288
Engleheart, John Cox Dillman 288
English BSA 50
English Dance of Death, The 52
Epstein, Jacob 26
Eragny Press 55
Eskimo 12
Essays on the Microscope 53
Etex, A. 61
Etuis 130
Eureka Clock Co. Ltd. 90
Evans, Lewis 155
Exclusive Bath Oil 30
Expert Columbia 49
Eye Baths 131, 132

Fairground Memorabilia 133, 134
Fairings 135-137
Famous Cricketers 391
Fans 138-140
Farlowe & Co. Ltd. 148
Farthing, I. H. 306
Feather Hotel, The 161
Feline, Edward 235
Fenton, H. 206
Fentun, Mary 318
Festiniog Railway 380
Fevre, D. 364
Field, John 337
Fieldings 217
Fiji Islands 334
Finger Plates 141
Fire Irons 142, 143
Firemarks 144-146
First and Last House 162
First National Bank of San Fran. 37
Fischer & Toller 223
Fisher, S. Ltd 89
Fishing Reels 147-149
Fitzgerald, E. 53
Fitzgerald, John 165
Flambe 150
Flameng, F. 255
Flannel Dance 380
Flatman, Thomas 286, 288
Fletcher & Sons 41
Flight & Robson 248
Flint 159
Flora Britannica, The 53
Florsheim, James 168
Footballers 391
Ford 394
Ford, Henry 194
Fornasetti, Piero 99
Forster, Wm. 418
Fowles, J. 55
Fragments 35
French Dragoon 177
French Royal Exchange 84
Freres, Geneve 89
Freres, Henri 330
Freres, Nicole 249
Fringing Reef 334
Frink, Dame Elizabeth 298
Frith, F. 338

Fry, J. S. & Sons Ltd. 392
Fuchi Kashira 151

G.W.R. Jigsaws 166
Gagliano, F. 419
Gagliano, G. 419
Gagliano, Joannes 417
Galle 152, 153
Ganshoshi Nagatsune 151
Garbott, Nellie 359
Gardiner's 300
Gardner, J. 208, 370
Gaskin, A. 191
Gasnier 89
Gathercole, Ellen 360
Gay & Sons 331
Gebhard, M. J. 241
General Ins. Co. of Ireland, The 145
Genroku 67
Gentleman's and Citizen's Almanack, The 54
Geschutzt 60
Gianutio 54
Gibson, Richard 286, 287
Gidman, Joseph 155
Gilbert, Sir Alfred 60
Gillinder 270
Gillman, Emily 21
Gimson, E. 143
Ginger Beer Bottles 154, 155
Gioachino, Greco 54
Girl on a Goose 64
Girod, Ducommun 249
Glenister, William 417
Godden, H. 251
Godefroy, J. 250
Godiana 276
Goldscheider 156, 157
Golf Book of East Lothian, The 159
Golfing 159
Golfing Books 158, 159
Golfing Idyll, A 159
Goodall, Chas. & Son 34
Gordon Highlanders, The 219, 229, 411
Gordon, George 165
Gorham Co. 59, 163
Goshu Hino Yoshihisa 308
Gosnell, John & Co. 330
Goss 272, 332
Goss Cottages 160-162
Goss Oven, The 161
Gossage, William & Sons Ltd. 392
Goulding, C. J/ 243
Grace, W. G. 105, 106
Gragnano, P. M. di 239
Grand Libellule 65
Grandfather's Ointment 266
Grant of Devizes 369
Grant, P. L. 276
Grant, Ulysses S. 339
Gray and Reynolds 91
Gray, T. 73
Grays of Cambridge 302
Great Expectations 55
Great Western Railway 166, 208, 379
Green Jackets Brigade, The 229
Green, James 287
Greene's 307
Greenly, A. H. 243
Greenock Apothecaries & Lawsons Ltd. 363
Greens, Stephen 164, 165
Gregson 424
Gretton, Cha. 83
Grimaldi, William 286
Grindlay, Capt. Robert Melville 55
Grose J. & Co 65
Groves, A. 243
Gruber, Jacques 350, 351
Grueby 163
Guibal 89
Guiness Bottles 164, 165
Gulliford 42
Gum, A. & B.C. Ltd. 391, 392
Gunn, T. E. 369, 370

Gyokumin 101

H.M.S. Centurion 258
Haakon VII 341
Hagenauer 70
Hagger, Jams. 427
Hair Clips 167
Halford 54
Hall 307
Halle, Lady 26
Hamano Noriyuki 406
Hamlet, Wm. 336
Hampshire and S. of Eng. In. 145
Hampston & Prince 111
Han Dynasty 68, 188, 189
Hancock, John C. 250
Hancock, R. 97
Handall's Celebrated Ointment 266
Handbags 168
Handwerck, Max 122
Hannell's 15
Hans Coper 169
Hardstone 170, 171
Hardy Bros. Ltd 147-149
Hardy, Thomas 161
Harris, J. B. 243
Harris, Robert 158
Harris, Thos. & Son 259
Harrods Ltd. 276
Harry Peck's 16
Hart, Chas. H. 115
Harvey, W. J. 281
Hase, Henry 37
Hat Pins 172-174
Hathaway, Ann 161
Hauer, B. G. 345
Haughton, Wm. 86
Hawkes & Co. 412
Hawksley, G. & J. W. 291
Haynes & Jeffy's 49
Heath & Middleston 126
Heckel, Erich 297
Helmets 175-177
Hemins, Edw. 85
Henry, Thomas 194
Hepple A. & Co. 170
Herbery, Victor 276
Hercules Fire Insurance 146
Hewitt, James L. & Co. 250
Hidekatsu 151
Hilderscheimer, S. 24
Hill, Wm. E. & Sons 418
Hine, W. 371
Hints on Golf 158
Hockney, David 298, 299
Hodder & Stoughton 314
Hollanby, H. 407
Holloway's Ointment 264
Holme Cardwell 61
Holmes, L. T. 115
Holmes, Sir Richard 315
Holtzmann 252
Hopi 13, 14
Horn 178
Horner, Charles 173, 378
Horoldt, Johann G. 224
Horsham Show 379
Houdon 372
Houghton, G. B. 236
Howard & Davis 87
Howard & Sons 74
Howett 64
Hoyle, Harroit 318
Hud Aftershave 29
Hudson's Soap 141
Hukin & Heath 82, 112
Hutchings, J. 371
Hutchinson 159
Hutchinson, Horace 158, 159
Hutton, John 351
Hutton, Wm. & Sons 278

Icons 179, 180

Iesson, Sarah 318
Illustrated London News, The 315
Imperial Airways 9
Indian Scout Vee Twin 247
Inglis, R. W. 40
Inhalers 181, 182
Inros 183, 184
Irish Railway Commission 208
Isaacs, Harry 379
Ishiguro Masa-yoshi 151
ISO Grifo 396
Isthmian Library, The 158
Ivalek 107
Ivory 185-187

Jade 188, 189
Jaguar 395, 396
James Starley Coventry 49
Jaques, J. & Son 300
Jarvis, Thos. 351
Jaschke, Ch. 331
Jean, Philip 287, 288
Jensen, Georg 191
Jetter, H. 301
Jewell & Co. 429
Jewellery 190-193
Johns, Capt. W. E. 51
Johnson 306
Johnson, Dr. Thomas 264
Jokasai 184
Jones Bros. 154
Jones, John 347
Jumeau 27
Jurine, M. le Prof. 99
Just William Books 194
Juster, Joe 118

Kaji-kawa 184
Kandler J. J. 224, 225
Kane, Michael 258
Kanshosai 184
Katsuchika 405
Kauba, C. 60
Kearsar 241
Kelvin & Hughes Ltd. 260
Kelvin & White Ltd. 259
Kelvin Bottomley & Baird Ltd. 259
Kemp. Dixon 239
Kennedy School 419
Kensitas 385
Kent Fire Ins. Co. 146
Kenworthy, K. R. F. 238
Kerr 159
Keys 195
Khayyam, Omar 53
Khecheong 414
Kidner, P. C. 243
Kingsware 196, 197
Kipling, Rudyard 341
Kirckman, Jacob 251
Kirk Braddon Cross 271
Kirschbaum, Weyersberg 362
Kirschner, Raphael 23, 24
Klinger, Gottfried 225
Klingert, Gustav 81
Knight, Laura 298
Knox, Archibald 277
Knox, John 162
Koch and Kellermeistern 53
Koen, J. J. 104
Kohler, J. A. 252
Koma Kyuhaku 183
Kondo Mitsuyasu 151
Kozan 186
Kramer, Jacob 297
Kress & Owen 131
Kronke, E. 422
Kruse, Kathe 122
Kyo-shoami 406
Kyoto School 263

Lacquer 198, 199
Lady Skater 64

Lafayette 430
Lagonda 393
Lalique 64, 65, 127, 200, 201
Lambardos, E. 179
Lancaster, Charles 309
Lancers, The 410
Landberg, Nils 113
Landulphus, Carolus F. 418
Lantern Clocks 85
Laundy, J. 222
Lawson, Oliver 114
Lazenby, E. & Son 15, 16
Le Guay 326
Le Protecteur 239
Le Roy 89
Leach 202
Leclerc, J. N. 419
Ledsam, Vale & Wheeler 415
Lee Enfield 309
Lee, Robert E. 340
Leeway 293
Lehrmittelwerke 222
Leithner, W. 307
Lejaune, Louis 64
Lens, Gernard 288
Leoni Taroni & Co 42
Lewis 9
Lewis, Esther 20
Liberty & Co. 191, 384, 245, 278
Libro nel Quale si tratta della Maniera 54
Light Cavalry 362
Lille 282
Lilley & Son 258
Limbert 352
Linderby, Wm. 91
Line, E. & Co 155
Lines Bros. 123, 390
Lingee, C. L. 256
Lingley, Annie 163
Linwood, Matthew 416
Lion Engineering Co. 244
Lione, Somalvico & Co 41
Liverpool Fire Office 144
Livingstone, David 26
Loncase Clocks 86, 87
London Assurance 145
Longman, Clementi & Co. 251
Loof, I. D. 134
Lorenzl 157
Lorenzo 418
Louis Wain Postcards 204
Loving Cups 205, 206
Low, J. L. 159
Low, Son & Haydon 331
Lowe, T. 236, 237
Lowne, W. 371
Lucci, Giuseppe 417
Lukutin Factory 99
Lunardi 53
Lupton, Edith 22, 359

Ma Shaoxuan 344
Macdonald, A. K. 23
MacHamlet 'Hys Handycap' 159
Machin's Infallible Pearl Ointment 265
Mackintosh, Charles Rennie 351
MacNiven & Cameron's Pens 141
Mahon, C. P. 38
Malacreda, G. L. 345
Malacrida 42
Malloch's 147
Mally, J. R. 300
Manchester Corporation 380
Manners & Sons 83
Mannlicher Schoenauer 309
Mansfield's 15
Mantel Clocks 88, 89
Manx Bank 38
Manx Cottage Nightlight 160
Maps 207-209
Marc, Hy 27
Maron, Flos 320
Marshall & Sons 82

Martin Bros 210, 383, 384
Martinware 210, 211
Mary Queen of Scots 351
Masakazu 263
Masanaga 404
Masanao 261
Masanori 262
Masatoshi 263
Masayuki 187
Masonic Items 212, 213
Match Strikers 214-217
Matisse, Pierre 99
Matsuda Sukenaga 262
Maurer, Johan 83
Maw, S. Son & Thompson 223, 330
Maws 132
McIntyre 215
McLennan, John H. 21
McPherson, W. J. 350
Medals 218-221
Medical Items 222, 223
Meiji 67
Meissen 224, 225, 345, 378
Mene, P. J. 61
Mercedes-Benz 394, 395
Mersey Tunnell Toll 380
Mettoy 390
Metzler & Co. 251
Meyer, F. F. 224
MG 395
Micro Mosaics 226
Miers and Field 337
Miers, John 338
Military Badges 227-229
Millot, F. 331
Mills, N. 347, 414-416
Millville 268
Mineral Water Bottles 230, 231
Ming Dynasty 60, 92, 199
Minic 389
Minton 232, 233, 272
Mirrors 234, 235
Mister Softee Ltd. 392
Mitchell, A. 293
Mitchells Patent 230
Mitsuhiro 186, 261
Mitsumasa 262, 405
Mobil Oil Co. Ltd. 392
Model Engines 236-238
Model Ships 239-241
Models 242-244
Momillon, X 99
Momo-yama 56, 58
Monroe, Marilyn 25
Montgomery, Bernard Law 339-341
Montgomery, C. & J. 330
Monzani & Co. 252
Moonseed Ointment 266
Moonwind 29, 30
Moorcroft Pottery 245
Moore 150
Moore, Fred 21, 22
Moore, Henry 298, 299
Morel Bro' Cobbett & Son 15
Morgan 394
Morrell, Abel 378
Morris's 141
Morris, R. J. 271
Motorbikes 246, 247
Mott, J. L. & Co. 429
Mount Washington 268, 269
Movado 424
Mucha, Alphonse 129
Muirhead, James 260
Muller, H. 61
Murdock 237
Murray, Keith 433
Musical Boxes 248, 249
Musical Instruments 250-252
Mustard Pots 253

N. Wei Dynasty 68
Nagamasa 406

Nagatsugu 406
Nagayasu 263
Nairne, J. G. 36
Napoleonic Memorabilia 254-257
Nasatoshi 262
Nash, A. H. 154
Nautical Items 258-260
Navajo 12, 14
Nelson Lee Library 391
Nelson, D. R. 181
Netsuke 261-263
New Book of Golf, The 159
Nexus 29, 30
Nez Perce 13
Nicholas, Jules 122
Nickolls, L. A. 314
Nicolas, Sir H. 52
Nikkosai 184
Nikolaiev, Dmitri 81
Nineteen Eighty-Four 54
Nixon, Harry 22
No Name Ointment 266
Noble Game of Cricket, The 106
Nock, H. 280
Noke and Moore 20, 22
Noke, C. J. & Fenton, H. 205
Noke, C. J. 21, 22, 206, 324, 325, 383
Nolan, L. 110
None, G. 59
North British Ins. 145
Northern Song Dynasty
Norton 247
Norwich General 146
Nunn, W. 381
Nyren, J. 105

O'Brien, M. P. 155
O'Hanrahan, James 164
Occur 30
Odhams 314
Ointment Pots 264-266
Old Maids Cottage 161
Old Market House 160
Old Thatched Cottage, The 162
Olfers, L. 103
Oliphant, Mrs. 315
Omori Eishu 151
On the Links 159
Ordnance Survey 208
Ortelius, Abraham 209
Orwell 54
Osborn, J. N. 15
Osborne, H. 331
Otto, F. 311
Owen, George 439
Owen, Will 122

Page, J. B. 37
Pajou 372
Paperweights 267-270
Parian 271, 272
Paris International Exh. 379
Parker Bros. 303, 363
Parker, S. 318
Pascall, James Ltd. 392
Passenger, Chas. 118
Passenger, Fred 118
Pasteur, Louis 339
Pastorelli J. 42
Patch Boxes 273
Patrick, John 40
Patterson, Richard 217
Pattison 308
Payne 89
Payne, A. & Sons 239
Peale, James 288
Pedestrian Hobby Horse 50
Pell, Sarah 319
Pellerin & Co. 255
Pemberton, Samuel 414
Pemberton, T. & S. 416
Penet, L. 128
Penn-Sayers, P. 243

INDEX

Peppiatt, K. O. 37
Persil 141
Petitot, L. 88
Pharaoh 64
Phelps, W. 337
Philippe, Patek & Co. 424-427
Philippes 53
Phillips, Godfrey 385
Phipps & Robinson 111
Phipps, T. 347
Phonographs 274, 275
Pianola Rolls 276
Piatnik 283
Picture Frames 277, 278
Pidduck & Sons 40
Pierotti 428
Ping-Pong 303
Pistols 279, 281
Pitt, Wm. 336
Place, George 287
Plantin, C. 209
Playing Cards 282, 283
Plimer, Andrew 287
Pogany, W. 53
Polyphones 284
Pomanders 285
Pomeroy National Bank, The 39
Pools Advertising Service 10
Poor Man's Friend 265, 266
Pope Manufacturing Co 49
Pope, Francis 359
Popeye 391
Porter, P. W. 307
Portman Lodge 161
Portrait Miniatures 286-288
Post, Wilaminia 163
Pot Lids 289, 290
Pottier and Stymus 74
Pouch Ball 302
Powder Flasks 291
Powers, Hiram 25
Prams 292-294
Preiss Figures 295, 296
Preissler, I. 378
Premier Vee Twin 246
Prescott, Wm. 87
Prescott-Westcar, C. W. 239
Primrose Confectionary Co. 391
Prints 297-299
Prior, Geo. 426
Prosser, T. H. & Sons 302
Prout, Samuel 25
Provincial Bank 37
Prowse, Keith & Co. 276
Prussian Regt. of Garde 19
Pugin, A. W. N. 73, 190
Punch 63
Puss in Boots 64
Pyne, G. 418

Qianlong 188, 198, 342
Qing Dynasty 92, 171, 343, 344
Queen's Own Cameron Highlanders 176

R.T.N. 15
Racketana 300-303
Rafaelli 226
Ramsden & Carr 278
Ramsden, Omar 81
Ranlite 388, 390
Ratseys and Lapthorn 100
Rattles 304
Ravenglass Eskdale Ry. 380
Rawlings & Sumner 110, 111
Rawlings, C. 58
Razors 305, 306
Reading Mineral Water Co., The 155
Record Watch Co. 427
Red Cross 35
Red-Ashay 64
Redford, Constance E. 359
Redoubtable 240
Reid, Robt. 252

Reilly, John 102
Rein, A. & Son 223
Reinicke, P. J. 224, 225
Remington 308
Renard, Louis 208
Renoir, Pierre-Auguste 298
Reymong, Pierre 128
Richardson, Charlotte 317
Richmond, Sir William 25
Ricketts 439
Ricks, Thomas 333
Rieder, F. 61
Rifle Brigade 229
Rifles 307-309
Riley & Storer 111
Rimbault, Stepn. 83
Rinaldi, G. 226
Risler & Carre 82
Roberte, Jane 96
Roberts, Dr. Giles 266
Robertson Sanderson & Co. 214
Robinson & Leadbetter 105, 272
Robinson, D. 87
Robinson, E. 347
Roger & Gallet 331
Roger, John 259
Rogerson, Sidney 159
Rolls Royce 388, 394-396
Roncheti, J. B. 41
Rookwood 310
Rosbach Table Waters 216
Rose, Jas. & Co. 165
Ross, Robert 26
Rothebusch, Frederick 310
Rouolle, L. C. 255
Rover 246
Rowlandson 52
Royal Bank of Canada 37
Royal Co. of Archers 361
Royal Doulton 20, 21, 97, 150, 196, 197,
    214, 216, 253, 324, 383, 384
Royal Dragoons 220
Royal Dublin Fusiliers, The 228
Royal Dux 311, 312
Royal Exchange Assurance 146
Royal Flying Corps 9
Royal Fusiliers, The 229
Royal Hussars 410
Royal Irish Assurance Co. 146
Royal Mail 50
Royal Welsh Fusiliers 177
Royal Wiltshire Yeomanry 411
Royall Game of Chess, The 54
Royalty Books 313-315
Roycrofters 55
Rumsey, P. 240
Ruskin Pottery 316
Ryuo 406
Ryuraku 187

S.S. Servia 236, 237
Sainsbury, J. Ltd. 392
Saint Patrick Ins. Co. 146
Salomon 418
Samplers 317-319
Sands' Ointment 266
Sandwich 270
Sanglier 64
Sannino, Vincenzo 417
Sansho 262
Sardine Dishes 320
Sare, A. 238
Sare, R. J. 236, 244
Saunders, E. C. 370, 371
Saxony Cavalry 362
Scarborough Cricket Club 106
Scenery Costume and Architecture 55
Schindler, P. E. 225
Schleiertanz 80
Schmit, Georg 426
Schneider Trophy 9, 10
Scott, James 54, 111
Scottish, Commercial Fire & Life 144

Scrimshaw 321
Seals 322, 323
Seddon & Moss 87
Sentinel 393
Series Ware 324, 325
Seth Thomas Clock Co. 91
Seutter, Mattheus 208
Sevres 326, 327
Shackleton, Sir E. H. 340
Shaker 328, 329
Shakespeare's Birthplace 162
Shakespeare's Cottage 160
Shand-Mason 242
Sharp's Toffee Co. 63
Shaver Cream Pot Lids 330, 331
Shaving Mugs 332, 333
Shaw, G. 114
Shaw, John 416
Shell Aviation Petrol 10
Shells 334
Ships Figureheads 335
Ships of the World 391
Shoveller, Harriatt 318
Showman's Road Locomotive 244
Shuho Yamakawa 299
Signed Photographs 339-341
Silhouettes 336-338
Simmance, Eliza 253, 360
Simon & Halbig 27, 122
Singleton's Eye Ointment 264
Sir Edward Lee's Old Scotch Whisky 215
Sir Kreemy Knut 63
Sirletti, Giacomo 347
Sixty Years of Golf 158
Skeaping, J. 433
Skeleton Clocks 90
Sketches Illustrative 55
Slade & Bullock Ltd. 392
Slazenger 302
Smart, John 286, 287
Smith, Benjamin 111
Smith, Edward 66
Smith, Gordon 158
Smith, R. 105
Snuff Boxes 10, 342-347
Societe des Bronzes de Paris 61
Solomon Islands 334
Solon, L. 233
Some Essays on Golf Course Architecture
    159
Some Poems 55
Soul of Golf, The 158
South Australia Militia Lancers 410
Southampton Tudor House 162
Spa 141
Spaco Ltd. 363
Sparklets 363
Speede, John 207, 209
Speilman, H. 133
Spencer 193
Spirit of the Wind 63
Sporting Stoneware 348, 349
Spratt's Perfect 331
Springer and Oppenheimer 135
St Catherine's Chapel 162
St Helens Corp. Transport 380
St Louis 267-270
St. Nicholas Chapel 161
Stag's Head 63
Stained Glass Windows 350, 351
Stands 352-354
Stanley Steamer 29
Star Manufacturing Co. 293
Steinlen, Theodore Alexandre 297
Steinway 250
Stephens' Gum 141
Stevengraphs 355, 356
Stevens, Betsey 317
Stevens, T. 10
Stevens, Thomas 355
Stewart, John Watson 54
Steyr 309
Stickley Bros. 353

INDEX

Stickley, Gustav 87, 354, 357, 358
Stickley, L. & J. G. 358
Stinton, H. 440
Stinton, John 440
Stone Sawing Plant 244
Stone, Anna 317
Stoneware 359, 360
Storr, Paul 305
Story of a Passion, The 55
Stubbs, Thos. 86
Sturton's Poor Man's Cerate 265
Styles, Susannah 317
Suffolk & Gen. Country Insurance 146
Suffolk Dredging 242
Sulgrave Manor 160
Summers, William 415
Suruga Takayoshi 405
Suss, Gerr 86
Sutcliff's Patent 231
Sutton, G. F. & Co 15, 16
Suzhou School 343
Swaine 421
Sweet Honesty 29
Swords 361, 362
Syphons 363, 364

T.M.C. 107
Tai Winds 29, 30
Tait, F. G. 159
Tang Dynasty 67, 68
Tang/Song Dynasty 189
Tapestries 365, 366
Taps 367
Tardy & Tandart 326
Tassie Medallions 368
Tatsuke Takamasu 184
Taxidermy 369-371
Taylor & Perry 415, 416
Taylor on Golf 158
Taylor Tunncliff 217
Taylor, H. A. 244
Taylor, Isaac 337
Teignbridge Cricket Club 106
Tell, E. 157
Tenantry, Percy 291
Tenkodo Hidekuni 405
Tennyson, Alfred Lord 53
Terracotta 372, 373
Terry, Eli & Son 89
Terry, Miss Ellen 160
Tete de Belier 65
Tete de Coq 64
Textiles 374-376
Thames Publishing Co. 51
Theaker, H. G. 21
Theroude 28
Thimbles 377, 378
Thirteen Star American Flag 98
Thomason 102, 103
Thomason, J. 336, 337
Thorn, C. E. 242
Tibbald's Blood Tonic 265
Tickets 379, 380
Tiffany 191, 350, 425
Tiles 381, 382
Tinworth, George 360
Tinworth, George 382
Tlingit 13
Tobacco Jars 383, 384
Tobacco Silks 385, 386
Tojo 184
Toleware 387
Tomohisa 151
Tomotada 261
Tompion, Tho. 426
Tonnecliff, Elizabeth 319
Touch Wud 64
Tour of Doctor Syntax, The 52
Toy Cars 388-390
Toyo and Kao 183
Trade Cards 391, 392
Transport 393-396
Trays 397, 398

Treen 399, 400
Triefus, Paul 159
Triumph 396
Trophies 401, 402
Trotmans, T. 293
Troughton & Simms 260
Truncheons 403
Tsubas 404-406
Tuck, Raphael 23, 24, 204
Tuke, Henry Scott 105
Tunbridgeware 407
Tunon, Carlo 419
Turner, Richard 111
Tyrolesse School 419

Uhlan Regt. 175
Ulster Bank 36
Umbrellas 408, 409
Underhill, H. A. 241
Uniforms 410-412
Union Assurance Soc. 146
Unione Militare 177
Unite, G. 110
Ute Reservation 13

Vacheron & Constantin 425
Vaile, P. A. 158
Vale Press 55
Valentien, Albert R. 310
Van Geelen, Johannes 103
Van Ysseldijk, Godert 46
Veilsdorf, Kloster 420
Velkonocni Pozdrav 23, 24
Venini, Paolo 113
Verneh 12
Veterinary Items 413
Vickery, J. C. 102
Victoire – Spirit of the Wind 65
Victoria Wine Co. 364
Victory 389
Views in Greece 55
Vile, Wm. 277
Villanis, E. 61
Villon, Jacques 299
Vinaigrettes 414-416
Vincent Brooks Day & Son 10
Vincent, Alfred 419
Violins 417-419
Visscher, Nicolaus 207
Vitesse 65
Volkert, Hans 23
Vom Hofe, Julius 149
Voyage Round Great Britain, A 54

Wagenfeld, Wm. 126
Wain, Louis 204
Walker, John 426
Walker, Thos. 260
Walking Sticks 420-422
Wall Clocks 91
Waller & Son 265
Wallingford Brewery Ltd. 155
Wallis, J. 283
Wallshale Lodge 213
Walsam, W. K. 236
Walton and Cotton 52
Walton, George 351
Walton, Isaac 161
Walton, Izaak 325
Ward Bros., L. T. 115
Ward, Robt. 85
Wardle 216
Warhol, Andy 298
Warth, C. 382
Waste Land, The 54
Watch Stands 423
Watches 424-427
Watkins, F. 42
Watson 147
Watson, Geoffrey 9, 10
Waugh's Patent 231
Wax Models 428

Weatherhill Pit Winding Engine 236
Weathervanes 429-431
Weaver, T. 154
Webenwein, M. 23
Wedgwood 432, 433
Weeks, L. G. & Sons 363
Weiss 223
Wellings, Wm. 336-338
Wells 388, 390
Welshpool & Llanfair Ry. 379
Wemyss 434
West of Scotland Ins. 144
Westbury, Cyril 276
Westley Richards 307
Westminster Insurance 144
Wethrell, Harriot 319
Wheatley, Samuel 253
Wheatley, Thomas 111
White Thomson & Co. 260
Whitman, Walt 341
Wiedekind & Co 216
Wiegand, G. 332
Wild Country 29, 30
Wilkie, I. H. 240
Wilkinson Sword Co. 412
Wilkinson, Henry 362
William Tapscot 241
Williams, M. 243
Willmore, Joseph 347, 415, 416
Wilmot, J. 81
Wilson, Gus Aaron 115
Wilson, Ino. 91
Wine Glasses 435-437
Wisden, J. 106
Withers, E. 419
Wogdon & Barton 280
Wolff, David 435
Wolverhampton Corp. Tramsways 380
Women's Royal Air Force 9
Wood, Ralph 438
Worcester 439
Wordsworth's home 160
World of Golf, The 158
Worrall, Thos. 112
Worthingtons 214
Wragg, Job. Ltd. 363, 364
Wright & Greig's Premier Old Scotch 217
Wright 9
Wrights 363

Yapp & Woodward 79, 346, 415, 416
Yasumasa 151
Yasuyuki 184
Yates Bros 155
Yavapai 14
Ye Zhongsan 342, 343
Yokohama Specie Bank 38
Yoshiharu 263
Yoshijuro Urishibawa 298
Yoshimasa 261
Young Cricketer's Tutor, The 105
Young, Grace 310
Yuan Dynasty 189

Zettel, J. 310
Zhou Dynasty 189
Zigang 344
Zwichl, F. 80